Sherlock Holmes

FOR

DUMMIES®

by Steven Doyle and David A. Crowder

WILEY

Wiley Publishing, Inc.

Sherlock Holmes For Dummies®

Published by
Wiley Publishing, Inc.
111 River St.
Hoboken, NJ 07030-5774
www.wiley.com

Copyright © 2010 by Wiley Publishing, Inc., Indianapolis, Indiana

Published by Wiley Publishing, Inc., Indianapolis, Indiana

Published simultaneously in Canada

WILEY

About the Authors

Steven Doyle has been a Sherlockian since the age of 14, when his parents gave him a copy of *The Adventures of Sherlock Holmes* for Christmas. Doyle is a member of the Baker Street Irregulars, as well as several other Sherlock Holmes societies, including the Illustrious Clients of Indianapolis.

Doyle has also had a long career in Sherlockian publishing. In 1987, Doyle founded and edited the quarterly journal *The Sherlock Holmes Review.* This critically acclaimed periodical ran for 10 years. In 1992 he cofounded Wessex Press, a high-quality small press specializing in Sherlock Holmes, Arthur Conan Doyle, and other topics of related interest. Wessex Press (and its imprint, Gasogene Books) is the premier Sherlockian publisher in the world. Finally, in 2008, Doyle assumed the role of publisher for *The Baker Street Journal,* the official quarterly publication of the Baker Street Irregulars. Doyle has also authored countless essays and articles and edited or co-edited five books: *The Illustrious Clients Fourth Casebook, The Illustrious Clients Second Case-Notes, Holmes in the Heartland: The Illustrious Clients Fifth Casebook, Murderland,* and *G. K. Chesterton's Sherlock Holmes.* He lives in Zionsville, Indiana, a suburb of Indianapolis, with his wife, Pamela, and their three cats.

David A. Crowder has authored or coauthored more than 25 books, including the bestsellers *Building a Web Site For Dummies* and *CliffsNotes Getting on the Internet.* His two most recent books were both listed as essential for all library collections by the magazine *Library Journal.*

Dr. Crowder is a professor in the School of Languages at the University of Antioquia in Colombia. He is equally at home with high technology or with working his way through the backcountry on horseback or in a dugout canoe. When he is not writing, he spends his time with his wife, Angela, wandering through villages in the Andes or frolicking in the Caribbean surf.

Dedication

To my parents, who gave their son a Christmas gift that never stopped giving, and to my wife, Pamela, who has always allowed Mr. Holmes to share our home.

— Steven Doyle

Author's Acknowledgments

Special thanks go out to a number of people who offered advice, help, and encouragement during the writing of this book. My team at Wiley Publishing was terrific; Michael Lewis, Tracy Barr, Tim Gallan, and Todd Lothery made the entire process a pleasure, and their feedback materially improved the book. Melanie Hoffman gave insight and encouragement — thanks, Mel! Mark Gagen gets special mention — our London photo safari provided many of the illustrations in this volume. Thanks also to my great friends Mike Whelan, Roy Pilot, Don Curtis, and my brother, Patrick. And finally, special thanks to my wife, Pamela Wampler, whose feedback and encouragement on this project helped keep me going. Thanks, everyone!

— Steven Doyle

Publisher's Acknowledgments

We're proud of this book; please send us your comments through our Dummies online registration form located at http://dummies.custhelp.com. For other comments, please contact our Customer Care Department within the U.S. at 877-762-2974, outside the U.S. at 317-572-3993, or fax 317-572-4002.

Some of the people who helped bring this book to market include the following:

Acquisitions, Editorial, and Media Development

Senior Project Editor: Tim Gallan

Acquisitions Editor: Mike Lewis

Copy Editor: Todd Lothery

Technical Reviewer: Pamela Bedore

Editorial Program Coordinator: Joe Niesen

Editorial Manager: Michelle Hacker

Senior Editorial Assistant: David Lutton

Editorial Assistants: Jennette ElNaggar, Rachelle Amick

Cover Photos: to come

Cartoons: Rich Tennant (www.the5thwave.com)

Composition Services

Project Coordinator: Katie Crocker

Layout and Graphics: Yovonne Grego, Joyce Haughey, Ronald G. Terry

Proofreader: Cynthia Fields

Indexer: Potomac Indexing, LLC

Publishing and Editorial for Consumer Dummies

> **Diane Graves Steele,** Vice President and Publisher, Consumer Dummies

> **Kristin Ferguson-Wagstaffe,** Product Development Director, Consumer Dummies

> **Ensley Eikenburg,** Associate Publisher, Travel

> **Kelly Regan,** Editorial Director, Travel

Publishing for Technology Dummies

> **Andy Cummings,** Vice President and Publisher, Dummies Technology/General User

Composition Services

> **Debbie Stailey,** Director of Composition Services

Contents at a Glance

Table of Contents

Introduction

*O*dds are, if you're sitting down to read this book, you believe that you don't know much about Sherlock Holmes. But you're wrong. You know he's a detective, even the most famous detective of them all. You know he's English. You likely know he has a friend named Watson. You probably even have a vague idea of what he looks like. But if that's the extent of your knowledge, then you're definitely ready to read on!

By any measure, Sherlock Holmes is the greatest character ever created in literature. Holmes's popularity extends around the world. His influence on popular culture is immense (and shows up in the most surprising places). He has inspired a following of enthusiasts and fans that's unprecedented for a fictional character from a work of literature. And the stories that comprise his adventures offer endless and fascinating new discoveries to his readers.

Over the past 100 years, enough articles, essays, periodicals, and books have been produced about the Great Detective to literally fill a library. Because of this, approaching the world of Sherlock Holmes can be daunting. But that's what *Sherlock Holmes For Dummies* is for. Here you'll find a general reference offering insight and entrance into the fascinating and exciting world of Sherlock Holmes.

However, this book isn't an encyclopedia. (There are actual Sherlock Holmes encyclopedias for that.) As in any field of study, some topics covered here are simply informational, while others venture into subjects that have been debated for decades. *Sherlock Holmes For Dummies* definitely has opinions, but it's never dogmatic. Half the fun of reading about the character is the variety of responses readers have to the stories and the evolving character of Holmes himself.

About This Book

When fans start to talk about their favorite detective, newcomers are often amazed at the number of topics that can fall under the umbrella of "Sherlock Holmes." You might presume that, because these are mystery stories, most conversations would revolve around the tales themselves — sort of like what you'd find in a book club, where everyone reads the same volume and discusses it. But there's so much more than that!

In this book, each chapter is devoted to a different area of interest, and subsections break down the chapter into more specific topics. The world of Sherlock Holmes covers an amazing array of subjects, including

- The origins of Sherlock Holmes and early detective fiction.
- The stories, including plots, characters, continuing themes, and common threads.
- The influence of Holmes on detective fiction, from his contemporaries to today.
- The life and work of Sir Arthur Conan Doyle, the creator of Sherlock Holmes.
- Holmes's life outside the stories, including film and TV adaptations, pastiche and parody, and fan clubs.

Unlike many of the Sherlock Holmes reference books, handbooks, and encyclopedias published over the years, this book is organized so that you can dive in anywhere. No chapter is dependent upon any other, so if you see something that grabs your attention in the table of contents, just turn to it and go. Think of the book as a sort of "random access" publication.

Conventions Used in This Book

I use some conventions in the book that you may not be familiar with. These are mostly terms that new Sherlock Holmes readers may not know, such as:

- *Sherlockian* is the term for American devotees of Sherlock Holmes. British fans are called *Holmesians*.
- *Sherlockiana* means of the Sherlockian universe. So, for instance, a book can be called a volume of Sherlockiana.
- *The canon* is what Sherlockians call the original 60 Sherlock Holmes stories.
- *The Great Detective* is another term for Sherlock Holmes himself.
- *The Good Doctor* refers to Holmes's friend and colleague, Dr. Watson.

Beyond the conventions specific to the Holmes stories, here are a few others it would help you to know:

- New words or terms appear in *italics*.
- **Bold** text makes it easy to spot keywords in bulleted lists.
- Monofont is used for Web addresses.

What You're Not to Read

This book has lots of great stuff throughout, but none of it needs to be read in order, and some of it can be skipped altogether! I've organized and designed it so that you can quickly identify what the subject is and easily understand what it's saying. Beyond that, I've put in a lot of extra stuff that may be of interest. This material amplifies or reinforces the main topic of the chapter, but it isn't vital to read it in order to get the major points. This optional material includes

  ✔ **Sidebars:** The shaded boxes that are scattered throughout the book contain extra material that I may touch on in the chapter but that isn't crucial to your understanding of the subject.

  ✔ **Anything with a Technical Stuff icon:** Text next to one of these icons is interesting (I hope) supplementary material that, again, isn't necessary to your understanding of the topic at hand.

Foolish Assumptions

If you're getting ready to plunge into this book, it's only fair to tell you that I made certain assumptions about you when writing it.

  ✔ You've heard of Sherlock Holmes. It's a basic assumption (Holmes would call it "elementary"), but that's where we start.

  ✔ You're literate, curious, and intrigued by the phenomenon of Holmes's popularity. You've had some vague sense that this character was special somehow, and now you've decided to look into it.

  ✔ You want to get up-to-speed on the subject quickly and easily. You want some good, insightful information and commentary, but you don't want to spend a lifetime getting it.

  ✔ You like stuff like this — detective fiction, mysteries, genre movies. You think this stuff is cool!

How This Book Is Organized

This book is organized into five parts to divide the material into broad subjects and help you quickly locate a topic on Sherlock Holmes you may be interested in.

Part I: Elementary Beginnings and Background

This first part is the basic introduction to Sherlock Holmes — the plots of the stories and the fascinating history of their publication. In addition, you meet Arthur Conan Doyle, the man who created the world's greatest detective, and you find out about Victorian London, the time and place that the Holmes stories take place.

Part II: What a Bunch of Characters!

Few stories in literature are populated with as many fascinating characters as the tales that make up the Sherlockian canon. In this part you get a detailed profile of Sherlock Holmes himself, and you'll be amazed at the depth of the characterization. You also meet his friend, Dr. Watson, as well as other characters, including cops, bad guys, victims, and damsels in distress.

Part III: Holmes and His Adventures

In addition to rich characters, the Holmes stories are full of atmosphere and history, providing a window into the Victorian age. This part describes the "typical" Sherlock Holmes story and takes a detailed look at the most famous Holmes novel of them all, *The Hound of the Baskervilles*. I also examine common themes that occur throughout the 60 stories.

Part IV: Beyond Baker Street

The influence of Sherlock Holmes has, from the beginning, spread far beyond the original stories, and even beyond the printed page. This part looks at how Holmes has inspired thousands of imitators, first in parody and pastiche, and then later in new detectives created to resemble the Great Detective. It also examines Holmes on the stage and screen and looks at the character's unprecedented fan following.

Part V: The Part of Tens

What are the ten unsolved mysteries found in the canon? If I want to visit the actual places where the stories happened, where should I go? What are the ten most important books about Holmes that I should have on my shelf? What are the most memorable quotes of Sherlock Holmes? You can find the answers to these burning questions in this part!

I also include an appendix that lists the hundreds of active Sherlockian societies in the United States. If you want to find a fan club to join, here's the list!

Icons Used in This Book

In the left margin throughout this book, I use icons to point to information that may be fun, interesting, memorable, or useful.

This icon points out important information that you want to remember.

This icon is next to material that helps reinforce information in the text but that isn't necessary to know. It's perfectly okay to skip the info that appears with this icon if you feel like it.

This icon alerts you to topics in the text that have parallels and relevance to similar subjects today, showing a continuity between events in the past and the present. Again, though not vital to a comprehension of the material, this information does add another level of understanding.

I use this icon primarily to give readers helpful tips. For instance, Chapter 17 discusses Sherlockian places to visit, and the Tip icon offers pointers on when to go and what to see.

Where to Go from Here

This book is organized so that you can jump in wherever you want. This nonlinear format lets you start wherever your interests take you and proceed according to your whims. Do you need a basic introduction to Sherlock Holmes? Head to Chapter 1. Perhaps you're more interested in film and television adaptations of the Great Detective. If so, you want to go to Chapter 14. For broad categories, turn to the table of contents. For more specific topics, check out the index.

If you're not sure where to start, you can begin at the beginning with Part I. It gives you a snapshot of Sherlock Holmes, the background of his creation, and the stories.

Part I
Elementary Beginnings and Background

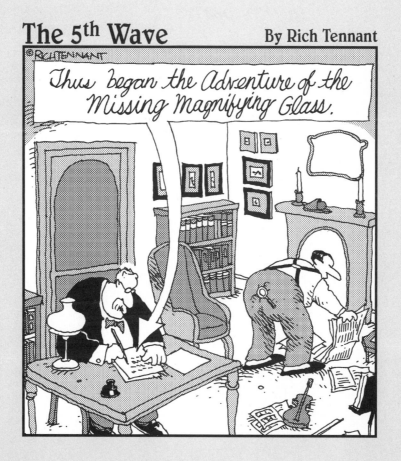

In this part . . .

This first part offers a basic introduction to Sherlock Holmes. I give an overview of the character of Holmes himself, the plots of the 60 Holmes stories, and the fascinating history of their publication. In addition, you meet Sir Arthur Conan Doyle, the man who created the world's greatest detective. This part also provides information about Victorian London — the time and place in which the Holmes stories take place.

Chapter 1

A Snapshot of Sherlock Holmes and the Stories That Made Him Famous

Try this experiment: Ask ten random people if they know who Sherlock Holmes is. Odds are they'll say yes. Then ask what they know about him. Chances are they'll say he's a detective, he has a friend named Watson, he smokes a pipe, and he wears a funny hat. Some will even think he was *real*. What's even more amazing is that if you were to try this experiment on every continent on the planet, you'd likely get the same results, demonstrating the grip that Sherlock Holmes has on the popular culture, even to this day.

Sherlock Holmes: Not Who You Think He Is

The popular image of Sherlock Holmes is largely made up of clichés that have become associated with the Great Detective over the years. Some of these do come from the actual character as written in the stories, while others have come from the countless adaptations on TV and in the movies. But if you're approaching the Holmes stories for the first time, you may be surprised at the person you find. Sherlock Holmes is not who you think he is. (And neither is his friend, Dr. Watson!)

Pop culture portrayal versus portrayal in the stories

The common picture of Holmes is of a square-jawed, well-off, middle-aged, stuffy do-gooder who lives with an elderly, slightly befuddled roommate in a quaint London apartment. Both men while away their time until Scotland Yard appears with a particularly baffling case of murder that's so mysterious it has the official police force stumped. (Well, this bit about the official police force being stumped *does* happen a lot in the stories!) Holmes comes off as a bit of a prig — stern, cold, scientific, and humorless. And always running around in an odd cape and funny hat.

Surprise! That is *not* Sherlock Holmes.

Who you meet in the stories is a young man (both Holmes and Watson are in their 20s when they meet) who's poor enough to need a roommate and untidy and strange enough that he has trouble finding one. Sherlock is musical (he plays the violin and loves to attend concerts), occasionally funny, and, as becomes clear over time, a loyal friend.

In the fashion department, it's top hat and frock coat for Sherlock, not a checked cape and hunting cap! Holmes has a dark side as well — impatience, vanity, depression, drug abuse, and an antisocial streak that keeps him from making many friends or forming romantic relationships. These are all personality traits that help define the real Sherlock Holmes.

In other words, you won't find the cartoon image of Holmes in the stories. Instead, you meet a character with virtues *and* vices, strengths *and* weaknesses, and professionally, successes *and* failures. It's a complex personality that has kept fans coming back to his adventures over and over for more than a century.

Why the confusion

As the famous poet T. S. Eliot once said when speaking of Holmes, it's hard "not to slip into the myth of his existence." And in fact, many people think Holmes was a real, living, historical person. So great is the impression he made, first on his readers and then on the popular culture, that thinking he actually lived is an understandable mistake. Of course, the myth of Sherlock's reality has been helped along by a number of factors.

His fans treated him as though he were real

From the moment Sherlock Holmes appeared in his first short story in 1891, fans began treating the detective as real. For instance, when readers learned that Holmes had died in "The Final Problem," a public outcry of shock and grief ensued that equaled, and even exceeded, that which would occur at the death of real-life persons. Young businessmen in London even wore black armbands in mourning.

He's been written about as if he were real

Since the early 1900s, fans and scholars have perpetuated the myth by writing about Holmes — his adventures, his methods, his world — as if he were real. The best example of this phenomenon is *The Baker Street Journal,* a quarterly publication by the Baker Street Irregulars, the oldest and most prestigious Sherlock Holmes society in the world. (For more on the Baker Street Irregulars and other Holmes organizations, go to Chapter 15.)

The Baker Street Journal was founded in 1946, and it's devoted to publishing essays, commentary, and research papers that "play the game," a term Sherlockians use for pretending that the stories are factual accounts of real persons and events. However, there have been quite literally tens of thousands of similar publications: books, articles, journals — the list is endless!

He still inspires the pros

To this day, Holmes continues to be held up as a role model in police departments around the world. He is cited in countless academic and professional articles and journals. College classes in forensic science, logic, chemistry, and scientific method, using Holmes as a model, are taught every day around the world.

For a fictional character, he gets a lot of kudos!

Imagine you're on vacation in Switzerland and you come to a small village in the Alps, and there outside an inn is a life-sized statue of Sherlock Holmes! Nearby is a plaque that reads, "At this fearful place, Sherlock Holmes vanquished Professor Moriarty, on 4 May 1891." The fact is that Holmes has more plaques, statues, and museums erected in his honor than most real-life historical figures!

> ✔ In the Criterion Bar in London's Piccadilly Circus, a plaque commemorates the place where Dr. Watson met his friend Stamford, who went on to introduce Watson to Holmes.

✔ A chemical laboratory in London's St. Bartholomew's Hospital has a plaque identifying it as the location where Holmes and Watson first met.

✔ On London's Baker Street, where Holmes lived, stands a museum dedicated to him. The museum not only re-creates his rooms down to the smallest detail but also has a blue plaque (see Figure 1-1).

For decades, the actual 221b Baker Street address was occupied by Abbey House, a financial institution. Abbey House opened for business on this location in 1932 and immediately began to receive letters addressed to Sherlock Holmes. Holmes received so much mail that Abbey hired a secretary to answer it, and the letters continue to arrive to this day, with many people asking for Holmes's help in solving a mystery!

Blue plaques are historical markers used in many European countries that are installed in public places to commemorate a link between the location and a famous person or event. It's believed that Holmes's residence is the only fictional location to receive such an honor.

✔ You can find more statues of Sherlock Holmes than of his creator, Arthur Conan Doyle! Commemorative statues of the Great Detective can be found in London, England (see Figure 1-2); Edinburgh, Scotland; Meiringen, Switzerland; Moscow, Russia; and Karuizawa Town, Japan.

Figure 1-1:
Sherlock Holmes Museum with blue plaque.

Photo courtesy of Steven Doyle.

Photo courtesy of Steven Doyle.

Given all these accolades and commemorative markers, what's a person to think?

Though Sherlock Holmes may seem more real to people than many actual historical figures, he is, of course, a work of fiction. But as a work of fiction, his identity has eclipsed the author of the stories. More people know of the creation than the creator. For even more details on Holmes, head to Chapter 2.

Arthur Conan Doyle: Holmes's Creator

Sir Arthur Conan Doyle was born in 1859 in Edinburgh, Scotland. His father was Charles Altamont Doyle, an artist and painter. His mother was Mary Foley. As a boy, his main interests were sports and storytelling. He attended private schools and entered Edinburgh University medical school in 1876. He completed work on his doctor's degree in 1885 and entered into private practice.

In his early career, in order to both pass the considerable time between infrequent patients and earn a little extra money, he began writing. He had a number of short stories published anonymously and wrote several novels of questionable quality. His main interests were in historical fiction and the supernatural. He didn't set out to be a mystery or detective fiction writer. When Doyle wrote the first Holmes story, *A Study in Scarlet,* he had no idea he had created the defining character of his career.

In medical school, Doyle was influenced and inspired by his professors, especially Dr. Joseph Bell. Bell was a master of diagnosis using observation and deduction. It was from Bell that Doyle learned the Sherlock Holmes method. Doyle's medical training and career were to be major sources of writing inspiration throughout his life, including the Holmes stories. For more on Doyle, the Holmes stories, and his other works, head to Chapter 3.

Sherlock Holmes's debut

In 1887, Doyle got the idea to write a detective story and to model the main character after his old medical school professor, Dr. Bell. He gave it the lurid title of *A Study in Scarlet.* This was the first Holmes story, and despite being the best thing Doyle had written up to this time, very few publishers were interested. Finally, out of desperation, he accepted an offer from Ward, Lock & Co. to purchase the copyright for £25. The novel appeared complete in 1887, in the seasonal publication *Beeton's Christmas Annual.* It was a great story, but to be honest, it just sort of came and went without a lot of hoopla.

That might have been it for Sherlock, but then, in 1890, Holmes made his second appearance in the novel *The Sign of the Four.* This exciting tale was commissioned by the publisher of *Lippincott's Monthly Magazine,* an American publication. (That's right, Sherlock Holmes owes his continued existence to an American.) *The Sign of the Four* did a little better than *A Study in Scarlet,* but bigger and better things were right around the corner for both Arthur Conan Doyle and Sherlock Holmes.

Changing the way stories were serialized

The Victorian era was a golden age of magazine publishing, especially from the 1860s to the first decade of the 1900s. These reasonably priced monthly publications appealed to a wide range of readers and featured essays, stories, poetry, and serialized novels.

Many famous authors serialized novels over a number of months in a magazine. For example, most of Charles Dickens's best-known works appeared as serialized installments in magazines before they were published in book form. The problem with this was that if readers missed an issue, they were lost!

In 1891, Doyle had an idea that revolutionized the way fiction was published in magazines. Instead of having a continuing story appear over numerous issues, Doyle decided to have a continuing *character* appear in a series of short stories. If you missed an issue, hey, no big deal — the character would be back the next month in a brand new, self-contained adventure. The character Doyle chose for this innovation was Sherlock Holmes, and he placed the stories in a new monthly called *The Strand Magazine.*

Holmes was an overnight sensation! Subscriptions to the magazine went through the roof. At the end of the first 12 stories, *The Strand* asked for more. Doyle in turn asked for more money and got it. And so it went until Holmes made Doyle a very rich man.

It turned out to be a long, profitable relationship. The first story appeared in *The Strand* in 1891, and the last one appeared in 1926. In England, new Holmes stories always made their first appearance in *The Strand,* and the detective and magazine are permanently linked.

The Canon of Sherlock Holmes

When Doyle wrote the very first Holmes story, he thought that was it. He never dreamed that he'd be writing stories about this character his entire life. The detective's enormous popularity and the love/hate relationship that Doyle had with the character (Doyle felt that Sherlock's popularity obscured his more important writing, which goes to show that an artist isn't always the best judge of his own work!) ultimately compelled him to write 60 official adventures of Sherlock Holmes. These 60 stories are what fans and scholars call *the canon.*

So, what kind of stories are they?

If you're unfamiliar with the Holmes adventures, you may think that every story finds Holmes and Watson solving a baffling case of murder. This *is* the case for many famous detectives who came in Sherlock's wake. Let's face it — murder sells.

However, this *isn't* the case with Holmes. Oh, the canon has plenty of dead bodies — in fact, 263 dead bodies and 119 murders! But despite the body count, a large percentage of the tales are *not* murder mysteries. For example, only 4 of the 12 stories from *The Adventures of Sherlock Holmes* have anything to do with murder. In fact, many of the tales have, in the end, nothing criminal about them at all. They're often more accurately described as *detective stories* than *murder mysteries.*

The Holmes stories can be classified into different categories. Following are some of these categories, and many tales actually fall into more than one:

- ✔ **The "locked-room" mystery:** This is a type of detective story in which a murder is committed under impossible conditions, usually in a place that the murderer couldn't have entered or left. Although he isn't given enough credit for it, Doyle was one of the earliest innovators of this classic subgenre of crime fiction. Examples of this type include "The Speckled Band," "The Empty House," and *The Valley of Fear.* (For more on locked-room mysteries, see the nearby sidebar.)

- ✔ **Crime prevention:** Often, Holmes's participation in a case results in crime prevention instead of crime detection. Whether thwarting a bank robbery, preventing a kidnapping and forced marriage, or stopping the embezzlement of money, Holmes is up to the task. "The Red-Headed League," "The Solitary Cyclist," and "The Three Garridebs" are examples of this type of tale.

- ✔ **Espionage:** Several stories find Holmes working on behalf of the British government, often recovering stolen state secrets, and in one unique instance, actually going undercover as a spy. These tales include "The Naval Treaty," "The Second Stain," "The Bruce-Partington Plans," and "His Last Bow."

- ✔ **Missing persons:** In real life, private detectives are often hired to find missing persons. It was the same for Sherlock Holmes. In "A Case of Identity," it was a missing bridegroom. In "The Noble Bachelor," it was a missing bride! Other missing-persons cases include "The Man with the Twisted Lip" and "The Priory School."

- ✔ **Weird tales:** Some of the stories just defy categorization! They aren't exactly crime stories, and they aren't really mysteries. Instead, although they have elements of adventures and romance, they're really just weird tales. "The Yellow Face," "The Crooked Man," and "The Veiled Lodger" are clearly in the realm of weird tales.

The long and the short of it

The Sherlock Holmes canon contains 4 novels and 56 short stories. Both forms have their strengths and weaknesses, but Doyle generally excelled at the short story format. He once explained that it took as much effort to concoct the plot of a short story as it did a novel, and it's clearly easier for him to sustain a tale over fewer pages. Three of the four novels have a lengthy flashback that explains the back story and motivation of the adventure at hand. Of course, there's an exception to every rule! The greatest of all Holmes adventures, *The Hound of the Baskervilles,* is a novel.

Masters of the locked-room tale

The "locked-room" mystery is perhaps the best-known subgenre of crime fiction. Arthur Conan Doyle wasn't the first author to write this style of story, nor was he the last. Some of his fellow locked-room authors include

✔ **Edgar Allan Poe:** Poe's tale "The Murders in the Rue Morgue" (1841) is a classic of the locked-room style. When a mother and daughter are brutally murdered, investigators discover that the room is locked from the inside and is too high up for window access. So who — or what — could have come down the chimney?

✔ **Dorothy Sayers:** Mystery writer (and Holmesian) Dorothy Sayers introduced a locked-room-style mystery into her Lord Peter Wimsey series in *Have His Carcase*

(1932). When a man is found with his throat cut on a rock, which is located in the middle of a smooth stretch of sandy beach, authorities are baffled!

✔ **John Dickson Carr:** Carr was one of the masters of the locked-room story. For instance, in "The Case of the Constant Suicides" (1941), a dead man is found in a Scottish castle at the top of the tower. All the evidence indicates that he was alone when he died and points away from suicide.

✔ **Ellery Queen:** The great Ellery Queen wrote a fair number of locked-room mysteries, including *The King is Dead* (1951). A millionaire locked in a room far away from his brother is found shot dead. But there's no gun in the room!

A Study in Scarlet

First published in 1887 by Ward, Lock & Co. in *Beeton's Christmas Annual* (see Figure 1-3), this novel is the first Sherlock Holmes story. In this landmark adventure, Dr. John H. Watson is looking for a roommate, and when he's introduced to Sherlock Holmes, their immortal partnership begins. As they take up residence together, Watson begins to wonder about the weirdo he has moved in with. What's with the mysterious chemical experiments? The endless parade of unusual visitors? What is his line of work? The mystery involves a case of revenge, murder, and obsession that dates back 30 years to the Mormons in Salt Lake City, Utah. Not a bad start!

The Sign of (the) Four

On August 30, 1889, Joseph M. Stoddart, the managing editor of the American publication *Lippincott's Monthly Magazine,* held a remarkable dinner party. The guests included Oscar Wilde and Arthur Conan Doyle, two British authors whom Stoddart greatly admired and wanted to publish in his magazine. Wilde went on to contribute *The Picture of Dorian Gray,* and Doyle wrote *The Sign of the Four,* the second Sherlock Holmes novel.

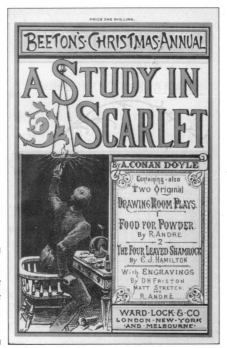

Figure 1-3:
*Beeton's
Christmas
Annual,
1887.*

In Doyle's sophomore effort, readers discover Holmes's drug abuse ("What is it today?" asks Watson in disgust. "Morphine, or cocaine?"), meet the Baker Street Irregulars (the ragtag group of street urchins Holmes uses as his eyes and ears around London), and head off on a treasure hunt featuring bloodhounds, savage natives, blowguns, and a boat chase on the Thames. Great stuff!

The Sign of the Four first appeared in the February 1890 edition of *Lippincott's Monthly Magazine.* In America it was called *The Sign of the Four,* but in Britain the title was shortened to *The Sign of Four.* However you title it, it's a classic.

The Adventures of Sherlock Holmes

The Adventures collects the first 12 Sherlock Holmes short stories into one volume. These tales were originally published serially in *The Strand Magazine* from July 1891 to June 1892. *The Adventures* was published in book form in 1892.

The 12 stories in this collection are

✔ **"A Scandal in Bohemia":** Hired to thwart a public scandal involving the king of Bohemia, Holmes encounters the beautiful Irene Adler, who, as he puts it, "has a face that a man might die for."

- ✔ **"The Red-Headed League":** This story begins with high comedy but ends with a dangerous vigil in a darkened bank vault full of French gold.

- ✔ **"A Case of Identity":** Holmes uncovers a heartless deception in a case he solves without ever leaving his rooms.

- ✔ **"The Boscombe Valley Mystery":** It's murder! Here Holmes uses his powerful forensic crime-scene investigation skills (see Figure 1-4).

- ✔ **"The Five Orange Pips":** Not a shining moment for Sherlock as he underestimates the power and reach of the Ku Klux Klan.

- ✔ **"The Man with the Twisted Lip":** Holmes uses one of his greatest tools — his pipe — to work out the solution to this case. It's a real "three pipe problem"!

- ✔ **"The Adventure of the Blue Carbuncle":** The only Christmas-time tale in the canon is a tour de force of detection as Holmes traces the journey of a stolen jewel from a hotel room to the crop of a Christmas goose.

- ✔ **"The Adventure of the Speckled Band":** One of the spookiest and best-known tales in the canon. What killed Julia Stoner as she lay in bed behind her locked bedroom door? What was the mysterious whistle in the night? And what did she mean by, "It was the band! The speckled band"? This story is one of the canon's best locked-room mysteries!

Figure 1-4:
Sherlock Holmes examining clues in "The Boscombe Valley Mystery."

Illustration by Sidney Paget, The Strand Magazine.

✔ **"The Adventure of the Engineer's Thumb":** One of the grisliest Holmes stories relates Victor Hatherley's unfortunate encounter with a meat cleaver.

✔ **"The Adventure of the Noble Bachelor":** Holmes investigates the case of a jilted groom and a missing bride. But is there a crime?

✔ **"The Adventure of the Beryl Coronet":** The theft of a priceless piece of jewelry allows Holmes to once again display his amazing crime-scene investigation skills.

✔ **"The Adventure of the Copper Beeches":** Definitely a weird tale. Why must the new governess obey her employer's strange rules, like wearing a blue dress and cutting her hair? And why must she never go into a certain wing of the house?

The Memoirs of Sherlock Holmes

This is the second collection of Holmes short stories, originally published in 1894 in *The Strand Magazine*.

✔ **"Silver Blaze":** An investigation into a stolen racehorse and a murdered trainer leads to a surprising suspect!

✔ **"The Adventure of the Cardboard Box":** This story of marital infidelity and murder was considered too racy for the American edition of *The Memoirs of Sherlock Holmes* and didn't appear in book form in America until *His Last Bow*.

✔ **"The Adventure of the Yellow Face":** Another strange tale with little detection and no crime. And yet, its surprising conclusion pays off.

✔ **"The Stockbroker's Clerk":** Holmes cracks a case of early identity theft and narrowly prevents a serious crime.

✔ **"The Gloria Scott":** The normally secretive Sherlock suddenly opens up and tells Watson about his very first case, an adventure that took place during college.

✔ **"The Musgrave Ritual":** Holmes must have been in a chatty mood as he follows "The Gloria Scott" with yet another tale of college-age mystery solving.

✔ **"The Adventure of the Reigate Squire":** While recovering from a nervous breakdown, Holmes investigates a strange burglary that led to murder.

✔ **"The Adventure of the Crooked Man":** The mysterious death of Col. Barclay unearths a terrible, heartbreaking secret.

✔ **"The Resident Patient":** Holmes looks into the hanging death of a wealthy but paranoid man in another crime-scene investigation tour de force.

✔ **"The Greek Interpreter":** This thrilling, horrifying tale of kidnapping and murder introduces readers to Holmes's brother, Mycroft.

✔ **"The Naval Treaty":** A stolen military treaty shakes the British government and afflicts another man with "brain fever." It also offers a surprising glimpse of the religious views of the Great Detective.

✔ **"The Final Problem":** This tale, which introduces Professor James Moriarty, the "Napoleon of crime," has a shocking conclusion that few readers can forget. "It is with a heavy heart" that Watson relates the death of Sherlock Holmes.

The Hound of the Baskervilles

This supposedly posthumous story is the greatest of all Sherlock Holmes adventures. *The Hound of the Baskervilles* is a Gothic masterpiece of suspense, atmosphere, and horror. Originally serialized in *The Strand Magazine,* it appeared in book form in 1902. It tells the tale of the Baskervilles, who live on the moor and are haunted by a spectral hound, "the hound from hell." When the current resident of Baskerville Hall dies under mysterious circumstances, Watson is sent to protect the new heir from harm. With mysterious neighbors, an escaped convict on the loose, and a glowing hellhound, *The Hound of the Baskervilles* is consistently named by fans as their favorite Holmes story of all.

The Return of Sherlock Holmes

When Arthur Conan Doyle killed Sherlock Holmes at the end of "The Final Problem," he immediately felt intense pressure to bring him back to life. He held out for ten years, but he finally gave in. *The Return of Sherlock Holmes* is the collected short-story adventures published after the Great Detective's return from the dead. It appeared in 1905.

The stories in this volume include

✔ **"The Adventure of the Empty House":** Holmes has been dead for three years when a lonely Watson becomes interested in the mysterious death of the young Ronald Adair. But then this classic locked-room mystery becomes secondary to a shocking revelation: Sherlock Holmes lives!

✔ **"The Adventure of the Norwood Builder":** Unrequited love and revenge drive this story of a retired builder who is murdered immediately upon making out his will.

✔ **"The Adventure of the Dancing Men":** This story has it all: mysterious codes, gangsters, a love triangle, murder, and one of Holmes's greatest crime-scene investigations.

✔ **"The Adventure of the Solitary Cyclist":** Violet Smith is being followed. Having no one to turn to, she appeals to Holmes for advice. This creepy story of a young woman being stalked by bicycle on a lonely country lane is a classic.

✔ **"The Adventure of the Priory School":** Kidnapping, murder, and high society result in a case that ends with Holmes becoming a very rich man.

✔ **"The Adventure of Black Peter":** The solution to one of the grisliest murders in the canon (the victim is pinned to the wall with a harpoon!) hinges on the location of a blood drop.

✔ **"The Adventure of Charles Augustus Milverton":** In an effort to save the reputation of an innocent woman, Sherlock resorts to housebreaking as he battles the "king of the blackmailers." Prepare yourself for the shocking climax!

✔ **"The Adventure of the Six Napoleons":** Why is someone smashing statues of Napoleon all around London? It looks like madness, but the Great Detective sees something else.

✔ **"The Adventure of the Three Students":** While doing research in one of England's "great university towns," Holmes is asked to look into an academic cheating scandal. Which of the three students is guilty?

✔ **"The Adventure of the Golden Pince-Nez":** When a bedridden scholar's personal assistant is murdered, Holmes solves the case by smoking cigarettes and looking into the killer's dropped eyeglasses.

✔ **"The Adventure of the Missing Three-Quarter":** This missing-persons case begins by looking like foul play, but it ends in brokenhearted tragedy.

✔ **"The Adventure of the Abbey Grange":** A husband is dead and his wife is tied to a chair. It's a clear case of home invasion. *Or is it?*

✔ **"The Adventure of the Second Stain":** This is one of the greatest cases in Sherlock's career! It has everything — blackmail, stolen state secrets, a jealous mistress, and murder. It also has one of the strangest crime-scene clues of all time!

The Valley of Fear

The Valley of Fear is the fourth and final Sherlock Holmes novel. Originally serialized in *The Strand Magazine,* it was published in book form in 1915. As in *A Study in Scarlet* and *The Sign of the Four,* the story is divided into two parts. The first part is a classic locked-room mystery. How did someone get into John Douglas's room and blow his head off with a sawed-off shotgun, especially when the drawbridge across his moat was up?

The second half reveals the back story, which is based on the real-life criminal activities of the Molly Maguires and their downfall at the hands of a Pinkerton Agency detective in Pennsylvania. And, oh yeah . . . it also has Professor Moriarty.

His Last Bow

Originally published in 1917 during World War I, *His Last Bow* collects into one volume the stories published between 1908 and 1913, plus the title story, "His Last Bow," which was published in 1917. The American edition of the book had an additional tale, "The Adventure of the Cardboard Box," which had been suppressed years before.

The seven stories are

- ✔ **"The Adventure of Wisteria Lodge":** When Mr. John Scott Eccles accepts an invitation from his new friend to visit Wisteria Lodge, little does he know what he's getting himself into. By morning, his host is dead, and he's a wanted man.

- ✔ **"The Adventure of the Red Circle":** A murderous secret society and a young, persecuted couple are at the heart of this story. When a young woman spurns the advances of a Mafia chief, her husband takes extraordinary action to protect her.

- ✔ **"The Adventure of the Bruce-Partington Plans":** How did the body get on the underground tracks, and how did the stolen submarine plans get in his pocket? Missing state secrets, murder, espionage, and another stint of Holmesian housebreaking can be found in this adventure.

- ✔ **"The Adventure of the Dying Detective":** Sherlock Holmes is dying! Having contracted a deadly infectious disease while working on a case, the Great Detective is feverish and delirious. He sends Watson to summon the only man in London who can cure him. But will he come?

- ✔ **"The Disappearance of Lady Francis Carfax":** "One of the most dangerous classes in the world," says Holmes, "is the drifting and friendless woman. She is the inevitable inciter of crime in others." So it is with Lady Francis Carfax.

- ✔ **"The Adventure of the Devil's Foot":** When an entire family is driven insane, the village priest is sure it's the work of the devil. Sherlock Holmes isn't so sure.

- ✔ **"His Last Bow":** Set in 1914 on the eve of World War I, this case of espionage and spying is, chronologically, the very last adventure that Holmes and Watson work on together. (Stories that Doyle wrote after "His Last Bow" were set in a time period before it.)

The Case-Book of Sherlock Holmes

The last volume of Sherlock Holmes adventures was published in June 1927. It collects the final 12 short stories, which Arthur Conan Doyle sporadically wrote over the last decade of his life. By the time *Case-Book* was published,

Holmes had been appearing for 40 years! The struggle Doyle had in sustaining the stories is evident; some of these adventures are a bit strained. But others are as good as anything he ever wrote.

The final adventures of Sherlock Holmes are

- ✓ **"The Adventure of the Mazarin Stone":** This story was adapted from a stage play by Doyle called *The Crown Diamond*. Holmes uses several tricks, including a wax dummy and a record player, to extract a confession and recover a stolen jewel. It's definitely the weakest story in the canon.

- ✓ **"The Problem of Thor Bridge":** Holmes makes a fine recovery in one of the *best* stories in the canon. It's another locked-room mystery, except this time the room is a bridge over a pond. There's a body with a bullet in the brain, but is it murder? Or suicide? If so, *where's the weapon?*

- ✓ **"The Adventure of the Creeping Man":** This story has a dash of science fiction in it. When an aging professor begins treating himself with a mysterious serum, he undergoes a startling transformation!

- ✓ **"The Adventure of the Sussex Vampire":** When Bob Ferguson finds his mysterious South American wife sucking blood from the neck of their infant son, he fears he's married to one of the undead.

- ✓ **"The Adventure of the Three Garridebs":** What begins as an odd story of misdirection ends with terror for Holmes when Watson is shot.

- ✓ **"The Adventure of the Illustrious Client":** When the daughter of a member of high society falls under the spell of the "Austrian murderer" Baron Gruner, an "illustrious client" hires Holmes to prevent the marriage. This dark tale takes Holmes and Watson into the underbelly of London life in a story of violence, sexual abuse, and revenge.

- ✓ **"The Adventure of the Three Gables":** Mrs. Maberley receives an unusual offer to purchase her house (the buyer wants *everything*). Thus begins another adventure of Sherlock Holmes.

- ✓ **"The Adventure of the Blanched Soldier":** James Dodd wasn't worried when he didn't hear from his friend Godfrey for over six months. But when he's told that Godfrey is taking a cruise around the world, he doesn't buy it, especially when he sees Godfrey looking in his window at night! This is the first of two stories told by Holmes instead of Watson.

- ✓ **"The Adventure of the Lion's Mane":** In this, the second story told by Holmes, he has retired to a cottage on the Sussex Downs near the coast. One morning a neighbor staggers up from the beach and dies, crying out, "The lion's mane!" Holmes finds that the man's back is covered with what looks like whip marks. What killed the man, and what do his dying words mean?

Arthur Conan Doyle's favorite stories

In 1927, Sir Arthur Conan Doyle made a list for *The Strand Magazine* of what he believed were the best Sherlock Holmes short stories.

- ✔ "The Adventure of the Speckled Band"
- ✔ "The Red-Headed League"
- ✔ "The Adventure of the Dancing Men"
- ✔ "The Adventure of the Final Problem"
- ✔ "A Scandal in Bohemia"

- ✔ "The Adventure of the Empty House"
- ✔ "The Five Orange Pips"
- ✔ "The Adventure of the Second Stain"
- ✔ "The Adventure of the Devil's Foot"
- ✔ "The Adventure of the Priory School"
- ✔ "The Adventure of the Musgrave Ritual"
- ✔ "The Adventure of the Reigate Squire"

- ✔ **"The Adventure of the Retired Colourman":** "Burglary has always been an alternative profession, had I cared to adopt it," remarks Sherlock Holmes. It's a skill he turns to in solving a case of a missing wife and her lover.

- ✔ **"The Adventure of the Veiled Lodger":** When summoned by a landlady to check out a mysterious tenant who never shows her face, Holmes finds himself in the role of confessor instead of detective. "The Veiled Lodger" is one of the most tragic tales in the canon.

- ✔ **"The Adventure of Shoscombe Old Place":** Sir Robert Norberton has everything riding on his horse winning a race. Winning will save him from financial ruin. But why is he visiting an ancient family crypt at night? And how do you explain the human bone in the furnace? Sherlock's love of dogs holds the key to solving this case.

Three Centuries and Counting

Sherlock Holmes debuted in 1887. The staying power of this eccentric, moody, drug-abusing Victorian bachelor is amazing. Holmes's popularity now spans three centuries. Other famous literary detectives, and even pop culture icons, have come and gone, but Holmes is still going strong.

His esteem has never really waned. At times, of course, his light has seemed to shine brighter than it normally does, but from the moment Holmes debuted in *The Strand Magazine* to this day, his popularity has manifested itself in an astonishing number of ways.

Foreign translations

Sherlock Holmes is well-known worldwide, so it comes as no surprise that the stories have been translated into over 80 languages. These include Arabic, Chinese, Czechoslovakian, Egyptian, Finnish, French, German, Greek, Hebrew, Hindi, Italian, Japanese, Latin, Portuguese, Russian, Sinhalese, Spanish, Swedish, and Urdu, as well as more than 60 others. In addition to spoken-language translations, the canon has also been rendered in Braille, Morse code, and Pitman shorthand!

Dramatic adaptations

Almost as soon as the stories appeared in *The Strand Magazine,* dramatic portrayals of the Great Detective began to emerge. Today, Sherlock Holmes is one of the most dramatized characters in history. His dramatic exploits have appeared in every entertainment medium, be it stage, screen, TV, radio, and now even video games!

- ✔ **Stage adaptations:** The earliest dramatic adaptations of Holmes appeared on the stage. The first known play was appropriately titled *Sherlock Holmes* and was written by an enterprising man named Charles Rogers. It was 1893, and Arthur Conan Doyle had just killed Sherlock Holmes. Rogers realized that a mourning public would love to see its hero alive on the stage, and he dashed off his melodrama — the first of literally hundreds.

- ✔ **Sherlock on the silver screen:** Holmes was also there at the dawn of the motion picture era. In 1900, the American Mutoscope & Biograph Company produced the very first Sherlock Holmes film. *Sherlock Holmes Baffled* had a running time of 30 seconds and was shown in Mutoscope machines in arcades. Since then, there have been over 260 motion pictures featuring Holmes.

- ✔ **Sherlock on TV:** In addition to a stellar career on the big screen, Holmes was the first fictional character adapted for TV. In 1937, the American Radio Relay League broadcast an adaptation of "The Three Garridebs" from New York City's Radio City Music Hall. Since then, Holmes has been a TV staple, appearing in both long-running series and made-for-TV movies in Canada, Czechoslovakia, England, Poland, Russia, the United States, and other countries around the world.

- ✔ **Radio:** From the golden age of radio up through the modern era, Holmes has appeared in over 700 radio adaptations.

Sherlock Holmes societies

Perhaps the most obvious sign of the amazing popularity of Sherlock Holmes is the phenomenon of clubs and literary societies devoted to his adventures. To date there are over 260 Sherlock Holmes societies around the world, including ones in such countries as Australia, Denmark, France, Iraq, Israel, Italy, Japan, Kyrgyzstan, Portugal, Russia, Spain, Sweden, and Switzerland!

Continuing adventures

So what happens when you finish the final Holmes story? Well, many people read them again! But others turn to the groaning bookshelves of Sherlockian *pastiche* (works that deliberately imitate the style of Doyle's Holmes stories) and *parody* (works that poke fun at the character and the stories) that make up the continuing adventures of Sherlock Holmes. (And some even go on and write their own. . . .)

No other character in history has appeared in as many stories written by other authors as has Sherlock Holmes. This phenomenon started early, with the first known parody appearing in 1893. What began as a trickle is now a tidal wave, as new stories appear every year, literally by the hundreds.

Whether in the form of pastiche or parody, or maybe somewhere in between, devoted followers often need a fix of extra-canonical Sherlock!

Chapter 2

The Great Detective and His Life in Crime

Many readers think that Sherlock Holmes was the first detective in fiction. After all, his image is legendary — the curved pipe, the deerstalker hat. He has to be the first, right? Well, no, not exactly.

When Arthur Conan Doyle created Sherlock Holmes, he had numerous sources of inspiration, both in literature and in real life. This chapter looks at where Holmes came from, how Holmes improved the embryonic genre of detective fiction, and just what kind of detective Holmes actually was.

Finding Sherlock's Origins

From the beginning, readers have believed that Sherlock Holmes and his biographer, Dr. John H. Watson, were actual living, historical persons, and that the stories Holmes appears in were actual historical events. This phenomenon dates back almost to the creation of the character in 1887. From the time Doyle created Holmes when he was 26 right on up to his death in 1930, Doyle felt he always stood in the shadow of the Great Detective.

When Doyle began his undistinguished medical career in 1881, he had a lot of time on his hands. He was new in town, he had very little medical experience, and he had no patients. In the early days, it was all he could do to pay the gas bill or put food on the table. To make a little extra money and to fill those long hours without any patients, he turned to writing. He wrote ghost stories and a couple of bad novels, and he wrote a lot of letters to his mother. As a doctor, he eventually began to get patients and make a living, and his career ended up being moderately successful. But he still had plenty of time — and need — to supplement his income by writing.

The more Doyle wrote, the better he got, and he soon found he was able to supplement his medical income by placing stories in popular magazines of the day. Eventually, he began resenting the appearance of patients because they interrupted his creative train of thought. And then one day he decided to write a detective story.

Literary inspirations for Holmes

For inspiration, Doyle turned to his predecessors in the field. They were Edgar Allan Poe, Émile Gaboriau, and Wilkie Collins. It's fair to say that Doyle borrowed a little from all three of these writers.

Traces of nearly everything Doyle ever read usually found its way into the Holmes stories — newspaper stories, magazine stories, even advertisements — so to find obvious elements of previous detective writers in his writing is no surprise.

Edgar Allan Poe

Edgar Allan Poe (1809–1849) was a great American writer, poet, and critic best known for his Gothic tales of mystery and horror. Both his poetry and short stories routinely betray an obsession with death, madness, and guilt ("The Raven," for example), as well as dismemberment and decomposition ("The Tell-Tale Heart"). He was a creepy guy! He's also credited with inventing the detective fiction genre.

Doyle was particularly fond of Poe, calling him "the supreme original short story writer of all time" — an opinion that's hard to challenge.

Doyle got numerous bits of inspiration from Poe's stories:

- ✔ **"Murder in the Rue Morgue" (1841):** This story was an obvious inspiration for the method of Col. Sholto's death in *The Sign of the Four.* In "Rue Morgue," an inaccessible room is reached by a murderous orangutan. In *The Sign of the Four,* an inaccessible room is reached by a murderous pygmy.

> ✔ **"The Gold Bug" (1843):** This story features cryptograms and encoded writing. It's an obvious inspiration for the famous Dancing Men code in "The Dancing Men."
>
> ✔ **"The Purloined Letter" (1845):** This story's theme of hiding something — in this case a letter — in plain site is echoed in "A Scandal in Bohemia," where instead of a letter, the desired object is an incriminating photograph.

Émile Gaboriau

Émile Gaboriau (1832–1873) was a French novelist and early author of detective fiction. His best-known books featured an amateur detective named Monsieur Lecoq, who was based on a real-life criminal turned police chief, Eugène François Vidocq.

From Gaboriau, Doyle got scientific and methodical crime scene investigation (the TV show *CSI* owes a lot to Émile Gaboriau!), the use of disguises, and the storytelling device of the *flashback,* which Doyle employs in three of the four Sherlock Holmes novels.

Wilkie Collins

Wilkie Collins (1824–1889) was a very popular English novelist and short story writer. His best-known novels are the mysterious *The Woman in White* and the detective story *The Moonstone.*

From Wilkie Collins came the image of Sherlock Holmes. Below is a description of Sergeant Cuff from Collins's masterpiece *The Moonstone:*

> . . . so lean that he looked as if he had not got an ounce of flesh on his bones in any part of him. He was dressed all in decent black, with a white cravat round his neck. His face was sharp as a hatchet, and the skin of it was yellow and dry and withered as an autumn leaf. His eyes, of a steely light grey, had a very disconcerting trick, when they encountered your eyes, of looking as if they expected something more from you than you yourself were aware.

Compare Collins's description of Cuff with one of Doyle's numerous descriptions of Holmes:

> In height he was rather over six feet, and so excessively lean that he seemed to be much taller. His grey eyes were sharp and piercing, save during those intervals of black reaction to which I have alluded; and his thin, hawk-like nose gave his whole expression an air of alertness and decision.

A few other literary inspirations for Sherlock Holmes

You can find elements of the following works in various Sherlock Holmes adventures:

- *Confessions of an English Opium-Eater* (1821): Doyle got the idea for a more bohemian Sherlock Holmes and his notorious drug addiction from Thomas de Quincey's book.

- *The New Arabian Knights* (1882): Robert Louis Stevenson's book influenced the surreal, fantastical atmosphere of *The Sign of the Four,* along with its Indian overtones.

- *The Dynamiters* (1885): The Mormon flashback sequence in *A Study in Scarlet* bears more than a passing resemblance to Stevenson's novel.

- *The Mystery of the Hansom Cab* (1886): This novel by Fergus Hume, published a year before *A Study in Scarlet,* is a model of the urban, late-Victorian crime novel.

The model for Holmes

Doyle had other literary inspirations and influences, but when he was directly asked, "Who was your model for Sherlock Holmes?" he didn't mention another writer or a story. Instead, he answered with a real-life person: "Dr. Joseph Bell," shown in Figure 2-1.

Dr. Joseph Bell was one of Doyle's former medical professors at Edinburgh University, where Doyle studied to be a doctor. Bell was (and actually, still is) legendary for specializing in accurate diagnoses based on the very Sherlockian method of observation and deduction.

Doyle wrote of Bell: "He would sit in his receiving room with a face like a Red Indian, and diagnose the people as they came in, before they even opened their mouths. He would tell them details of their past life; and hardly would he ever make a mistake."

And again, in his autobiography, Doyle recounted the merging of his literary influences with his old medical school teacher:

> I felt now that I was capable of something fresher and crisper and more workmanlike than many of the detective stories that had been written up to that time. Gaboriau had rather attracted me by the neat dovetailing of his plots, and Poe's masterful detective, M. Dupin, had from boyhood been one of my heroes. But could I bring an addition of my own? I

thought of my old teacher Joe Bell, of his eagle face, of his curious ways, of his eerie trick of spotting details. If he were a detective he would surely reduce this fascinating business to something nearer an exact science. I would try it if I could get this effect. It was surely possible in real life, so why should I not make it plausible in fiction?

Doyle wrote a letter to Bell in 1892, after Sherlock Holmes had exploded on the scene:

It is most certainly to you that I owe Sherlock Holmes, and though in the stories I have the advantage of being able to place [the detective] in all sorts of dramatic positions, I do not think that his analytical work is in the least an exaggeration of some effects which I have seen you produce in the out-patient ward.

Bell wrote back and told Doyle that "you are yourself Sherlock Holmes and well you know it."

Figure 2-1:
Dr. Joseph
Bell.

A new kind of detective

As I explain in the preceding sections, Sherlock Holmes wasn't the first detective in literature, but he was the first of a new *style* of detective. Early in Doyle's first published Holmes story, the novel *A Study in Scarlet,* Holmes uses the term "consulting detective" (and in later stories, "private consulting detective") to describe what he does.

The "world's only private consulting detective"

Victorian London at the time of Sherlock Holmes was full of detectives, and these real-life investigators fell into the same categories as the fictional ones. As Holmes tells Watson in *A Study in Scarlet,* "here in London we have lots of government detectives [police officers] and lots of private ones." But as a *consulting* detective, Holmes is a sort of "court of last appeal." So when one of these professional investigators is stuck and can't solve whatever mystery he's working on, the stumped investigator comes to Holmes and, for a fee, Holmes will "put [him] on the right scent."

Though the character of Sherlock Holmes shares traits with his predecessors, his professionalism and investigative methods are crucial distinctions. For instance, Poe's detective Dupin isn't a professional detective but merely a gifted amateur who investigates crime for personal amusement. Gaboriau's Monsieur Lecoq is a police officer, as is Collins's Sergeant Cuff. But Sherlock Holmes is clearly different.

Some crime fiction authors have debated whether Poe's detective Dupin is a professional or an amateur. It's true that Dupin receives a fee at the end of his stories, but he's clearly not in the same class as Holmes. For instance, in "The Murders in the Rue Morgue," Dupin takes up the case by saying, "As for these murders, let us enter into some examinations for ourselves, before we make up an opinion respecting them. *An inquiry will afford us amusement*" (italics mine). William Crisman, in the article "Poe's Dupin as Professional, the Dupin Stories as Serial Text," argues that Dupin evolves from amateur to professional over the course of his stories.

Holmes's status as "the world's only private consulting detective" was an innovation that still sets him apart to this day. It has often been imitated, such as in Agatha Christie's popular detective Hercule Poirot. Christie openly acknowledged Holmes as an inspiration when she created her famous Belgian detective. The similarities are striking:

✔ Just as Holmes has his friend Dr. Watson tell the story, Poirot has Captain Arthur Hastings, who also acts as an assistant and storyteller.

✔ In the Holmes stories, Inspector Lestrade is the Scotland Yard detective whom Holmes both works with and gets the best of. Sure enough, Poirot has his own version, a Chief Inspector Japp.

✔ Poirot even has a smarter older brother! Sherlock has Mycroft. Hercule has Achille!

Like doctor, like detective

Arthur Conan Doyle based the unique model of private consulting detective on his knowledge and experience as a medical doctor. Plenty of doctors were general practitioners, as Doyle was himself. Then and now, when a patient's illness requires knowledge or skill beyond the general practitioner's abilities, he turns to a specialist. When Doyle applied this model to detective fiction, Sherlock Holmes became a specialist in crime. He became the detective the other detectives turned to.

This doesn't mean that Holmes didn't get cases on his own, just like a doctor who specializes in a specific branch of medicine doesn't only get patients through referral from other doctors. But it does mean that Holmes worked on a higher professional plane than other detectives, and this special status brought him the most interesting, challenging, and often most bizarre cases — cases that, if he wanted to, he was free to refuse.

The best example of a modern private consulting detective is TV's Adrian Monk (from the show *Monk*). Like Holmes, Monk takes in cases on his own, but he's also the go-to detective when the police find themselves stumped (which is a lot of the time!).

Doyle's experiences and career as a medical doctor greatly influence the Holmes stories in both tone and detail. Consider these examples:

✔ When Holmes first meets Watson, Holmes is working on a test to detect blood stains in a chemical lab in St. Bartholomew's Hospital, which was also a medical school.

✔ In the early stories, Holmes struggles to make ends meet, just as Doyle did when he first established his own medical practice.

✔ As a specialist in crime detection, Holmes has profound scientific knowledge in specific areas, just as a doctor who specializes in certain diseases would have.

✔ For Holmes, the detective/client relationship is very much like the doctor/patient relationship. When meeting a client for the first time, for example, Holmes inquires into the person's life and history, just as a doctor learns his patient's history on first meeting. And as in a doctor/patient relationship, there is the presumption of confidentiality. On more than one occasion, Holmes has refused to divulge details of both a client's case and the client's identity. And in a more indefinable way, Holmes often takes on the role of comforter and counselor, just as a doctor does when consulting with a patient over a distressing diagnosis.

✔ Holmes's fees and payment structure are modeled after a doctor's: "My professional charges are upon a fixed scale. I do not vary them, save when I remit them altogether."

> ✔ Holmes's method of observation and deduction is based on the diagnostic technique of Doyle's medical school teacher, Dr. Joseph Bell (refer to the earlier section "The model for Holmes" for details).

The influence of Doyle's medical training and experience gives the Sherlock Holmes stories a richness and authenticity that's often lacking in other works of detective fiction, especially everything that came before them.

The Methods of Sherlock Holmes

I have trained myself to see what others overlook.

—Sherlock Holmes

Sherlock Holmes's methods of detection can be divided into two categories: crime scene investigation and deductive reasoning. Many people unfamiliar with Sherlock think of him only as a crime scene investigator or as a sort of human computer. But to really understand his methods, it's important to look at both sides of his technique.

Victorian CSI: Holmes at the scene of the crime

Holmes didn't invent the detailed crime scene investigation that has become familiar through popular TV shows like *CSI*. But it's fair to say that Holmes not only popularized this relatively new branch of science in detective fiction and the public's mind but also showed real-life law enforcement agencies the potential of forensic science.

Throughout the 60 stories, Holmes investigates many crime scenes. His method of analysis and evidence collection is detailed and scientific:

- ✔ **He pays attention to subtle clues as well as the more obvious ones:** He examines tobacco ashes and cigar and cigarette butts, and is even cognizant of odor, whether it's a type of perfume or poison on a dead man's lips. Holmes often lectures the Scotland Yarders on the need to notice these "trifles."

- ✔ **He meticulously analyzes the evidence he finds:** He examines bloodstains, uses tracings of footprints (both human and animal), preserves impressions with plaster of Paris, has handwriting analyzed, and studies bullet holes and firearms.

- ✔ **He uses his vast knowledge to recognize clues that others miss:** He can recognize and distinguish between death by hanging, poison, stabbing, gunshot, and blunt force trauma.

A case study: "The Resident Patient"

Though the Sherlock Holmes stories have many examples of Holmes's investigative and forensic ability, none presents a better case study of Sherlockian crime scene investigation than "The Resident Patient." It's a tour-de-force!

Holmes is summoned to the home of Dr. Percy Trevelyan, who has a resident patient named Blessington who has been found hanged in his bedroom. Blessington had a fear of intruders. Now he's dead, hanging by the neck from a hook in the center of his ceiling. The police detective believes it's a suicide, but Holmes's examination of the bedroom convinces him otherwise. Several clues, including the discovery of four cigar ends and tobacco ashes, tell him that Blessington was visited by three intruders in the middle of the night.

First, Holmes examines Blessington's cigar case, which was in the victim's coat pocket. Inside it he finds a single cigar. It's a Havana, but the other four cigar ends are an unusually thin type of cigar imported from East India. Holmes therefore knows immediately that Blessington didn't smoke these cigars.

Further examination reveals that two were smoked with a holder and two without a holder. That means that more than one cigar smoker had been present. Holmes then examines the room, paying close attention to where the ashes of the cigars fell. He's able to deduce that the man with the cigar holder sat in a wicker chair, a second man sat in a chair near a chest of drawers (he repeatedly knocked his ash off against it), and a third man paced up and down on the opposite side of the room. This evidence also tells Holmes that they had been there for a long period of time, and so some kind of deliberation must have been going on. Ultimately, Blessington was hanged.

"This is no suicide," said Sherlock Holmes to inspector Lanner. "It is a very deeply planned and cold-blooded murder."

The meticulous portrayal of Holmes's investigative and evidence-gathering style is still held up as an example by law enforcement agencies.

The "ideal reasoner"

Just as important as Holmes's scientific method of crime scene investigation was his use of observation and deduction. Collecting evidence was one thing; being able to reason what it meant was another. His reasoning ability was usually the key to solving the mystery or catching the criminal.

As Sherlock says in *A Study in Scarlet:* "From a drop of water a logician could infer the possibility of an Atlantic or a Niagara without having seen or heard of one or the other."

Holmes's method, then, is relatively straightforward. He would draw inferences based on careful study of the evidence he observed and gathered. When several theories were possible, he'd opt for the one that covered the most facts in the case until proven wrong. "It is an old maxim of mine," he tells Watson, "that when you have excluded the impossible, whatever remains, however improbable, must be the truth."

Many of the stories begin with a display of Sherlockian deductive reasoning:

- **"A Scandal in Bohemia":** Holmes deduces that Watson had gotten very wet lately and that he has a clumsy and careless servant girl. He knows this by observing that the inside of Watson's left shoe is scored by six parallel cuts. He deduces that they were made by a careless servant girl after Watson was out in bad weather.

- *The Hound of the Baskervilles:* The novel begins with an amusing yet instructive demonstration of Holmes's method. By examining the marks and inscription on a walking stick that was left behind by a prospective client while Holmes and Watson were out, Holmes deduces that the owner was "amiable, unambitious, and absent-minded." He also concludes that he has a medium-sized dog. And of course, he's right!

The canon contains many other outstanding examples of deductive reasoning. On several occasions, Holmes is able to state a total stranger's occupation. In *A Study in Scarlet,* it's a retired military man. In "The Red-Headed League" it's a ship's carpenter who is now a pawnbroker. In "The Greek Interpreter," it's a retired artillery officer.

Holmes also makes astonishing deductions by observing objects and personal items including hats, pipes, shoes, and the knees of someone's pants. From the examination of a pocket watch, Holmes discovers that Watson's late brother was an alcoholic gambler.

Holmes was often accused of being insensitive in his pursuit of "that true cold reason which I place above all things." Watson once accused him of being "an automaton — a calculating machine," adding that "there is something positively inhuman in you at times." It's not that Holmes is uncaring. But when a client comes to him with a case, Holmes deliberately approaches the person and the situation as a cipher or puzzle to solve. As Watson explains, "grit in a sensitive instrument, or a crack in one of his own high-power lenses, would not be more disturbing than a strong emotion in a nature such as his." Sherlock's rationalism occasionally caused him to be insensitive to his client's feelings.

Stocking his brain attic

In pursuit of his role as the world's first and only consulting detective, Sherlock Holmes embarked upon a unique and specialized course of study. He describes his brain as an *attic,* which he prefers to stock with only the information that helps him as a detective. Without taking any formal classes, Holmes becomes a first-class chemist. As he says, his studies were "eccentric," and those who knew him couldn't figure out what use he was going to put all that learning to. As someone describes him in *A Study in Scarlet,* "he has amassed a lot of out-of-the-way knowledge which would astonish his professors."

This practice of studying subjects that would further his skill as a detective is one that Holmes pursues throughout his career. And he draws on this knowledge when taking on a case, comparing his current puzzle to thousands of prior crimes, looking for similarities and patterns. He tells Scotland Yard Inspector Stanley Hopkins that "the most practical thing that you ever did in your life would be to shut yourself up for three months and read twelve hours a day at the annals of crime."

Holmes's research often leads him to write papers, articles, and *monographs* (treatises), which were usually technical publications that he recommended to other detectives. They include:

- ✔ "Upon the Distinction Between the Ashes of the Various Tobaccos": This work describes 140 different tobacco ashes and includes color plates.

- ✔ "The Polyphonic Motets of Lassus": Holmes printed this work for private circulation, said by some experts to be the last word on the subject. (We'll take their word for it!)

- ✔ Two articles on ears in the *Anthropological Journal.*

- ✔ A monograph on secret writings in which 160 different ciphers are analyzed.

- ✔ A monograph on the dating of documents.

- ✔ A contribution to the literature of tattoos.

- ✔ A monograph on the tracing of footsteps.

- ✔ A monograph on the influence of the trade on the form of the hand.

- ✔ "The Book of Life," a magazine article laying out his theory of observation and deduction.

- ✔ "The Practical Handbook of Bee Culture," on, you guessed it, bee behavior.

Holmes on the "brain attic"

In *A Study in Scarlet,* Watson confesses amazement that Holmes is ignorant of the Copernican theory that the planets orbit the sun. Holmes goes on to explain his theory of brain capacity. "I consider that a man's brain originally is like a little empty attic," he says, "and you have to stock it with such furniture as you choose." After saying only a fool jumbles up his brain with useless knowledge, he adds that "the skilful workman" will "have nothing but the tools which may help him in doing his work, but of these he has a large assortment, and all in the most perfect order."

Sherlock Holmes didn't know everything

Shortly after Sherlock Holmes and Dr. Watson begin sharing rooms, Watson finds himself fascinated by his strange new friend — his peculiar habits, the odd visitors, and most of all, what Holmes knows and doesn't know.

"His ignorance was as remarkable as his knowledge," Watson writes of his roommate. "Of contemporary literature, philosophy and politics he appeared to know next to nothing.... My surprise reached a climax, however, when I found that he was ignorant of the Copernican Theory and of the composition of the Solar System."

Finally, Watson draws up a list of Sherlock's knowledge and entitles it "Sherlock Holmes — His Limits."

1. Knowledge of Literature — Nil.

2. Philosophy — Nil.

3. Astronomy — Nil.

4. Politics — Feeble.

5. Botany — Variable. Well up in belladonna, opium, and poisons generally. Knows nothing of practical gardening.

6. Knowledge of Geology — Practical, but limited. Tells at a glance different soils from each other. After walks has shown me splashes upon his trousers, and told me by their colour and consistence in what part of London he had received them.

7. Knowledge of Chemistry — Profound.

8. Anatomy — Accurate, but unsystematic.

9. Sensational Literature — Immense. He appears to know every detail of every horror perpetrated in the century.

10. Plays the violin well.

11. Is an expert singlestick player, boxer, and swordsman.

12. Has a good practical knowledge of British law.

Over the course of the stories, Holmes demonstrates a wide degree of knowledge, but he doesn't know everything (see the sidebar "Sherlock Holmes didn't know everything" for a list of the limits of Sherlock's knowledge). Most of his knowledge relates to his career as a detective and covers the criminal world of London, including such subjects as

- The details of continental crime
- Foreign languages, including French, German, and Latin
- The Bible (but this is a bit "rusty")
- Dogs
- An exact knowledge of the geography of London
- Newspaper typefaces

✔ Perfumes

✔ The typewriter and its relation to crime

✔ Bicycle tires

✔ The names and trademarks of the world's major gun makers.

Tools of the trade

While the best tool Sherlock Holmes uses is his great brain, as a detective he also uses a variety of objects. Some help him gather evidence, and some are for personal defense. Most are legal, but some are decidedly illegal!

Holmes doesn't carry a crime scene bag like modern detectives, but he does have items in his pockets to help him. These include a magnifying glass, a tape measure, and an envelope for collecting evidence such as tobacco ash.

For personal protection, Holmes's weapon of choice is the riding (also known as hunting) crop. For instance, Holmes uses it to strike out at the poisonous snake in "The Speckled Band," and he nearly thrashes the heartless stepfather in "A Case of Identity."

He also carries a cane, which he uses as a weapon when needed. He is, according to Watson, an expert at "singlestick," a form of fighting using a stick or cane. And on rare occasions, both Holmes and Watson use pistols, although Holmes usually prefers that Watson carry the gun. Some have speculated that this may mean Holmes isn't a very good shot!

As a private consulting detective, Holmes was a free agent and therefore could employ methods not open to the police — like housebreaking (see Figure 2-2)! There are two examples in the stories of Sherlockian burglary: In both "The Adventure of Charles Augustus Milverton" and "The Bruce-Partington Plans," Holmes and Watson resort to illegal entry in pursuit of justice. When playing burglar instead of detective, the tools of the trade included black silk face-coverings, rubber-soled tennis shoes, a glass cutter, a jemmy, a dark lantern, and a chisel.

Other skills that come in handy

In addition to possessing obvious detective skills, Sherlock Holmes had other talents that came in handy. These gave him an added edge over the average official police detective.

An actor and a rare one

When someone who has never read a Sherlock Holmes story is asked to say what they know about the Great Detective, one of the most frequent answers is, "He often uses a disguise!" This is one of the best-known characteristics of Sherlock Holmes, and it was a powerful and effective tool in his arsenal as detective.

Watson describes Holmes as a talented actor. Holmes often goes undercover, adopting a disguise to penetrate the criminal's lair or to gather evidence that may not be available under normal circumstances. His skill as an actor and at adopting disguises was so remarkable that he was even able to fool his close friend Watson. In "A Scandal in Bohemia," Holmes adopts the identity of a drunken groom and is so convincing that Watson has to look three times before he's certain that the groom is actually Sherlock Holmes. "It was not merely that Holmes changed his costume," says Watson. "His expression, his manner, his very soul seemed to vary with every fresh part that he assumed."

Figure 2-2: Holmes and Watson as burglars in "The Adventure of Charles Augustus Milverton."

Illustration by Sidney Paget, The Strand Magazine.

Athletic skills

While seldom taking exercise for exercise's sake, Sherlock Holmes was nevertheless a remarkable athlete, and this physical ability was a great aid in his chosen career. It allowed him the strength to follow a bloodhound through the streets and alleyways of London in *The Sign of the Four,* to climb a tall fireplace mantle in "The Abbey Grange," and to climb a slippery rock wall out of the Reichenbach Falls in "The Empty House."

It's at the Reichenbach Falls that Holmes fights Professor Moriarty to the death. The climactic battle is won by Holmes, thanks to his knowledge of the obscure martial art of bartitsu, or the Japanese system of wrestling, which Holmes said had "more than once been very useful to me."

Holmes is also a formidable boxer, a skill that comes in handy on several occasions. The first mention of this talent comes in *The Sign of the Four,* in which it says that Sherlock "fought three rounds" in a benefit fight four years earlier. In "The Solitary Cyclist," Holmes is challenged to a fight in a pub by Jack Woodley, the villain of the tale (see Figure 2-3). It isn't wise to pick a bar fight with Sherlock Holmes — Woodley went home in a cart.

Figure 2-3: Sherlock Holmes's fistfight with Jack Woodley in "The Solitary Cyclist."

" A STRAIGHT LEFT AGAINST A SLOGGING RUFFIAN."

Illustration by Sidney Paget, The Strand Magazine.

A Few (Not So Small) Quirks

One of the reasons readers return to the Sherlock Holmes stories over and over, even when they know the solution to the mystery, is the character of Holmes himself. Holmes seems like a real person, full of contradictions, both virtuous and flawed. He's not a superhero but instead a real character with real issues.

Melancholy

Did Holmes suffer from depression? Many readers have wondered. When you read Watson say that Sherlock has periods of "excellent spirits" that "alternated with fits of the blackest depression," a pretty clear picture begins to emerge. Time and again, Holmes is seen slipping into a funk:

> "Stand at the window here. Was ever such a dreary, dismal, unprofitable world? See how the yellow fog swirls down the street and drifts across the dun-coloured houses. What could be more hopelessly prosaic and material?"

Watson speaks of a "dual nature" and how under the strain of work, Holmes has what looks exactly like a nervous breakdown:

> His iron constitution, however, had broken down under the strain of an investigation which had extended over two months, during which period he had never worked less than fifteen hours a day and had more than once, as he assured me, kept to his task for five days at a stretch. Even the triumphant issue of his labours could not save him from reaction after so terrible an exertion, and at a time when Europe was ringing with his name and when his room was literally ankle-deep with congratulatory telegrams I found him a prey to the blackest depression.

It was while in this state that Holmes often resorted to drugs.

Drug use

"Which is it to-day," I asked, "morphine or cocaine?"

That Sherlock Holmes is a drug addict in the early years of his detective career is undeniable. You find out about this unfortunate habit in *The Sign of the Four*. Watson says that for several months he has witnessed Holmes take drugs three times a day:

Sherlock Holmes took his bottle from the corner of the mantelpiece, and his hypodermic syringe from its neat morocco case. With his long, white, nervous fingers he adjusted the delicate needle and rolled back his left shirtcuff. For some little time his eyes rested thoughtfully upon the sinewy forearm and wrist, all dotted and scarred with innumerable puncture-marks. Finally, he thrust the sharp point home, pressed down the tiny piston, and sank back into the velvet-lined armchair with a long sigh of satisfaction.

Evidence indicates that Holmes alternated between morphine and cocaine, both of which were perfectly legal in Victorian London. Legal or not, Watson implored his friend to quit and often lectured him on the damage to his body and mind that his drug use was causing.

Holmes explained that drugs were a response to boredom and lack of work. Once, when Watson asks Holmes if he currently has a case, Holmes responds by saying, "None. Hence the cocaine."

As his doctor and his friend, Watson is finally able to wean Sherlock from his drug addiction. In later years, while Holmes was able to resist the craving for drugs, Watson knew a relapse was always possible, especially during slow times between cases. It was then that Watson would see a drawn, brooding look in his friend's face and know that the urge "was not dead, but sleeping."

Smoking

Despite being a fictional character, Holmes is one of the great smokers in history. While partial to pipes and cigarettes, he also smokes cigars. He's often portrayed as smoking a large, oversized calabash pipe.

The calabash pipe, shown in Figure 2-4, wasn't a feature in Doyle's tales. It was actually an invention of the actor William Gillette, who portrayed Holmes on the stage in the early 20th century. Gillette used the calabash because it was easier to deliver his lines while smoking it. The calabash has been associated with Sherlock Holmes ever since.

Holmes's pipe tobacco of choice was called "shag." Shag is not a flavor but a method of cutting the tobacco leaves into a very fine, narrow leaf. Doing so made it suitable for rolling into cigarettes as well.

Sherlock had several peculiar smoking habits. One was keeping his tobacco in the toe-end of a Persian slipper tacked to the mantle of his fireplace, a practice that left the tobacco in the hot, dry air near the fire, making it smoke hot and fast. Even worse was his disgusting habit of the "plugs and dottles."

Holmes's first pipe of the morning "consisted of all the plugs and dottles of the previous day." Yuck!

Finally, Holmes smokes *a lot!* He smokes when he wakes up. He smokes when he's reading or just hanging out at Baker Street. And he really smokes when he's on a case. The smoky atmosphere of the Baker Street rooms and the soothing tobacco helps him think and meditate on the problem. A case that's particularly mysterious is called "a three-pipe problem." Tobacco use was an addiction that, unlike drugs, Sherlock Holmes never gave up.

Figure 2-4: The calabash pipe is commonly associated with Sherlock Holmes but is actually found nowhere in the canon.

Photo courtesy of Steven Doyle.

Case Files: A Rundown of Significant Cases

Any list of the best or most significant cases of Sherlock Holmes is by necessity up for debate. Even Doyle's own list (see the sidebar "Arthur Conan Doyle's favorite stories" in Chapter 1) is disputed by fans! But some cases are definite landmarks. Following is a list of some of Holmes's more significant cases:

- *A Study in Scarlet:* This short novel is the first Sherlock Holmes story. It's notable for its account of the first meeting of Holmes and Watson and the beginning of their immortal partnership. The book is split into two halves. The first half is Watson's account of the investigation of a strange murder in a deserted house. The second half is called "The Country of the Saints" and is a flashback that provides motivation and a back story to the murder in England. It takes place among the Mormons in the state of Utah in the U.S. By the end of the book, the link between the two halves is made, and it's revealed that the motive for the crime is revenge.

- *The Sign of the Four:* This novel is the second Holmes story to be written and published. *The Sign of the Four* is a more mature, complicated book than *A Study in Scarlet* and paints a far more bohemian and textured picture of the Great Detective. For instance, it's here that Holmes's drug habit first appears. It's also in this book that Watson meets his first wife, Mary Morstan.

The Sign of the Four was commissioned on August 30, 1889, at a dinner party held by the managing editor of *Lippincott's Monthly Magazine,* Joseph M. Stoddart, at the Langham Hotel in London. This memorable meal also had another prospective contributor, Oscar Wilde, who went on to write *The Picture of Dorian Gray* for the magazine.

- "A Scandal in Bohemia": This is the first of the 56 Sherlock Holmes short stories to be published in *The Strand Magazine.* Holmes is hired by the king of Bohemia to thwart an anticipated blackmail attempt by the "adventuress," Irene Adler. As Watson says in the very first line of the tale, "To Sherlock Holmes she is always *the* woman. I have seldom heard him mention her under any other name. In his eyes she eclipses and predominates the whole of her sex." "A Scandal in Bohemia" has fueled endless speculation about a potential romance between Holmes and Irene Adler, of "dubious and questionable memory."

- "The Speckled Band": One of the most famous tales in the Sherlockian canon, this story of creeping murder has it all: an evil stepfather, an old Gothic English manor house, a midnight vigil in the dark, and a thrilling climax. Doyle adapted this story into a successful stage play in 1910.

- "Silver Blaze": On the eve of an important race, the racehorse Silver Blaze has been stolen, and his trainer has been found murdered. It's up to Holmes and Watson to find the killer and recover the horse before race day. With its atmospheric portrayal of Dartmoor, this is one of the most popular stories in the canon. It's also the origin of the popular reference to "the dog that did nothing in the night-time."

- "The Final Problem": "It is with a heavy heart that I take up my pen to write these the last words in which I shall ever record the singular gifts by which my friend Mr. Sherlock Holmes was distinguished." So begins this story, which introduces the greatest villain in all of detective fiction, the criminal mastermind Professor James Moriarty. "The Final Problem" includes Holmes's long investigation into Moriarty's criminal organization, a chilling visit by the professor himself to Holmes's rooms on Baker Street, three murderous attempts on Holmes's life, and the hair-raising flight to the continent to escape. And of course, it has the most shocking ending of any story in the canon: "An examination by experts leaves little doubt that a personal contest between the two men ended, as it could hardly fail to end in such a situation, in their reeling over, locked in each other's arms."

✓ ***The Hound of the Baskervilles:*** This novel is a masterpiece of Gothic suspense and atmosphere and is often cited as one of, if not *the* greatest mystery story of all time. The Baskerville family of Dartmoor has a family legend that says they're cursed to die violent deaths and be haunted by a ghostly hound of hell. When elderly Sir Charles is found dead and a ghastly hound is seen on the moor, Holmes and Watson are enlisted to protect the young new heir. With its melancholy, gloomy atmosphere and supernatural overtones, this story ranks as the all-time favorite Sherlock Holmes story.

✓ **"The Empty House":** Holmes returns from the dead in this tale. His surprising reappearance causes his landlady, Mrs. Hudson, to go into hysterics, and his friend Watson to faint! Holmes recounts how he narrowly escaped death at the Reichenbach Falls, spent three years abroad letting criminal London believe he was dead, and returned to capture the remaining member of Professor Moriarty's gang.

✓ **"The Dying Detective":** Upon learning that his friend Holmes is dying from an infectious disease, Watson hurries to his aid. He finds Holmes delirious and on death's door. In between bouts of raving and abuse, Watson learns that there is one man in London capable of helping him. Can Watson persuade him to come? And why must he hide behind the headboard of the bed when he does?

✓ **"The Illustrious Client":** It's here that Holmes goes up against one of the worst villains in all the stories — Baron Adlebert Gruner, the Austrian murderer. This hypnotic womanizer is engaged to a prominent member of society's daughter, and Holmes is persuaded by an "illustrious client" to intervene. Despite not having an actual mystery to solve, this story — with its overtones of sexual perversion and violence and the thinly-veiled member of the royal family who hires Holmes — is one of the most memorable of the later tales.

✓ **"His Last Bow":** On the eve of World War I, German spy Von Bork is preparing to leave England the intelligence he has gathered. He's waiting for one last piece of crucial information, which is to be delivered by an Irish-American spy named Altamont. This story provides a glimpse of a 60-year-old Sherlock Holmes and Dr. Watson called out of retirement to foil the German's plans. It gives us a final glimpse of our old friends. "Stand with me here upon the terrace," Holmes says to Watson, "for it may be the last quiet talk that we shall ever have." (This was intended to be the last Sherlock Holmes story ever published, but financial need and popular demand forced Doyle to write more stories in later years.)

Chapter 3

Arthur Conan Doyle: The Doctor Who Created the Detective

*F*rom childhood, Arthur Conan Doyle was a natural storyteller. At first glance, you wouldn't have taken the tall, athletic boy for someone with an artistic nature. But from his earliest days, Doyle spun tales. His first audience was his mother, who filled her child's imagination with stories of knights, chivalry, and adventure. Later in school, Doyle regularly kept his classmates spellbound with tales of bloodthirsty pirates and scary ghost stories. In retrospect, Arthur Conan Doyle was born to be a writer.

The adage "write what you know" certainly fit Doyle's approach. Much of his work contains autobiographical elements. For example, his 1895 novel *The Stark Munro Letters,* the story of a young doctor's struggle to establish himself in medical practice, is clearly autobiographical. Throughout his career, he drew on both his personal and professional life for inspiration, writing an astonishing number of tales with an English doctor like himself as the protagonist. These obviously include the Sherlock Holmes stories.

Doyle's Early Life and Education

Arthur Conan Doyle, shown in Figure 3-1, was the son of an Irish father who was born and raised in England and an Irish mother who lived in Edinburgh, Scotland. Arthur was born in Edinburgh in 1859. With his Irish ethnicity, his Scottish burr, and his English citizenship, Doyle embodied the United Kingdom and was thoroughly British in his outlook.

Figure 3-1:
Sir Arthur
Conan
Doyle.

"Art in the blood"

Doyle once had Sherlock Holmes say that "art in the blood is likely to take the strangest of forms." As usual, he was writing from personal experience. Doyle came from an artistic family. His grandfather was John Doyle, a famous political cartoonist. Arthur's uncles were artists, too. One was Henry Doyle, who was the director of Ireland's National Gallery, and the other was Richard "Dicky" Doyle, famous for illustrating *Punch* magazine.

Arthur's father was Charles Altamont Doyle. Charles also had artistic talent but never reached a high level of fame. He was an architectural draftsman in the Scottish Office of Works and held this job for 30 years, supplementing his meager pay with book and magazine illustrating.

Charles married Mary Foley, and together they had ten children, but only seven survived. Arthur inherited his storytelling skills from his mother. Mary Doyle often read to her children or made up stories with such skill that, as an adult, Arthur would say in his autobiography, "the vivid stories she would tell me stand out so clearly that they obscure the real facts of my life."

Unfortunately, the family was not without its problems. Charles was a chronic alcoholic, an affliction that worsened through the years, causing emotional and financial hardship for his wife and children. As Charles's alcoholism (and later epilepsy) worsened, the family found its financial fortunes in a slow downward spiral. Ultimately, Charles was committed to an asylum, and the family was forced to take in lodgers to make ends meet. Arthur's strong, resourceful mother kept the family together and forever earned the devotion of her son.

This period had a profound impact on Doyle, and that impact is reflected throughout his writing. Young women in financial need, abusive alcoholic husbands and fathers, and households with sometimes unsavory lodgers all find their way into his fiction, including the Sherlock Holmes stories.

You may have heard Arthur referred to as "Conan Doyle" enough that you think "Conan Doyle" was a compound last name. However, "Conan" was Arthur's *middle* name. Shortly after he graduated from high school he began using Conan as a sort of surname. But technically, his last name is simply "Doyle."

Boarding school

Throughout most of his childhood, Doyle didn't live at home. At the age of 9, he was sent to England to attend a Jesuit preparatory school and then to Stonyhurst, a Jesuit secondary school. These weren't happy times for Doyle. The school was very strict, and corporal punishment was common. As Doyle characterized himself in his autobiography, he was "wild, full blooded and a trifle reckless." This brought Arthur his fair share of discipline. He graduated in 1876 at the age of 17.

Coming from a Catholic family, it wasn't unusual for Arthur to attend a private Catholic boarding school (with the help of wealthier relatives). But it was here that the young man began to question his faith, heading down a path that would land him in a very different spiritual place years later.

During this time, Doyle began writing regular letters to his mother and cultivating the lifelong habit of correspondence. He also worked on his storytelling skills by entertaining his fellow students with exciting tales he would make up.

Medical school

Given his family background, his artistic nature, and his admittedly wild adolescence, it's surprising that Doyle chose to go into medicine. He was accepted into the University of Edinburgh to study medicine in 1876. His medical training and the impressions left by his instructors laid the foundation for the rest of his life. These experiences trained him in science, fueled his literary career, and even helped form his religious and philosophical outlook on life. Perhaps the greatest influence came from his instructors, two of which memorably show up later in his writing:

- ✓ **Professor William Rutherford:** With his Assyrian beard, booming voice, and bombastic personality, Rutherford was the model for Professor George Edward Challenger of Doyle's landmark science fiction novel *The Lost World.*

- ✓ **Dr. Joseph Bell:** Bell had, without question, the greatest influence on Doyle. He was legendary for his ability to make a diagnosis without the patient ever saying a word by using observation and deduction. This seemingly magical ability was a lesson Doyle never forgot. (For more detail about Bell and his role in the creation of Sherlock Holmes, go to Chapter 2.)

Even before he graduated from medical school, Doyle had become a published author. His short story "The Mystery of Sasassa Valley" was published in *Chamber's Journal.* He followed it up with "The American Tale," which was published in *London Society.*

Writing wasn't the only way Doyle earned money while in medical school. In 1880, he took a job as a doctor on the whaling ship *Hope.* (Whaling was considered a normal commercial activity back in those days.) In his auto biography, he cites this adventure as one of the greatest experiences of his life. "I went on board the whaler a big straggling youth," he later wrote. "I came off a powerful well-grown man."

Upon graduation, Doyle hoped to have another adventure similar to his arctic voyage. This time he signed on to the *Mayumba* as the ship's surgeon and sailed to Africa in 1881. He had many adventures on these voyages, ranging from dealing with tropical fevers to battling fire at sea.

Early practice and hard lessons

In 1882, Doyle returned to England and settled in Plymouth, a bustling southern port city. Arthur was invited to join the practice of an eccentric friend, Dr. George Budd, who had a well-deserved reputation for being hot-headed. Budd also had a profitable practice. In fact, it was booming! Doyle accepted Budd's invitation, and it didn't take long to find the secret of Budd's success: He saw every patient for free but charged heavily for the medicines he prescribed. In Budd's defense, he didn't prescribe unnecessary medicine, and this strange business plan seemed to work.

Then the relationship between the two men went bad. Budd, it turned out, was paranoid and had been reading Doyle's mail. He learned that Doyle and his mother had been discussing the practice, and Mary Doyle clearly stated her disapproval of Dr. Budd. Even though Doyle had defended Budd in the letters, Budd took it badly and ended the partnership, making a promise of financial aid so that Doyle could set up his own practice — aid that never materialized. Doyle left Plymouth and went to Southsea, Portsmouth, to set up his own private practice. At first it wasn't very profitable, but the young doctor's rather quiet offices would be remembered forever as the place where Sherlock Holmes came to life.

Early literary pursuits

Doyle wrote his first story at the age of 6. It was a tale about a man who was eaten by a tiger. In his autobiography, *Memories and Adventures,* he says that he never finished the story, because ". . . when the tiger had absorbed him, I found myself slightly embarrassed as to how my story was to go on . . . It is very easy to get people into scrapes, and very hard to get them out again." Doyle relearned this lesson decades later when, after killing Sherlock Holmes, he decided to revive him. (See the section "The Death (And Rebirth) of Holmes" for more on that.)

Although Doyle gave up on that first story, he never lost his fascination with writing. His early successes came while still in medical school. Some of these better known early tales include

- ✔ **"The Gully of Blueman's Dyke" (1881, *London Society*):** In this tale set in the Australian gold fields, many men head off to the diggings, but none come back. What is it that's waiting for them in Blueman's Dyke?

- ✔ **"The Captain of the Pole-Star" (1881, *Temple Bar*):** This spooky ghost story is one of Doyle's classics. The crew of the arctic whaler *The Pole Star* find that their captain is a haunted, troubled man. As days turn into weeks among the frigid waters of the Arctic Ocean, stories about ghosts begin to circulate among the crew.

- ✔ **"My Friend the Murderer" (1882, *London Society*):** Told in the first-person, this tale centers on a prison doctor who has an extraordinary interview with a notorious killer. The title of this story is one of Doyle's best.

Many of Doyle's stories were published anonymously, a normal custom for Victorian magazines. This practice enabled critically-acclaimed authors to write popular romances or adventure fiction for magazines purely for money, and it protected reputations (a key reason why some people choose to publish anonymously today!) Doyle, however, concluded that for him, publishing anonymously was a dead end. He decided to try writing books and make a name for himself.

The Case of the Bored Doctor and the Birth of Sherlock Holmes

The year was 1887. With the slow pace of his relatively new medical practice, Doyle had spare time on his hands, and so he again turned to writing as a way of increasing his income.

A popular myth about Doyle is that he was a failure as a doctor. But that's only a myth. Doyle's practice was very slow for the first six months, but within the year he was making a living as a doctor. Records indicate that by the third year he was making £300 annually — four times the wage of a skilled craftsman like a carpenter or printer. In London, a physician could make as little as £150 annually, with an average annual wage being £350. He was clearly not a failure.

His powerful imagination strayed to the mesmerizing memory of his old medical school professor, Dr. Joseph Bell. Reflecting on his mentor's uncanny ability at observation and deduction, Doyle began to see the outlines of what would be his greatest creation: Sherlock Holmes.

Holmes made his debut in the novel *A Study in Scarlet* in the 1887 issue of *Beeton's Christmas Annual,* a seasonal publication that featured short stories, novellas, and drawing-room plays, usually written by new, relatively unknown authors. It came out in November at a price of one shilling. It was a true "shilling shocker," and was usually sold out before Christmas.

If at first you don't succeed

Beeton's Christmas Annual wasn't Doyle's first choice as publisher. In fact, it was his last. Doyle's luck at finding a home for *A Study in Scarlet* was so bad that Sherlock Holmes almost didn't happen. He had been regularly submitting his previous novel, *The Firm of Girdlestone* (the story of a family business run by an unethical father and son, who try to murder a young woman for her inheritance), to a series of publishers and garnering a collection of rejection notices in return. But with his new detective novel, he thought he was onto something big. In his autobiography, *Memories and Adventures,* Doyle says,

> I knew that the book was as good as I could make it, and I had high hopes. When *Girdlestone* used to come circling back with the precision of

a homing pigeon, I was grieved but not surprised, for I acquiesced in the decision. But when my little Holmes book began also to do the circular tour I was hurt, for I knew that it deserved a better fate.

After numerous rejections, he finally received an offer from Ward, Lock & Co., the publishers of *Beeton's Christmas Annual.*

An (underwhelming) offer he couldn't refuse

The publishers of *Beeton's Christmas Annual* obviously didn't understand the huge opportunity that had come to them with *A Study in Scarlet.* They wrote Doyle and said

> Dear Sir,
>
> We have read your story *A Study in Scarlet,* and are pleased with it. We could not publish it this year, as the market is flooded at present with cheap fiction, but if you do not object to its being held over until next year we will give you £25 for the copyright.
>
> Ward, Lock & Co.

As desperate to get published as he was, Doyle still hesitated to accept the offer. But in the end, he figured this deal was better than no deal at all. "Therefore I accepted," he admits in his autobiography, "and the book became 'Beeton's Xmas Annual' of 1887. I never at any time received another penny for it."

It was here, between the precarious pages of *Beeton's Christmas Annual,* that the public first met the immortal duo of Sherlock Holmes and Dr. Watson, whose partnership quite literally changed history.

Arthur Conan Doyle didn't choose Sherlock as the name for his detective right away. At first he called him Sherrinford Holmes, and Watson almost got stuck with the name of Ormond Sacker! Fortunately, Doyle changed his mind before he got too far into *A Study in Scarlet.*

Catching on with the public

The reception Holmes received upon his debut was less than great. In fact, despite a few positive reviews, *A Study in Scarlet* just sort of came and went. When Sherlock made his second bow in *The Sign of the Four,* the results were a little better, but still, that could have been it for the Great Detective. But then came *The Strand Magazine.*

Holmes's appearance in *The Strand Magazine* was an instant sensation. The editor, Herbert Greenhough Smith, instantly recognized he was onto something special when the first few Sherlock Holmes stories landed on his desk. The magazine ended up being the permanent home of every new Holmes story. Every time the magazine's cover boasted a new Holmes tale, circulation soared and people stood in lines just to snatch up a copy.

The first batch of stories ran from July 1891 to June 1892 and were then published in book form as *The Adventures of Sherlock Holmes* in October 1892. They were:

- "A Scandal in Bohemia"
- "The Red-Headed League"
- "A Case of Identity"
- "The Boscombe Valley Mystery"
- "The Five Orange Pips"
- "The Man with the Twisted Lip"
- "The Blue Carbuncle"
- "The Speckled Band"
- "The Engineer's Thumb"
- "The Noble Bachelor"
- "The Beryl Coronet"
- "The Copper Beeches"

The Death (And Rebirth) of Holmes

The public was wildly enthusiastic about Sherlock Holmes, but one man didn't share that feeling. Incredibly, it was Arthur Conan Doyle himself. He had greater ambitions in mind as a writer; he believed he'd make his mark in literature by writing historical novels (for more on these works, see "Other Literary Endeavors" later in this chapter). The public, however, wanted more Sherlock Holmes. Doyle began to see the detective as an impediment to his work instead of as a part of it.

Economic realities kept Doyle writing about Holmes for a while longer, but he soon began to plot a way out. While vacationing in Switzerland, he found a way to make sure Sherlock never bothered him again.

"Killed Holmes!"

To kill off Sherlock Holmes, Doyle created another character who was as great a villain as Holmes was a hero: Professor Moriarty, the "Napoleon of crime," the most serious threat Holmes would ever face (see Chapter 7 for more on Moriarty).

It was on that vacation in Switzerland that Doyle found the crime scene: Reichenbach Falls (see Figure 3-2). With its thundering cascade plunging over 800 feet and its mist rising out of a fearful chasm far below, it seemed a perfectly dramatic place for Holmes to end his career. Upon his return to England, Doyle wrote "The Final Problem," and on the night he finished it, he wrote in his diary just two words, "Killed Holmes."

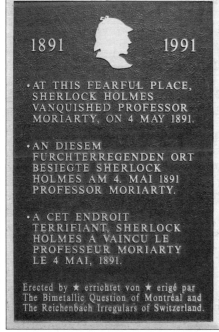

Figure 3-2: Plaque placed near Reichenbach Falls, Switzerland, to commemorate the spot where Sherlock Holmes and Professor Moriarty fought to the death.

Doyle never realized how popular Sherlock Holmes was until he killed him. "I was amazed at the concern expressed by the public," he wrote in his autobiography. "They say a man is never properly appreciated until he is dead, and the general protest against my summary execution of Holmes taught me how many and numerous were his friends. 'You Brute!' was the beginning of the letter which one lady sent me. . . ."

Over 20,000 people canceled their subscriptions to *The Strand Magazine* in protest. Young men in London took to wearing black mourning bands. Some young women wore black. The Prince of Wales expressed dismay, and it was rumored that Queen Victoria herself "was not amused."

In the timeline of the Sherlockian canon, Sherlock Holmes was officially dead from 1891 to 1894. In reality, ten years passed before Doyle decided to officially reverse the death sentence and bring Holmes back to life.

Doyle moves on, despite a few backward glances

In retrospect, it wasn't long before the first hints of regret at killing off Holmes began to show up. While publicly he was firm in his conviction to keep Holmes dead, Doyle kept getting ideas for Holmes-like stories. Clearly, one can find the ghost of Sherlock Holmes in a series of tales Doyle called *Round the Fire Stories*. Many Holmes scholars believe that two of the stories, published in *The Strand Magazine,* actually include cameos by Holmes himself:

✔ **"The Story of the Man with the Watches" (July 1898):** Holmes fans believe that Sherlock Holmes himself appears as the author of a letter to the *Daily Gazette.* The letter's author is described as "a well-known criminal investigator" who writes:

> In the absence of data we must abandon the analytic or scientific method of investigation, and must approach it in the synthetic fashion. In a word, instead of taking known events and deducing from them what has occurred, we must build up a fanciful explanation if it will only be consistent with known events.

No doubt about it . . . that's Sherlock Holmes.

✔ **"The Story of the Lost Special" (August 1898):** This tale also has a letter-writer, this time to the *Times* of London. The author comments "over the signature of an amateur reasoner of some celebrity" who writes:

> It is one of the elementary principles of practical reasoning that when the impossible has been eliminated the residuum, however improbable, must contain the truth.

If you remember Holmes's famous doctrine, "when you have eliminated the impossible, whatever remains, however improbable, must be the truth," then you recognize the letter-writer as Holmes.

By 1900, Doyle was working on an eerie novel about a phantom hound that haunted a family named Baskerville (see Chapter 9) when he realized that it needed something more — it needed a hero. Realizing he had already created the perfect central character that could tie the story together, he once again turned to Sherlock Holmes. But Sherlock wasn't back from the dead yet. It would be another couple of years before that would happen. No, this would be a posthumous adventure, set before Holmes's fateful encounter with Professor Moriarty. Needless to say, the public welcomed this story with open arms.

Sherlock Holmes's unlikely rebirth

By 1903 much had changed for Arthur Conan Doyle. In the 12 years since Sherlock Holmes first appeared in *The Strand Magazine,* the struggling doctor with literary aspirations had become a wealthy full-time author. He had taken a wife, Louise, and they now had two children (see "His marriages" later in the chapter for more on his personal life). The ten years following his decision to kill off Holmes had given him the chance to write on an impressive array of subjects: ghost stories, adventure stories, nonfiction essays, and the historical fiction he so dearly wanted to write.

Age and time had helped soften his feelings toward Sherlock Holmes. It's a common myth that Doyle hated Holmes. This is untrue. He did, after all, create the character. What he hated was the level of popularity Holmes received, which, in his opinion, obscured his other writing. Now, finding himself in a different place in life, he was ready to revisit Sherlock.

Finally, in 1903, after ten years of public pressure, Doyle revealed the astounding news that Sherlock Holmes was alive! In "The Empty House," Holmes returns to England in disguise and reveals himself to Dr. Watson. The story is set in 1894, three years after his presumed death. Holmes explains away the "evidence" Watson found at Reichenbach Falls, tells how he faked his death, traveled around the world, and finally returned to London to catch the last of Moriarty's gang.

Some readers may have found Holmes's explanation a bit farfetched, but no one cared. "It was indeed like old times," wrote Watson, "when, at that hour, I found myself seated beside him in a hansom, my revolver in my pocket and the thrill of adventure in my heart."

Other Literary Endeavors

Doyle was a prolific writer, and the depth and breadth of his writing over his lifetime is staggering. He wrote short stories, novels, and plays. He wrote in a variety of genres, including romance, science fiction, mystery, horror, and adventure. He was a poet and a playwright. He wrote a history of World War I (as it was happening). He was a journalist, a propagandist, and an advocate for justice. And he continued to write Sherlock Holmes stories. Although a complete overview of his work is impossible here, I highlight a few of his best non-Sherlockian works in the following sections.

Brigadier Gerard

Following the supposed death of Holmes, Doyle created a new recurring character in a series of comic short stories, Etienne Gerard, a soldier in the French Army during the Napoleonic Wars. Gerard is very brave, very vain, and not always the sharpest tool in the box. This combination puts him in some very entertaining situations. (It turns out that Doyle could write comedy!)

Originally published in *The Strand Magazine,* the Brigadier Gerard stories appeared between 1894 and 1903 and were later collected into two books, *The Exploits of Brigadier Gerard* (1896) and *The Adventures of Gerard* (1903). A final story was published in 1910, entitled "The Marriage of the Brigadier."

The Lost World

Even without Sherlock Holmes, Sir Arthur Conan Doyle would be remembered today for his science fiction masterpiece, *The Lost World.* The novel tells the story of Professor George Challenger, a brilliant but unorthodox scientist who claims to have discovered living dinosaurs on an isolated plateau in an unexplored region of South America. Fascinated by recent discoveries of dinosaur fossils near his home, Doyle placed his story deep within the Brazilian rain forest and sent Challenger and a band of fellow explorers up the Amazon River in search of this lost world.

Doyle based his characters on several real-life explorers: Everard Im Thurn, J. W. Boddam-Whethem, Roger Casement, and P. H. Fawcet, who, during expeditions through unexplored Amazonian jungles, reported remote, isolated plateaus exactly like Doyle describes in *The Lost World.* He also relied on state-of-the-art Edwardian paleontology, citing a real-life book by scientist Edwin Ray Lankester titled *Extinct Animals.*

Doyle loved the character of Professor Challenger and brought him back in two novels (*The Poison Belt* in 1913 and *The Land of Mist* in 1926) and two short stories ("When the World Screamed" in 1928 and "The Disintegration Machine" in 1929). He never tired of his brilliant scientist, as he did with Sherlock Holmes. In fact, he loved Challenger enough to convert him to spiritualism in *The Land of Mist*.

The influence of *The Lost World* can't be overstated. In 1925 the book was adapted as a silent movie (it came right at the end of the silent era). The great Willis O'Brien did the special stop-motion dinosaur effects. Doyle himself loved the effects and the film. O'Brien went on to make *King Kong* just a few years later. It's clear now that *Kong* is merely a remake of *The Lost World*. In fact, every living dinosaur movie made in its wake, right up through *Jurassic Park*, owes a nod to *The Lost World*.

The White Company

Doyle always believed his true calling was writing historical fiction. *The White Company* (1891) is by far his most popular and best-known work in this field. It's set during the Hundred Years' War. After attending a lecture on the Middle Ages, Doyle began detailed research into his tale, which tells the exciting story of Alleyne Edricson and his band of knights known as the White Company.

Life Outside of Literature

No doubt about it . . . Arthur Conan Doyle will always be remembered primarily for Sherlock Holmes. This probably would have both astounded and disappointed him. He not only left us with an amazing and varied body of writing but also led an amazing and varied life.

His marriages

In 1885, Doyle married Louise Hawkins (nicknamed "Touie"). Their marriage produced two children, Mary and Kingsley, and was a happy one until the summer of 1893, when Louise was diagnosed with tuberculosis. Tuberculosis is an often deadly infectious disease that attacks the lungs and, in a time before antibiotics, was usually a death sentence. Arthur was devastated. "I am afraid we must reconcile ourselves to the diagnosis," wrote Doyle in a letter to his mother. Louise lived another 13 years, but it was the restricted life of a live-in patient.

During the years of Louise's illness, Doyle channeled his energy and feelings into travel, sports, writing, and any number of other activities, almost certainly as a coping mechanism. And then, in March 1897, he met a young, strikingly beautiful woman named Jean Leckie and fell madly in love. Despite his wife being an invalid, and being in love with another woman, it's believed that Doyle remained faithful to Louise, living a celibate life until her death on July 4, 1906.

A little over a year later, on September 18, 1907, Arthur and Jean Leckie were married in a large, public wedding. The two remained devoted to each other for the rest of their lives. The new Mr. and Mrs. Conan Doyle moved to Sussex, to a new home they called Windlesham, and had three children together. The first was a boy named Denis, who was born in 1909. Then came Adrian in 1910, and finally a girl named Jean in 1912.

Hitting the road

Throughout his life, Doyle loved to travel. Sometimes he traveled for pleasure; other times it was to lecture on literature or, later, spiritualism. But whatever the reason, his far-flung travels gave him an appreciation for the larger world and new raw material for his writing. Some of his more significant journeys include

- **Switzerland (1893):** Doyle took his family to Switzerland in hopes that the air would help his wife's tuberculosis. While there, he visited the Reichenbach Falls and decided that it would be the place he would kill off Sherlock Holmes. (For more info, see the earlier section "Killed Holmes!")

- **United States (1894):** The now famous author took a lecture tour of the United States, visiting many cities, including New York, Cincinnati, Indianapolis, and Chicago. While Doyle hoped to lecture on non-Sherlockian subjects, he couldn't escape questions about Sherlock Holmes.

- **Egypt (1895):** The Doyle family cruised up the Nile and visited the Pyramids. The adventure provided vivid material for one of Doyle's most under-appreciated adventure novels, *A Desert Drama, Being the Tragedy of the Korosko*.

- **South Africa (1900):** Doyle volunteered as field doctor during the Boer War. (See the next section for more information.)

- **United States and Canada (1914, 1922–1923):** By this stage of his life, Doyle was the world's leading advocate of spiritualism. He toured extensively promoting his faith.

Patriotism and public service

In 1899, war broke out in South Africa between Britain and Dutch settlers (known as Boers) over colonization. It was a long, bloody war, but it appealed both to Doyle's sense of adventure and his patriotism. In 1900, he volunteered as a medical doctor behind the lines. During his time in Africa, he saw as many soldiers die of infectious disease as war wounds and campaigned for better aseptic methods in field hospitals.

Upon his return he wrote an account of the conflict entitled *The Great Boer War.* He also vigorously defended the honor of the British soldier against charges of war crimes. The following year, in recognition of his services to the Crown during the Boer War, King Edward VII knighted Doyle. The creator of Sherlock Holmes was now Sir Arthur. (It was rumored that the king was also unofficially thanking Doyle for reviving Holmes. Edward VII was a Sherlock Holmes fan.)

He really is Sherlock Holmes!

Dr. Joseph Bell, who taught Doyle the Sherlockian method, once told him, "You are yourself Sherlock Holmes and well you know it." It turns out that he was right. On two occasions, Doyle successfully undertook criminal investigations to free wrongly accused men. In both cases, he employed the methods of Sherlock Holmes.

The George Edalji case

In 1907, Doyle met a young man named George Edalji who had been convicted of a series of cattle and horse mutilation incidents in the village of Great Wyrley.

Edalji was a Parsee Indian. For years, both George and his family had endured hateful and threatening anonymous letters. Then things took a turn for the worse. In 1893, farm animals in the area were being mutilated in the middle of the night. The animals bled to death from long, shallow cuts to their abdomens. Then an anonymous letter to the police named George Edalji as the perpetrator. Edalji was arrested and charged not only with the cattle mutilations but also with writing the threatening letters to himself! He was sentenced to seven years' hard labor.

Many were convinced that this was a clear miscarriage of justice. When 10,000 people signed a petition protesting the sentence, Edalji's sentence was reduced to three years. After his early release, Edalji sought to clear his name and contacted Arthur Conan Doyle. Doyle decided to look into the case. What he found was overwhelming. He was convinced that Edalji was innocent and that racial prejudice had played a part in his conviction.

Upon meeting him, Sir Arthur knew he was innocent. As he reported in his book *The Case of Mr. George Edalji,* the accused man's eyesight was so bad that it would have been impossible for him to have done it:

> He had come to my hotel by appointment, but I had been delayed, and he was passing the time by reading the paper. I recognized my man by his dark face, so I stood and observed him. He held the paper close to his eyes and rather sideways, proving not only a high degree of myopia, but marked astigmatism. The idea of such a man scouring fields at night and assaulting cattle while avoiding the watching police was ludicrous. There, in a single physical defect, lay the moral certainty of his innocence.

All the evidence against Edalji fell apart. Blood on razors found in Edalji's home turned out to be rust. Mud on his boots was soil that was different from the soil from the field where the mutilations occurred. A handwriting expert demonstrated that he wasn't the author of the anonymous letters. Animal mutilations continued after Edalji was arrested! And most of all, George Edalji was certainly legally blind.

Doyle outlined the results of his investigation in a series of newspaper articles. They caused enough pressure that in the spring of 1907, a judicial committee reversed the conviction on the mutilations. (However, they maintained his guilt in the letter-writing conviction.)

The George Edalji case, a real-life mystery with the creator of Sherlock Holmes investigating the crimes, still fascinates. In 2006, award-winning novelist Julian Barnes wrote the best-selling novel *Arthur and George,* which offers a fascinating psychological examination of the case.

The Case of Oscar Slater

On the morning of December 21, 1908, in Glasgow, Scotland, an elderly woman named Marion Gilchrist was found bludgeoned to death. She was discovered by her servant girl, Helen Lambie, who had briefly gone out to buy a newspaper. While Lambie was out, a man named Arthur Adams, who lived in the apartment below Gilchrist, heard three knocks on his ceiling and, knowing his upstairs neighbor was elderly, went to investigate.

The door was locked, but he met Helen Lambie, who had just returned from her errand. While outside Gilchrist's door they noticed a strange man in the building's hallway, but the man left, and they had no reason of suspecting him of being anything other than another tenant in the building. Upon entering they discovered the body and that a diamond brooch had been stolen.

The police fixed on a petty criminal named Oscar Slater. Two pieces of evidence raised a red flag. Slater had recently pawned a diamond brooch and had just set sail for America under a false name. When authorities caught up to Slater, he was immediately willing to return to Scotland to clear his name.

Once back in Scotland, it was shown that the pawned brooch didn't match the stolen brooch. He also had an alibi for the time of the murder. Despite this, the police were convinced he was the culprit, and a trial was held in 1909. Oscar Slater was found guilty and sentenced to death. Two days before his execution, his sentence was commuted to life with hard labor.

When Doyle reviewed the case, he was convinced that Slater was innocent. He published *The Case of Oscar Slater,* which methodically examined the evidence. *The Case of Oscar Slater* sparked demand for a new trial, but the fight for Slater's innocence went on for years. Finally, in 1927, the secretary of state issued the following statement:

> Oscar Slater has now completed more than eighteen and a half years of his life sentence, and I have felt justified in deciding to authorize his release on license as soon as suitable arrangements can be made.

Oscar Slater was finally a free man. He was awarded £6,000 and cleared of all charges.

The First World War

When World War I started in August 1914, Arthur Conan Doyle, at 55 years old, was too old to fight, so instead he decided to write an account of the war. *The British Campaign in France and Flanders* ended up being six volumes long and was written while the war was still being waged. During a visit to the front lines, he was asked if Sherlock Holmes was fighting. Doyle replied that Holmes was retired and too old for military service!

The First World War devastated an entire generation of young men in England and France. The Doyle family shared in this loss. Sir Arthur lost his oldest son Kingsley, as well as his brother, his two brothers-in-law, and two nephews. The grief he felt at these losses helped turn Doyle's curious interest in spiritualism into a passion.

Speaking with the dead

Many have understandably wondered how the man who created the ultimate scientific thinker could have come to believe in spiritualism, a religion focused on communication with the spirits of the dead. Spiritualists believe that life after death is not only true but also provable, and that the living can communicate with those who've died. Had Doyle lost his mind?

Spiritualism began in 1848 in Hydesville, New York, when two sisters named Maggie and Katie Fox claimed to be communicating with the ghost of a murdered man who was buried in their cellar. In less than a decade, nearly 2 million people had become spiritualists. Between 1900 and 1914, the movement's popularity began to fade, but then, with the horrific number of deaths in World War I, millions flocked to the faith as a way to cope with the loss of so many loved ones. Arthur Conan Doyle was one of them.

The key to understanding Doyle's conversion is his analytical mind. That may seem strange, because spiritualism deals in mediums, séances, and other spooky but seemingly faked elements. But spiritualism appealed to Doyle because, to him, it offered proof of life after death. What could be more convincing to a man trained in science than to actually communicate with the dead? That's the secret to understanding his passionate adoption of this seemingly illogical faith.

When Doyle took up a cause, he did it with all he had, whether it was fighting to clear a man's name, upholding the honor of England against false charges, or spreading the word of the "new revelation" of spiritualism. It became the defining cause of the last 15 years of his life.

He became a regular participant in séances, joined the British Society for Psychical Research, and opened a store called the Psychic Bookshop. He wrote numerous books, articles, and essays advancing the cause. He engaged in a series of high-profile debates with skeptics (often coming out on top) and traveled the world promoting the faith he so strongly believed in.

It wasn't all clear sailing, however. Occasionally, his zeal blinded him to the undeniable fakers and charlatans that were making names for themselves. Unfortunately, because Doyle was such a public figure, these blunders often became public embarrassments. The two best known examples involve the Cottingly fairies and a very public feud with illusionist Harry Houdini.

The Cottingly fairies

In 1920, two young girls from the village of Cottingley took, in the woods near their home, photographs that purported to show fairies. A story was published in *The Strand Magazine* about the pictures, and Doyle decided to investigate.

When experts stated that the negatives hadn't been tampered with and the photos were genuine, Doyle very publicly threw his support behind the photographs by writing a book, *The Coming of the Fairies.* He just couldn't believe that children could perpetrate a fraud of this kind. Unfortunately, they were indeed capable and admitted the fraud years later, after Doyle's death. Nothing damaged Doyle's reputation as much as the Cottingly fairies.

Harry Houdini versus Jean Conan Doyle

Harry Houdini, the world's greatest escape artist, and Arthur Conan Doyle were unlikely friends, but they found common ground in an interest in spiritualism. After the death of his mother, Houdini hoped to contact her using mediums. But he was a magician, and he soon found that the psychics he was consulting were frauds. From then on he was on a crusade to expose these charlatans.

The Doyle/Houdini friendship ended in 1922, when Doyle's wife Jean, who had adopted spiritualism and who specialized in automatic writing, offered to help contact Houdini's mother. Unfortunately, it didn't go well. Jean wrote down messages she was supposedly receiving from Houdini's mother, but when the writing was in English (she didn't speak English), made no mention that it was his mother's birthday, and used a Christian cross drawn on the top of the page (Houdini was Jewish), Houdini was insulted. The disagreement went public and proved to be another embarrassment for Doyle.

Spiritualists believe that messages from the spirits of the dead can come to us from the other side. One of these forms of communication is "automatic writing," where the writer enters a trance and unconsciously transcribes messages from a communicating spirit.

His Last Bow

Doctor, author, sportsman, patriot, journalist, amateur detective, historian, scientist, adventurer, husband, father, religious advocate. All these titles, and more, are applicable to Arthur Conan Doyle. With this list in mind, he might cringe to know that he'll always be best remembered for the creation of Sherlock Holmes. But he should be proud. No other author has ever created a character that transcended the boundary of the printed page to become, in the mind of the public, a living person. It's been said that an artist isn't the best judge of his own work, and certainly this is the case with Arthur Conan Doyle.

After an amazing life of adventure and accomplishment, Doyle died on Monday, July 7, 1930. He is buried at Windlesham, and his tombstone reads, "Steel True, Blade Straight."

Chapter 4

Life in the Days of London Fog

Sherlock Holmes has been a popular character for well over 100 years. His adventures have never been out of print. Radio, film, and television adaptations have kept him fresh for each new generation, and yet Holmes will always be firmly rooted in Great Britain's late-Victorian era. Because England in the 19th century was, in many ways, quite a different place than the modern, 21st-century world, it's helpful to understand the culture that Holmes lived and worked in and how it shaped him.

England, the Center of the World

At its peak, the British Empire was the largest empire the world had ever known. It was said that "the sun never sets on the British Empire," and while this statement may sound like bragging, it was true. At the height of its power, the British Empire ruled over 450 million people around the globe. That worked out to one-quarter of the entire world's population, and covered one-quarter of the planet!

Britain was a world power long before Sherlock Holmes was born (1854). But by the time Holmes appeared, the empire's influence and power were so great that many began to take for granted that the empire was not only indestructible but also naturally superior.

The white man's burden — as they saw it

Take up the White Man's burden —

The savage wars of peace —

Fill full the mouth of Famine

And bid the sickness cease

Perhaps the best example of how the British understood their empire, including its rights and responsibilities, can be found in Rudyard Kipling's poem "The White Man's Burden." Written for Queen Victoria in 1899, the poem was both a justification for the empire and a statement of its costs. It sought to cast the British Empire as a noble cause, as shown in the few lines quoted earlier.

To the average Englishman of Arthur Conan Doyle's time, the empire represented the very foundation of civilization itself. The Royal Navy ruled the seas, and English commercial vessels plied their trade in all the ports of the world. The most powerful factors driving the British Empire, especially in the late 19th century, were trade and religion.

Colonization brought trade and fueled a rising tide of prosperity. The rise of the empire and the growth of trade went hand in hand. The rapid expansion of overseas colonies brought an increased demand for manufactured goods to be shipped from England throughout its empire. On the flip side, the opening of trade routes from the colonies to England brought back a dizzying array of natural resources to England. Sugar, tobacco, rice, rubber, and other materials, never before available, now flowed in, fueling a new economy of merchants and manufacturers. They then sold their wares at home and exported to the far-flung reaches of the empire. It was a symbiotic relationship.

All this required a strong military to preserve and defend these valuable assets. The global reach of the empire imposed a long period of relative peace. In an age in which Darwin's theory of survival of the fittest gained widespread acceptance, the very fact of the power and reach of the British Empire instilled a feeling of cultural superiority among its citizens.

It was also a time when the British public enthusiastically supported Christian missionary work around the world. For instance, Anglican churches sprang up throughout India, fulfilling what many felt was the proper role of the British Empire — the spreading of British culture and religion to India's masses, and proclaiming the Gospel of Christ to the "heathens." While not officially supported by the English government, missionary work was a vital component in the spread of the British Empire because it helped to instill some degree of uniformity in language and cultural identity.

A brief history of British empire-building

England wasn't the first European nation to embark on the path of empire-building. That distinction belongs to Spain and Portugal. It was during the 15th and 16th centuries that these two powers kicked off the Age of Discovery, which led to global exploration, the creation of profitable trade routes and overseas colonies, and ultimately, large empires.

England was actually rather late to the party. It didn't start down this road until the early 17th century. Before then, England was a typical European nation that either formed alliances with its continental neighbors or fought them in wars. But when England (along with France) established colonies in America and Asia, it also established lucrative trade routes, and a global empire began to form. Even the loss of the American colonies was only a temporary setback, as victory in the Napoleonic Wars with France turned Britain toward Africa, India, and other areas of the world. As England entered the Victorian age, its powerful navy, medical advances, and new communication technology helped grow the empire even more.

English territory around the world fell into several different categories. The British government directly controlled some territories, and British-run companies controlled others, but all fell under the rule of British law:

- **Colonies:** These were territories that the British government ruled directly. Appointed governors who had broad powers ran the colonies. These were the most common form of foreign territory in the British Empire.

- **Company rule:** These were regions run by private British companies for commercial trading.

- **Protectorates:** These were territories where local government continued ruling but gave a degree of allegiance to the British government.

- **Dominions:** These colonies had a large degree of self-rule. Canada, Australia, and New Zealand are examples of dominions to this day.

It's easy to see colonialism and empire-building as exploitative and oppressive enterprises (even some British believed this to be true), and it's undeniable that in some cases, this was so. But that's a modern understanding. At the time, the average Englishman had a much different view; power, wealth, and civilization imparted a moral obligation to export their culture to poorer, "less civilized" people. Misguided? In many cases, yes. But done with evil intent? Not always.

The Sherlock tales: Spanning two eras

The majority of the Sherlock Holmes stories were written in a time that's now known as the Victorian era, which spans the reign of Queen Victoria.

Victoria's reign was a long one, lasting from 1837 to 1901 — nearly 64 years! Her reign saw the British Empire grow, and this brought peace and prosperity to Britain. The Industrial Revolution began on her watch as well, creating a large, literate middle class — exactly the readership that embraced Holmes in *The Strand Magazine*. The Victorian era is generally cited as the beginning of the modern age.

Victoria wasn't only the queen of England; she was also the ruler of Scotland, Wales, and Ireland, as well as the Empress of India. Her actual full (and long) title was Queen of the United Kingdom of Great Britain, and the first Empress of India of the British Raj.

Though the Holmes tales began in the late-Victorian era, Doyle was still writing them well after Victoria's reign ended. In 1901, Victoria's son Edward VII succeeded her to the throne. Historians refer to his reign as the Edwardian era. Even though Edward died in 1910, the Edwardian era lasted until 1914, with the outbreak of World War I.

The Edwardian era was definitely influenced by King Edward himself. His mother had been reserved and even a bit repressed, but Edward openly enjoyed life, indulging in art, fashion, travel, and many romances. During the Edwardian era, the English class system was still in place, but changes in both economics and society were afoot. Many social and political movements became prominent during this time, including women's suffrage, socialism, and upward mobility within the classes.

It was an age of change — more modern, more progressive, and in some cases, more coarse. The Holmes adventures that Doyle wrote during the Edwardian era tend to be more violent and often deal with sexual and social themes that would have been unheard of back in the 1890s.

London, the Heart of Empire

Watson called London "that great cesspool into which all the loungers and idlers of the empire are irresistibly drained." Holmes called it a place where "four million human beings [are] all jostling each other within the space of a few square miles."

To the people of Holmes's time, London wasn't a city — London was *The City,* period. If Britannia ruled the waves that washed the shores of the perpetually sunlit empire, then London ruled Britannia.

Of course, London was the center of government, but it was much, much more than just a bureaucratic or political center — it was the heart of the nation. The Thames River flows right through the center of the city, making it a commercial center as well, importing and exporting the wares of the world.

A cosmopolitan environment

Victorian London, the center of global power that was the British Empire, was composed of many races, nationalities, religions, and classes. Immigrants from around the world gravitated to London from the far-flung reaches of the empire. As in modern times, immigrants tended to gather into their own ethnic communities. For instance, in east London you would find a Jewish ghetto, made up of people who fled the czar's persecutions in Russia, as well as an Irish ghetto. An area called Saffron Hill was mainly Italian.

In London's kaleidoscope of people you could find Welsh, Germans, Indians, Chinese, and Africans, all contributing to the cosmopolitan nature of the London of Sherlock Holmes. The canon reflects not only the diversity of London, but the British Empire as well:

- ✔ **"The Man with the Twisted Lip":** This story begins with Holmes going undercover in a Chinese opium den located near the river.

- ✔ **"The Greek Interpreter":** The victim in this tale is a Greek immigrant who makes his living as an interpreter for the government and for new immigrants to London.

- ✔ **"The Six Napoleons":** This adventure takes Holmes and Watson deep into the Italian immigrant community as they track a stolen pearl.

While undoubtedly a man of his time, Doyle had a more advanced attitude than many of his contemporaries when it came to other people and different races. For example, in "The Yellow Face," he has Holmes display a positively enlightened attitude toward interracial marriage. At the end of the story, when it's discovered that Holmes's client has a biracial child from a previous marriage to an African American, both Holmes and Watson are charmed by the child and cast no judgment on the woman. Her husband proves himself a good man as well, but only after ten long minutes of silence.

However, the canon also undoubtedly reflects the cultural tensions of both London as a worldwide melting pot and the British Empire. For example, numerous stories are tinged with tragedy resulting from England's rule in India. The entire plot of *The Sign of the Four* is driven by a back story of greed and murder during the Indian Mutiny of 1857, a rebellion against Britain's occupation of India. The most tragic tale of them all, "The Creeping Man," is also set against the backdrop of Britain's military conquest of India. Holmes encounters numerous characters who've been permanently wounded by foreign occupation and war. (Watson himself is permanently scarred in the shoulder and leg from his involvement in the Second Afghan War). And don't forget that, in a nation with a long history of political distrust and religious discrimination for their Irish neighbors, the greatest criminal of all, Professor Moriarty, has an Irish name.

How classy are you? Social status

Victorian England was an extremely class-conscious society with very low social mobility. In early Victorian society, people had little opportunity to move up the social ladder. (Moving down was always a possibility, should financial disaster strike.) However, by Holmes's time, increased industrialization, capitalists, a growing skilled labor force, trade unions, and political pressure from socialists began to put cracks in the class system.

The rungs on the social ladder were as follows:

- ✓ **Upper class:** This included royalty, as well as the landed aristocracy (meaning landowners). The aristocracy were usually born into their positions, but when the Industrial Revolution began, many gained positions in society through wealth. An example of the aristocracy in the canon is Lord Robert St. Simon from "The Noble Bachelor."

- ✓ **Middle class:** The Victorian middle class appeared with the growth of the economy. Businessmen, manufacturers, small entrepreneurs, shopkeepers, and merchants are examples of the middle class. In "The Red-Headed League," pawnbroker Jabez Wilson "bore every mark of being an average, commonplace British tradesman" and was a perfect example of the middle class.

- ✓ **Working class:** Members of the working class were physical laborers. Men were unskilled, and women were often servants in upper-class households. Even children worked, which eventually triggered child labor laws to curb abuses and slave-like conditions. Working-class living conditions were usually overcrowded, with no gas or sewage systems, and few had opportunities for education. A good example of the working class in the canon is the cleaning lady from "The Naval Treaty" who is suspected of stealing a document.

For Sherlock Holmes, the social order is something to be both upheld and defied. On one hand, his bohemian nature rebels at class distinction and privilege, while on the other hand he takes extreme measures to rescue the aristocracy from scandal. Sherlock tends to be more polite to the lower and middle class than those in the upper classes. In "The Blue Carbuncle," Holmes shows mercy to James Ryder, a member of the poor working class, even after he steals a precious jewel. On the other hand, Holmes treats a king ("A Scandal in Bohemia") with barely concealed contempt, knowing that he has treated a woman wrongly. His disdain for wrongdoing knows no class distinction.

Living conditions

Just like today, the difference between how the rich lived and how the poor lived was striking, only the gap was even greater than it is now. The rich upper class lived in fashionable west London (the "West End"), in homes with servants and gaslight. The canon has numerous examples of the upper class, but a particularly good example of their life can be found in "The Empty House," where the young Ronald Adair is murdered in the bedroom of his family's Park Lane home. Holmes's lifestyle and residence on Baker Street was solidly middle class, even after he had prospered financially in later years.

The poorest of the poor lived in conditions scarcely imaginable by today's standards. In the East End, poverty, drink, and overcrowding led to disease, prostitution, and homelessness. Some unfortunates were so utterly destitute that they squeezed out a living combing the mud and muck along the riverbank for anything that could be sold or salvaged. Holmes's Baker Street Irregulars are perfect examples of children caught in the cycle of extreme poverty. Watson describes them as a dozen barefoot, dirty, "ragged little street Arabs."

The problem with pollution

London was one of the most populous cities of its time — and perhaps the single most polluted. In addition to being a government and commercial nexus, it was also the home of the vast majority of the nation's factories. In the early days of the industrial society, little if any thought was given to pollution control or effects on the environment.

The streets were covered with horse manure. The Thames River was a convenient dumping place for everything from raw sewage to manufacturing waste to the latest murder victim's body. The air, fed by the smokestacks of countless factories, was so bad that, on a bad day, it was nearly unbreathable. In fact, the famous London fog was really nothing more than smog. In modern, pollution-conscious London, London fog is a thing of the past.

Keeping in Touch

Without cell phones, e-mail, Twitter, text messages, or any of the other communication methods we take for granted, you may think that Victorian Englishmen had real difficulty staying in touch. But in reality, they did pretty well, and had a variety of ways to send a message.

- ✓ **Personal messengers:** The fastest way to send a message for immediate delivery was by personal messenger. The messenger often was from a delivery service and was known as a *commissionaire.* Commissionaires were usually retired military men who worked as uniformed attendants or messengers, or did other duties as needed. Peterson, from "The Blue Carbuncle," is a commissionaire.

- ✓ **Postal service:** Within London, mailing a letter was actually a pretty fast way of sending a message. The Victorian postal system delivered mail an astounding *seven times a day!*

- ✓ **Telegrams:** The telegraph was the most widely used method for sending important messages over large distances in Victorian England. When you needed to know something right away, you wouldn't wait days for a letter to be carried to a correspondent, then days for a response to arrive. Instead, you paid for a timely delivery and an immediate response. Sherlock Holmes, however, used the telegraph even for short distances. Watson says that Holmes "never wrote a letter when a telegram would suffice."

- ✓ **Telephones:** Even though London's first public telephone exchange was opened in 1879, large scale telephone use didn't happen until the early 1900s. Affordable and widespread service across the nation didn't occur until 1912. Holmes wasn't an early adopter of the telephone, but it does start appearing in the canon relatively early. The telephone shows up in the 1890 novel *The Sign of the Four,* when Inspector Athelney Jones offers to step across the street and make a call from the public phone bank on Baker Street to get a boat. Ironically, he had come to see Holmes in response to his telegram!

The first evidence of Holmes using a telephone doesn't occur until 1924, in the story "The Illustrious Client" (see Figure 4-1). Although he doesn't actually use the phone in the story, he shows Watson a message he has received that asks him to confirm an appointment with a telephone call.

Finally, in the 1926 story "The Retired Colourman," there is definitive evidence of 221b Baker Street getting a telephone. "Thanks to the telephone and the help of the Yard," says Holmes, "I can usually get my essentials without leaving this room."

Figure 4-1:
Holmes
goes
hi-tech.

Illustration by Sidney Paget, The Strand Magazine.

From Peelers to the First Detectives: The Rise of Scotland Yard

According to the book *A History of Police in England,* "at the beginning of the nineteenth century . . . in no department were ignorance, corruption, and inefficiency so pronounced as in that of [the] police." Low pay, poor training, and the overwhelming nature of crime, particularly in the poorer areas of London, made keeping order difficult and made officers vulnerable to corruption, bribes, and graft.

Many areas of London were dangerous, especially after dark. (A good illustration in the canon is in "The Man with the Twisted Lip," where the respectable, upper-middle-class woman accidentally finds herself in a bad neighborhood.) The city took some measures to increase public safety, like installing gaslights to make streets safer for walking, but most people continued to rely on their own measures to stay safe. Finally, the need for a professional police force could no longer be ignored.

The first modern police department

The Metropolitan Police Force was created in 1829. The creation of the new police force took an act of Parliament, which was introduced by Sir Robert Peel. Soon afterwards, the newly minted police officers were nicknamed *peelers* or *bobbies* in his honor. While the term peelers isn't used much today, London police officers are still known as bobbies.

The first police offices were located in a private house on a courtyard called the Great Scotland Yard. It didn't take long for the entire police force to get the name *Scotland Yard.* Over time, Scotland Yard became the prototype for modern police departments the world over.

Prior to the advent of Scotland Yard, police in London had been a confusing hodgepodge of local officers who gained their authority from a variety of sources. Scotland Yard brought them all together into a single administrative unit. The only exception was the City of London police, who continued to operate as an independent group, the same situation you have in most urban areas today.

The old building isn't used anymore. The Metropolitan Police, since 1890, have been in a newer one called — you guessed it — New Scotland Yard.

Bobbies, constables, and inspectors: A who's who of crime fighters

All police operating out of Scotland Yard were technically *constables* — meaning that they were government officials who had the power of making an arrest — although the term was usually only applied to the uniformed street patrols. The *inspectors,* however, were the elite of the new police force. They were the plainclothes detectives who were called upon to use their brains rather than their brawn.

Holmes rarely deals with constables, but instead works with the official detectives, the inspectors. Inspector Lestrade is Holmes's most familiar Scotland Yard colleague, but he also worked regularly with Inspector Tobias Gregson and Inspector Stanley Hopkins.

"The Second Stain" provides good examples of constables on the scene. It was Constable Barrett who, while passing along Godolphin Street, observed an open door and discovered a dead body. And later in the same story, it was Constable MacPherson who was tricked into letting someone see the crime scene.

Early in the canon, the Scotland Yarders are portrayed as incompetent buffoons, jealous of Holmes's success, suspicious or contemptuous of his methods, and at times openly hostile. As for Holmes, the contempt was mutual. But then, art begins to mirror life. As the years pass, and the real-life detectives of Scotland Yard gain a reputation as a leading crime-fighting force, Holmes and the professionals start sharing a mutual respect for each other. The transformation is complete when Lestrade tells Holmes the following at the conclusion of "The Six Napoleons":

> "Well, I've seen you handle a good many cases, Mr. Holmes, but I don't know that I ever knew a more workmanlike one than that. We're not jealous of you at Scotland Yard. No, sir, we are very proud of you, and if you come down to-morrow, there's not a man, from the oldest inspector to the youngest constable, who wouldn't be glad to shake you by the hand."

Holmes Gets Around

When not moping around his rooms in a funk, Sherlock Holmes can be a very active man. Whether he's on a case, heading out to hear a concert at St. James's Hall, or visiting Cox and Company (his bank) to do a little banking, Holmes had to get from one place to another. In Victorian England, that usually meant either by horsepower or steam locomotives.

The original taxi: Horses and hansom cabs

Although mechanical forms of transportation were beginning to change the face of Victorian society during the time of the Sherlock Holmes stories, the horse was still the main source of power for most people. The earliest automobiles weren't much more than very expensive toys (Doyle bought himself one) and the British highway system left a great deal to be desired when it came to motoring.

Automobiles don't appear in the stories until "His Last Bow," which is set in 1914. Here Watson chauffeurs Holmes in a small Ford. But otherwise, the canon contains a wide variety of horse-drawn vehicles, and Holmes's fans have to wade their way through such odd designations as dogcarts, gigs, wagonettes, broughams, and four-wheelers, among others:

- **Dogcart (also known as a gig):** This is a light cart, drawn by a single horse, with two seats placed back to back. A box under the rear seat was used for carrying dogs, giving the vehicle its unique name.

- **Bus (full name is *omnibus*):** Just like now, this was cheap public transportation. A bus is a long-bodied enclosed carriage with seats along the sides. It was drawn by two horses and ran on regular routes throughout the city, just like city busses do now.

- **Wagonette:** This is a four-wheeled open carriage with two seats facing each other. It was drawn by two horses.

- **Brougham:** Named after a British statesman named Lord Henry Brougham, this single-seat carriage was closed and pulled by a single horse.

- **Four-wheeler (also known as a growler):** This is an enclosed, four-wheeled cab. It was pulled by a single horse and was primarily used in cities, like London. To summon a four-wheeler, a patron would blow one blast on a cab whistle.

- **Landau:** This is a style of four-wheeled, convertible carriage, often drawn by a team of four horses. The landau was a vehicle of luxury, with a low body type good for seeing and being seen. In "A Scandal in Bohemia," Holmes tells Watson that he considered sneaking a ride on the back of a landau while tracking a suspect.

- **Hansom cab:** The most iconic vehicle in all of London was the hansom cab, a two-wheeled vehicle pulled by a single horse, shown in Figure 4-2. The driver rode high up behind the passengers. To hail a hansom, a patron would blow two blasts on his cab whistle.

Hansom cabs were a scandalous, shocking thing to the more prudish-minded Victorians, because the driver, sitting in back, couldn't see his passengers. This meant that his riders could, heaven forbid, kiss without him knowing about it.

The Victorian railway: Holmes makes tracks!

For long distance travel, nothing beat the railroad. It was fast (for its day), modern, reliable, and you could depend on the schedules when it came to getting around. *Bradshaw's Railway Guide* published every train schedule in Great Britain. If you couldn't find a suitable train that fit your needs, you could — assuming you had money to burn — hire a "special" that would take you where you needed when you needed. In "The Final Problem," Professor Moriarty hires a special to pursue Holmes and Watson as they flee to the continent.

Illustration by Sidney Paget, The Strand Magazine.

Figure 4-2:
Hailing a
hansom
cab.

Although early train travel was a bit primitive, by Sherlock's time, train service was getting to be pretty comfortable. Compartments featured armrests, upholstered seats, and oil lamps for light. Most passengers shared compartments with other travelers, but first-class travelers could get a private compartment.

Train travel was generally fast and safe. But accidents occasionally happened, and just like today, mass transportation accidents can have a lot of casualties. Even this gets referenced in the canon. In "The Speckled Band," Helen Stoner tells Sherlock Holmes that her mother was killed in a railway accident, forcing her and her sister to live with their evil stepfather.

Baker Street and the Underground

London had the world's first subway system, called the Underground, and it was already a quarter of a century old when Holmes came onto the world stage in *A Study in Scarlet*. The Underground (or the Tube, as it's called now) opened to the public on January 10, 1863. In its first year, 9.5 million Londoners rode it.

The Underground trains were powered by steam, and with all the smoke and steam belching out of the engines, keeping a supply of breathable air in the tunnels was a big problem. Those tunnels contained a lot of poisonous, smoky air!

Finally, "blow holes" were created along the Underground routes. They were capped with gratings in the roadways up above. It was common for pedestrians or passengers in carriages to be surprised by sudden blasts of steam shooting out of them.

The Underground appears more rarely than the aboveground railroads. In "The Beryl Coronet," a client named Alexander Holder takes the Underground to Baker Street. In "The Bruce-Partington Plans," the corpse of a murder victim named Cadogan West is found by the tracks of the Underground, and the details of its operations form part of the solution to the case.

Holmes's rooms are right down the street from the Baker Street Underground station, a fact that's mentioned several times. Yet, in 60 stories, he and Watson only take it once, in "The Red-Headed League," when they travel on it from Baker Street to Aldersgate. But perhaps Holmes took it more often, for he speaks of his "experience" in traveling on the Underground.

Part II
What a Bunch of Characters!

The 5th Wave · By Rich Tennant

"Diabolical, Watson. It can only be the work of Prof. Moriarty, no doubt with some help from the Baskervilles' hound."

In this part . . .

Few stories in literature can rival the adventures of Sherlock Holmes for memorable characters. This part provides a detailed profile of Holmes, showing the amazing depth of the Great Detective's characterization. You also meet his friend and colleague, Dr. Watson, as well as many of the secondary and supporting characters, including cops, bad guys, victims, and damsels in distress.

Chapter 5

Sherlock Holmes and Dr. Watson

Throughout this book I talk about Arthur Conan Doyle, the Sherlock Holmes stories, Victorian history, and lots of other fascinating topics. But in this chapter, I discuss the personalities at the center of the whole Sherlockian phenomenon — Sherlock Holmes and his friend and biographer, Dr. John H. Watson.

So what is known about Holmes and Watson? And where does that knowledge come from? Though numerous biographies of the Great Detective have been written (yes, that's right — *more than one*), I draw the information in this chapter from the stories themselves. By combing the canon and reading closely, you can get a pretty good idea of who these guys are, their personal histories, and even their virtues and vices. The portraits that emerge, built up over time and the 60 stories, really leave the impression that these are real, complicated people. So it's time, as T. S. Eliot put it, to "slip into the myth of [their] existence." It's time to look at Holmes and Watson as if they were real people.

Sherlock Holmes: A Character Study

Everything known about Sherlock Holmes and Dr. Watson comes from their own words. This is especially true of Sherlock's family history, which is still shrouded in much secrecy. The fact that Holmes seems reluctant to speak much about his family (Watson calls it a "complete suppression of every reference to his own people") has led some to speculate that the Holmes family's past holds a terrible secret, and many articles, essays, and stories have been written proposing various theories. All that's really known is what Holmes tells Watson directly and what can be gleaned from other comments in the canon.

Family history

Sherlock Holmes was extremely reticent about his family history, but in "The Greek Interpreter," he divulges a treasure-trove of personal information. (In fact, this story is the primary source of Sherlockian family history — including the introduction of his brother, Mycroft.) The story reveals two direct facts about Sherlock's family history. The first pertains to Sherlock's bloodline. In the story, he tells Watson that his grandmother was the sister of "Vernet, the French artist."

Émile Jean-Horace Vernet (1789–1863) was a member of the famous Vernet family of French artists and is the most likely candidate for Holmes's ancestor. He was best known as a painter of battles and Arab scenes. His father, Carle Vernet, was another famous painter, and Carle's father, Claude Joseph Vernet, was also an artist. Art was the family business! Holmes attributes his own abilities and his nature to this branch of his family tree. "Art in the blood is liable to take the strangest forms," he remarks.

Also in "The Greek Interpreter," Holmes makes the second direct statement about his family history when he tells Watson, "My ancestors were country squires, who appear to have led much the same life as is natural to their class." But what is a "country squire," and what does it mean for our understanding of Sherlock Holmes?

A country squire was a gentleman landowner in the country who rented his land to tenants instead of using it for farming. A squire lived with his family in what's known as an English country house, which was a local seat of influence in its county. This is an important bit of information. Sherlock's casual comment indicates that he came from a family with some money and prestige, and you can see the influence of his family background in everything from his education to his attitudes about money and the upper classes. You also see it in his brother Mycroft.

For instance, Sherlock relates easily to the men who take care of Irene Adler's horse in "A Scandal in Bohemia," and a familiarity with horses comes with country life. But he is equally comfortable moving among the upper class, who neither impress nor intimidate him. Surely this comes from his family having some degree of social status as country squires.

Then there's his brother Mycroft (see Figure 5-1), who, as the story "The Bruce-Partington Plans" reveals, draws a modest annual salary and remains a subordinate in government service. And yet he's not only a member but a *founder* of a private gentleman's club, known as the Diogenes Club. Mycroft obviously is living on family money.

Brother Mycroft

Poor Watson. There he was, living on Baker Street with his friend Sherlock Holmes for five years, thinking that his friend was "an orphan with no relatives living." Or, as he put it, "an isolated phenomenon." Then one day, out of the blue, Holmes tells him that he has a brother. "This was news to me indeed," says Watson in a classic understatement.

Mycroft Holmes is seven years older than his more famous brother. Sherlock says that Mycroft's abilities at observation and deduction are even greater than Sherlock's, implying that these abilities are some kind of hereditary trait.

And yet, despite having this skill, Mycroft is no detective. Unlike his brother, Mycroft is lazy. As Sherlock puts it, he "would rather be considered wrong than take the trouble to prove himself right."

Also unlike his brother, Mycroft is "heavily built and massive" but with "a head so masterful in its brow, so alert in its steel-gray, deep-set eyes, so firm in its lips, and so subtle in its play of expression, that after the first glance one forgot the gross body and remembered only the dominant mind."

Mycroft holds a position in the British government, but it isn't exactly clear what his position is. In "The Bruce-Partington Plans," Sherlock describes his brother as "the central exchange, the clearing-house" of government information and policy, and calls him "the most indispensable man in the country."

Even the great Sherlock Holmes turns to Mycroft when he's stuck on a case. "Again and again I have taken a problem to him, and have received an explanation which has afterwards proved to be the correct one," says Sherlock in "The Greek Interpreter." "If the art of the detective began and ended in reasoning from an armchair, my brother would be the greatest criminal agent that ever lived."

When not in his government office, Mycroft can be found in the Diogenes Club, a private club founded for "the most unsociable and unclubable men in town. No member is permitted to take the least notice of any other one." Mycroft was a founding member.

His education

Because Sherlock's family were country squires, you can be pretty certain he had a good education as a child. Illiteracy was high, especially in the first half of the Victorian age, and many children never went to school. Some schools were run by churches, which taught poorer children. Middle-class kids usually went to small, private schools in their local towns. For wealthier families, including the Holmeses, there was something else.

Going to public school

The norm for many prominent families was private tutoring by a governess. Think of it as the Victorian version of modern home schooling. Privately tutored boys, when they reached a certain age, then went off to public school. (Girls stayed home, where they were taught more domestic skills, like sewing and cooking. They also often learned to read music and to play the piano.)

The term "public school" in this case is actually misleading. Public schools were actually *private* schools that charged tuition. Life at a Victorian public school could be grueling, and the classes were very demanding. The whole idea was to get the boys prepared either for a profession or to go on to college. The curriculum included lessons in Greek and Latin (and other languages) and the classics of literature. You can see the influence of this education on Sherlock Holmes, who speaks French, quotes Latin, and often references classical literature. He's clearly the product of a public school education.

Daily life at these schools often included physical punishment, and older boys tended to bully younger ones. Parents often used the schools to be rid of children they didn't want to care for. It all makes you wonder if Sherlock's lack of friends and general antisocial behavior (see "The antisocial Holmes" section later in the chapter) can be traced to his time in public school.

Figure 5-1:
Mycroft
Holmes.

Illustration by Sidney Paget, The Strand Magazine.

Attending college

The stories leave no doubt that, after he graduated from public school, Sherlock Holmes attended college. In "The Gloria Scott" and "The Musgrave Ritual," Holmes mentions a little about his university life. Evidence in the stories indicates that he attended either Oxford or Cambridge, but it's impossible to know for certain which one was Sherlock's alma mater.

Holmes didn't make many friends while in college. In fact, he says that someone named Victor Trevor "was the only friend I made during the two years I was at college." (This comment also divulges something else — Holmes never graduated.)

Holmes and Trevor (see Figure 5-2) meet when Trevor's bull terrier bites Holmes on the leg! "It was a prosaic way of forming a friendship," says Holmes, "but it was effective." It's while visiting Trevor on summer vacation that the events of "The Gloria Scott" occur, first giving Holmes the idea that he might make a living by using his gift of observation and deduction.

At school, Sherlock did participate in extracurricular activities, including fencing and boxing, but he admits that "I was never a very sociable fellow . . . always rather fond of moping in my rooms and working out my own little methods of thought, so that I never mixed much with the men of my year."

Figure 5-2: Sherlock visiting college friend Victor Trevor from "The Gloria Scott."

" 'HUDSON IT IS, SIR,' SAID THE SEAMAN."

Illustration by Sidney Paget, The Strand Magazine.

The one other person Sherlock got to know in college was Reginald Musgrave, who was in the same college as Holmes. Musgrave was a member of one of the oldest families in Britain, with a large manor house in Hurlstone. Musgrave was only an "acquaintance," but like Holmes, he "was not generally popular among the undergraduates." Four years after graduation, when a mystery occurs at Musgrave's manor house, he invites Holmes to investigate. (For details, read "The Musgrave Ritual.")

His early professional life

Perhaps it was the events of "The Gloria Scott" that persuaded Holmes to leave school early and become the world's first and only consulting detective, or, as he tells Reginald Musgrave, "living by my wits."

As he tells Watson, "When I first came up to London I had rooms in Montague Street, just round the corner from the British Museum, and there I waited, filling in my too abundant leisure time by studying all those branches of science which might make me more efficient." His early caseload wasn't overwhelming. "Now and again cases came in my way, principally through the introduction of old fellow-students, for during my last years at the university there was a good deal of talk there about myself and my methods." When he wasn't working on cases, Holmes could be found in the reading room of the British Museum, or, as Watson was soon to discover, the chemical lab at St. Bartholomew's Hospital.

Over the next five years, Holmes patiently worked to establish his reputation, courting police contacts, offering help to Scotland Yard detectives, and slowly gaining clients through word of mouth. It was also during these slow years that Holmes turned to drugs to relieve his boredom. "I cannot live without brainwork," he later tells Watson.

By 1881, Holmes had "many acquaintances, and those in the most different classes of society." His professional relationship with Scotland Yard had gotten strong enough that Inspector Lestrade was turning to Holmes "three or four times in a single week." Shortly after he and Watson began living together, Watson noted that, in one week, his visitors included a young, fashionably dressed girl; an excited, gray-headed, seedy man; a slipshod elderly woman; an old, white-haired gentleman; and a railway porter in his velveteen uniform — quite a cross section of society!

His first meeting with Watson

In 1881 (or 1882 — it's difficult to be exactly sure), Sherlock Holmes was looking for a roommate. He had been living near the British Museum, but as his detective practice grew, he found he needed better rooms. Unfortunately, his bank account hadn't grown quite as fast, so he needed a roommate to share expenses. He had his eye on a suite of rooms on Baker Street, and in *A Study in Scarlet,* he mentions his desire to share them with a man known only as "Stamford," whom he knows from the chemical lab at St. Bartholomew's Hospital.

Later that afternoon, Stamford stops in at the Criterion Bar in Piccadilly Circus to meet his old friend, Dr. John H. Watson. It turns out that Watson is looking for a roommate, too, and so, after lunch, they go to find Holmes.

There, in St. Bartholomew's Hospital chemical lab, they find Holmes, who has just discovered a revolutionary new test for blood stains. When he calms down, Stamford introduces Watson to him.

"Dr. Watson, Mr. Sherlock Holmes," says Stamford. Holmes shakes hands with Watson and immediately demonstrates his extraordinary powers: "You have been in Afghanistan, I perceive."

And the rest is history. Holmes and Watson took the rooms on Baker Street, at the address 221b, and forged a partnership that lasted on and off for the next 32 years. Along the way, Sherlock Holmes established the model method for crime detection.

The ascent to professional prominence

Holmes and Watson became roommates out of financial need. In the early days of their partnership when money was tight, Holmes loved getting a wealthy client. For instance, when spotting a carriage pull up to the curb outside their door in "A Scandal in Bohemia," Holmes comments, "A nice little brougham and a pair of beauties. A hundred and fifty guineas apiece. There's money in this case, Watson, if there is nothing else."

Over the years, Sherlock's reputation grew, not only among the police but also in high society and the government. Though Holmes never stopped seeing the frightened governess or the lowly shopkeeper, his list of cases and clients grew to include kings, popes, various European governments, and the upper crust of British society.

Several big cases finally put Holmes in a position of financial security. In "The Final Problem," he tells Watson, "Between ourselves, the recent cases in which I have been of assistance to the royal family of Scandinavia, and to the French republic, have left me in such a position that I could continue to live in the quiet fashion which is most congenial to me, and to concentrate my attention upon my chemical researches." Even though he's still relatively young (approximately 37), Sherlock Holmes has begun to think of retirement.

Sherlock's lessons in detection

Sherlock Holmes often shared the secrets of his detective skills. The canon is littered with little Sherlockian lessons in detection. Many of these statements are still cited by law enforcement professionals when teaching criminal investigation:

✔ "You know my method. It is founded upon the observation of trifles."

✔ "It is a capital mistake to theorize in advance of the facts."

✔ "See the value of imagination . . . We have imagined what might have happened, acted upon the supposition, and find ourselves justified."

✔ "We approach the case, you remember, with an absolutely blank mind, which is always an advantage. We had formed no theories. We were simply there to observe and to draw inferences from our observations."

✔ "I never guess. It is a shocking habit — destructive to the logical faculty."

The retired detective (who can't quite stay retired . . .)

Even as early as 1891, Holmes was thinking of retirement. In "The Final Problem," he tells Watson, "Of late I have been tempted to look into the problems furnished by nature rather than those more superficial ones to which our artificial state of society is responsible."

Finally, in 1903, Sherlock Holmes retired. Watson had already left 221b Baker Street for marriage, and so Holmes packed up and took a cottage on the Sussex Downs near the sea. There, he took up beekeeping and agriculture, living the life of a hermit, all alone but for a housekeeper named Martha.

He didn't plan on forgetting about detective work entirely, at one point saying he intended to devote his "declining years to the composition of a textbook which shall focus the whole art of detection into one volume." Despite his retirement, mystery had a way of finding him.

Three recorded cases take place after Sherlock Holmes retires to the Sussex Downs. They are:

✔ **"The Blanched Soldier":** Holmes investigates the case of a man who's gone missing, even though no one will admit it. This is the first of two stories that Holmes narrates, and, after years of criticizing Watson's accounts, Holmes grudgingly admits that Watson knew what he was doing!

➤ **"The Lion's Mane":** When a neighbor dies from whip marks after swimming, Holmes decides to investigate. At the start of the story, Holmes says that he had given himself up "entirely to that soothing life of Nature" which he had often yearned for "during the long years spent amid the gloom of London." He adds, "At this period of my life the good Watson had passed almost beyond my ken. An occasional week-end visit was the most that I ever saw of him."

➤ **"His Last Bow":** When Britain's foreign minister and premier both visit Sherlock in his humble cottage to ask for the Great Detective's help in foiling a German spy ring, the case proves to be too much to resist. The request sets Holmes on a three-year odyssey resulting in the capture of a German spy on the eve of World War I. This story also reveals how Holmes really spent his retirement years. He shows Watson the magnum opus of his latter years, a small blue book titled *A Practical Handbook of Bee Culture, with Some Observations upon the Segregation of the Queen,* by Sherlock Holmes. "Behold the fruit of pensive nights and laborious days when I watched the little working gangs as once I watched the criminal world of London!"

His complicated personality

"I confess how much this man stimulated my curiosity," says Watson after he moves in with Holmes. The longer he lived with Holmes, the more fascinating a person the detective became. "My interest in him and my curiosity as to his aims in life gradually deepened and increased," Watson says in *A Study in Scarlet.* Most readers who pick up the canon and start reading will end up feeling the same way.

Sherlock's "racing engine"

Watson once characterized his friend as "the most perfect reasoning and observing machine that the world has seen." Holmes would have agreed. For Holmes, mental exercise was life itself.

Idleness or lack of work usually put Holmes into a bad mood. Sometimes it made him short-tempered. Other times it sent him into a depression. And still other times, when things were particularly slow, Holmes turned to drugs. "My mind rebels at stagnation," he explains to Watson when the doctor objects to his cocaine use. "Give me problems, give me work, give me the most abstruse cryptogram, or the most intricate analysis, and I am in my own proper atmosphere. I can dispense then with artificial stimulants."

The need for mental stimulation was a common condition of Holmes throughout the canon. As early as the second story, *The Sign of the Four* (1890), Holmes says, "I abhor the dull routine of existence. I crave for mental exaltation." And as late as "The Adventure of Wisteria Lodge" (1908), he exclaims, "My mind is like a racing engine, tearing itself to pieces because it is not connected up with the work for which it was built."

The antisocial Holmes

Sherlock Holmes was not a sociable man. "I do not encourage visitors," he says in "The Five Orange Pips," following an unexpected knock at the door. In "The Noble Bachelor," when Holmes receives what looks like an invitation in the mail, he responds by saying, "This looks like one of those unwelcome social summonses which call upon a man either to be bored or lie." Watson says that Holmes "loathed every form of society with his whole bohemian soul."

But why was he like this? Was he just a jerk? Or was there some other, more sympathetic reason? For the discerning reader, Holmes's antisocial nature is clearly related to his tendency toward depression. "I get in the dumps at times, and don't open my mouth for days on end," he tells Watson when they first decide to share rooms. "You must not think I am sulky when I do that. Just let me alone, and I'll soon be right."

Sherlock's brother Mycroft shares his antisocial tendency. Mycroft was a founding member of the Diogenes Club, which was created for men who, "some from shyness, some from misanthropy, have no wish for the company of their fellows." Holmes tells Watson that "no member is permitted to take the least notice of any other one." He adds that "I have myself found it a very soothing atmosphere."

A touch of drama

Despite being antisocial in his personal life, Holmes did crave recognition. He wasn't shy about his own abilities, once saying, "I cannot agree with those who rank modesty among the virtues." This tendency often led Holmes to withhold what he was up to in order to spring an exciting resolution to a case. Watson says that Holmes could "never resist the touch of the dramatic."

In *The Valley of Fear,* Holmes comments: "Watson insists that I am the dramatist in real life. Some touch of the artist wells up within me, and calls insistently for a well-staged performance." Holmes's flair for the dramatic has caused some to wonder if, in his youth, he took acting lessons, or even performed on the stage. For the record, the canon has no mention of a theatrical background, but Holmes often spoke in theatrical terms. For instance, toward the end of "The Second Stain," he says, "Come, friend Watson, the curtain rings up for the last act."

Holmes's ability at disguise and makeup was extraordinary. His disguises include everything from a priest to a "drunken groom." His makeup and performances were so good that they often fooled Watson himself. "The best way of successfully acting a part," says Holmes, "is to be it."

His love life (or lack thereof)

Aside from Holmes's drug abuse, no aspect of his personality has inspired more speculation than his feelings for and relationships with women. If you've only watched Holmes movies, you may think that he had an on-again, off-again affair with a notorious woman named Irene Adler. Brace yourself — that's all wrong.

Irene Adler makes her one and only appearance in "A Scandal in Bohemia." She comes to Holmes's attention when his client accuses her of blackmailing him. Adler was an "adventuress," or what's nowadays known as a gold digger. An American born in New Jersey, Irene was a contralto who performed at La Scala and was prima donna of the Imperial Opera of Warsaw until she retired from the operatic stage. And at the time of the story, she was engaged to be married (but not to Sherlock Holmes!).

"It was not that he felt any emotion akin to love for Irene Adler," Watson says. "All emotions, and that one particularly, were abhorrent to his cold, precise but admirably balanced mind." No, Sherlock Holmes and Irene Adler never hooked up.

Despite Watson's disclaimers, Holmes wasn't entirely unaware of the effect a woman could have on him. For instance, upon seeing Irene, Holmes tells Watson that "she was a lovely woman, with a face that a man might die for." And decades later, in "The Lion's Mane," Sherlock encounters a woman named Maud Bellamy. In all the canon, no woman inspires such an honest expression of admiration and attraction in Sherlock Holmes as does this woman.

"Women have seldom been an attraction to me, for my brain has always governed my heart," confesses Holmes, "but I could not look upon her perfect clear-cut face, with all the soft freshness of the Downlands in her delicate coloring, without realizing that no young man would cross her path unscathed." Or older men either, evidently!

No, the problem wasn't that Holmes was immune to the charms of a woman. But as Watson put it, "Grit in a sensitive instrument, or a crack in one of his own high-power lenses, would not be more disturbing than a strong emotion in a nature such as his." The real issue was that Holmes didn't trust women.

"The motives of women are so inscrutable," he explains. "Their most trivial action may mean volumes, or their most extraordinary conduct may depend upon a hairpin or a curling tongs." On another occasion he puts it more bluntly: "Women are never to be entirely trusted — not the best of them."

Though he didn't understand what motivates women and, therefore, as an analytical reasoner, couldn't trust them, Holmes did understand the ways of love. When one of his young, female clients is getting unwanted attention from a man, Holmes remarks that "it is part of the settled order of nature that such a girl should have followers." He also shows remarkable insight into the human heart when he comments in "The Musgrave Ritual" that "a man always finds it hard to realize that he may have finally lost a woman's love, however badly he may have treated her." Who knows? Perhaps he speaks from personal experience.

By his own confession, Holmes admits that "I have never loved." And yet, even with that straightforward statement, it's hard to get Irene Adler out of your mind. Not only is she one of the few opponents who ever bested the Great Detective, but also, as Holmes tells Watson, "She is the daintiest thing under a bonnet on this planet." And then there's the famous conclusion to "A Scandal in Bohemia." Watson's words will always make readers wonder: "He used to make merry over the cleverness of women, but I have not heard him do it of late. And when he speaks of Irene Adler, or when he refers to her photograph, it is always under the honorable title of *the* woman."

His religious beliefs

Despite the influence of Charles Darwin and Karl Marx, late 19th-century England identified itself overwhelmingly as a Christian country, with Anglicanism being the official church of the state. (That fact hasn't changed, as the queen is still head of the Church of England.) Sherlock Holmes reflected his country's Christian nature in both word and deed.

One of Holmes's most attractive personality traits is his moral character. Though he's not one to indulge in false modesty about his own abilities, when faced with real moral and ethical situations, he displays the humility of England's Christian faith. For example, in *The Hound of the Baskervilles,* Dr. Mortimer expresses a belief that the hound may be supernatural. Holmes replies by saying, "In my modest way I have combated evil, but to take on the Father of Evil himself would, perhaps, be too ambitious a task."

This trait, in balance with his great mental ability, gives a moral depth to a person who otherwise would be nothing more than a "reasoning machine." On numerous occasions in the canon, Holmes feels compassion for wrong-doers, essentially telling them to "go and sin no more." His sense of justice is clearly coupled with an instinct for mercy.

So was Sherlock Holmes religious? Did he believe in God? As seen in the following examples, the answer is clearly yes.

✔ "God help us!" says Holmes after hearing the murderer's confession in "The Boscombe Valley Mystery." He goes on to say, "Why does fate play such tricks with poor, helpless worms? I never hear of such a case as this that I do not think of Baxter's words, and say, 'There, but for the grace of God, goes Sherlock Holmes.'"

✔ At the end of "The Cardboard Box," when the tragic story of jealousy, marital infidelity, and murder is revealed, Holmes asks, "What is the meaning of it, Watson? What object is served by this circle of misery and violence and fear? It must tend to some end, or else our universe is ruled by chance, which is unthinkable."

✔ The most explicit statement of Holmes's theology comes from "The Naval Treaty." While listening to his client's story, Holmes picks up a rose from a vase on the table and delivers an extraordinary little theological lecture. "What a lovely thing a rose is!" he says. "Our highest assurance of the goodness of Providence seems to me to rest in the flowers. All other things, our powers, our desires, our food, are all really necessary for our existence in the first instance. But this rose is an extra. Its smell and its color are an embellishment of life, not a condition of it. It is only goodness which gives extras, and so I say again that we have much to hope from the flowers."

Sherlock Holmes was a deep guy!

His life's purpose: Pursuit of the greater good

Armed with the gift of a great mind and fueled by the religious morality of his era, Holmes plied his trade in pursuit of the greater good. "I think that I may go so far as to say, Watson, that I have not lived wholly in vain." He adds, "The air of London is the sweeter for my presence. In over a thousand cases I am not aware that I have ever used my powers upon the wrong side."

When Holmes writes what he believes is his goodbye letter to Watson in "The Final Problem" (just before his fight to the death with Professor Moriarty), he pens, "I am pleased to think that I shall be able to free society from any further effects of [Moriarty's] presence, though I fear that it is at a cost which will give pain to my friends, and especially, my dear Watson, to you." Holmes takes on a Christ-like aura here, willing to sacrifice himself for his fellow man. (He even eventually returns from the dead.) These unconscious motifs add a surprising depth to his character.

As he once stated, "It's every man's business to see justice done."

Meet Dr. Watson

Dr. John H. Watson is the friend and biographer of Sherlock Holmes. Readers get most of their information about Holmes through Watson's accounts of their adventures together. Of the 60 tales in the canon, Watson wrote at least 56 of them. (Two were told by Holmes himself, and two others were told in the third person, making it impossible to identify who the author is supposed to be.)

Much speculation has gone into what Watson's middle name is. The stories only say that his middle initial is "H," but the famous mystery author Dorothy Sayers (creator of Lord Peter Wimsey) theorized that the "H" stands for "Hamish," the Scottish version of "James." She cited as evidence the fact that Watson's wife once called him James instead of John, his first name. Most Sherlockians embrace this clever theory and now consider his full name to be Dr. John Hamish Watson.

Watson reveals some biographical details right at the start of the first novel, *A Study in Scarlet*. You can glean the rest of what's known about him from reading the stories, as insights and biographical tidbits are sprinkled throughout the tales.

A brief biography

Watson mentions that he earned the degree of Doctor of Medicine from the University of London in 1878. He then took a course to become a surgeon in the British Army.

Working back from that date, it's believed that he was born sometime in 1852, making him approximately two years older than Sherlock Holmes. The fact that Holmes and Watson are close in age often comes as a shock to new readers, who are used to Watson being portrayed in the movies as a much older man.

Watson's early life is a bit sketchy, and you can't deduce nearly as much about him as you're able to about Holmes. This isn't surprising, as Watson was telling Sherlock's story, not necessarily his own. But a few things are made clear, such as the fact that his parents are dead and that he had an older brother who died from alcoholism.

In *The Sign of the Four*, Watson asks Holmes what he can discover from Watson's old pocket watch. Holmes deduces that it belonged to Watson's older brother, but he doesn't stop there: "He was a man of untidy habits — very untidy and careless. He was left with good prospects, but he threw away his chances, lived for some time in poverty with occasional short intervals of prosperity, and finally, taking to drink, he died."

Needless to say, Holmes was right, but you'll have to read the story to know how he figured it out! With the death of his brother, Watson was all alone. At the start of *A Study in Scarlet* he says, "I had neither kith nor kin in England."

From references and his own statements in the stories, it's clear that Watson had traveled extensively before he met Holmes. He explicitly says that he has traveled to "many nations and three separate continents," and some of these locations become apparent in the stories. Among his many travels, Watson visited Australia, the United States, the continent of Europe, and Afghanistan.

Watson served in the military during the Afghan war. He was wounded and shipped home on a wound pension of "eleven shillings and sixpence a day." He gravitated toward London, "leading a comfortless, meaningless existence, and spending such money as I had, considerably more freely than I ought." He was nearly out of money and out of luck. And then came the great turning point in his life, when Dr. John H. Watson was introduced to Sherlock Holmes.

His military career

Watson's military career was short and tragic, but like many military men, his experiences in the British Army stayed with him throughout his entire life. "I was duly attached to the Fifth Northumberland Fusiliers as assistant surgeon," he says in *A Study in Scarlet*. His regiment was stationed in India. Upon his arrival, the Second Afghan War broke out. He was reassigned to a new regiment, the Berkshires, and while he was with them, disaster struck.

His company was caught up in the Battle of Maiwand, one of the main battles of the Second Afghan War. Casualties were high, and it was one of the few times the British Army was defeated in battle. Over 2,000 Afghan warriors were killed, and approximately 1,500 were wounded. On the British side, over 900 were killed, and 177 were wounded. Watson was one of them: "I was struck on the shoulder by a Jezail bullet, which shattered the bone and grazed the subclavian artery." Laying wounded on the battlefield, Watson would surely have died or been killed if not for an orderly named Murray, who picked him up, threw him across a packhorse, and brought him back to safety.

He was then shipped out, "worn with pain, and weak from the prolonged hardships," to a base hospital at Peshawar. It was there that he had his second round of bad luck — he was struck down with "enteric fever," otherwise known as typhoid fever, spread by poor sanitation techniques.

Finally, after months of suffering and recovery, Watson found himself on a ship bound for England "with my health irretrievably ruined." Thus ended the short, inglorious military career of Dr. John H. Watson.

Watson's war wound can be confusing because it seems to move from story to story! In *A Study in Scarlet,* he says, in technical detail, that "I was struck on the shoulder by a Jezail bullet, which shattered the bone and grazed the subclavian artery." In the very next book, the wound has moved to his leg! "I had had a Jezail bullet through it some time before, and though it did not prevent me from walking, it ached wearily at every change of the weather." Did he forget where he was wounded? Was he shot twice? Or was it a single "magic bullet," as in the JFK assassination, that was able to turn and pass through his shoulder *and* his leg?

His love life

No doubt about it, Watson was a ladies' man, once boasting "an experience of women which extends over many nations and three separate continents." Wow! But it seems he wasn't exaggerating. Even Sherlock Holmes acknowledges it, saying, "Watson, the fair sex is your department."

In the stories, Watson always lingers on the physical descriptions of women, greatly appreciating feminine beauty. For instance, he describes his first glimpse of one of their clients, Mrs. Neville St. Clair, with much detail:

> The door flew open, and a little blonde woman stood in the opening, clad in some sort of light mousseline de soie, with a touch of fluffy pink chiffon at her neck and wrists. She stood with her figure outlined against the flood of light, one hand upon the door, one half-raised in her eagerness, her body slightly bent, her head and face protruded, with eager eyes and parted lips, a standing question.

Watson must have had a way with women. In "The Retired Colourman," Holmes says, "With your natural advantages, Watson, every lady is your helper and accomplice." But Watson wasn't always Mr. Smooth with women. While riding in a cab with Mary Morstan, whom Watson had fallen in love with and who would eventually become his wife, the good doctor gets tongue-tied and tells her a "moving anecdote as to how a musket looked into my tent at the dead of night, and how I fired a double-barrelled tiger cub at it." Uh, right. . . .

We know for certain that Watson was married twice. His first wife was Mary Morstan, whom he meets in *The Sign of the Four.* They were married in 1882, but sadly, by 1892, Watson was a widower.

He stayed single for approximately 20 years, but finally, in "The Blanched Soldier," Holmes says that "the good Watson had deserted me for a wife, the only selfish action which I can recall in our association."

Watson as doctor

Though Watson was indeed a doctor, his heart never seemed to truly be in it. Life with Sherlock Holmes had spoiled him. How could treating someone's gout compare to mysterious coded messages or murderous pygmies? How could diagnosing a head cold stand up to analyzing a bloody crime scene? It couldn't, and Watson himself admits that "my practice is never very absorbing."

And yet, for a while after his first marriage, he made a go of it. "Shortly after my marriage I had bought a connection in the Paddington district. I had confidence . . . in my own youth and energy and was convinced that in a very few years the concern would be as flourishing. . . ." For a time, Watson seemed to have the best of both worlds — a happy marriage and career, while still occasionally joining his friend for a thrilling adventure. His wife never begrudged his being called away by Holmes, and Watson always had an accommodating neighbor who could see his patients for a day or two.

So how good a doctor was Watson? In "The Dying Detective," in a terrible moment of (feigned) delirium, Holmes declares, "Facts are facts, Watson, and, after all, you are only a general practitioner with very limited experience and mediocre qualifications." But you can't take this as an honest appraisal of Watson's medical skills. At the end of the story, Holmes himself explains that he had to say those things to convince Watson that he was really sick and out of his mind with fever. "Do you imagine that I have no respect for your medical talents?" Holmes tells his friend.

Actually, despite his lack of enthusiasm, Watson seems to be a pretty good physician. He quickly diagnoses an aortic aneurism in *A Study in Scarlet,* and at a glance he recognizes that the murder suspect in "The Boscombe Valley Mystery" is "in the grip of some deadly and chronic disease." Evidence even exists that he worked at keeping his medical skill current. In "The Resident Patient," he mentions having read a monograph on "obscure nervous lesions," the kind of thing only a curious, interested doctor would read.

Watson as biographer and partner

As a partner in his detective practice, Holmes valued Watson highly. "A trusty comrade is always of use," he once said, "and a chronicler still more so." But how highly did Holmes value Watson as a "chronicler"?

Well, there's no denying the fact that for most of their association, Holmes felt Watson was lacking as his biographer. On one occasion, Holmes says, "Your fatal habit of looking at everything from the point of view of a story instead of as a scientific exercise has ruined what might have been an instructive and even classical series of demonstrations."

Holmes believed that Watson's accounts should be "cold and unemotional" lessons in scientific detection. "You have attempted to tinge it with romanticism," he says in another critique of his friend's writing, "which produces much the same effect as if you worked a love-story or an elopement into the fifth proposition of Euclid."

Quite understandably, Watson finds Holmes's literary criticism irritating. "Why don't you write them yourself?" he asks. And finally, Holmes gives it a shot. "For a long time [Watson] has worried me to write an experience of my own." And when he does, Holmes gets a big surprise: "I am compelled to admit that, having taken my pen in my hand, I do begin to realize that the matter must be presented in such a way as may interest the reader."

The fact is, Watson was a very good storyteller, and his ability to recognize what makes a good tale, as opposed to merely a clinical account of observation and deduction, helped make him Holmes's superior in the writing department. Plus, he was simply a good writer. Even Holmes admits this latter point: "I must act as my own chronicler," he writes in "The Lion's Mane," one of the few stories Holmes wrote himself. "Ah! had he but been with me, how much he might have made of so wonderful a happening and of my eventual triumph against every difficulty!"

It may have taken decades for Holmes to appreciate Watson as a writer, but he made up for it by recognizing Watson's value as an investigative partner almost immediately. "I am bound to say that in all the accounts which you have been so good as to give of my own small achievements you have habitually underrated your own abilities," he tells Watson in *The Hound of the Baskervilles*. "It may be that you are not yourself luminous, but you are a conductor of light. Some people without possessing genius have a remarkable power of stimulating it. I confess, my dear fellow, that I am very much in your debt."

Watson at play

Unlike his friend Sherlock Holmes, who usually moped around his rooms when not occupied, Watson was a regular guy who enjoyed a number of fun activities. In his youth he must have been athletic, for you find out in "The Sussex Vampire" that he at one time played rugby for Blackheath.

The game of rugby, a form of English football, was invented in 1823 at England's Rugby School in Warwickshire. In 1830, Blackheath Proprietary School opened in Blackheath, England. Blackheath wasn't a public school (see the earlier section "Going to public school"), but it nonetheless set out to provide an education on par with the best public schools in England. The school adopted rugby as its favorite sport, and soon, matches were regularly schedule on its heath.

When alums of the school founded the Blackheath Football Club in 1858, they made it an open club, meaning that membership wasn't restricted to association with the school. It became the first and most prestigious rugby club in the world. The fact that Watson played for this club says a lot about his athleticism, and the stories reveal that Watson keeps up on sports.

Another of Watson's leisure-time pursuits wasn't so good for him. Watson liked to gamble! It's pretty clear he bet on horse racing. In "The Adventure of Shoscombe Old Place," Holmes asks, "By the way, Watson, you know something about racing?" Watson answers by saying, "I ought to. I pay for it with about half my wound pension."

Watson also regularly played billiards at his club with a friend named Thurston. Knowing Watson, it's hard to imagine that he didn't have something riding on it!

A Study in Friendship

It's been said that you first read the Sherlock Holmes stories for the mysteries and adventures, but you read them again for the portrait of Holmes and Watson's friendship. Much of the pleasure in reading the canon comes not in the action or mystery but in the quiet domestic scenes on Baker Street, with our two heroes reading, chatting, or just enjoying each other's company. "You have a grand gift of silence," Holmes once said to his friend. "It makes you quite invaluable as a companion."

They are close enough that they can criticize each other without jeopardizing their friendship, compliment each other without embarrassment, and support each other in times of need. It's a deep friendship that shines through the more formal Victorian manner.

And there are a few moments where the affection in the relationship is obvious rather than implied. In "The Three Garridebs," when "Killer" Evans, the bad guy, is cornered, he pulls a gun and shoots Watson! Holmes knocks out the villain and turns to Watson.

> "You're not hurt, Watson? For God's sake, say that you are not hurt!"

> It was worth a wound — it was worth many wounds — to know the depth of loyalty and love which lay behind that cold mask. The clear, hard eyes were dimmed for a moment, and the firm lips were shaking. For the one and only time I caught a glimpse of a great heart as well as of a great brain. All my years of humble but single-minded service culminated in that moment of revelation.

> "It's nothing, Holmes. It's a mere scratch."

It wasn't serious, but it didn't stop Holmes from turning once more to the man who shot his friend. "By the Lord, it is as well for you. If you had killed Watson, you would not have got out of this room alive."

But no words in the canon speak to the affection and friendship between Sherlock Holmes and John H. Watson more than the closing words of "The Final Problem." Watson writes them under the impression that his friend has died following the showdown with the arch-criminal Professor Moriarty. He simply calls Sherlock Holmes "the best and the wisest man whom I have ever known."

Chapter 6

Cops, Landladies, and Others: The Supporting Characters

In This Chapter

▶ Getting to know the inspectors from the Holmes stories

▶ Introducing Mrs. Hudson

▶ Heralding some of Holmes's little helpers

Sherlock Holmes doesn't live his life in a vacuum, of course. He's not defined simply by his personal habits, his background, or his work. As with everyone, a key factor is the company he keeps. Holmes interacts with a variety of people, ranging from the police inspectors with whom he both collaborates and competes against to the servants who prepare his breakfast. He's in contact with everyone from kings to commoners to homeless children. The relationships he forms with those he lives and works with help complete the picture of Holmes's life and world.

The Police

Right out of the gate, Arthur Conan Doyle established the official police force as both collaborators with and competitors to Sherlock Holmes. This unique relationship accomplishes several things:

- ✓ **It sets up Holmes as a "consulting detective."** Holmes is "the court of last appeal," meaning that when a professional investigator is stuck, he turns to Holmes, who, for a fee, will "put [him] on the right scent." (For more on Holmes's unique profession, see Chapter 2.)

- ✓ **It juxtaposes Holmes's skills against Scotland Yard's abilities.** When Holmes began his detective practice, police work, especially crime detection, was primitive and unscientific. Portraying the official force in this manner helps establish the gulf between Holmes and the Scotland Yard inspectors.

> ✔ **It highlights Holmes's revolutionary methods.** Logical application of observation and deduction, meticulous evidence collection, and scientific forensic analysis, all coupled with a vast knowledge of criminal history, stand in stark contrast to the standard policing methods used at the start of Holmes's career.

To give credit where credit's due, the official detective force did in real life begin to adopt many methods similar to those of Holmes, and this is reflected in the canon. In the stories, Scotland Yard and Holmes are competitors *and* collaborators, but the balance between the two shifts over time. Older, more established detectives like Inspector Lestrade come to see Holmes as a colleague, while younger, less experienced Scotland Yarders haven't had time to reach this understanding.

You can find a classic example of this in "The Naval Treaty." The Scotland Yard detective assigned to this stolen document case is Inspector Forbes, "a small, foxy man with a sharp but by no means amiable expression." Forbes is on the case from the night the crime occurs, but in the nine weeks that elapse before Holmes is called in, he's made no progress. Upon meeting him, Watson says that Forbes "was decidedly frigid in his manner to us, especially when he heard the errand upon which we had come."

"I've heard of your methods before now, Mr. Holmes," says the younger, less experienced inspector. "You are ready enough to use all the information that the police can lay at your disposal, and then you try to finish the case yourself and bring discredit on them."

Forbes is definitely more in the competitor camp, but Holmes soon sets him right.

"On the contrary," replies Holmes, "out of my last fifty-three cases my name has only appeared in four, and the police have had all the credit in forty-nine. I don't blame you for not knowing this, for you are young and inexperienced, but if you wish to get on in your new duties you will work with me and not against me."

Working with Holmes instead of against him is a lesson Forbes's colleagues learned a long time ago. As time passes and the stories progress, the relationship between the pros and the gifted amateur becomes more collaborative than competitive.

In the early days, presenting a crack team of professional inspectors would have been historically inaccurate and also would have undermined the image of Sherlock Holmes. The portrayal of the official detective force as a bunch of bumblers created the environment for someone like Holmes to appear on the scene. As a result, while feeling a natural sense of professional competitiveness, the police actually end up being some of Holmes's best customers.

Just as the canonical police changed over time, the real-life Scotland Yard evolved throughout most of the 19th century. In 1829, with the passing of the Metropolitan Police Act (see Chapter 4), the Metropolitan Police Force stood at 1,000 men. By 1890 the force had grown to about 13,000, and the job of policeman became a full-time profession. All the modern principles of the force originated during this time, including the patrolling of streets by uniformed police officers (see Figure 6-1), a centralized command structure, and a detective force.

London Life.—City Police.

Figure 6-1:
A uniformed
London
police officer.

"The pick of a bad lot": Inspectors Gregson and Lestrade

Over the course of the entire Sherlockian canon, you meet 21 different Scotland Yard detectives. Taking into account that three of these detectives make repeated appearances, Scotland Yard appears in 42 of the 60 stories! Sherlock's professional counterparts are vital, not only to his career as a consulting detective but also to the entire canon.

Sherlock Holmes versus the Yard . . . for real!

The tension between Sherlock Holmes, gifted amateur, and his Scotland Yard rivals is well known. However, you may be surprised to find out that this rivalry spilled over into real life! *The Encyclopedia of Police Science* states,

> It is well known that the Sherlock Holmes series served as the seminal base for many of the modern scientific methods used in criminal investigations. His use of tobacco, dust, plaster casting, and even document examinations to identify perpetrators prompted Dr. Edmond Locard, a leading criminologist of the time, to comment, "Sherlock Holmes was the first to realize the importance of dust. I merely copied his method." A careful reading of the mysteries suggests that Sherlock Holmes also used a form of psychological profiling.

Edmond Locard was a pioneer in forensic science who became known as "the Sherlock Holmes of France" and founded the first forensic police laboratory in France in 1910. He was clearly a fan of the Great Detective.

But across the Channel in London, just like in the stories, Holmes gets no love from the Yard.

Sir Basil Thomson led Scotland Yard's Criminal Investigation Division from 1913 to 1921. During Thomson's time in office, Doyle was still writing the Holmes stories. Following Thomson's retirement, he wrote *The Story of Scotland Yard* and became a frequent lecturer on police matters. In a 1922 interview he was asked, "Has the scientific detection of crime made much progress in England in recent years?" In stark contrast to his peers, Sir Basil answered:

> It undoubtedly has made remarkable headway, but not in the direction of the Sherlock Holmes method of working by deduction. If I had followed such a plan when I was at Scotland Yard I should probably have landed the Lord Chief Justice or the Archbishop of Canterbury in prison before I had finished. I take my hat off to Sherlock, but I sincerely hope that I shall never meet him in the flesh when I am engaged in the work of criminal investigation.

Looks like the real-life Scotland Yarders felt a lot like their fictional counterparts — he sounds exactly like Inspector Lestrade!

The two most famous Scotland Yard detectives — Inspector Tobias Gregson and Inspector G. Lestrade — first appear in *A Study in Scarlet*, Arthur Conan Doyle's first Holmes novel. Although they make numerous other appearances in the Holmes stories, Lestrade and Gregson don't work together again on the same case after this first tale. Holmes clearly prefers to work with Inspector Lestrade, who appears in three times as many adventures as does Inspector Gregson.

Although Holmes is fond of baiting the official police force, often finding their efforts at detection lacking, he grudgingly admits that Lestrade isn't a total loss, calling him "the best of the professionals" in *The Hound of the Baskervilles.* In the earlier *A Study in Scarlet,* however, he said much the same thing about Gregson, calling him "the smartest of the Scotland Yarders." But he quickly throws in the qualifier, "he and Lestrade are the pick of a bad lot."

Holmes's biggest complaint regarding Lestrade, Gregson, and all of Scotland Yard is their inability to appreciate his revolutionary methods and employ them themselves. Although Holmes's opinion of his two regular Scotland Yard colleagues' intelligence and skill does rise over the years, this one complaint never changes.

Early in their careers, Gregson and Lestrade seemed to be in professional competition. Considering that *A Study in Scarlet* takes place in either 1881 or 1882, and Holmes is still working with both of them in 1902 (Lestrade in "The Three Garridebs"; Gregson in "The Red Circle"), both men were young and professionally ambitious. When you consider that the average Scotland Yard inspector's income was less than £100 per year (that's approximately $11,000 in today's value), you may have a little more sympathy for their competitive natures.

Whatever their motivations are, Holmes seems to enjoy the situation, saying, "They have their knives into one another . . . They are as jealous as a pair of professional beauties. There will be some fun over this case if they are both put upon the scent."

Inspector Tobias Gregson

Surprisingly, Holmes calls Gregson "the smartest of the Scotland Yarders." However, given Holmes's low opinion of the police force at this point in his career, this isn't necessarily high praise.

Gregson reappears in "The Wisteria Lodge" and "The Red Circle," stories that appeared decades after his initial turn in *A Study in Scarlet.* The reasons for this are unknown, but Holmes clearly preferred to work with Inspector Lestrade, Gregson's professional rival, and so perhaps Gregson never quite got over the professional contempt and jealousy that seems to characterize Scotland Yard (even in real life — see the "Sherlock Holmes versus the Yard . . . for real!" sidebar).

Inspector Lestrade

Inspector G. Lestrade is the Scotland Yarder who makes the most appearances in the canon. Of all the professional policemen in the Holmes stories, Lestrade is the one who undergoes the greatest transformation. When he and Holmes first meet, they can barely contain their contempt for each other, despite the fact that the inspector prevails upon the amateur detective several times a week. Holmes tells Watson in *A Study in Scarlet* that "he knows that I am his superior . . . but he would cut his tongue out before he would own it to any third person." However, 17 years later, when "The Six Napoleons" was published, Inspector Lestrade admits to Holmes that "we're not jealous of you at Scotland Yard. No, sir, we are very proud of you." He also tells Holmes, upon seeing him for the first time after his return from the dead, "it's good to see you back in London, sir."

Holmes's opinion of Lestrade changes as well. In "The Cardboard Box," although Holmes still finds Lestrade lacking imagination, he goes on to say that "he is as tenacious as a bulldog when he once understands what he has to do, and, indeed, it is just this tenacity which has brought him to the top at Scotland Yard." It's clear that, in Sherlock's opinion, though Lestrade will never be a perfect detective, what he does know how to do he does very well.

Doyle never reveals Lestrade's first name; the fullest version that appears in the stories is "G. Lestrade." Doyle likely acquired the inspector's unusual name from a medical school acquaintance. Doyle knew a Joseph Alexandre Lestrade, who was two years behind him in school from his days at both Stonyhurst and the University of Edinburgh.

Their mellowing relationships with Holmes

Although Sherlock Holmes may enjoy yanking Scotland Yard's chain from time to time, he has no genuine bad feelings toward the inspectors. Though Gregson and Holmes don't work together as frequently as Lestrade and Holmes do, when they do meet, the greeting is usually a cordial one. In "The Adventure of Wisteria Lodge," Holmes's client, Scott Eccles, is in the middle of telling Holmes his story when a "robust and official-looking" Inspector Gregson shows up to arrest the man. Watson describes Gregson as "energetic, gallant, and, within his limitations, a capable officer." Gregson's professional behavior bears this out — he allows Eccles to finish his statement to Holmes, but not before adding, "it is my duty to warn Mr. Scott Eccles that it may be used against him."

And in "The Red Circle," when Holmes meets Gregson in a darkened street while staking out a house, he exclaims, "Why, Gregson! Journeys end with lovers' meetings."

Yes, things seemed to have mellowed between the Yard and Sherlock Holmes in later years. It's true, in the early days Holmes ruefully, and even resentfully, acknowledges that credit for his work will go to Scotland Yard: "My dear fellow, what does it matter to me? Supposing I unravel the whole matter, you may be sure that Gregson, Lestrade, and Co. will pocket all the credit."

Later, by the time of "The Norwood Builder," it seems that Holmes's resentfulness has given way to resignation. He actually tells Lestrade to take the official credit for solving the case. Patting him on the back, he says:

> "Instead of being ruined, my good sir, you will find that your reputation has been enormously enhanced. Just make a few alterations in that report which you were writing, and they will understand how hard it is to throw dust in the eyes of Inspector Lestrade."

> "And you don't want your name to appear?"

> "Not at all. The work is its own reward."

This passage, of course, reveals a bit about Holmes — that by this time in his career, he had attained such a degree of success that he was no longer concerned with publicly getting credit. But it also reveals something about Gregson and Lestrade — they don't mind a bit taking credit they don't deserve.

And yet, again, late in the canon, we get this appreciative paragraph from Watson, talking about Inspector Gregson:

> Our official detectives may blunder in the matter of intelligence, but never in that of courage. Gregson climbed the stair to arrest this desperate murderer with the same absolutely quiet and businesslike bearing with which he would have ascended the official staircase of Scotland Yard.

It's a far more respectful attitude, and it reflects the mutual respect that had grown between Scotland Yard and Holmes and Watson.

The rest of the Scotland Yard inspectors

As I mention earlier, Scotland Yard appears in 42 of Holmes's adventures. But the Yard wasn't alone! As you may expect from a series of detective stories, a variety of official policemen and detectives appear throughout the saga. Sometimes you find out more about them, sometimes less. But while they may take the stage for only a brief moment, many of them are quite memorable.

Inspector Algar: "My friend of the Liverpool force"

In "The Cardboard Box," Holmes says he sent a telegram to "my friend Algar, of the Liverpool force." Readers never meet Inspector Algar, but this statement shows that Holmes's connections now stretch to the north of England. Additionally, the two must have collaborated enough that Holmes considers him "my friend."

Inspector Bardle: The Sussex Constabulary

Inspector Bardle appears in "The Lion's Mane," a story written by Holmes himself in retirement. Holmes says that Inspector Bardle is from the Sussex Constabulary and is "a steady, solid, bovine man with thoughtful eyes." When a man ends up dead on the beach with terrible, whip-like wounds, the country constable feels a bit in over his head and turns to his famous neighbor for advice. "I know your immense experience, sir," he says. "This is quite unofficial, of course, and need go no farther. But I am fairly up against it in this McPherson case. The question is, shall I make an arrest, or shall I not?" The passage seems to show that the more humble an officer's position, the less ego he has regarding working with the Great Detective.

Inspector Barton: Scotland Yard

Inspector Barton is the first of two official detectives named in "The Man with the Twisted Lip," and he doesn't appear quite as confident as his counterpart, Inspector Bradstreet. Barton, who has charge of the case, makes a serious mistake by delaying to arrest the murder suspect, thus allowing him to communicate with some of his comrades.

Inspector Baynes: The Surrey Constabulary

Inspector Baynes, of the Surrey Constabulary, makes his one and only bow in "The Adventure of Wisteria Lodge." Despite appearing in only one tale, he is one of the few professionals who earns Holmes's respect. Baynes is the only uniformed police officer in all the canon who was a match for Sherlock's investigative skills. The two detectives work along different lines, coming together at the end to catch the criminal. Holmes bestows a rare thing on his rival — a compliment! — and concludes with the belief that the inspector's detective career is promising.

Inspector Bradstreet: Scotland Yard

Inspector Bradstreet, who Watson describes as "a tall, stout official," is stationed in the Bow Street Station. He makes three appearances in the canon, first showing up in "The Man with the Twisted Lip." In "The Blue Carbuncle," a newspaper account of the crime reveals that Inspector Bradstreet belongs to B division and was the arresting officer. Finally, in "The Engineer's Thumb," it was Bradstreet who accompanied Holmes, Watson, and Victor Hatherley on a train trip to Berkshire in an attempt to locate the house where Hatherley had his thumb chopped off.

Inspector Forrester: Scotland Yard

In "The Reigate Squires," Holmes is recuperating from a nervous breakdown at the home of Watson's friend in Surry. Inspector Forrester is "a smart, keen-faced young fellow" on the scene investigating a murder committed during a burglary. When the young, ambitious Scotland Yarder hears the Great Detective is nearby, he pays a visit. "We thought that perhaps you would care to step across, Mr. Holmes."

Inspector Gregory: Scotland Yard

Inspector Gregory, of "The Adventure of Silver Blaze," is another official high on Holmes's list. Watson calls him "a man who was rapidly making his name in the English detective service," and Holmes backs him up by later saying "Inspector Gregory, to whom the case has been committed, is an extremely competent officer." But, as with many of his official colleagues, there is a catch. "Were he but gifted with imagination," says Holmes, "he might rise to great heights in his profession."

He also asks a question that leads to one of the most quoted passages in all the canon:

"Is there any point to which you would wish to draw my attention?"

"To the curious incident of the dog in the night-time."

"The dog did nothing in the night-time."

"That was the curious incident," remarked Sherlock Holmes.

Wilson Hargreave: The New York Police Bureau

Wilson Hargreave demonstrates that Holmes's professional contacts stretch beyond England. In "The Dancing Men," Holmes needs information on an American gangster and sends a cable "to my friend, Wilson Hargreave, of the New York Police Bureau, who has more than once made use of my knowledge of London crime." Sherlock's reputation had spread across the Atlantic!

Inspector Stanley Hopkins: Scotland Yard

Inspector Stanley Hopkins appears in four of the Sherlock Holmes stories: "The Adventure of Black Peter, " The Adventure of the Golden Pince-Nez," "The Adventure of the Missing Three Quarter," and "The Adventure of the Abby Grange." Hopkins is perhaps the most enthusiastic student of Holmes's methods and frequently consults Holmes for advice.

Watson calls him "an exceedingly alert man, thirty years of age, dressed in a quiet tweed suit, but retaining the erect bearing of one who was accustomed to official uniform." He is a young police inspector, and Holmes has high hopes for his future. Hopkins in turn openly confesses admiration and respect for his role model.

Inspector Athelney Jones: Scotland Yard

Memorable for both his strange first name and his incompetence, Inspector Jones makes his only appearance in *The Sign of the Four*. Watson describes him thus: "A very stout, portly man in a gray suit . . . red-faced, burly, and plethoric, with a pair of very small twinkling eyes which looked keenly out from between swollen and puffy pouches." Jones distinguishes himself by denigrating Holmes's methods, coming to a completely wrong conclusion about the crime and then arresting the wrong man! His is clearly the least-flattering portrait of a Scotland Yard detective in the canon.

Inspector Peter Jones: Scotland Yard

Inspector Peter Jones, found in "The Red-Headed League," is the perfect embodiment of the canon's image of a Scotland Yard detective. He's no-nonsense, practical, brave, and simultaneously admiring and dismissive of

Holmes and his methods. "You may place considerable confidence in Mr. Holmes, sir," he tells the manager of a bank that is about to be robbed. "He has his own little methods, which are, if he won't mind my saying so, just a little too theoretical and fantastic, but he has the makings of a detective in him."

Inspector Lanner: Scotland Yard

Described as "a smart-looking police-inspector," Mr. Lanner represents a different kind of Scotland Yard detective, one that wholeheartedly welcomes Holmes's help on a case. In "The Resident Patient," when Holmes arrives on the scene, he exclaims, "Ah, Mr. Holmes, I am delighted to see you." Not all of the Yard's detectives were as dense as Athelney Jones!

Inspector Alec MacDonald: Scotland Yard

Though Inspector Alec MacDonald only appears in *The Valley of Fear,* his reputation as a detective, both in the eyes of Scotland Yard and Sherlock Holmes, is great. When we see him in the story, Watson says it is back "in the early days at the end of the '80s, when Alec MacDonald was far from having attained the national fame which he has now achieved." Evidently, MacDonald went far in his chosen profession.

MacDonald is described as having a "tall, bony figure" that "gave promise of exceptional physical strength," with a "great cranium and deep-set, lustrous eyes" that told of a "keen intelligence." Watson goes on to say he "was a silent, precise man with a dour nature and a hard Aberdonian accent."

That he was a favorite of Holmes is clear: "Twice already in his career had Holmes helped him to attain success, his own sole reward being the intellectual joy of the problem."

The admiration went both ways:

> The affection and respect of the Scotchman for his amateur colleague were profound, and he showed them by the frankness with which he consulted Holmes in every difficulty. Mediocrity knows nothing higher than itself; but talent instantly recognizes genius, and MacDonald had talent enough for his profession to enable him to perceive that there was no humiliation in seeking the assistance of one who already stood alone in Europe, both in his gifts and in his experience. Holmes was not prone to friendship, but he was tolerant of the big Scotchman, and smiled at the sight of him.

It's too bad we don't see more of Alec MacDonald!

Inspector MacKinnon: Scotland Yard

Some things never change. Here, right at the end of the canon in "The Retired Colourman," a Scotland Yarder gets credit for Holmes's work, just like in the early days. At the end of the case, the newspaper reports that the mystery was solved because of "the remarkable acumen" of Inspector MacKinnon, who is an "example of the intelligence of our professional detectives."

"Well, well, MacKinnon is a good fellow," says Holmes with a tolerant smile. "You can file it in our archives, Watson. Some day the true story may be told."

Inspector Martin: The Norfolk Constabulary

Inspector Martin of the Norfolk Constabulary appears in "The Dancing Men." Watson describes the local police inspector as "a dapper little man, with a quick, alert manner and a waxed moustache." The murder of a prominent citizen, and the shooting of his wife, is certainly the biggest case Inspector Martin has ever had. And then Sherlock Holmes arrives! As Watson puts it, "he was considerably astonished when he heard the name of my companion."

Holmes's reputation was, by this story, known far and wide, and Martin tells the famous detective, "I should be proud to feel that we were acting together, Mr. Holmes."

Inspector Martin proves to be a good partner. As Holmes examines the room, "the country inspector's face had shown his intense amazement at the rapid and masterful progress of Holmes's investigation. At first he had shown some disposition to assert his own position, but now he was overcome with admiration, and ready to follow without question wherever Holmes led."

And when a particularly brilliant deduction is explained to him, Martin exclaims, "Capital! Capital!" It's clear that the local investigator is completely dazzled by the world-famous detective.

While the police, and especially the Scotland Yard detectives, can and do solve crimes on their own, they rarely do it in the Holmes stories. But they come to Holmes because they have a particularly strange or difficult case, and so they need to call in a specialist. Not every crime has a Professor Moriarty behind it, and even the likes of Gregson and Lestrade obviously have some degree of success on their own.

Other private detectives

Holmes's professional acquaintances aren't limited to the official side of the street. As Holmes tells Watson early on in *A Study in Scarlet,* "Here in London we have lots of government detectives and lots of private ones." Although there were indeed lots of private detectives around, the canon doesn't contain many. But a couple are definitely worth noting.

Mr. Barker: Private detective

In "The Retired Colourman," Holmes introduces another private detective, Mr. Barker, "a stern-looking, impassive man." Watson goes on to add that he's "a dark man with gray-tinted glasses and a large Masonic pin projecting from his tie." Very ominous sounding!

Holmes calls Barker a friend and "my hated rival upon the Surrey shore." The Surrey shore is the far side of the Thames from the richer and more fashionable area north of the river, the heart of the true city, where Holmes's base lies. Holmes may be simply telling Watson innocently where Barker lives, but under the circumstances, he seems to intend it as a dig, as if he needs to establish his superiority over a professional rival in any way he can. Yet it's abundantly clear that he has a genuine respect for Barker, and the two of them, finding themselves working on the same case, decide to work on it together, one of the few times Holmes accepts a partner other than Watson.

Holmes then asks a police detective the rhetorical question, "He has several good cases to his credit, has he not, Inspector?" to which the policeman gives the same kind of answer you would expect Lestrade or Gregson (or any of the other police) to give about Holmes: "He has certainly interfered several times." That's pure Scotland Yard!

Mr. Leverton: The Pinkerton Detective Agency

In "The Red Circle," Holmes encounters Scotland Yard detective Gregson lurking in the shadows outside a house on a stakeout. Gregson is accompanied by a Mr. Leverton, whom he introduces to Holmes by saying, "This is Mr. Leverton, of Pinkerton's American Agency."

"The hero of the Long Island cave mystery?" Holmes immediately replies. "Sir, I am pleased to meet you."

Leverton is a Pinkerton agent, and Holmes is well aware of that agency's reputation. It wasn't the first time he had encountered Pinkerton agents. Decades earlier, in *The Valley of Fear,* Holmes had his first brush with this legendary organization.

Its full name was the Pinkerton National Detective Agency. Founded in 1850 by Allan Pinkerton, this private detective agency gained fame when it foiled a plot to assassinate President-elect Lincoln on his way to the inauguration. Lincoln was impressed enough to then hire Pinkerton agents as security guards during the Civil War.

The agency's second greatest claim to fame came during periods of labor unrest, particularly in the Pennsylvania coal fields of the 19th century. Mine owners hired Pinkertons to infiltrate the unions, who were resorting to violence, to gather evidence against them. This was actually the backdrop of *The Valley of Fear.*

Servants in Victorian England

In an era before such luxuries as dishwashers and microwaves, things that we now take as minor tasks had to be done by hand and consumed a great deal more time. Those well off enough paid other people to deal with the daily necessities of life such as cooking and cleaning. In the class-conscious society of Victorian England, the master-servant relationship reflected that of queen and subject.

A long succession of anonymous servants underlies the entire canon, faceless and nameless, constantly answering doors, delivering messages, receiving and delivering visiting cards, mending clothing, and running other errands.

Even when Watson isn't living at 221b Baker Street, he still has servants to tend to his needs: his unnamed valet from "The Final Problem," the maid who brings a telegram to him and his wife in "The Boscombe Valley Mystery" and the other one who gathers up some evidence at Holmes's request in that same story, and a maid named Mary Jane who butchers his shoes in "A Scandal in Bohemia."

It comes as no surprise that Leverton is known to Sherlock Holmes. Holmes was a student of crime, and his contacts stretched from Europe to the United States. It's a certainty that Holmes and the Pinkertons were well aware of each other.

Mrs. Hudson, the Landlady

221b Baker Street's cozy domesticity is only fully achieved with the presence of Mrs. Hudson, the landlady of Sherlock Holmes and Dr. Watson. The Mrs. Hudson of the stories, however, was more than simply a landlady. Sure, she did make sure that breakfast was ready on time or the coffeepot was polished. But she did a lot more than that. She was also the gatekeeper to the shrine of justice, the person who stood between the street and the Great Detective. As such, like Watson, Mrs. Hudson is a vital member of Holmes's team.

In Victorian England, life was a lot more like living in a hotel than in a modern apartment, and both Holmes and Watson lived like Victorian gentlemen, in a world where all the drudgery was taken care of behind the scenes by a variety of servants. For more information about life during this period, go to Chapter 4.

Mrs. Hudson described

Everybody knows what Mrs. Hudson looks like, right? She's the matronly, white-haired, pleasantly plump landlady . . . the den-mother of Baker Street, isn't she? But to many readers' great surprise, Mrs. Hudson is never physically described in the canon. She is, more often than not, presented more as a series of actions than as a person. Mrs. Hudson "came up to lower the blinds," "had the good sense to light the fire," "entered with the tea and coffee," "appeared with a lady's card upon her salver," "brought up a message," and so on. The stories say a lot about what she does, but they don't say whether she's tall or short, young or old, or anything else about what she looks like.

But doing a little math, Mrs. Hudson was not an elderly woman when Holmes and Watson moved into Baker Street. Remember, Holmes lived there for over 20 years. No, it's more probable that Mrs. Hudson was middle-aged, certainly older than Sherlock and Watson (who were in their mid-20s when they met). She was a young widow, probably in her late 30s or 40s. If you fix a younger Mrs. Hudson in your mind, suddenly, a woman who not only tolerates but actually enjoys the adventure and excitement of her mysterious lodgers becomes far more likely. No, it wasn't an elderly grandmother who was crawling around on the floor, moving the wax bust that Holmes placed in the window as a decoy for Col. Moran's air gun. It was a younger, and young at heart, Mrs. Hudson who enjoyed the adventure of participating in her tenant's exploits, especially after the loss of her husband.

Her feelings about Holmes

Her feelings toward Holmes also parallel those of Watson; she "stood in the deepest awe of him and never dared to interfere with him, however outrageous his proceedings might seem." In other words, she too recognized in Sherlock Holmes something above human law.

For instance, she never protested the constant parade of humanity in and out of her house — everyone from dirty, homeless children to murderers to kings. Well, maybe the dirty children, as you'll soon see!

Holmes kept strange hours. Occasionally, there was a struggle, accompanied by smashed objects and broken windows. Holmes's unanswered correspondence was transfixed by a jackknife into the very center of his wooden mantelpiece. Once, the place was set on fire! And the perpetual mess! Watson says that "month after month his papers accumulated until every corner of the room was stacked with bundles of manuscript which were on no account to be burned, and which could not be put away save by their owner."

Who's the landlady?

"A Scandal in Bohemia" contains a passage where, as in so many other stories, Holmes and Watson are sitting down to eat in their Baker Street rooms. Speaking of their current case, Holmes says,

> "When Mrs. Turner has brought in the tray I will make it clear to you. Now," he said as he turned hungrily on the simple fare that our landlady had provided, "I must discuss it while I eat, for I have not much time."

These few simple lines would pass unnoticed in a dozen Sherlock Holmes stories. After all, there was usually a good table set at Baker Street.

There's just one question: *Who is Mrs. Turner?* There are about as many explanations for this odd passage as there are Sherlockians, some more reasonable than others. It's pretty safe to assume that Doyle was just being a trifle sloppy here, as he was known to be in other instances, but perhaps Mrs. Turner is simply a minor character, a housemaid whose name just happened to be mentioned. After all, the passage doesn't actually say that Mrs. Turner is "our landlady" but that the landlady was the one who provided the meal. For other "mysteries" sprinkled throughout the canon, go to Chapter 16.

The catalog of abuses was indeed long. Watson characterizes Mrs. Hudson by saying she "was a long-suffering woman." You know Holmes was special in some way to her, as Watson says that "Holmes, in one of his queer humours, would sit in an armchair with his hair-trigger and a hundred Boxer cartridges and proceed to adorn the opposite wall with a patriotic V. R. done in bullet-pocks." There can be no doubt that Watson spoke for Mrs. Hudson when he deadpanned, "I felt strongly that neither the atmosphere nor the appearance of our room was improved by it."

That Mrs. Hudson put up with such things can be partially explained by the "princely" rent on the rooms. Watson says that he has "no doubt that the house might have been purchased at the price which Holmes paid for his rooms during the years that I was with him." Yet there's a bit more to things, it appears, for the good doctor also says that "she was fond of him [Holmes], too, for he had a remarkable gentleness and courtesy in his dealings with women." Just as a portrait of a great friendship emerges between Holmes and Watson over the course of the stories, it also becomes apparent that there's real affection between Holmes and Mrs. Hudson.

As I mention earlier, in "The Empty House," Mrs. Hudson gladly risks her life to help capture an assassin who is gunning for Holmes, even to the point of putting herself in the line of fire. It's unlikely that she would do so simply for money. It seems more than likely that she was willing to risk her life for Holmes because her fondness for him was very deep, indeed.

Pageboys and Urchins

In the universe that Sherlock Holmes had constructed for himself, Watson and Mrs. Hudson are like family. But others not only provided useful service but also did in fact have a relationship with the Great Detective.

Billy the page

A *page* or *pageboy* was what we would today call a "gofer" — a young person (always male in those days) employed by both private residences and hotels and used for errands and light chores. Billy the page first shows up in the novel *The Valley of Fear* and then reappears by name in "The Mazarin Stone." About a dozen other tales have an unnamed page. In addition to running errands, the page also shared a portion of Mrs. Hudson's gatekeeping, such as ushering in clients, as he does in "A Case of Identity." In that tale, he's identified only as "the boy in buttons," a colorful bit of phrasing that simply meant a uniformed pageboy.

Sherlockians have often just sort of assumed that any mention of a page refers to Billy, but given the dates these stories appear, it's unlikely that it's the same boy. The first pageboy appears in 1889. A page makes his appearance in 1903, and this time he's identified as Billy. Watson says to him, "It all seems very unchanged, Billy. You don't change, either."

This is, in one sense, a bit of nonsense; if it was the same boy he would certainly have grown to be a man by then. In another sense, though, it's a metaphor for the way that the world had changed so much around Holmes. By 1903, the time of horse-drawn travel — even land-bound travel, for that matter — was drawing to a close and the reliable comforts of the Victorian and Edwardian ages were about to be obliterated by the disaster of World War I and the horrors of the 20th century (see Chapter 11 for more on this transition to a more modern era). In this sense, Billy was a symbol of an earlier, simpler time and his being frozen in time was a pleasant reassurance.

The Baker Street Irregulars

Sherlock Holmes, no matter how good he was, couldn't be everywhere at once. He needed other eyes from time to time that could see things and watch people in places and situations that he couldn't be in himself. Among other assistants, he employed a group of "street Arabs" — the contemporary phrasing for homeless children — as his eyes and ears. As he explains to Watson, they can "go everywhere, see everything, overhear everyone."

Routinely described as "dirty and ragged," the Baker Street Irregulars reflected a real-life fact of Victorian London. Though many homeless, destitute families lived on the streets of the great city, numerous homeless children had also been left to fend for themselves at an early age. Others had run away from abusive homes. It was estimated that the metropolis of London had 30,000 deserted children.

Many of these destitute children lived by stealing, and the reader can surely see the street-savvy Baker Street Irregulars helping themselves to food and other necessities. To the respectable Mrs. Hudson and Dr. Watson, they must have seemed like a pack of wild animals. The good doctor at one point describes their departure as if they were vermin who "scampered away downstairs like so many rats, and we heard their shrill voices next moment in the street." And when they later return, Watson writes, almost with a shudder, that "the spokesman of the street Arabs" is a young man named Wiggins.

Holmes, however, is amused by the temporary invasion of his home, even though it has caused Mrs. Hudson alarm. He has a simple business arrangement in hand: He hires the "street Arabs" because they can go places he can't. However, in deference to his landlady, he tells Wiggins not to bring the whole gang again, but to simply report by himself what the others find out.

The sad and simple fact is that these urban poor were invisible to their fellow Londoners (see Chapter 4 for more on London society). Thus, they're the perfect spies for Holmes to send out into the city. He pays them each a daily wage along with incentives for success.

Wiggins and his band of ragamuffins first appear in *A Study in Scarlet* (1887). In *The Sign of the Four* (1890), they make a reappearance — a reenactment, really, the scene differing only in that a dozen instead of half a dozen street urchins invade Baker Street, along with their "disreputable little scarecrow" of a leader, Wiggins. Once more, Watson is at a loss to understand what's happening as he "could hear Mrs. Hudson, our landlady, raising her voice in a wail of expostulation and dismay." The whole situation gets explained again, and Holmes once again tells their leader, "In future they can report to you, Wiggins, and you to me. I cannot have the house invaded in this way."

After *The Sign of the Four,* the Irregulars dropped out of sight for a few years, showing up once more in "The Crooked Man" in 1893, then fading from the scene forever. In 1893, Wiggins had been replaced by a leader named Simpson; what happened to Wiggins is never revealed.

Although they played a relatively small role in the stories, these street urchins turned out to be among the most appealing supporting characters in all the canon and are forever part of the overall world of Sherlock Holmes.

Chapter 7

Villains, Victims, and Damsels in Distress

In This Chapter

▶ Chronicling the life and exploits of Professor James Moriarty

▶ Rounding up some other canonical criminals

▶ Holmes's clients: Classifying the victims of crime

*O*f course, no detective story can get by without a bad guy and a victim. Among the 60 Sherlock Holmes adventures, you'll find plenty of both. A survey of villains and victims spanning the entire canon reveals a lot about Sherlock's career, as well as the world in which he lived and worked.

Perpetrators and victims represent two sides of any crime. With a set of stories spanning 40 years, Holmes encounters examples from every class of society. On the victim side, everyone from kings to shopkeepers petition the Great Detective for help. And the criminal side of the equation represents a similar gamut, from petty thieves to the head of a mighty criminal organization.

Professor Moriarty: The Anti-Holmes

In his unique role as the world's first (and at that time *only*) consulting detective, most of the problems, mysteries, and crimes that were referred to Holmes were outside the commonplace. And usually, that meant a particularly bad criminal. Of all the crooks in the canon, one towers over the rest: Professor James Moriarty.

It's impossible to even think of Sherlock Holmes without thinking of Professor Moriarty, whose very name suggests the idea of death. Who is this incredible nemesis who, as Holmes says, "pervades London," and yet "no one has heard of"? Who is this "abstract thinker" with "a brain of the first order"? Seriously, just who is this evil criminal genius? Even Watson, Holmes's closest companion and ally, never heard of the professor.

Holmes's suspicions

For having such an immense reputation, Professor Moriarty appears in only three stories. He is introduced to Watson (and hence the reader) in "The Final Problem," which tells of the deadly encounter between him and Sherlock Holmes. Readers find out more about what happened at that showdown in "The Empty House," which recounts Holmes's return from the dead. Moriarty also appears in *The Valley of Fear,* where he is offstage pulling the strings on a revenge murder. (This story is set prior to "The Final Problem.") But it's that first encounter with Moriarty in "The Final Problem" that stays with the reader.

After being absent from Baker Street for three months on a case for "the French government upon a matter of supreme importance," Holmes suddenly appears, with bleeding knuckles and a morbid fear of air guns. He's had a day of horror, dodging one assassination attempt after another, and now that he's back, he feels it's time to come clean to Watson.

No one knows the criminal underworld as well as Holmes does. But as his career progresses, Holmes begins to see patterns in criminal activity that make him suspicious. "For years past I have continually been conscious of some power behind the malefactor," he tells Watson, "some deep organizing power which forever stands in the way of the law, and throws its shield over the wrong-doer."

The extent of this power must be immense. After Holmes realizes the reality of it, he sees its malign influence everywhere. "Again and again in cases of the most varying sorts — forgery cases, robberies, murders — I have felt the presence of this force." Holmes sees it not only in his own cases, but also, as he tells his friend, "I have deduced its action in many of those undiscovered crimes in which I have not been personally consulted."

So who's in charge of this organization? "You have probably never heard of Professor Moriarty?" Holmes asks Watson, who replies with "Never."

"Ay, there's the genius and the wonder of the thing!" cries Holmes.

The professor's illustrious early career

Professor James Moriarty began his extraordinary career as a "man of good birth and excellent education." At an early age young James was "endowed by nature with a phenomenal mathematical faculty." He was so advanced in mathematics that by the age of 21, "he wrote a treatise upon the binomial theorem, which has had a European vogue."

TECHNICAL STUFF

The binomial theorem

The binomial theorem is the result that allows the expansion of a binomial

$$(a + b)^5 = a^5 + 5a^4b + 10a^3b^2 + 10a^2b^3 + 5ab^4 + b^5$$

where the coefficients a_i are called binomial coefficients. Got that? No? Me either. But Professor Moriarty did — he was an expert at it by the age of 21!

On the strength of his work with the binomial theorem, Moriarty won the mathematical chair at a small university. At some point during this time, he scored a second success with a new publication titled *The Dynamics of an Asteroid* — "a book," says Holmes, "which ascends to such rarefied heights of pure mathematics that there was no man in the scientific press capable of criticizing it."

Truly a genius. As Holmes put it, Moriarty had "a most brilliant career before him." But then something changed.

Scandal leading to a career change

The canon doesn't reveal which university the brilliant young mathematics prodigy taught at, but wherever it was, something started to go wrong. As Holmes put it, "Dark rumors gathered round him in the university town, and eventually he was compelled to resign his chair and to come down to London." Because Holmes provides no further information, readers can only speculate what the "dark rumors" were about.

In London, Moriarty set up as an *army coach,* a sort of private tutor. That's quite a comedown for the celebrated, twice-published professor. The life of a private tutor isn't one destined for riches. *The Valley of Fear* reveals that Moriarty made £700 a year as a university professor — not bad, but certainly not an extravagant income. As a tutor, his income had to be even less.

And yet, he had something else going on, because he was able to afford a painting by Jean-Baptiste Greuze (see the nearby sidebar). Moriarty also had enough money to pay his bills with funds held in six different banks.

And even more shockingly, he paid his right-hand man, Colonel Sebastian Moran, an astronomical income of £6,000 a year! "It's more than the Prime Minister gets," comments Holmes. "That gives you an idea of Moriarty's gains and of the scale on which he works."

Jean-Baptiste Greuze

Professor Moriarty had good taste in art. The French painter Jean-Baptiste Greuze (1725–1805) enjoyed a great reputation during most of his lifetime. Both critics and the public greatly admired his work, and art collectors sought many of his paintings. Most of them were portraits of heads and faces, and during his life, experts associated him with *neoclassicism,* a late-18th-century and 19th-century movement that drew upon the classical art and culture of Western civilization. However, art historians now see his work as unique. So did the public, and by the end of the century, his paintings were some of the most popular in the Louvre. They also saw record prices at auction. For Moriarty to own one was indeed remarkable.

So what were his "works"? What did this professor with an extraordinary brain do? What was he up to in the small university town that made people suspicious of him? Why did he need to move to London? Holmes can tell us:

> "He is the Napoleon of crime, Watson. He is the organizer of half that is evil and of nearly all that is undetected in this great city. He is a genius, a philosopher, an abstract thinker. He has a brain of the first order. He sits motionless, like a spider in the centre of its web, but that web has a thousand radiations, and he knows well every quiver of each of them. He does little himself. He only plans."

Professor Moriarty's criminal business

Organization seems to have been the unique strength that Professor Moriarty brought to his criminal organization. There were other crime syndicates, Mafia families, and all sorts of criminal gangs prior to the professor, but with Moriarty's unique gift, he was able to create an organization unlike his predecessors.

Holmes's investigation gave him insight into how the business worked. "His agents are numerous and splendidly organized," he tells Watson in "The Final Problem." "If there is a crime to be done, a paper to be abstracted, we will say, a house to be rifled, a man to be removed — the word is passed to the professor, the matter is organized and carried out."

So well organized is Moriarty's organization that, should something go wrong and the perpetrator get caught, money is found for his bail and legal defense. "But the central power which uses the agent is never caught," comments Holmes, "never so much as suspected."

Sir Francis Galton

Sir Francis Galton (1822–1911) was an immensely influential, English Victorian scientist whose fields of interest and research included geography, anthropology, eugenics, meteorology, statistics, and, perhaps most importantly, genetics.

Galton's cousin was Charles Darwin, author of the landmark *The Origin of Species*, a work that had a significant influence on Galton. Using rigorous scientific methodology, Galton embarked on a study of human abilities and characteristics, carefully measuring and logging them. This revolutionary approach spread rapidly throughout the social and biological sciences.

Galton researched a large number of prominent Victorian men and discovered that most had prominent, accomplished relatives, leading him to conclude that whatever traits lead to social and professional success must run in families. (Time and research have shown that inheritance is a much more complicated subject than Galton could have imagined, dependent on genetics, environment, and other factors.) He published his research in two volumes, *Hereditary Genius* (1869) and *English Men of Science* (1874). *Hereditary Genius* was an especially influential work.

This incredible criminal system prompted Holmes to call Moriarty, in grudging admiration, "The greatest schemer of all time, the organizer of every deviltry, the controlling brain of the underworld, a brain which might have made or marred the destiny of nations." It was a fearsome, ruthless enterprise. As Moriarty himself tells Holmes in their first of only two face-to-face meetings (the first was at Baker Street; the second on the ledge over Reichenbach Falls): "You stand in the way not merely of an individual but of a mighty organization, the full extent of which you, with all your cleverness, have been unable to realize."

And as Holmes tells Watson, "This was the organization which I deduced, Watson, and which I devoted my whole energy to exposing and breaking up."

The idea of "bad blood"

When discussing his own background and heredity, Sherlock Holmes comments that "art in the blood is liable to take the strangest forms." He's referring to his belief that the artistic traits of his famous Vernet relatives (see Chapter 5), a family of French painters, account in part for his (and his brother Mycroft's) uncanny ability at observation and deduction.

In Moriarty, Holmes sees a similar phenomenon at work but in an entirely different direction. Of Moriarty he says, "The man had hereditary tendencies of the most diabolical kind. A criminal strain ran in his blood, which, instead of being modified, was increased and rendered infinitely more dangerous by his extraordinary mental powers."

In both Sherlock Holmes and Professor Moriarty, Arthur Conan Doyle is giving a reflection of the Victorian scientific understanding of heredity and genetics. That understanding was especially influenced by the work of Sir Francis Galton (see the nearby sidebar), a Victorian scientist whose research led him to the conclusion that, though individual human ability varied greatly, some traits could run strongly within families. Holmes's statement that "art in the blood is liable to take the strangest forms" reveals Galton's influence on Arthur Conan Doyle.

Why Moriarty looms so large

No doubt about it, the number one criminal in all of detective fiction is Professor James Moriarty. No other master criminal even comes close. And yet, despite his legendary reputation, the professor is active in only two actual tales in the canon:

- ✔ **"The Final Problem" (1893):** This is the story in which the "Napoleon of crime" is first introduced. Holmes says to his friend Watson, "You have probably never heard of Professor Moriarty?" And with that introduction comes the greatest criminal in literature. What ensues is, in the words of Moriarty himself, "a duel between you and me, Mr. Holmes." Its horrifying ending finds the "the most dangerous criminal and the foremost champion of the law" locked in each other's arms, plunging into the Reichenbach Falls.

- ✔ *The Valley of Fear* (1914): In this novel of revenge, set before the events of "The Final Problem," Moriarty provides a valuable consulting service to an American bent on murder.

In addition to these two turns, Moriarty's henchman, Col. Sebastian Moran (more about him later), is the villain of "The Empty House," and then, periodically until the end of his career, Sherlock refers to the "late, lamented Professor Moriarty." (It actually sounds like he misses him!) But with such a small number of appearances, why does Moriarty loom so large? For two reasons, which I discuss in the following sections.

Absence makes the heart grow (in this case) more fearful

The first reason for Moriarty's prominence in the Holmes stories is the theory of absence. Moriarty's absence doesn't diminish his status — it actually enhances it. The professor is a sort of Sherlockian boogeyman, haunting the stories through to the end of the canon. Indeed, his attraction is so great that writers and filmmakers simply can't resist including him.

Think about it: Moriarty is like some kind of ghost, and few but Sherlock Holmes himself have ever laid eyes on him. In "The Final Problem," Moriarty pays a visit to Holmes at Baker Street, but readers only get the account of the visit secondhand, from Holmes himself.

Later, when Watson and Holmes are fleeing the professor on the train, Watson only sees "a tall man pushing his way furiously through the crowd, and waving his hand as if he desired to have the train stopped." It was Watson's only glimpse of the Napoleon of crime. "It was too late . . . for we were rapidly gathering momentum, and an instant later had shot clear of the station."

And then later, the tragic, fatal encounter on the ledge of the Reichenbach Falls happens only after Watson has been lured away. When the doctor returns, all he finds is Holmes's walking stick and a note.

In *The Valley of Fear,* Moriarty's involvement, as serious and fatal as it is, is entirely offstage. He's there, behind the scenes, pulling the strings on a grisly crime.

We often fear most that which we can't see. That's why a filmmaker cuts away just as the killer strikes. The viewer's imagination is often worse than whatever the filmmaker would show. That fear of what we can't see is what causes us to sleep with the lights on. It also helps explain Moriarty's towering reputation.

In Nicholas Meyers's novel *The Seven-Per-Cent Solution* (and the movie of the same name), Professor Moriarty is treated as an innocent man who had been Sherlock Holmes's math tutor when he was a boy. The title refers to Holmes's preferred dosage of injected cocaine, and the whole confrontation between the Great Detective and his arch-nemesis is reduced to a drug-induced hallucination, a self-made prison from which Sigmund Freud frees him (see Chapter 2 for more on Holmes's drug use).

The Sherlockian doppelgänger

The second reason for Moriarty's grip on the imagination is that he's the Sherlockian doppelgänger. A *doppelgänger* is, in legend, a person's disturbing, ghostly double. The word is German, meaning "double walker," and when a doppelgänger appears, either to the person it's mirroring or to his family, it's regarded as a harbinger of bad luck, illness, danger, or even death — especially when a person and his doppelgänger come face to face.

Holmes, "the foremost champion of the law," and Moriarty, the world's "most dangerous criminal," are mirror opposites, as physically similar as they are morally different. Both are tall and thin, with a receding hairline (see Figure 7-1). Yet Moriarty's "face protrudes forward and is forever slowly oscillating from side to side in a curiously reptilian fashion," and he is stooped. Holmes stands straight.

Whereas Holmes is a consultant to the law, Moriarty is a consultant to the underworld of crime. Whereas Holmes breaks the law for the sake of justice, Moriarty breaks it for the sake of personal profit. Whereas Holmes brings peace and safety to the world, Moriarty fills it with terror and tragedy.

Figure 7-1:
Sherlock
Holmes and
Professor
Moriarty.

Illustration by Sidney Paget, The Strand Magazine.

Holmes himself gives hints throughout the canon that Moriarty is his doppelgänger and that he is Moriarty's doppelgänger as well. As I mention earlier, Holmes does break the law on more than one occasion, and though he does it for virtuous ends, he admits to the lure of a life of crime. "I don't mind confessing," he once told Watson, "that I have always had an idea that I would have made a highly efficient criminal." There's no doubt, even in his own mind, that Holmes would bring the same degree of organization and efficiency to the business that his nemesis does.

Doyle built up the character of Moriarty as the opposite of Holmes in "The Final Problem" because he wanted to kill off his detective and concentrate on other books he was more interested in writing (see Chapter 3). To give the Great Detective a fitting sendoff, the agent of his departure from our world had to have a certain stature of his own; it just wouldn't have been plausible for Holmes to be killed by a lesser man.

The real-life inspiration for Moriarty

Just as Sherlock Holmes was modeled on one of Doyle's real-life medical school professors, Dr. Joseph Bell (for more on Bell, see Chapter 2), Professor Moriarty had real-life inspiration as well. In the case of the Napoleon of crime, he seems to have been an amalgamation of several sources.

Adam Worth

There can be no doubt that the German-American criminal Adam Worth was a prototype for Moriarty. Worth was actually given the nickname "the Napoleon of the criminal world" by Scotland Yard. Furthermore, Arthur Conan Doyle himself confirmed it.

Worth was born in 1844 in Prussia. His family was Jewish, and they emigrated to America when Worth was 5, landing in Cambridge, Massachusetts. Worth left home in 1854 and held a variety of jobs until the Civil War broke out. At the age of 17, he enlisted in the Union Army and was eventually promoted to sergeant. He was then wounded at Bull Run and sent to a hospital in Washington, DC. While recovering from his wounds, he discovered that he had been listed as "killed in action." He immediately left the hospital.

Worth then began a pattern of reenlisting in the army under an assumed name, getting paid, and then deserting his new unit. Ultimately, this brought him to the attention of the Pinkerton Detective Agency, which the government hired to investigate this kind of fraud. Worth fled to New York City when the Pinkertons got on his trail.

It was there that Worth embarked on a life of crime in earnest, starting as a pickpocket. He became the leader of a gang of pickpockets, which led to even more organized crimes, including robberies and burglaries. Eventually, he was caught and sent to Sing Sing prison, but he escaped after only a couple of weeks!

Worth went into partnership with Fredericka Mandelbaum, a well-known criminal organizer. Together they grew the business, expanding into bank robberies, but eventually, Worth went out on his own. On November 20, 1869, he tunneled into the underground vault of a Boston bank, starting from the basement of a neighboring store. (This is the exact scenario that the villains use in "The Red-Headed League," again showing that Doyle was well acquainted with the career of Adam Worth!) When the bank hired the fearsome Pinkertons to track the criminals, Worth moved to Europe with Charley Bullard, a safecracker colleague.

Over the years, Bullard and Worth took various names and identities as they moved through Europe robbing, pickpocketing, and pulling heists. They eventually landed in Paris, where they opened a restaurant and bar, which also featured gambling on an upper floor. Gambling, of course, was illegal, but that didn't deter Worth. Eventually, after numerous raids by the police, the place got too hot and Worth moved to London.

Adam Worth worked his way into London society while forming a new criminal organization devoted to larger, more serious robberies. But Scotland Yard took notice of the group's activities, and a series of bad breaks began to undo Worth and his crime syndicate.

Then, in 1876, came a career-defining crime. Worth stole a famous Thomas Gainsborough painting, *Georgiana Duchess of Devonshire,* which had been hanging in a prominent London art gallery. However, instead of selling it, Worth decided to keep it. With the Pinkertons and Scotland Yard on his trail, Worth left England, traveled the world, kept financing himself through theft, got married, and had children, all the while keeping the Gainsborough painting with him. Finally, he returned to New York, painting in hand. Just like Moriarty in *The Valley of Fear,* he had a stolen masterpiece in his possession.

After further criminal adventures, Worth was eventually arrested in Belgium after a botched robbery, and he stood trial on March 20, 1893. He was found guilty and sent to prison, and he was released in 1897 for good behavior. Worth then met William Pinkerton, of the very agency that had pursued him for decades. In a strange turn of events, Worth related the story of his colorful, crime-filled life, and Pinkerton turned his notes of the account into a book.

After meeting with Pinkerton, Worth returned the stolen *Duchess of Devonshire* to the gallery that he had stolen it from years before, but not before he received $25,000 for it! Worth then returned to London with his children, where he died on January 8, 1902. In an odd twist, Worth's son later went on to become a Pinkerton agent himself!

Jonathan Wild

Doyle compares Moriarty, in *The Valley of Fear,* to the real-life 18th-century criminal mastermind, Jonathan Wild. Wild lived about a century before the Holmes stories, and he was quite a colorful character who was written about by both Henry Fielding *(The History of the Life of the Late Mr. Jonathan Wild the Great)* and Daniel Defoe *(The True and Genuine Account of the Life and Actions of the Late Jonathan Wild).*

Wild lived in the days before England had a police force, and the government relied on civilian bounty hunters, or "thief-takers," to curb serious crime. Wild was the premier thief-taker of his time and earned a handsome living while making himself into a public folk hero.

What the public didn't know, however, was that Wild was himself the mastermind behind a great deal of the crime in London. Although he provided a variety of services to the criminal community, he specialized in fencing stolen goods. He developed the technique of hiring thieves to steal specific items and then ransoming those items back to the victims. Those grateful souls actually believed him to be a hero akin to Sherlock Holmes, a paladin who sniffed out the guilty and recovered his clients' lost goods from them. But his activities as a thief-taker were simply his own way of eliminating the competition — he turned in anyone who didn't work for him and protected his hirelings.

He eventually fell afoul of the law and, after years of successfully living his double life, ended on the gallows. Despite his long career as the premier crime lord of London, he was convicted only of conspiring to steal £40 worth of lace, intending to sell it back to its owner.

In *The Valley of Fear,* Holmes sums up the identity between the real criminal mastermind and the fictional one when he says to Dr. Watson: "Everything comes in circles — even Professor Moriarty. Jonathan Wild was the hidden force of the London criminals, to whom he sold his brains and his organization on a fifteen per cent commission. The old wheel turns, and the same spoke comes up. It's all been done before, and will be again."

Other candidates

It's believed that Doyle used other people in creating Moriarty, and he's known to have used his former school, Stonyhurst College, as inspiration for many details of the Holmes series. In the case of Moriarty, Stonyhurst may have provided the Reverend Thomas Shay. Shay was the prefect of discipline at Stonyhurst, and it's said that the Stonyhurst priests instantly thought of Father Shay when they read the description of Moriarty.

Later, during his life and medical practice in Portsmouth, Doyle made the acquaintance of a Rev. James Moriarty, who may have at least lent his name to Doyle's character.

And finally, in 2000, Professor Franco Eugeni, a mathematician from the University of Teramo in Italy, discovered an old letter referring to a relatively obscure mathematician of Doyle's time named James Moriarty who did some work on the binomial theorem, just as Doyle's Professor Moriarty did. (Interestingly, the real-life James Moriarty had an older brother who was a railway employee, much like Doyle's literary Moriarty, and a younger brother who was involved in the London criminal element.)

Moriarty's minions

The greatest criminal mastermind didn't exist in a vacuum, of course, any more than Holmes himself did (see Chapter 6 for more on Holmes's supporting cast). He had both family and hirelings to help him.

The Moriarty brothers

Professor Moriarty had at least two brothers. In *The Valley of Fear,* an unnamed younger Moriarty brother "is a station master in the west of England." Although the stationmaster is never named, it would be a strange career path for a high-ranking army officer to become master of a train station, so it's safe to assume that James is probably the older brother. Then, in "The Final Problem," Moriarty is defended in the press by his other brother, Colonel James Moriarty.

Why two children in the same family should be named James is anyone's guess, but it appears to be a simple slip of the kind that Doyle made throughout the Holmes stories. When Professor Moriarty is first introduced in "The Final Problem," Doyle provides no first name for him, although his brother is called James Moriarty. When "The Empty House" appeared many years later, Doyle called the arch-criminal James, too, apparently forgetting that he had already used the name James for Moriarty's sibling. But the reality of the situation is not nearly as fun as what many Sherlockians prefer to believe — that because two of the three brothers are named James, the third must be as well!

Henchmen

Readers are granted only the slightest glimpse of Moriarty's gang. In "The Final Problem," Holmes relates how, as he "went out about midday to transact some business," he was nearly run down by a two-horse van that, as he puts it, "was furiously driven" and that "whizzed round and was on me like a flash." Holmes "sprang for the foot-path and saved [himself] by the fraction of a second."

Later that same day, as Holmes walked down Vere Street, a brick from the roof of one of the houses fell and shattered at his feet. Clearly, Moriarty had minions everywhere.

In the story "The Empty House," Holmes says of one of Moriarty's lookouts (a "sentinel," actually) that he is "a harmless enough fellow, Parker by name, a garroter by trade, and a remarkable performer upon the jew's-harp."

A *garrote* is a tool for strangling people, usually made from a rope or chain. It's odd that Holmes should speak of the professional assassin who was expert in its use as "harmless," but undoubtedly, relative to the horrors of the deadly air gun, a run-of-the-mill garroter seems harmless!

Beyond this, the only major player is Colonel Sebastian Moran. Moran is a key figure in Holmes's saga and is described as Moriarty's chief of staff: "I happen to know who is the first link in his [Moriarty's] chain — a chain with this Napoleon-gone-wrong at one end, and a hundred broken fighting men, pickpockets, blackmailers, and card sharpers at the other, with every sort of crime in between. His chief of staff is Colonel Sebastian Moran, as aloof and guarded and inaccessible to the law as himself."

In short, Doyle sets the colonel up as a nasty villain, "the second most dangerous man in London." Moran was a hit man and a card cheater, but he was never convicted of any of these crimes. In fact, Moran didn't end up on the gallows as Holmes predicted — even after the Great Detective caught him red-handed trying to kill him with several police officers as witnesses (one assumes that the colonel had a *very* good lawyer). This skilled assassin is referred to in "The Illustrious Client" as still living and "dangerous" eight years after he was arrested (see Figure 7-2) for trying to kill Holmes in "The Empty House."

Figure 7-2:
The capture
of Colonel
Sebastian
Moran.

Illustration by Sidney Paget, The Strand Magazine.

Doyle's description of Moran is that of a typical *shikari,* or tiger hunter, in the India of the British Empire, "once of Her Majesty's Indian Army, and the best heavy-game shot that our Eastern Empire has ever produced." Moran "was always a man of iron nerve, and the story is still told in India how he crawled down a drain after a wounded man-eating tiger."

So Moran is, on the surface, a pillar of the British Empire. "This is astonishing," says Watson after reading Moran's biography in Holmes's notebook. "The man's career is that of an honorable soldier!" Holmes responds by saying that "it was undoubtedly he who gave me that evil five minutes on the Reichenbach ledge."

Other Unsavory Characters

Of course, the canon is full of criminals other than Moriarty and his henchmen. Their crimes run the gamut from running an entire criminal syndicate to crimes of passion to justifiable homicide. Here's just a sampling of canonical criminals:

✔ **Enoch Drebber, Joseph Stangerson, and Jefferson Hope:** Though Drebber and Stangerson are both murdered at the hands of Jefferson Hope, there's no doubt that they're villains. In the flashback of *A Study in Scarlet,* they kidnap Lucy Ferrier, murder her father, and force her into a marriage that causes her to die of a broken heart. Right out of the gate, Doyle produces a tale in which the guilt of the killer, Jefferson Hope, is more ambiguous than it seems at first glance.

✔ **John Clay:** Canonical criminals come from all levels of society. "The Red-Headed League" contains one of the most colorful. John Clay, whose grandfather was a royal duke, has a fine Eton and Oxford education. Upon his arrest, he announces, "I have royal blood in my veins. Have the goodness, also, when you address me always to say 'sir' and 'please.'" Despite his upbringing and social advantages, in the end he's nothing more than a forger, a thief, and a con man — or even a murderer as necessity demands.

✔ **James Windibank, a.k.a. Hosmer Angel:** Though he doesn't technically commit any crimes, James Windibank is one of the most reprehensible villains in the canon. In "A Case of Identity," he schemes with his wife, assumes a disguise, and starts dating his stepdaughter, Mary Sutherland. Taking the name of Hosmer Angel, he causes the poor, near-sighted woman to fall in love, only to vanish on their wedding day. Miss Sutherland promises to wait for her missing fiancé, all so that the parents can keep control of her money. "The law cannot, as you say, touch you," says Holmes to the unrepentant man, "yet there never was a man who deserved punishment more. If the young lady has a brother or a friend, he ought to lay a whip across your shoulders." And then Holmes nearly did just that!

✔ **John Turner:** In "The Boscombe Valley Mystery," after an early life of crime in Australia, John Turner went to England to lead a quiet life. However, once there he endures years of being blackmailed by someone who knows his shameful past. Finally, when his tormentor demands that Turner's daughter marry his son, Turner turns to murder. "God help us!" says Holmes after hearing the man's confession. "Why does fate play such tricks with poor, helpless worms?"

✔ **Dr. Grimesby Roylott:** "The Speckled Band" features a truly outstanding bad guy, Dr. Grimesby Roylott, another evil stepfather. When he's forced to leave India after killing a man, Roylott brings an explosive temper home to England, where he terrorizes the neighborhood and begins murdering his stepdaughters for their money. "When a doctor does go wrong he is the first of criminals," Holmes tells Watson. "He has nerve and he has knowledge."

✔ **Wilson Kemp:** Torture, starvation, asphyxiation . . . these are the particular tools of Wilson Kemp, the terrible villain of "The Greek Interpreter." His thick glasses and "nervous, jerky fashion" of speaking, punctuated with "little giggling laughs," makes him even more terrifying.

✔ **Biddle, Hayward, Moffat, Sutton, and Tobin:** These are the names of the Worthingdon bank gang from "The Resident Patient." When robbing the bank, this group of criminals murders a guard in cold blood. There's no honor among thieves, however, as Sutton turns state's evidence and testifies against his fellow crooks, sending them to prison in exchange for his own freedom. Unfortunately, his old mates eventually leave him dangling from the end of a rope.

✔ **Jack Stapleton:** A true all-star canonical criminal, Jack Stapleton is the evil manipulator behind *The Hound of the Baskervilles.* His sins are many — murder, spousal abuse, animal abuse, and even promising marriage in order to manipulate a poor, lonely woman to further his plan. But readers should begrudgingly give credit where credit is due — using the legend of the hound of the Baskervilles was a stroke of genius!

✔ **Charles Augustus Milverton:** "I've had to do with fifty murderers in my career, but the worst of them never gave me the repulsion which I have for this fellow." So says Holmes of the master blackmailer, Charles Augustus Milverton, from the story of the same name. Holmes makes it perfectly clear how low he regards Milverton: "I would ask you," he says, "how could one compare the ruffian, who in hot blood bludgeons his mate, with this man, who methodically and at his leisure tortures the soul and wrings the nerves in order to add to his already swollen money-bags?"

✔ **Abe Slaney:** Just as Holmes's professional ties stretch to the United States, so do the criminals he deals with. In "The Dancing Men," Abe Slaney is a Chicago gangster obsessed with regaining an old girlfriend — so obsessed that he travels all the way to England to woo her back. Only problem is, he doesn't realize that shooting her husband isn't a good approach.

✔ **Jack Woodley:** Surely one of the most disgusting crooks in all the canon is Roaring Jack Woodley, found in "The Solitary Cyclist." A "coarse, puffy-faced, red-moustached young man, with his hair plastered down on each side of his forehead," Woodley was constantly coming on to Violet Smith, music teacher to the daughter of Woodley's friend, Bob Carruthers. "Mr. Woodley seemed to me to be a most odious person," she confides to Holmes. Too bad, because she ends up marrying him at gunpoint!

✔ **Boss McGinty and the Scowers:** For sheer scope, these guys from *The Valley of Fear* are nearly unrivaled. The Scowers, with their bearded, brutal leader Boss McGinty, held an entire region of Pennsylvania in their evil grip. Part crime syndicate, part terrorist organization, this twisted fraternity had business owners, politicians, and police under their thumb. Torture, intimidation, and cold-blooded murder were their methods of choice.

An all-star lineup of bad guys

Which villains did Sherlock Holmes believe were the standouts of his time? In making a "most memorable" list as defined by the Great Detective himself, Holmes repeatedly uses the device of labeling a character in a very specific way, with the typical description style constructed like this: "The [adjective]-[person type] in [location]." For example, Holmes may have labeled someone "the most notorious burglar in England." With this in mind, here's a pretty definitive list of who, according to Sherlock himself, are the outstanding villains in the canon:

1. Professor Moriarty: "The greatest schemer of all time."

2. Sir George Burnwell: "One of the most dangerous men in Europe."

3. Charles Augustus Milverton: "The most dangerous man in London" as well as "the worst man in London."

4. Col. Sebastian Moran: "The second most dangerous man in London."

5. Alec Cunningham: "The most accomplished swindler in Europe."

6. Abe Slaney: "The most dangerous crook in Chicago."

7. Pietro Venucci: "One of the greatest cutthroats in London."

8. John Clay: "The fourth smartest man in London" and "the third most daring man in London."

9. Baron Adelbert Gruner: "The aristocrat of crime."

✔ **Jim Browner:** If ever there was a murderer in the canon that evokes pity rather than horror, Jim Browner of "The Cardboard Box" is him. With an evil, scheming sister-in-law and an unfaithful wife, poor, haunted Browner is practically driven to murder. "I have to make a clean breast of it all," he confesses to Holmes. "You can hang me, or do what you like with me, but you cannot punish me as I have been punished already. I cannot shut my eyes but I see those two faces staring at me . . . I killed them quick, but they are killing me slow; and if I have another night of it I shall be either mad or dead before morning." And then, just as Holmes prepares to leave, Browner asks, "You won't put me alone into a cell, sir? For pity's sake don't, and may you be treated in your day of agony as you treat me now."

✔ **Von Bork:** In "His Last Bow," Sherlock Holmes's final case, the arrogant German spy Von Bork brags about the dim, hoodwinked English as he prepares to return to Germany on the eve of World War I. He's satisfied that he has gained valuable information to help win the war, but little does he know that, for two years, Holmes has been working against him. Boy, is he in for a big surprise!

Victorian Victims: The Clients of Sherlock Holmes

Sherlock Holmes was the court of last resort for the most perplexed people in England. They came to him for a variety of reasons. Perhaps they were the victim of a crime, like robbery or fraud, or maybe they had an utterly inexplicable experience that left them frightened and confused. Sometimes they just needed advice from someone well-known for "knowing things that others don't." And even, on one or two occasions, they came to him because they just needed someone to confess to.

The victims of crime in the canon often offer as much insight into the world of Sherlock Holmes, the culture of Victorian England, and human nature itself as the criminals do. Doyle's deft touch at character creation infuses them with depth and believability.

Holmes's clients are an eclectic array, coming from every spectrum of society. In the early days, Holmes's clientele came from the mostly lower and middle classes and the police, but as his fame and reputation grew, so did the status of those who came to Baker Street for help. Throughout the stories, Holmes occasionally name-drops the king, the pope, a government official, and sometimes even the government itself, which has used his services. Wealthier clients often bestow great rewards upon him, but the Great Detective doesn't take these cases for the money. Nor does he turn away a poor man or woman.

"I play the game for the game's own sake," he says. It's the problem that draws his attention, not the profit. If your problem presents a strange puzzle that needs the application of a brilliant mind to solve, then Holmes will take your case.

Their dilemmas

Though most mystery stories today deal with murder, only around half of Holmes's cases dealt with murder (or attempted murder). The subjects of the remainder range from kidnapping to fraud to theft to the occasional odd offense such as illegal medical experiments or other offbeat situations. Because Sir Arthur took such odd roads, the stories have never failed to capture their audience. The tales have the ring of truth because they often reflect real life. Doyle instinctively knew that the smallest, most unusual circumstance can offer the opportunity for mystery.

For instance, in "A Case of Identity," Holmes delivers a little speech to Watson about the odd dilemmas and situations that life can present, and these are undoubtedly Doyle's own views, spoken by his detective:

> "My dear fellow," said Sherlock Holmes as we sat on either side of the fire in his lodgings at Baker Street, "life is infinitely stranger than anything which the mind of man could invent. We would not dare to conceive the things which are really mere commonplaces of existence. If we could fly out of that window hand in hand, hover over this great city, gently remove the roofs, and peep in at the queer things which are going on, the strange coincidences, the plannings, the cross-purposes, the wonderful chains of events, working through generations, and leading to the most outre results, it would make all fiction with its conventionalities and foreseen conclusions most stale and unprofitable."

Despite the stories being set in a much earlier time, with sensibilities that are in some cases quite different than today, many of the crimes and the victims are timeless. Sometimes, the client has a secret and faces blackmail, as is the case in "A Scandal in Bohemia," a socially devastating possibility then and now. Many of the victims can be classified in broad categories. Some of the more unusual include the following.

Damsels in distress

This category is particularly rich in the Holmes stories. Doyle's own sisters were forced into work as governesses by dire family finances, making him keenly aware of the vulnerability of financially desperate women. Many examples of this show up in the tales.

- ✔ **Violet Hunter:** In "The Copper Beeches," Violet Hunter is in dire financial circumstances and takes a job as governess to a strange family. They offer her a salary far greater than the market rate. She says, "You may imagine, Mr. Holmes, that to me, destitute as I was, such an offer seemed almost too good to be true." It was.

- ✔ **Lady Francis Carfax:** "One of the most dangerous classes in the world," says Holmes in "The Adventure of Lady Francis Carfax," is "the drifting and friendless woman . . . She is helpless. She is migratory . . . She is a stray chicken in a world of foxes." Lady Francis Carfax is such a woman, and just as Holmes says, she becomes prey to a terrible con man.

- ✔ **Violet Smith:** "The Solitary Cyclist" is a tale of a woman who is stalked by a bearded man on a bicycle. The young music teacher Violet Smith (again in financial straits and lured by a large paycheck) accepts the job and goes to work in an isolated country home. There she falls prey to the advances of two unscrupulous criminals, and they decide to force her into marriage, with the groom determined by a card game.

Victims of bad karma

It's common in the Sherlockian canon to find, when a case is solved, that the murder victim gets what's coming to him. Though the stories don't exactly condone murder, it's sometimes hard for the reader (and occasionally Holmes and Watson as well) to muster much sympathy for the victim.

- ✔ **Charles McCarthy:** In "The Boscombe Valley Mystery," Charles McCarthy spends decades blackmailing his victim, until one day the victim strikes back, killing his tormentor. "I did it, Mr. Holmes," the killer confesses. "I would do it again. Deeply as I have sinned, I have led a life of martyrdom to atone for it."

- ✔ **Mr. Blessington:** One of the best examples of bad karma coming back on someone is in "The Resident Patient." Mr. Blessington thinks he's gotten away with letting his fellow bank robbers take the fall. That is, until he's woken up in the middle of the night by a noose around his neck.

- ✔ **Giuseppe Gorgiano:** "The Red Circle" offers the story of brutal Mafia chief Giuseppe Gorgiano, who sets his sights on a younger man's wife. When the couple flees Italy for London, Gorgiano follows. The message? Don't mess with another man's wife.

Robbery victims

Even this classic set of victims offers up some oddities. But keep in mind, only the strange ones come to Sherlock Holmes. Examples include

- ✔ **Alexander Holder:** In "The Beryl Coronet," Mr. Holder, of the banking firm of Holder & Stevenson, has taken what sounds like one of the crown jewels as collateral on a loan. Uh-oh . . . someone has broken off the jewels!

- ✔ **The Countess of Morcar:** The fabulous jewel known as the blue carbuncle already has a sinister history. "There have been two murders, a vitriol-throwing, a suicide, and several robberies," says Holmes, "brought about for the sake of this forty-grain weight of crystallized charcoal." The current owner is the countess of Morcar — that is, until the jewel is stolen from her hotel room, only to be swallowed by a goose!

Victims of fraud

Many of Holmes's clients come with baffling tales recounting some mysterious experience they've had — something so out of the orbit of their normal lives that it's a true mystery. In the end, it often turns out to be a case of fraud. For instance:

✔ **Victor Hatherley:** In "The Engineer's Thumb," Victor Hatherley, a young hydraulic engineer, is hired to go in the middle of the night to fix a broken hydraulic press. Upon his arrival, he realizes that all is not what it seems. Let's just say he has a hard time thumbing a ride back to the city!

✔ **Hall Pycroft:** "The Stockbroker's Clerk" is the story of Hall Pycroft, who accepts an unexpected job offer as the business manager of the Franco-Midland Hardware Company, Ltd., "with a hundred and thirty-four branches in the towns and villages of France, not counting one in Brussels and one in San Remo." It seems too good to be true. And it is.

Part III
Holmes and His Adventures

The 5th Wave   By Rich Tennant

I'm no Sherlock Holmes, but I've got a hunch we're looking for someone well over six feet tall.

In this part . . .

In addition to the many characters found in the canon, the Sherlock Holmes stories are rich in both atmosphere and history. The tales provide a window into the Victorian age, a time of gaslight, fog, and hansom cabs. This part looks at the elements that make up the "typical" Sherlock Holmes story. I also discuss the most famous Holmes novel of them all, *The Hound of the Baskervilles,* and I examine common themes found throughout the 60 stories.

Chapter 8

The "Typical" Sherlock Holmes Story

In This Chapter

▶ Looking at the common elements of Doyle's novels

▶ Identifying some of the typical tropes of Doyle's short stories

▶ Exploring 221b Baker Street

*T*he Sherlockian canon consists of two styles of story — the novel and the short story. Generally speaking, each is a distinct form of storytelling. The novel allows an author to develop his plot over a longer period of time and has space for subplots, numerous characters, and intricate plotting. The short story, on the other hand, typically provides a tighter-paced, plot-driven experience with little time for character development.

At least that's the conventional wisdom. However, when it comes to Sherlock Holmes, things aren't always what you may expect. Both the Sherlock Holmes novels and the short stories often contradict the generalizations that are normally associated with the respective forms. For example, novels typically have subplots woven in the main story, but none of the Holmes novels employs this device. And conversely, short stories are generally light on character development, but character development is Arthur Conan Doyle's greatest strength as a writer. The result is that the Holmes stories are full of deftly drawn characterizations that live and breathe on the page.

Doyle's novels and short stories share a number of characteristics, but each form also has elements that are distinctly its own. This isn't to say that the structure and style of Doyle's novels and stories are without consistency — they just have their own set of "typical" elements that, with some exceptions, Doyle uses repeatedly.

The Long of It: The Novels

Sherlock Holmes was intended to be a creature of the detective novel. Indeed, the first two Holmes stories make up two of the four novels in the Sherlockian canon. It wasn't until Doyle had the brain wave of magazine publication that the Great Detective moved to the short story.

Most Sherlockians believe that the canonical novels are less successful than the short stories, but this isn't true. They aren't less successful; they're just different. Each form has its own set of unique virtues and limitations. In addition to having plots and stories that play out over a greater number of pages, the longer-form books introduce vital information that helps readers better understand the history and nature of the characters.

A quick rundown of the longer tales

Of the four novels, I can say the following: One is a landmark, one is a perfect Sherlock Holmes story, one is an acknowledged masterpiece, and one is an underappreciated gem.

Although the Holmes adventures first appeared in the form of novels, despite their popularity and quality, the reputation and fame of Sherlock Holmes exploded when Doyle's creation debuted in *The Strand Magazine* in 1891 with "A Scandal in Bohemia."

A Study in Scarlet

Written in 1887 when Doyle was only 27, this is the first recorded adventure of Sherlock Holmes. (For more on the history of this novel's publication, see Chapter 2.) It not only introduced Holmes to the reading public and began his enduring partnership with his friend and companion, Dr. John H. Watson, but also established many of the conventions that appear throughout the entire run of the stories.

The original title of the book was *A Tangled Skein* . . . not a bad title, but not as good as what Doyle changed it to. At one point early in the book, Holmes tells Watson, "there's the scarlet thread of murder running through the colorless skein of life, and our duty is to unravel it, and isolate it, and expose every inch of it." Holmes also describes the case of murder they're investigating as his "study in scarlet."

A Study in Scarlet is really a two-part work. (I discuss this feature in more detail in the later section "The novel elements of the novels.")

✔ The first half is Dr. Watson's first-person account of his unfortunate military experience, his introduction to Sherlock Holmes and how they came to share lodgings, and the investigation into the mysterious murder of a man in an abandoned house who is found with the word "RACHE" written in blood on a nearby wall. It is Watson's first case with Holmes.

✔ Part two of the book is a flashback that gives the back story to the investigation in London. This flashback takes readers to the U.S. and tells a tale set in Mormon Utah during the time of Brigham Young. It provides a motive for the London murders and is a thrilling tale in its own right.

Following the flashback, the story returns to London, with Holmes clearing up any lingering questions about the mystery and tying the two parts of the book together.

A close, honest reading of *A Study in Scarlet* reveals that, though it's an entertaining, landmark book, Doyle was still maturing as a writer. For instance, it's hard to imagine the writer of *The Strand Magazine* short stories or *The Hound of the Baskervilles* resorting to the strained plot device of having an actor impersonate an old woman right there on Baker Street in order to get back Lucy's ring. Doyle had written himself into a corner, and many readers have cringed at his solution for getting out of it. It's the kind of clumsy moment that rarely, if ever, happens in his writing again. When compared with the brilliance Doyle would attain in just another year or two with *The Sign of the Four,* his lack of maturation as a writer is easier to see.

The Sign of the Four

Published complete in *Lippincott's Monthly Magazine* in February 1890, *The Sign of the Four* was more successful financially than its predecessor. Given its unusual origins (it was commissioned by the publisher of *Lippincott's*), it easily could have been the final adventure of Sherlock Holmes. But then, this was before Doyle switched to writing short stories.

The Sign of the Four is a romance as much as a mystery. It has everything: swirling fog, a fortune in treasure, a chase, Holmes's cocaine use, and even a damsel in distress. Each year on the anniversary of her father's death, Miss Mary Morstan receives a beautiful pearl in the mail from an anonymous sender. One day she is told to come and meet the sender, and being young and uncertain, she turns to Holmes and Watson. What follows is a wild chase through London, with blowguns, cannibalistic pygmies, a one-legged man, and a thrilling boat chase on the Thames. This is followed by a flashback to the Indian uprising — the first example in the canon of a tragedy in the British Empire coming home to England.

It's unlikely that Doyle was making a conscious statement about the empire. It's far more likely that he was simply reflecting the sentiment held by most of his fellow countrymen — that the farther you travel out into the empire, the more dangerous it becomes.

Saving Sherlock from obscurity

With two less-than-overwhelming appearances in the novels *A Study in Scarlet* and *The Sign of the Four*, Sherlock could have simply faded from his creator's imagination and the public's memory. But then, in early 1891, Arthur Conan Doyle turned to his detective for a continuing character to appear in a series of short stories. And where would these short stories be published? In *The Strand Magazine*.

The Strand Magazine was published in Britain from January 1891 to March 1950 during an era of great magazine publication and readership. The magazine itself, even before the Holmes stories appeared within its pages, was an immediate hit. Right out of the gate, it sold 300,000 copies. Then, in the spring of 1891, an extraordinary gift arrived on the desk of editor Herbert Greenhough Smith — the manuscripts of the first Sherlock Holmes short stories.

Sometimes the stars just line up, and this was one of those moments. First, there was this fresh new magazine with an exciting philosophy of "a picture on every page." Then, this exciting new character — a "consulting detective" named Sherlock Holmes — was added at precisely the time when the reading public was primed for precisely this product, and the result was a runaway hit. For a complete list and discussion of all the Holmes stories, refer to Chapter 1.

The novelty of this seemingly simple idea revolutionized periodical publication and set the scene for the explosion of Sherlock Holmes onto the world stage. Holmes was immediately popular, and the press run of *The Strand Magazine* rose from an initial run of 300,000 to an average of 500,000 copies a month, largely on the strength of the Great Detective.

The Strand Magazine was reincarnated in 1998 as *The Strand Mystery Magazine.* It regularly makes the Great Detective the centerpiece of its issues, with frequent essays on Sherlock Holmes. Check out www.strandmag.com.

In stories throughout the canon, events in countries in the distant reaches of the British Empire often have tragic consequences back in England:

- ✔ **Australia:** "The Boscombe Valley Mystery" and "The Gloria Scott"
- ✔ **India:** "The Speckled Band" and "The Crooked Man"
- ✔ **South Africa:** "The Solitary Cyclist" and "The Blanched Soldier"
- ✔ **U.S.** (though technically no longer in the British Empire, the U.S. was certainly seen as just as wild and untamed, especially the farther west a person went): *A Study in Scarlet,* "Five Orange Pips," "Yellow Face," "Dancing Men," and *The Valley of Fear*

Many other Sherlockian story staples make their first appearance in *The Sign of the Four:* cocaine use, bloodhounds, Watson's floating wound, the Baker Street Irregulars, and Watson's romantic ability.

The Hound of the Baskervilles

Like most of Holmes tales, this one starts at 221b Baker Street, opening with an account of an early 18th-century legend. Holmes's visitor, Dr. Mortimer, reads an old parchment telling how "a hound of hell" has haunted the Baskerville family, who live out on the moors. He goes on to relate how the latest member of the family died under mysterious circumstances.

The novel is clearly in the Gothic tradition, combining elements of mystery, romance, and horror. The tension between the seemingly supernatural evil in the story and Holmes's science and logic helps make *The Hound of the Baskervilles* an acknowledged masterpiece. It's one of Arthur Conan Doyle's greatest works.

The tale is told entirely in first-person by Watson, who uses narrative, letters, and diary extracts. Doyle doesn't employ a flashback, as he does in other Holmes novels.

The Hound of the Baskervilles (1901) was published after Doyle killed his hero at the Reichenbach Falls in "The Final Problem" (1893). The novel is presented as a posthumous Holmes adventure, and when it appeared in *The Strand Magazine,* it was a sensation. (For more on *The Hound of the Baskervilles,* see Chapter 9.)

The Valley of Fear

The Valley of Fear (1914) is undoubtedly the least popular and least read of the Sherlock Holmes novels, and that's too bad, because in plotting, characterization, and sheer thrills, it's second only to *The Hound of the Baskervilles.*

The Valley of Fear is really two independent stories that only dovetail at the end of the book.

- ✔ **Story 1:** The first story begins with what seems like a terrible murder in an English country home. The owner's face has been blown off by a sawed-off shotgun.

- ✔ **Story 2:** The second story is a flashback based on the true-life events involving the Molly Maguires, an Irish-American labor organization that used terror and violence to fight abusive mine owners in Pennsylvania. This story (both in real life and in the novel) involves a Pinkerton detective going undercover to catch the bad guys. Some Sherlockians contend that this flashback is so well-written that *The Valley of Fear* should be considered to contain not one but *two* detective stories.

History in the flashbacks

All three flashbacks in the Sherlock Holmes novels are based on or rooted in actual historical events. The flashback to Utah in *A Study in Scarlet* has, as its foundation, the controversy and fascination with the Mormon Church in the 19th century. Utah was in a distant, isolated wilderness, and back east in the U.S., as well as in England, lurid tales of polygamy, plural marriage, forced marriage, and "avenging angels" circulated in the popular press. Doyle's take on Mormonism reflected the popular understanding of the day.

In *The Sign of the Four*, during Jonathan Small's lengthy account (which is merely a flashback to his time in India), he tells his listeners, "suddenly, without a note of warning, the great mutiny broke upon us." He's referring to the Indian Rebellion of 1857, when native Indian soldiers under the command of the British Army mutinied. The violence spread, sparking other mutinies and then civilian uprisings. The rebellion posed a great threat to the English Empire in India until it was finally put down on June 20, 1858.

In *The Valley of Fear*, the flashback toward the end of the book is inspired by the secret, real-life Irish society called the Molly Maguires. The Mollies were active in the coal fields and coal mining towns of Pennsylvania following the Civil War. They organized to resist what they believed to be tyrannical rule by the owners and management of the coal fields. Some historians view them as a sort of labor union, others see them as an innocent social fraternity, and still others believe they were terrorists who resorted to murder and violence to achieve their ends. What historians do agree on are the approximately 50 unsolved murders in this region at this time. Just as in the book, the real-life Molly Maguires were infiltrated by a Pinkerton detective, who then testified against them in order to bring down the organization.

The novel elements of the novels

Three of the four Holmes novels are, in general terms, structurally similar, with common elements, themes, and storytelling devices. *A Study in Scarlet, The Sign of the Four,* and *The Valley of Fear* were, from their inception, conceived as Sherlock Holmes adventures, so it comes as no surprise that they're structurally similar. The notable exception is *The Hound of the Baskervilles,* which is completely different in style and wasn't originally conceived as a Holmes adventure. (For more on *The Hound of the Baskervilles,* see Chapter 9.)

In this section, I discuss the peculiar storytelling conventions that Doyle uses in writing the Holmes novels, as well as the common motifs and themes that are found in them.

The flashback

Arthur Conan Doyle's use of flashback served several functions: It provided back story to and motivation for the plot's crime; it gave him a chance to write about an exotic foreign location and time; and it helped to bring his books up to novel length.

None of the Sherlock Holmes novels is lengthy, and occasionally, you may see either of the early novels *A Study in Scarlet* or *The Sign of the Four* referred to as a novella. A *novella* is a story that's too long to be considered a short story but not long enough to be considered a novel. A novella is generally considered to be less than 40,000 words, and though all four Holmes novels are longer than this, *A Study in Scarlet* and *The Sign of the Four* both come in at just over 43,000 words.

Exotic foreign influence

With the exception of *The Hound of the Baskervilles,* the plots of the Sherlock Holmes novels are motivated by foreign crime and influence:

- **Mormonism in *A Study in Scarlet:*** In the first published tale, Holmes and Watson find themselves investigating the death of two victims from the U.S. America was a pretty far-off place in the 1880s, but it turns out that the victims were Mormons from the state of Utah. Mormonism, with its early history of polygamy and violence, was about as scandalous and foreign to the average British citizen as you could get.

- **India and *The Sign of the Four:*** This tale's back story and plot are rooted in mysterious India — then the eastern, subcontinental possession of the empire — and so is the very spirit of the book. At every turn you encounter the intrusion of wild, exotic India into the ordered world of London.

  For example, upon answering a mysterious summons to Pondicherry Lodge, Holmes, Watson, and their client Mary Morstan are ushered into a strange, disorienting room: "We were all astonished by the appearance of the apartment into which he invited us," Watson says. "The richest and glossiest of curtains and tapestries draped the walls, looped back here and there to expose some richly mounted painting or Oriental vase." As the visitors await their host, they notice "two great tiger-skins" on the floor that give a "suggestion of Eastern luxury, as did a huge hookah which stood upon a mat in the corner. A lamp in the fashion of a silver dove was hung from an almost invisible golden wire in the centre of the room. As it burned it filled the air with a subtle and aromatic odor." Indeed, the very air of *The Sign of the Four* reeks with exotic foreign overtones.

Revenge and murder

Unlike the short stories, the Holmes novels — even *The Hound of the Baskervilles* — all deal with murder. A Sherlockian short story may also deal with murder, but just as often it deals with robbery, espionage, blackmail, or occasionally no crime at all. But in the long-form Holmes tales, it's always murder.

In *A Study in Scarlet,* the plot revolves around death by poison and a double homicide. In *The Sign of the Four,* the plot includes death by a poisonous dart! *The Hound of the Baskervilles* brings death by induced heart attack and attempted murder by a vicious dog. Finally, *The Valley of Fear* has perhaps the grisliest murder of them all — death by a sawed-off shotgun blast to the face. You have to hand it to Arthur Conan Doyle — he was creative in coming up with violent deaths!

Exciting events

Objectively reading the Holmes novels makes it pretty clear that sustaining the mystery over an entire book was difficult for Doyle. Because of that he uses flashbacks, which take the reader out of the mystery plot by providing a sort of prequel to the main plot. He also employs much more action in the novels — because the longer format has more room and because the action helps cover and stretch the plot. Not that this is a bad thing. Some of the best sequences in the canon — involving boat chases, bloodhounds, spectral dogs, and a return visit from Professor Moriarty — all come from the Sherlockian novels.

The Short of It: The Short Stories

Arthur Conan Doyle once wrote that it was as hard for him to concoct the plot of a Sherlock Holmes short story as it was to do so for a novel, and judging from the intricacies of many of the short-story plots, we must take him at his word. However, that doesn't mean that the short stories were like the novels, only shorter. True, some of the elements in the long stories — foreign influence, revenge, and so on — can occasionally be found in the short ones. But those elements are rarely handled in the short story the way they are in the novels.

The primary literary device of the novels, the flashback, rarely appears in the short stories. The short tales contain only four lengthy, back-story flashbacks — in "The Gloria Scott," "The Crooked Man," "The Golden Pince-Nez," and "The Veiled Lodger."

Writing for the English commuter

The late Victorian era was a golden age for magazine publishing. At a time before radio, television, and motion pictures, the Victorian magazines were the unifying entertainment of the popular culture in both England and the U.S. They presented serialized novels and short fiction by the era's greatest writers, as well as puzzles, profiles of famous celebrities, true-life accounts of travels to the empire's far-flung corners, political commentary, and a host of other valuable and entertaining items. Magazine advertising spread commerce and new products to a rising middle-class readership and helped homogenize the culture. These magazines undoubtedly provided many of the office "water-cooler" moments that would later come from radio and TV.

In addition to *The Strand Magazine,* some of the most popular magazines included *Scribner's Magazine, Harper's Monthly, Leslie's Magazine,* *McClure's, Pearson's Magazine, Harmsworth's Magazine, Century,* and *Puck Magazine.* With their short, punchy prose, illustrations, and interesting topics, these publications met the rising demand of Victorian commuters, who wanted to be entertained by exciting short stories on short railway journeys to and from the office. This was a time when the suburbs began to bloom, and many middle-class workers moved out of the city but still worked there. Tracks were laid to these new suburbs, and commuter trains ran to and fro. This was the perfect time for the medium of the magazine, and especially for Sherlock Holmes.

It's interesting to note that the decline of Victorian (and then Edwardian) magazines like *The Strand* began with the end of WWI and paralleled the decline of the commuter train in England.

The short story "formula"

The Sherlockian short stories collectively have a pattern or formula all their own. This isn't to say that Doyle followed some kind of template but that, over the course of reading the 56 short tales, common elements become apparent.

Of course, not every story has every one of these features, but these traits happen enough that, despite the variability, you can use them to construct a "typical" Sherlock Holmes short story.

The following sections outline how the typical Holmes short story proceeds from beginning to end.

No. 1: The opening domestic scene

Often, Watson opens his account in the apartment at 221b Baker Street. It's a scene of cozy, domestic tranquility, with Holmes and Watson engaged in some personal pastime before something or someone arrives, bringing a fresh case. Sometimes it's morning, as in "The Blue Carbuncle," where Holmes is "lounging upon the sofa in a purple dressing-gown, a pipe-rack within his reach upon the right, and a pile of crumpled morning papers, evidently newly studied, near at hand."

On another occasion it may be nighttime. The start of "The Five Orange Pips" offers about as evocative an example of an opening scene in 221b Baker Street as there is.

"It was in the latter days of September, and the equinoctial gales had set in with exceptional violence," says Watson, setting the scene. He describes how the storm's "wind had screamed and the rain had beaten against the windows" like "untamed beasts in a cage." He goes on to say:

> As evening drew in, the storm grew higher and louder, and the wind cried and sobbed like a child in the chimney. Sherlock Holmes sat moodily at one side of the fireplace cross-indexing his records of crime, while I at the other was deep in one of Clark Russell's fine sea-stories until the howl of the gale from without seemed to blend with the text, and the splash of the rain to lengthen out into the long swash of the sea waves.

No. 2: A demonstration of the Sherlockian method

Sherlock Holmes enjoys demonstrating his deductive "method" on Watson, who never fails to be amazed. This display usually comes before the arrival of a visitor to usher in a new case.

In "A Scandal in Bohemia," Holmes discovers much information about an impending visitor from a letter sent earlier in the day. In "The Dancing Men," Holmes surprises Watson by suddenly saying, "so, Watson, you do not propose to invest in South African securities?"

> "How on earth do you know that?" Watson responds.

> With a "gleam of amusement in his deep-set eyes," Holmes says, "now, Watson, confess yourself utterly taken aback."

> "I am."

> "I ought to make you sign a paper to that effect."

> "Why?"

> "Because in five minutes you will say that it is all so absurdly simple."

And it was, after it was explained!

No. 3: The introduction of the case

Following all the nice, domestic coziness comes the mystery. It can come via a cryptic letter or telegram, as in "The Dancing Men" or "The Sussex Vampire." In the former, Holmes receives a letter with "a number of absurd little figures dancing across the paper upon which they are drawn." In the latter, it's a note from a law firm referring its client to Holmes regarding vampires.

Often the case comes from Scotland Yard, with perhaps Inspector Lestrade himself paying a visit to the Great Detective. In "The Six Napoleons," the inspector comes for what seems like a social visit, until Holmes asks him, "anything remarkable on hand?"

> "Oh, no, Mr. Holmes — nothing very particular."

> "Then tell me about it."

But often the case arrives with the client himself. These moments are some of the most memorable in the canon. For example, in "The Beryl Coronet," Holmes and Watson's new client Alexander Holder is in such distress that "he beat his head against the wall with such force that we both rushed upon him and tore him away to the centre of the room."

In "The Priory School," Watson says that "we have had some dramatic entrances and exits upon our small stage at Baker Street, but I cannot recollect anything more sudden and startling than the first appearance of Thorneycroft Huxtable, M.A., Ph.D., etc." This gentleman enters their rooms, closes the door, and faints!

There's often less drama when the new client is a woman. For instance, in "The Solitary Cyclist," the new potential client is Miss Violet Smith. "Her visit was, I remember, extremely unwelcome to Holmes," says Watson, "for he was immersed at the moment in a very abstruse and complicated problem." Nonetheless, Holmes helps her out.

The fact is, it's just as likely for a king or a pawnbroker to pass through the door of 221b Baker Street seeking aid from the Great Detective. And each is as likely to get it. It all depends on the problem.

No. 4: The client's problem

After the client has Holmes's attention, the problem, crime, or mystery is presented. Holmes often starts the proceedings by introducing his associate. "This is my friend, Dr. Watson," he explains, "before whom you can speak as freely as before myself."

Then he makes a few deductions about the visitor — perhaps the tattoo on his wrist indicates he was a sailor, or the dents on the side of his nose show nearsightedness — and then, following a moment where Holmes indicates his "fees are on a fixed basis," they get down to business with an admonition to "omit nothing."

Typically, with men, Holmes is much more direct, less sympathetic, and even impatient. With women, however, Sherlock adopts an entirely different approach, revealing not only Doyle's own attitudes about women (he once slapped his son for referring to a woman as "ugly") but also Victorian society's. Holmes's interactions with women add an unexpected dimension that makes the character more complicated.

Watson says that, in the case of Violet Hunter (the canon has *four* Violets), "Holmes was favorably impressed by the manner and speech of his new client."

In "The Speckled Band," when Holmes notices that the young woman who has just arrived is shivering, he wonders if she's cold.

> "It is not cold which makes me shiver," Helen Stoner replies.

> "What, then?"

> "It is fear, Mr. Holmes. It is terror."

And then Holmes comforts and reassures the young woman, soothing her fears and making her feel safe. And it works. "My heart is lightened already since I have confided my trouble to you," she says as she leaves.

After the problem is presented, Holmes listens to the facts, the client departs, and he and Watson talk it over before heading off to investigate.

No. 5: On-site investigation

Holmes isn't an "armchair detective" — someone able to solve the case without ever leaving his chair. (That's more like his brother, Mycroft!) No, Holmes isn't afraid of getting his hands dirty looking into the case himself.

Sometimes he heads out alone, leaving Watson to wait and worry back at Baker Street. Sometimes Watson goes on his medical rounds, and other times he stays back and passes the time by reading. In "The Boscombe Valley Mystery," he says that "I lay upon the sofa and tried to interest myself in a yellow-backed novel. The puny plot of the story was so thin, however, when compared to the deep mystery through which we were groping, and I found my attention wander so continually from the action to the fact, that I at last flung it across the room." Poor Watson!

Holmes may return in disguise, as he does in "A Scandal in Bohemia," where he shows up as a "drunken groom." Following a good day of investigating, he may show up as he did in "The Black Peter," with a harpoon under his arm! Or, if things go badly, he may have an entirely different demeanor. In "The Norwood Builder," Watson says, "it was late when my friend returned, and I could see, by a glance at his haggard and anxious face, that the high hopes with which he had started had not been fulfilled. For an hour he droned away upon his violin, endeavouring to soothe his own ruffled spirits."

But the most common event is for Holmes and Watson to go to the scene of the crime and investigate. Time and again the famous duo is on the case together, and these scenes are often crowned by an exciting example of forensic crime-scene investigation by the Great Detective.

In "The Beryl Coronet," Holmes deciphers events by reading footprints in the snow. "The Speckled Band" has Holmes discovering alterations to his client's bedroom that indicate foul play. In "The Resident Patient," by examining cigar ashes, Sherlock learns that what looks like a suicide is really cold-blooded murder. I could go on and on, but you get the picture!

Eventually, by personally investigating the case, Holmes discovers what happened and devises a plan to catch the criminal.

No. 6: The Vigil

Holmes typically keeps his plans to himself and often prefers to stage-manage the climax of the case for dramatic effect. He often uses the device of keeping a vigil (sometimes in the dark), lying in wait for the perpetrator to appear and thus catching him red-handed.

Notable examples include

- ✔ **"The Red-Headed League":** Holmes, Watson, a Scotland Yard detective, and a bank manager wait in the total darkness of a bank vault to catch a robber.

- ✔ **"The Dancing Men":** Holmes says, "I think, gentlemen, that we had best take up our position behind the door. Every precaution is necessary when dealing with such a fellow. You will need your handcuffs, Inspector. You can leave the talking to me."

  Watson observes: "We waited in silence for a minute — one of those minutes which one can never forget. Then the door opened and the man stepped in. In an instant Holmes clapped a pistol to his head, and Martin slipped the handcuffs over his wrists."

- ✔ **"The Speckled Band":** "We must sit without light," says Holmes to Watson. "Do not go asleep; your very life may depend upon it. Have your pistol ready in case we should need it."

However Sherlock Holmes manages it, he usually ends up with his man in police custody.

No. 7: Summation of the case

Whether it's back at Baker Street or right there at the crime scene, Holmes usually explains how he worked out the solution to the case, highlighting the clues he discovered and the deductions he made from them. He may even wrap the whole thing up with a quote in Latin!

Holmes once quoted Horace, saying, *Populus me sibilat, at mihi plaudo, Ipse domi simul ac nummos contemplar in arca.* Translated, it means, "The public hisses at me, but I applaud myself in my own house, and simultaneously contemplate the money in my chest."

Arthur Conan Doyle recycles

The strain of plot construction, in part, drove Doyle to kill Holmes at the Reichenbach Falls. But the difficult task of devising plots also caused him to recycle a few of the better ones. Examples include

- ✔ **The too-good-to-be-true diversion plot:** In this plot, an unwitting victim is presented with a too-good-to-be-true opportunity that requires him to be out of his home or workplace. This opportunity is a diversion that allows the bad guys access to the victim's property or position in order to commit a crime.

  The first appearance of this ingenious plot was in "The Red-Headed League." Pawnbroker Jabez Wilson has a head of vivid red hair, which gets him into the League of Red-Headed Men. More important, it gets him out of his shop, giving a chance for his criminal assistant to tunnel into the neighboring bank vault!

  This plot type shows up again in "The Stockbroker's Clerk." A young stockbroker's clerk named Pycroft is offered a job at a prestigious firm without actually ever being seen in person by the employers. Before he can show up for the job, he's offered another job by a different firm for £500 a year (approximately $58,000 in today's money) — a wage far above his entry-level clerk status. What a great opportunity, even if the position is up in Birmingham, far from London! But wait . . . why does his new employer insist that Pycroft not write and decline the first offer?

- ✔ **The hide-the-rare-jewel-in-something-weird-and-look-all-over-town-for-it plot:** This plot shows up in two stories. The first is "The Blue Carbuncle," in which a thief steals a rare jewel. To keep it from being found, he forces it down the throat of a goose. But unfortunately for him, the goose gets sold, and Holmes ends up tracking him as he tracks the lost goose.

The curious case of the Mazarin stone

"The Adventure of the Mazarin Stone" took a long, tortured path to existence. It's an adaptation into story form of a short, one-act play called "The Crown Diamond." It's believed that "The Crown Diamond" is, in turn, a dramatic adaptation of the Holmes story "The Adventure of the Empty House." From short story, to play, to short story, this tale recycles the same material several times. It's also written in the third person, reading like a thin, one-act play. With its regurgitated story elements, improbable plot points, and a style that comes off almost as pastiche (even parody!), "The Mazarin Stone" tops most polls as the worst Sherlock Holmes story of all time. Give it a read and you'll know why!

The second is "The Six Napoleons," in which a thief again steals a rare jewel. To keep it from being found, he runs into a plaster statue factory and hides it in a bust of Napoleon. But unfortunately for him, that bust — along with five others — gets sold, and Holmes ends up tracking him as he tracks the lost Napoleon.

✔ **The put-a-wax-dummy-in-the-window-as-a-decoy plot:** In "The Empty House," Holmes puts a wax dummy in the window of Baker Street as a decoy to catch Col. Sebastian Moran. He does the same thing in "The Mazarin Stone."

It All Starts on Baker Street

221b Baker Street is the most famous address in all of detective fiction, and indeed, one of the best-known in the whole world. Nearly every case either starts or ends (or both) on Baker Street. Above all, it's the home of Sherlock Holmes and Dr. Watson.

Exploring the apartment

As you read the Holmes stories, a pretty clear picture of 221b begins to emerge (see Figure 8-1). Obviously, Arthur Conan Doyle had the famous flat pretty clearly fixed in his mind. But for a couple of minor incongruities, the residence of Sherlock Holmes is consistent throughout the tales.

Photo courtesy of Steven Doyle.

Figure 8-1:
The sitting room of 221b Baker Street.

First and foremost is the fireplace, which is the centerpiece of the sitting room. On either side of the fireplace are two chairs, one for Holmes and the other for Watson. Next to the fireplace is a coal scuttle where Holmes keeps his cigars. His pipe tobacco is in the toe-end of a Persian slipper hung on the wall next to the fireplace. Up on the fireplace mantle, along with criminal relics, a collection of pipes, and other debris, you find Holmes's unanswered correspondence transfixed to the mantle with a jackknife.

In one corner of the room would be Holmes's chemical table. "The Naval Treaty" provides a typical description: "Holmes was seated at his side-table clad in his dressing-gown and working hard over a chemical investigation. A large curved retort was boiling furiously in the bluish flame of a Bunsen burner, and the distilled drops were condensing into a two-litre measure."

Also found in the room is a desk where Watson wrote his stories, an unframed portrait of Henry Ward Beecher (it was Watson's), a sideboard with a tantalus and gasogene on it, and a "basket chair," which was a sort of wicker chair that was often offered to visitors.

Of course, fans of the Sherlock Holmes films have seen a wide variety of depictions of the famous rooms. In _The Private Life of Sherlock Holmes_ and _Murder by Decree,_ 221b is depicted as a vast labyrinth of spacious rooms, all tastefully appointed and decorated with stylish potted plants. This, of course, is ridiculous.

The most faithful representations of the Sherlockian digs can be found in the 1958 _The Hound of the Baskervilles_ starring Peter Cushing, as well as in the Granada Television _Sherlock Holmes_ series from the 1980s, starring Jeremy Brett as Holmes. Both show the apartment with rather small rooms, cozy if not a bit claustrophobic, and untidy.

To really experience the rooms, you should visit the Sherlock Holmes Museum on London's Baker Street. Here the rooms are faithfully re-created down to the most minute detail! (For more about the Sherlock Holmes Museum, see Chapter 17.)

A _tantalus_ was a contraption that held two cut-glass liquor bottles and had a locking mechanism that came down over the top. It was a popular device during an age when homeowners were worried that their servants would help themselves to the master's whiskey. The _gasogene_ was a device used to produce carbonated water. It had two globes surrounded by a wire mesh or cage. It needed the mesh because as it produced carbonation, it was possible for the globes to explode under pressure! It used tartaric acid and sodium bicarbonate to produce the carbon dioxide needed for carbonation and employed a siphon to discharge the mixture of water and gas into a glass.

Where was 221b?

One pastime that Sherlockians have engaged in is trying to locate exactly where 221b Baker Street would have been in real life. You may think, "Well, this couldn't be too hard . . . after all, we have the address, right?" Well, it isn't as easy as that.

During the time that the stories were written, Baker Street addresses only went to 100. To further complicate things, the middle section of what is now Baker Street was, during the time of the stories, actually called York Place. The street north of Marylebone Road and up to Regent's Park was called Upper Baker Street. Curiously, in the original manuscript notes for _A Study in Scarlet,_ Doyle originally named Holmes's street "Upper Baker Street," so perhaps this was indeed where it was meant to be located. In all this confusion, one thing is certain — there was no 221b.

Sometime in the 1930s, the entire place was renamed Baker Street, and all the addresses were renumbered. This finally did create a 221 Baker Street, which was the home of a financial firm called Abbey National (which for years employed a secretary to answer mail for Mr. Sherlock Holmes!).

Sherlockians have proposed several locations for the Great Detective's home, but in the end, all you really need to know for sure is that, in the canon, it was at 221b Baker Street.

Chapter 9

Delving into "The Hound of the Baskervilles"

*T*he Hound of the Baskervilles isn't just a great read. As Arthur Conan Doyle's magnum opus in the early years of the mystery genre, this novel occupies a pivotal role in modern literature. The intricacy of its plot, the depth of its characterizations, and the artfully developed mood of the setting combine to produce an extraordinarily powerful work. The novel sweeps readers out of the everyday world and into the clash between science and the unknown, into that ill-defined gap between rationality and terror, and leaves them trapped — for a while, at least — somewhere between heaven and hell, out there in the wastelands, all alone in the night.

For more on Sir Arthur's lifelong conflict between science and spirit, see Chapter 3.

Plot Points: How "The Hound" Is More Than Just a Dog's Tale

At the book's beginning, as Sherlock Holmes amuses himself with a string of deductions based on a walking stick "of the sort which is known as a 'Penang lawyer,'" the would-be client, one Dr. Mortimer, puts in an appearance and lays an incredible tale of murder at the detective's feet, a tale that involves an ancient crime and a supernatural beast called the Hound of the Baskervilles.

What's a Penang lawyer?

The Hound of the Baskervilles begins with Holmes amusing himself with a string of deductions based on a walking stick "of the sort which is known as a 'Penang lawyer.'" Penang is a part of Malaysia that belonged to the British Empire in the days of Sherlock Holmes (see Chapter 4). It had a reputation for a rough-and-tumble lifestyle back then, and Watson calls the walking stick with a heavy knob on top a "Penang lawyer" as a humorous way of saying that it could be used to quickly settle an argument.

It seems that this demonic beast has killed the most recent master of Baskerville Hall, just as it did the first one. And it's probably going to do the same thing to the next one unless Holmes can find a way to stop it. As the novel progresses, Dr. Watson goes with Sir Henry Baskerville, the new heir to the Baskerville estate, into the heart of the eerie moorland in an attempt to solve one murder and prevent another while Holmes works behind the scenes.

The Hound of the Baskervilles isn't just a story of some supernatural monster. From the beginning, Watson is caught up in an uncanny situation, surrounded by those who swear the hound is real — and at times, even he thinks it may be so. He struggles to uncover the truth in an intricate game of deception and violence, compounded by an escaped prisoner, a mysterious stranger, and enough shameful secrets and double-crosses to satisfy the most demanding reader.

A devilish game is afoot

From the very beginning, the Baskerville case is anything but ordinary. Sure, Holmes has real evidence to consider, but it's always tinged with the fantastic. Consider these examples:

- ✔ **The footprint:** As Holmes listens to the tale of murder for the first time, he's impressed by Dr. Mortimer's careful observation of the crime scene. When Mortimer speaks of footprints, Holmes asks him, "A man's or a woman's?" — a natural question for any detective to ask. But the answer is anything but natural when Mortimer whispers back, "Mr. Holmes, they were the footprints of a gigantic hound!"

- ✔ **The warning:** The ancient parchment that tells the tale of the hound warns the Baskerville heirs "to forbear from crossing the moor in those dark hours when the powers of evil are exalted." As kind of a series of

> booster shots, this phrase is repeated twice more, about 100 pages apart — once by Holmes on the threshold of the gateway, so to speak, at the railroad station, and again by Sir Henry, just before the hound sounds its chilling cry across the moor.

> ✔ **The sounds:** From his first night in Baskerville Hall, Watson lives in an emotional soundscape. A woman's sob in the night, the scratch of ivy on the wall — and then those shuddering howls from out in the moor. The mystery of the moor engages all the characters' — and vicariously, the reader's — five senses.

As the mystery deepens through each chapter, Doyle manages to both steadily build suspense and increase the reader's suspension of disbelief. Each event takes the characters and the reader one more pace away from the tale's relatively safe Baker Street origins to a place much removed from security and certainty — and, perhaps in the process, takes them one more pace toward the unthinkable. Could the evil of the moor, and the threat of the hound from hell, indeed be supernatural?

A word about Holmes's absence

Sherlock Holmes is physically absent through a large part of *The Hound of the Baskervilles*. Following the initial presentation of the case and some early investigation in London, Holmes turns the case over to Watson. Then, through the middle of the novel, Watson is the man on the ground, providing the eyes and ears for his absent friend. It's only later that Holmes reappears after some solid investigation by Watson. Watson comes with Holmes's highest recommendation. The Great Detective tells Sir Henry, "There is no man who is better worth having at your side when you are in a tight place. No one can say so more confidently than I."

The absence of Holmes and the actions of Watson are important story elements for two reasons:

> ✔ **They show Watson in a different light than the other Holmes stories.** In many of the stories, Watson faithfully and bravely works side by side with Holmes, often in very dangerous situations, but Doyle presents a new side of him here. In *The Hound of the Baskervilles*, Watson is an independent, competent investigator. Out on the moor, acting as Holmes's agent, he discreetly and capably discovers vital information.

> ✔ **They indicate that the character of Holmes was a bit of a latecomer in the novel's developmental cycle.** Holmes's peripheral involvement and Watson's presence at the center of the action are lingering traces that *The Hound of the Baskervilles* wasn't originally conceived as a Sherlock Holmes story. See the later section "Who Told the Hound Story First?" for more on this idea.

Examining Characterization: Henry and the Hound

Sir Henry, the foreign heir (he's Canadian), and the hound, the ancient nemesis of his family, define the novel. The impending, seemingly inevitable death of the likable Sir Henry under the fangs of the demonic beast establishes a sense of urgency from the beginning that carries through until the final confrontation between innocence and evil.

The hellhound

The star of the book isn't Sherlock Holmes, Dr. Watson, or Henry Baskerville. No, the star of *The Hound of the Baskervilles* is the hellhound (see Figure 9-1) — kept offstage, only fleetingly glimpsed, haunting the moors with his blood-chilling howls and his glowing muzzle. Is the hound merely a product of superstitious locals' fevered imaginations fed by old legends and rumor? Or is it something *else?* Is this hellhound real?

Figure 9-1:
The hound hunts in the night.

Illustration by Sidney Paget, The Strand Magazine.

The hound in *The Hound of the Baskervilles* is based on a local myth of a dog called the "black dog of Dartmoor," but the British Isles have no shortage of tales about devilish hounds. Legend has it that the entire realm is infested with dark beasts roaming through the darkness in a restless quest for their next victim. Consider these other canine legends:

- **Whisht hounds:** Also called *whist hounds* or *wish hounds,* these are ghostly versions of normal hounds, accompanying a huntsman in pursuit of his prey through the night.

- **Farvann:** The book *Folk Lore in Lowland Scotland* compares this fairy hound with Baskerville's bane, saying that it "moved silently, but for all its gliding gait, the print of its paws, as big as a human hand, were found on mud or sand or snow. Its voice was sonorous and far reaching, being heard even by those sailing on the seas. It paused between each bark and at a time gave vent to only three roars. Its baying struck terror into the pursued, who was invariably overtaken and destroyed after the third bark if he had not hidden himself from his unearthly pursuer."

Hellhounds have been around for a long time, going way back to Cerberus, the three-headed canine guardian of Hades. So the devilish hound in *The Hound of the Baskervilles* is one in a long line of such mythological creatures — preternatural dogs dispensing divine justice (or protection) and fulfilling ancient curses. In fact, just about every region seems to have a similar tale with its own special, local twist.

Most of these legends spring from rural or undeveloped locations, places where nature is omnipresent and the rhythms of daily life are pretty much set by its patterns. At the same time, the less urban the setting, the less light there is to push back the night — and consequently, the stronger the tendency to populate the unknown with the imaginary. See "A Sense of Place" later in this chapter for more on how the setting of *The Hound* impacts its mood.

The Baskerville heir

Although the story doesn't begin with Henry Baskerville (he isn't even the one who first asks for Holmes's help), Henry, shown in Figure 9-2, is a key character. The newest Baskerville heir because of the death of Charles Baskerville, Henry travels from Canada to see his family's home.

Poor Henry doesn't seem to be at home anywhere. From the start, he's awkward switching from the role of Canadian farmer to English squire. He's lost in a bewildering new world, complaining to Holmes and the others, "It seems to me that all you gentlemen know a great deal more than I do about my own affairs." His trip to London, though, is the least of the challenges he faces.

Figure 9-2:
Sir Henry
Baskerville.

Illustration by Sidney Paget, The Strand Magazine.

As he soon discovers, he has a few problems to contend with — affairs that are far more dangerous and complicated than he can imagine. Aside from the looming supernatural threat (as heir, the Baskerville curse falls on him), human forces are at work. Someone steals his things. Someone follows him (and Holmes). Someone sends him a note, although it's impossible to tell whether it's a threat or a warning. All he can do is put his trust in these strangers called Holmes and Watson and hope that it all turns out right somehow.

With the character of Sir Henry Baskerville, Doyle was able to inject a continuing note of strangeness into the story. The Americanized character of Henry represented a foreign or exotic element to Doyle's main audience in the UK. Although an Englishman, he had lived in Canada for so long that his customs, dress, and outlook were different; fitting into his new role would prove difficult for him. For more on Doyle's use of foreign characters, head to Chapter 4.

"The Hound" as Gothic Masterpiece

The Hound of the Baskervilles fall squarely in the literary tradition known as Gothic fiction. This genre of literature began in the late 1700s and combines elements of the romance novel and the horror story. Gothic fiction is dependent on a brooding, pervasive sense of mounting anxiety and fear — even horror.

Scholars and critics have identified common elements of Gothic fiction. As you can see, *The Hound of the Baskervilles* hits every point on the list:

- **A setting with an old castle, mansion, or manor house:** This old building often includes gloomy hallways, mysterious passages, and ruined or abandoned wings. The overwhelming feeling of the house is one of shadows, darkness, and a sense of entrapment. This fits Baskerville Hall to a T.

- **An atmosphere of mystery and suspense:** A pervading sense of fear and mystery is a hallmark of the Gothic novel. The plot is usually built around a mystery involving unknown parentage (parentage and inheritance are vital to the plot of *The Hound of the Baskervilles*), a disappearance or death, or some strange, uncanny event.

- **An ancient prophecy:** This plot element is usually connected to the house or its inhabitants. Clearly, the ancient legend of the hound and its relationship to the Baskerville family satisfies this requirement.

- **Visions, omens, portents:** In Gothic fiction, a character often has a disturbing dream or experience that seems to be a portent of coming events. In *The Hound of the Baskervilles,* when Sir Henry hears the howling of a hound in the middle of the night, it strikes fear into his heart and makes him believe the legend may be true.

- **Supernatural or otherwise inexplicable events:** Hauntings, voices, apparitions, and other supernatural occurrences are common in Gothic fiction. In some works, the events are ultimately given a natural explanation, while in others the events are truly supernatural. *The Hound of the Baskervilles* certainly fits this criterion.

- **High, overwrought emotion:** Characters in Gothic fiction often betray heightened emotion, including sorrow, terror, and impending doom. Several characters in *The Hound of the Baskervilles* fit this description, including Mrs. Barrymore, the housekeeper at Baskerville Hall, who is prone to creepy crying spells in the middle of the night.

- **Women in distress:** Female characters in Gothic fiction are usually oppressed and victimized by a tyrannical male figure and are often kept in some lonely, isolated location. Gothic women are usually abandoned, having no one to protect them. Beryl Stapleton and Laura Lyons are perfect examples of this type found in *The Hound of the Baskervilles.*

A Sense of Place

Doyle set *The Hound of the Baskervilles* in Dartmoor in the late-19th century. Although the story has elements of the supernatural, the setting itself is real. Dartmoor, in southwestern England, is an area that was familiar to Doyle's readers. Of course, it wasn't just a matter of putting a fantastic tale in a familiar setting. Doyle deliberately chose that area because of its wild, undeveloped terrain and because, as claimed in a contemporary guidebook, "there is a black dog which haunts the waste." This is precisely the legend that inspired what many think is Doyle's greatest novel.

Baskerville Hall

Inspired by Doyle's visit to the real-life Cromer Hall, Baskerville Hall is vital in establishing the novel's Gothic credentials. Sir Henry first sees Baskerville Hall through a "sombre tunnel" of trees, and he "shuddered as he looked up the long, dark drive to where the house glimmered like a ghost at the farther end." Inside is no better. The hall is vast, and "the dark bulk of the house" is overwhelming as "the door clanged heavily behind us."

On his first encounter with the interior, Watson feels that it's the kind of place where "one's voice became hushed and one's spirit subdued." Sir Henry's only comment is, "My word, it isn't a very cheerful place." Sir Henry rouses himself and makes plans to banish the darkness with a touch of science: "I'll have a row of electric lamps up here inside of six months, and you won't know it again, with a thousand-candle power Swan and Edison right here in front of the hall door."

While the hall is a fortress guarding them against the dangers outside in the night, it's also almost a tomb for the living, a sense that Doyle certainly intended as part of the overall mood. When Watson first meets Stapleton, one of the neighbors, he muses, "It is asking much of a wealthy man to come down and bury himself in a place of this kind."

Although sunshine occasionally pours through the windows, those moments are teasing contrasts pitted against the coming fog and rain — perhaps a mirror for the hopes of the characters and their fears. The dark confines of the hall also mirror the evil forces outside its walls — darkness both inside and out.

The lonely moor

Forget Shakespeare and *Othello;* Dartmoor isn't that kind of moor. This kind of moor is a desolate wasteland where nothing much grows except tangled thickets of shrubs called *heath* or *heather* (because of this, a moor can also be called a heath).

Scattered among the dry spots are *peat bogs,* perilous swamps in which you find decaying vegetable matter (called — you guessed it — peat). Peat is gathered, dried, and used as a fuel in lieu of firewood in this area where few trees grow.

The accidental artist

Sidney Paget was originally hired by mistake. *The Strand Magazine* intended to engage his brother Walter but signed on the wrong Paget.

It was a match made in heaven, though. Paget's illustrations struck a powerful chord with the public from the very beginning. His association with Sherlock Holmes would stretch from 1891 to 1904, running to over 500 drawings for both books and magazines. Those drawings of Holmes's adventures would influence the public's image of the Great Detective for all time.

The *tors* — craggy upthrusts of granite — rise in sharp contrast to the low marshland, and the whole scene seems to have been transplanted straight from some other planet. Indeed, one of Baskerville's neighbors has a telescope, watching the moor as if it were akin to the surface of the moon.

The setting is so far outside the experience of the typical Londoner that Holmes has to send out for a map.

As desolate and unwelcoming as a moor is, why would anyone want to live there? Because the area had more than just the moor. This description from *Devonshire Scenery,* an 1884 guidebook, tells the tale:

> Fair meadows bathed in sunshine, with the Otter river winding through them, lie below; yonder are the red Devon steers grazing up to their dewlaps in buttercups; beyond them dusky moors melt into purple haze, and every here and there you catch a glimpse of the far-off Tors on Dartmoor simmering in the mid-day glare.

Yet it was the moor proper that drove the dark, moody sense of *The Hound of the Baskervilles.*

From the time he gets off the train, even before reaching the vicinity of Baskerville Hall, Watson finds the setting oppressive — tinged, as he puts it, with melancholy: "The rattle of our wheels died away as we drove through drifts of rotting vegetation — sad gifts, as it seemed to me, for Nature to throw before the carriage of the returning heir of the Baskervilles."

The wildness of the moors is an important element in creating the forbidding and foreboding setting. For more on how the setting informs the story, see the later section "From civilized to primitive."

Doyle's word craft was perfectly matched by Sidney Paget's illustrations (see the nearby sidebar "The accidental artist"). Figure 9-3 shows Paget's rendering of the line, "There, outlined as black as an ebony statue on that shining background, I saw the figure of a man upon the tor." His stark renditions and blend of dark grays and blacks helped to bring the eerie setting to life.

Illustration by Sidney Paget, The Strand Magazine.

Figure 9-3:
Paget's
illustrations
were dark,
moody, and
eerie.

Key Themes in the Novel

The contest between science and superstition runs through *The Hound* in a powerful way. Doyle shows how thin the veneer of modern civilization is, artfully exposing the primitive that lies within us all. Just hours away from home and comfort, just inches beyond the edges of the firelight, all the ancient terrors still lurk in the night.

Going backward in time

The novel has an underlying movement backward through time. This is most evident in Sir Henry's travels:

✔ He first sails from the New World of Canada to the Old World of England.

✔ When Sir Henry travels from London to Devonshire, he takes the train — at that time the fastest, most modern form of transportation in existence. Upon his arrival at the railroad station, he switches to a kind of carriage called a *wagonette,* making the backward leap from machine power to horsepower. When he steps down from the carriage, he is back on foot, the most primitive form of transport. When Henry takes the last step of his long journey, passing at last through the doors of Baskerville Hall, he's not just arriving from Canada, not just taking possession of the Baskerville estate, but, perhaps, settling an ancient curse upon himself as well.

✔ Finally, on the moor, he walks among the prehistoric huts found scattered over the landscape.

All these elements are part of a distancing process. To make the supernatural seem real to a sophisticated city audience, Doyle carefully took them away from their day-to-day world in both space and time, moving them gradually into a strange place where things happen that "are hard to reconcile with the settled order of Nature."

From civilized to primitive

If the transition from London to Baskerville Hall is a step back in time of a few centuries, the transition from the hall to the moor is a much longer one. The hall, although centuries old, is actually a sign of civilization: a home and even a fortress that separates and protects the inhabitants from the wilderness beyond. So even though it's old compared to contemporary London, not to mention dark and gloomy, it's still protective.

The moors, on the other hand, represent an ancient, pagan wildness. The desolate land, covered with hedges and Stone Age ruins, traces of a magic older than history, constantly calls to the most primitive in the characters, challenging them to set aside their science and logic and just listen to the cries and howls in the darkness beyond the firelight. Even in the daylight, the sense that things aren't the same is overwhelming, and the prehistoric past dominates the landscape. As Watson puts it, once you enter the moor,

> . . . you have left all traces of modern England behind you, but on the other hand you are conscious everywhere of the homes and the work of the prehistoric people. On all sides of you as you walk are the houses of these forgotten folk, with their graves and the huge monoliths which are supposed to have marked their temples. As you look at their grey stone huts against the scarred hillsides you leave your own age behind you, and if you were to see a skin-clad, hairy man crawl out from the low door, fitting a flint-tipped arrow on to the string of his bow, you would feel that his presence there was more natural than your own.

When a neighbor named Stapleton takes Watson and Sir Henry to see the scene of the original hound story, the nattily dressed, so nicely civilized people (see Figure 9-4) seem comically overwhelmed by their surroundings, dwarfed both individually and as a group. Their scientific outlook seems like a helpless child before the ancient magic of the monoliths.

Figure 9-4:
Civilization
intrudes on
the moor.

Illustration by Sidney Paget, The Strand Magazine.

Superstition versus science

If Holmes has a professional definition aside from crime detection, it's as a logician. Watson, despite his writing talents, is essentially a medical man. As men of science, their attitudes lean toward the rational approach rather than the theological one. In the beginning of *The Hound of the Baskervilles,* Holmes asks the country doctor about his superstitions regarding the legendary hound from hell: "And you, a trained man of science, believe it to be supernatural?"

Watson likewise scoffs, more than once calling the whole idea "nonsense." Yet both of them experience at least a few instants of unreasoning fear before the affair is over. Watson writes that "the barren scene, the sense of loneliness, and the mystery and urgency of my task all struck a chill into my heart." Later, he listens to the baying of the hound in the night "with a chill of fear in my heart."

He even says at one point that his soul "quivered at the vagueness and the terror" while waiting for an encounter with a mysterious man in the wilds of the moor.

Even the staunchly scientific Holmes, once outside of London and in the midst of the moor, finds himself affected:

> "It does not seem a very cheerful place," said the detective, with a shiver, glancing round him at the gloomy slopes of the hill and at the huge lake of fog which lay over the Grimpen Mire.

When the mystery is finally solved, it's no surprise to the admirers of the rational Sherlock Holmes that the solution is matter-of-fact rather than supernatural. Indeed, the crimes could hardly have been committed without the help of scientific knowledge. In the final lines of the story, Sir Henry Baskerville is making practical plans to banish superstition from his corner of the moor. The reader has to wonder whether he can succeed. Meanwhile, Holmes and Watson turn to a healthier form of escapism — namely, music.

Who Told the Hound Story First?

The basic plot idea for *The Hound of the Baskervilles* was a collaborative effort between Sir Arthur and a friend of his. That much is for sure. Beyond that, however, a debate has raged for a long time about which one contributed how much to the book as a whole.

The basic core of the story goes back to the 17th century, when Richard Cabell, a local man with an evil reputation, inspired a local legend. Cabell was the biggest landowner of Buckfastleigh, a town in Devonshire. Depending on who's telling the story, he either murdered his wife and was killed by her pet hound, or he was just so plain wicked that the devil sent a pack of hounds to hunt his soul over the moors every night.

Who came up with the story

Sir Arthur, while returning from a visit to South Africa, met Bertram Fletcher Robinson, a Devonshire journalist. The two became fast friends and, over the course of a few visits, Doyle became fascinated by Robinson's tales of old legends. Two in particular caught his attention: the tale of Richard Cabell and another, the one about the dark hound that haunted the moors. The two men decided to collaborate on a novel about this eerie combination, one that Doyle told his publisher would be "a real creeper." (Robinson's coachman, by the way, was named Baskerville.)

Occasional odd claims over the years have maintained that Sir Arthur somehow stole the story from Robinson, taking credit for the whole thing. Yet interviews with Doyle and publishing notes indicate that nothing could be further from the truth. Not only was Robinson paid, but in negotiations with his publisher, Doyle wrote that Robinson "gave me the central idea and the local colour." In addition, the first page of the story in *The Strand Magazine* carried the note:

> This story owes its inception to my friend, Mr. Fletcher Robinson, who has helped me both in the general plot and in the local details. –A.C.D.

Finally, when the book was published in book form, Sir Arthur once again publicly thanked Robinson for his part in the dedication:

> MY DEAR ROBINSON,
>
> It was to your account of a West-Country legend that this tale owes its inception. For this and for your help in the details all thanks.
>
> Yours most truly,
>
> A. CONAN DOYLE.

As late as 1907, Doyle received a letter asking about the origins of *The Hound*, and he replied:

> My story was really based on nothing save a remark of my friend Fletcher Robinson's that there was a legend about a dog on the Moor connected with some old family.

Some question has also persisted about how much of the writing is Robinson's and how much is Doyle's. It's clear that Doyle meant from the beginning to do the actual writing himself, writing to his publisher that the story would be "in my own style without dilution." It's obvious to anyone who knows that style that he did exactly that, from beginning to end.

How the story developed

The Hound of the Baskervilles was originally conceived as a supernatural thriller, not as a Sherlock Holmes novel. When Doyle wrote a letter calling it "a real creeper" in March 1901, he certainly didn't mention Holmes, but by April he reported that "Robinson and I are exploring the moor over our Sherlock Holmes book."

Whatever the original story had been, Doyle made serious changes by bring-ing in the detective. This was a bit of a feat, given that prior to writing *The Hound of the Baskervilles,* Doyle had killed off his famous detective. In order to include Sherlock Holmes in *The Hound,* Holmes would have to rise from the dead — sort of.

Doyle solved this dilemma by making it a posthumous adventure of Sherlock Holmes, set before his unfortunate tumble over Reichenbach Falls. So although *The Hound of the Baskervilles* was written after Holmes's "death," the story itself relates events prior. Note that this wasn't Holmes's only resurrection. Doyle brought Sherlock back in the flesh, so to speak, in "The Adventure of the Empty House," a story in which readers discover how Holmes managed to escape death at Reichenbach Falls. (Check out Chapter 3 for more on the period during which Holmes was officially dead.)

When the publishers of *The Strand Magazine* learned that Holmes would be resurrected, they leapt at the chance to publish a new Holmes story. When Doyle asked for double the normal payment, they didn't hesitate for a second. The public reacted with similar enthusiasm, once again forming long lines outside the *Strand* offices, aching for one more tale of their favorite character.

Chapter 10

The Gaslight Goes Away: The "Modern" Stories

*F*or Sherlockians, one of the most famous quotations about Sherlock Holmes comes from a sonnet by Vincent Starrett, who concludes his poem about Holmes by writing, "it is always 1895." This sentiment perfectly evokes the popular image of Holmes, who forever lives in a world of gas lamps, fog, and hansom cabs. But the fact is, nearly a third of the canon was written after the upheaval of World War I.

These "modern" Holmes stories bear the imprint of being written in a world coping with the great disillusionment that followed that devastating conflict. The three volumes of the canon that fall into this time period are *The Valley of Fear, His Last Bow,* and *The Case-Book of Sherlock Holmes.* (If you want to get technical, *The Valley of Fear* was actually published serially in *The Strand Magazine* from September 1914 [just after the war started] to May 1915.)

Suddenly, It's No Longer 1895

Sherlock Holmes exploded in popularity during the late Victorian era of the 1890s. This era was the height of the British Empire's power and reach (for more on the era in which Holmes was created, refer to Chapter 4). The Industrial Revolution, which began in the late 18th century, brought massive change to all areas of society, including transportation and manufacturing, and sparked a period of urbanization throughout the United Kingdom. A scientific revolution was also underway, with major advances in astronomy, medicine, and natural sciences. Charles Darwin's theory of natural selection and evolution sparked not only a scientific revolution in biology but also a social revolution.

These changes weren't confined to England. In America, this period was known as the *Gilded Age,* a time when immigration was high, supplying workers to fuel the creation of great industries and businesses across America. "Captains of Industry" in the late 19th century amassed great wealth and power while creating new towns, factories, and railroads.

It was an age when the commissioner of the U.S. Office of Patents could say, "Everything that can be invented has been invented" and actually mean it. It was a world, both in England and America, that was supremely confident and secure in itself. This was the world of both Sherlock Holmes and his readers.

But then came the war.

The war to end all wars

It has many names. Early on it was *The War in Europe.* Some knew it by the now-ironic title *The War to End All Wars.* At the end of the shooting, it had become *The Great War.* And a couple decades down the road we were forced to call it *World War I.* Whatever it was called, the conflict engulfed Europe in a terrible, mechanized, total war, with all the industry and science of the Victorian era's Industrial Revolution behind it. By war's end, over 15 million people were killed, a third of whom were civilians, making it one of the deadliest conflicts in history. In England alone, 703,000 young men were killed and 1,663,000 wounded — nearly an entire generation in such a relatively small country.

The world that existed before August 1914 was gone. In its wake was a world that had lost the confidence and optimism of the Victorian era. The Gilded Age of possibility was replaced by an age of grim pessimism, as the nations of the West coped with the war's aftermath.

The psychological effect of World War I created a sense of distrust in political leaders who, after all, had led the world over the abyss. The horror of this modern, mechanized warfare — with its tanks, airplanes, machine guns, barbed wire, and, worst of all, poison gas — left those who witnessed it cynical and hardened. Around the world, in the aftermath of the war, grief and disillusionment replaced optimism.

The Roaring Twenties

In some sense, the 1920s can be seen as the inevitable outcome of both the repressed, proper Victorian era and the devastation of World War I. Just as the baby-boom generation did following World War II, the generation that followed the First World War rebelled against society's morality and mores. Social patterns, political ideas, the automobile, mass media, music, and entertainment — they all experienced radical changes during this time.

The disillusionment that was World War I, which cast its shadow to the end of the century, began to fully manifest itself in the 1920s. This shadow fell on both sides of the Atlantic. A decade that saw Western prosperity and societal freedom also ushered in coarseness and brutality, leaving no doubt that the gilded Victorian and Edwardian eras were history.

It was the Jazz Age, an era named after a new form of sexy, risqué (for its time) music, in which both technology and social trends seemed to break down barriers and speed up the pace of life. In England, the horrors of war had made the younger generation old before their time. Trench warfare, horrific wounds, shell shock, and wholesale slaughter had instilled a feeling that life was short, cheap, and meant to be enjoyed. To add to the general gloom, throughout the 1920s, over 2 million people in Britain remained unemployed.

In the United States, it was a time epitomized by the Algonquin Round Table, a celebrated group of New York City writers, celebrities, and critics, whose wisecracks and comments made at daily lunches at the Algonquin Hotel began to be reported in the popular press. There was Prohibition, the Great Depression, and the Dust Bowl. More disturbingly, there was lurid and high-profile crime, including Sacco and Vanzetti (two Italian immigrants sent to the electric chair for murder) and Leopold and Loeb (two thrill-seeking University of Chicago students who murdered a 14-year-old out of nothing more than a desire to commit the perfect crime). Add in Al Capone and Chicago's organized crime and the rise of the Ku Klux Klan, and it's easy to see that the country had definitely entered a new era.

No matter which side of the Atlantic you lived on, after World War I, the world got a lot smaller, and England and America shared many of the same cultural trends.

Crime and crime fiction also underwent radical changes during the 1920s, and the Holmes stories reflect this shift. Arthur Conan Doyle wasn't writing historical fiction when he penned an adventure of the Great Detective. The Holmes books were never intended to be period pieces. Quite the contrary: Doyle was always writing contemporary detective stories and crime fiction. For readers who see Holmes only existing in the cozy, gaslit, Victorian age, it may come as a shock to learn that the adventures of Sherlock Holmes were not immune to the spirit of the age.

Postwar Canonical Crime

In the U.S., into this coarser, postwar era, when everything seemed to be changing, came a new age of crime as well. In 1919, government passed the 18th amendment to the Constitution, beginning the age of Prohibition. From 1919 to 1933, all alcohol sales, manufacturing, and consumption were banned. This created an instant black market, and a golden opportunity for organized crime.

Battles ensued between rival mobs and between criminals and federal agents. In an age that was throwing off the restrictions of the past, Prohibition made millions of ordinary citizens lawbreakers, hardening the culture and blurring sympathies for criminals. It was in this fevered era of the 1920s that crime fiction began to change.

The rise of the hard-boiled detective

The decade of the 1920s is seen as the transitional era for crime fiction, with the rise of new styles within the genre. Critics regard the golden age of detective fiction as beginning in 1920, when Agatha Christie created Hercule Poirot and Dorothy L. Sayers gave us Lord Peter Wimsey. But more interestingly for this discussion, this period also saw the rise of another literary form, one that's clearly reflected in postwar Sherlock Holmes stories: the hard-boiled school of detective fiction.

Pulp fiction: "Black Mask"

The *hard-boiled school* saw its birth in the pages of *Black Mask,* a pulp magazine launched in April 1920 by publishers H. L. Mencken and George Jean Nathan. After only eight issues, *Black Mask* was sold, and under the direction of editor "Cap" Joseph Shaw, the magazine began publishing a new school of tough crime writers. Shaw believed that crime fiction could promote the ideal of law and order on the increasingly lawless streets of real-life America, leading many of the crime fighters in the *Black Mask* stories to be private detectives. This tougher, darker style was unlike earlier detective stories, which seemed like fairy tales next to the realistic, gritty adventures appearing in *Black Mask.* To quote writer William Marling, as their popularity increased, the stories "grew more violent, the style harder, the dialogue blacker, and the wit drier."

Luminaries of this new literary school included

- **Dashiell Hammett:** This ex-Pinkerton agent was the first breakout success. He published his first story in *Black Mask* in December 1922. His best know works include *The Maltese Falcon,* with detective Sam Spade, and his series of *Thin Man* books.

- **Erle Stanley Gardner:** Gardner made his hard-boiled debut in *Black Mask* in 1923. Gardner was prolific, writing under at least seven pseudonyms in addition to his own name. His most famous creation is the crime-solving lawyer, Perry Mason.

- **James M. Cain:** Despite a varied writing career, Cain is most strongly associated with the hard-boiled school. This gritty, unsentimental author's best-known book is *The Postman Always Rings Twice.*

> ✔ **Raymond Chandler:** Following his debut in a 1933 edition of *Black Mask,* Chandler went on to write *The Big Sleep.* Considered his finest work, this novel introduces his famous detective, Philip Marlowe.

Hammett and Gardner became *Black Mask*'s most popular writers. By 1926, *Black Mask* had a circulation of 66,000 and was available on newsstands across America.

In the 1920s, during the rise of the *Black Mask* and its new style of detective story, Arthur Conan Doyle and his family repeatedly toured the U.S. on lecture tours promoting his belief in spiritualism (refer to Chapter 3 for more on that). These tours would typically last months at a time and extended from New York to Los Angeles. One can imagine the Doyle boys, or perhaps Arthur himself, picking up copies of *Black Mask* in the train stations of America to entertain themselves as they crossed the country on their latest tour. And back home in England, a British edition was equally as popular. There's no doubt that the influence of the hard-boiled detective and *Black Mask* was felt across the Atlantic.

Arthur Conan Doyle invents the form

It's clear that the later Sherlock Holmes stories, which I detail in the following sections, reflect the times they were written in. Doyle never intended them to be nostalgia (that view of them would come later). Instead, Doyle intended the Holmes tales to be contemporary, modern (to that time period) detective stories.

Knowing this, it's no wonder that elements of the emerging hard-boiled detective story find their way into the adventures of Sherlock Holmes. Holmes was being written contemporaneously with the hard-boiled school. Indeed, some even believe Doyle's connection to the hard-boiled genre is even deeper.

Different schools, common roots

In the 1920s, detective fiction began to split into different genres. In England, a host of Sherlock Holmes-like detectives appeared on the scene, creating a model for the British mystery story that's still valid today. In America, the heroes of crime fiction changed from the brilliant, amateur detective model found in Holmes to a flawed private eye of the hard-boiled school.

American detective stories drew inspiration from the changing culture of the post-World War I era, as well as from the *dime novel.* These cheap paperbacks included several types of stories, detective tales among them. They commonly told their tales from the perspective of the bad guy. A popular subset of the dime novels had tales full of action and violence, set in the American West. Much of the spirit of the dime novel was inspired by the work of frontier authors like James Fenimore Cooper and Brett Harte. Interestingly, Doyle cites Harte as one of his early literary inspirations.

Few would deny that Doyle revolutionized the infant literary form of the detective story with his character Sherlock Holmes. But what most readers don't know is that Doyle pioneered a number of literary trends and genres throughout his long writing career. Several writers and historians of mystery and detective fiction (including Leslie S. Klinger and Gary Lovisi) believe another one should be added to the list: the hard-boiled detective story.

Officially, the first hard-boiled detective story appeared in the early 1920s in the pages of *Black Mask* (see the preceding section). But in reality, the tough undercover Pinkerton agent Birdy Edwards, from the flashback half of *The Valley of Fear,* is clearly a hard-boiled detective, and the half of the book that's set in the terrible, mean streets of Vermissa Valley is the world's first hard-boiled detective story. For more on *The Valley of Fear,* see the upcoming section "'The Valley of Fear': Doyle Goes Hard-Boiled."

The collection of Holmes stories written during this time, especially the ultra-violent *The Case-Book of Sherlock Holmes,* is a clear reflection of this harder, more violent age. Gone are gas-lit puzzles to entice a consulting detective. In its place is a disturbing parade of vitriol-throwing, sexual depravity, obsession, psychotic rage, suicide, and disfigurement. In addition to these new manifestations, the newer Holmes stories are sometimes violent updates on previous Sherlockian motifs. We're a long way indeed from the good old days.

"The Valley of Fear": Doyle Goes Hard-Boiled

Written at the start of this transitional era in crime fiction, *The Valley of Fear* perfectly embodies the fork in the road where hard-boiled split from the traditional forms of the Victorian and Edwardian eras. One half of the novel is the traditional Sherlock Holmes/British locked-room mystery (refer to Chapter 8).

Set in an English manor house, the story features a mysterious (if particularly gruesome) murder, with a hinted subplot of possible romantic involvement for some of the suspects in the case. Holmes himself is at the top of his game, a mature, middle-aged detective in prime form. Many of the standard elements are in place: a doubting official police detective, a peculiar clue, a foreign influence on the case, and a midnight vigil to catch the perpetrator red-handed. Indeed, the English half of this novel is about as perfect a Holmes story as you could hope for. But then there's the other half.

The long flashback, set in the gritty, dark coal fields of Pennsylvania, couldn't be more different from the first half of the book. It has private detectives, brutal beatings, secret organizations, assassinations, intimidation, and a town in the grip of crime. It's about as dark a story as you can find.

The scenario

Readers of *The Valley of Fear* undergo the shock of a complete change in time, location, and most importantly, tone. The second half of the book tells the tale of the terrible secret criminal society known as the Scowrers. The members of this organization use terrorism to battle the mine owners and murder and intimidation to rule the region and maintain and fund their criminal organization. Into this dangerous situation comes the undercover Pinkerton detective, Birdy Edwards.

Edwards comes to Vermissa Valley from Chicago, one of the classic cities of hard-boiled crime fiction. Using the name of John McMurdo, he comes off as a perfect hard-boiled detective. He's an aggressive, wisecracking, streetwise guy who quickly comes to the attention of the Scowrers. Soon, he has infiltrated the organization and begins collecting evidence against them. The fact that Edwards's true identity isn't revealed to the reader until the end of his adventure reflects the ambiguous nature of the hard-boiled detective story.

The dialogue

Both the scenario and the dialogue are reminiscent of the hard-boiled detective story. At one point, someone asks Edwards why he left Chicago.

> "In trouble?"

> "Deep."

> Was it a "penitentiary job?"

> "And the rest," he replies.

> "Not a killing!"

Edwards/McMurdo responds by saying, "I've my own good reasons for leaving Chicago, and let that be enough for you. Who are you that you should take it on yourself to ask such things?" Doyle adds that the Pinkerton's gray eyes gleamed with "sudden and dangerous anger from behind his glasses."

The location

Typically, hard-boiled detectives don't find themselves in cozy seaside villages, or English manor houses. No, if you're hard-boiled, you're an urban detective, working the dangerous, crime-ridden streets of your city or town. With this in mind, there's no doubt that Vermissa Valley meets the criteria of a gritty, dangerous, hard-boiled location.

Doyle describes Edwards's first view of the town as well as any of his successors would a decade later:

> The town showed a dead level of mean ugliness and squalor. The broad street was churned up by the traffic into a horrible rutted paste of muddy snow. The sidewalks were narrow and uneven. The numerous gas-lamps served only to show more clearly a long line of wooden houses, each with its veranda facing the street, unkempt and dirty.

In both style and tone, there's no doubt that this Pinkerton agent is undercover in a city as rough and dangerous as anything described by his hard-boiled contemporaries eight years later.

The violence

For readers of *The Strand Magazine,* whose last encounter with Sherlock Holmes was "The Second Stain," one of the classics of the canon (but nothing at all like what they were about to encounter), *The Valley of Fear* must have had them wondering what on earth had happened.

Of the four novels, *The Valley of Fear* has always been ranked last in popularity polls. It even ranks pretty low overall. Objectively speaking, it's an underrated masterpiece, a perfect amalgam of classic Holmes with hard-boiled detective story, with both halves succeeding. But the sheer shock of this change in tone has come at a cost to its popularity.

Part of that shock is in reaction to the book's violence. *The Valley of Fear* has more violent crime per volume than any other book in the canon. Just a few of the more notable examples include attempted strangulation, extortion, the shooting of two policemen, a double murder done to repay a "favor," and the brutal beating of the publisher of the local newspaper. The last two are described in explicit, gruesome detail.

In describing the double murder, Doyle writes:

The manager clapped his two hands to the wound and doubled himself up. Then he staggered away; but another of the assassins fired, and he went down sidewise, kicking and clawing among a heap of clinkers. Menzies, the Scotchman, gave a roar of rage at the sight and rushed with an iron spanner at the murderers; but was met by two balls in the face which dropped him dead at their very feet.

The beating of the newspaperman (see Figure 10-1) is equally as terrible:

From the room above came a shout, a cry for help, and then the sound of trampling feet and of falling chairs. An instant later a gray-haired man rushed out on the landing. He was seized before he could get farther, and his spectacles came tinkling down to McMurdo's feet. There was a thud and a groan. He was on his face, and half a dozen sticks were clattering together as they fell upon him. He writhed, and his long, thin limbs quivered under the blows. The others ceased at last; but Baldwin [the bad guy], his cruel face set in an infernal smile, was hacking at the man's head, which he vainly endeavored to defend with his arms. His white hair was dabbled with patches of blood. Baldwin was still stooping over his victim, putting in a short, vicious blow whenever he could see a part exposed, when McMurdo dashed up the stair and pushed him back.

"You'll kill the man," said he. "Drop it!"

Figure 10-1:
The brutal beating from *The Valley of Fear,* originally in *The Strand Magazine.*

Illustration by Sidney Paget, The Strand Magazine.

His Last Bow

This short collection of stories, published in 1917, again shows evidence of this period of transition. Three of the eight stories are rather conventional Sherlock Holmes tales, but five others clearly contain elements reflecting the disillusionment following the war, crime's threat to family and society, and the coarsening of the culture in general:

✔ **"The Adventure of Wisteria Lodge":** In this strange story, many commentators detect Doyle hinting at a homosexual liaison between the suspect and murder victim — an element that would never have been included back in the 1890s. But Doyle — who read of, remembered, and often used events from real life — may have had the trial of Oscar Wilde in mind.

The celebrated playwright had been caught up in a homosexual scandal, went on trial, and was convicted of "gross indecency" and sentenced to two years of hard labor in 1895. Doyle knew Wilde, both having been guests at a dinner party held by J. M. Stoddard, the publisher of *Lippincott's Monthly Magazine.* It was at this dinner that each author was commissioned to write a story for the magazine. Doyle came out with the second Sherlock Holmes novel, *The Sign of the Four,* and Wilde produced *The Picture of Dorian Gray.*

✔ **"The Red Circle":** Here's a second story of secret society and mafia involvement in the canon. But unlike the earlier story, "The Six Napoleons," which revolved around a stolen pearl, the motive here is driven in part by the unwanted sexual attentions of the head of the organization for the wife of a young, married couple whose husband is in the gang. Unlike the much earlier "Adventure of the Solitary Cyclist," in which a young *unmarried* woman is menaced and forced into marriage, this story shows crime and predatory behavior now having no respect for the boundaries of marriage.

✔ **"The Dying Detective":** Yes, I know that Holmes is only pretending to be sick. And yes, I also know that over the years he's been rude and inconsiderate to his one and only friend, Watson. But in the line of duty or not, never before has Holmes been so unutterably mean and heartless as he is in this story. Below is one of the most painful passages in the canon:

> "Holmes," said I, "you are not yourself. A sick man is but a child, and so I will treat you. Whether you like it or not, I will examine your symptoms and treat you for them."
>
> He looked at me with venomous eyes.
>
> "If I am to have a doctor whether I will or not, let me at least have someone in whom I have confidence," said he.
>
> "Then you have none in me?"

"In your friendship, certainly. But facts are facts, Watson, and, after all, you are only a general practitioner with very limited experience and mediocre qualifications. It is painful to have to say these things, but you leave me no choice."

I was bitterly hurt.

That level of cruelty and coldheartedness only appears in these later adventures of Sherlock Holmes.

✔ **"The Cardboard Box":** This story of domestic violence and marital infidelity was originally published in *The Strand Magazine* in 1892. It would have been collected into the volume entitled *The Memoirs of Sherlock Holmes,* but Doyle had second thoughts about the appropriateness of the tale. Extramarital affairs were just not something you casually wrote about for entertainment purposes in 1892, and so it was suppressed and left out of the book collection. However, by 1917, things had clearly changed, and this story, with its racy themes, felt right at home in this collection.

✔ **"His Last Bow":** Written in 1917 but set on the eve of war ("It was nine o'clock at night upon the second of August — the most terrible August in the history of the world"), this, the title story of the collection, is fraught with the despair and grief that the Great War inflicted on Europe and the world. "One might have thought already that God's curse hung heavy over a degenerate world," writes Doyle in the opening paragraphs of the story, perfectly capturing the disillusionment of the new age.

The Case-Book of Sherlock Holmes

Things don't cheer up much in *The Case-Book of Sherlock Holmes,* the final volume in the Sherlockian canon. In fact, they get worse. The *Case-Book* is replete with shocking motifs and elements unique in all the canon. Brutal beatings, disfigurement, paranoia, sexual perversion, suicide — you name it and it's probably in there! It even has, in addition to these new manifestations, violent updates on previous Sherlockian motifs. And worst of all, Sherlock Holmes writes his own stories.

Just a sampling of the delights to be found in *The Case-Book of Sherlock Holmes* includes:

✔ **Paranoia, jealousy, and psychotic rage:** "Never did I realize till that moment how this poor creature hated me," writes Grace Dunbar, governess in the home of millionaire Neil Gibson, of his wife Maria Gibson. When Mrs. Gibson detects that her husband wants more than a professional relationship with the young governess, it drives the woman mad with jealousy and rage. "She was like a mad woman — indeed, I think she was a mad woman, subtly mad with the deep power of deception which insane people may have. How else could she have met me with unconcern every day and yet had so raging a hatred of me in her heart?" How, indeed. Finally, the woman's hatred drives her to lure the young woman to a meeting at Thor Bridge, where she will commit suicide, framing her romantic rival for murder. "She poured her whole wild fury out in burning and horrible words. I did not even answer — I could not. It was dreadful to see her. I put my hands to my ears and rushed away. When I left her she was standing, still shrieking out her curses at me, in the mouth of the bridge."

✔ **Lust-driven science:** Some consider "The Creeping Man" to actually be a science fiction story. Well, it is fiction, and there is "science," but really, it's the story of a retirement-age professor's distasteful desire for a woman young enough to be his (at least) daughter. In an effort at "rejuvenation," the professor starts injecting himself with a serum made from monkey "glands," hoping to, as Holmes puts it, "gain his wish by turning himself into a younger man." At the end of the tale, Holmes asks the timely question, "What sort of cesspool may not our poor world become?"

✔ **A lonely, self-pitying Holmes:** After decades of heaping abuse and criticism on Watson's stories — the very stories that made him rich and famous — Sherlock Holmes grudgingly says, "I am compelled to admit that, having taken my pen in my hand, I do begin to realize that the matter must be presented in such a way as may interest the reader." Gone is the Sherlock who "loathes every form of society with his whole bohemian soul." That was a much younger man. Here is a Holmes who says, "The good Watson had at that time deserted me for a wife, the only selfish action which I can recall in our association. I was alone."

✔ **Savage physical assault and disfigurement:** The *Case-Book* has not one, but *two* facial disfigurements! "The Veiled Lodger" is the terrible story of a Mrs. Ronder, a former circus worker who had suffered having her face torn off by a lion! Then again, in "The Illustrious Client," the villain Baron Gruner has his face horribly disfigured by a vitriol attack. This story also has Holmes being beaten so badly it makes the papers. (For more on this story, see the later section "'The Illustrious Client' — A canonical villain gets really creepy.")

All in all, the later stories of Sherlock Holmes get progressively rougher as they go along. The times had changed, and Holmes had changed with them.

What's vitriol?

Vitriol is another term for sulfuric acid. When Baron Gruner got vitriol thrown in his face, he undoubtedly suffered the burning of the skin and damage to the underlying tissue. Sometimes the sulfuric acid can even dissolve the bones of the face. If vitriol is thrown in the eyes, it can cause blindness. This terrible form of assault did actually happen and is still common in many Asian countries, where the victims are usually female.

The Three Garridebs

By the time the dutiful Sherlockian has read his way deep into the collection known as the *Case-Book* to "The Three Garridebs," it's likely that a distinct feeling of unease will have set in. Watson makes it clear that most of these tales are late in the career of Sherlock Holmes, and supposedly take place somewhere in the first decade of the 20th century. And yet, whenever they're supposed to have occurred, there's no mistaking the fact that these stories were penned in the decade known as the Roaring Twenties.

The Valley of Fear may have introduced the hard-boiled detective story to readers of *The Strand Magazine* — and Doyle may have even invented the form — but no story brings the spirit of violence and danger home to the London of Sherlock Holmes like "The Three Garridebs" does.

A harder, more violent spirit

Many Sherlockian commentators have observed how Doyle recycled the plot of "The Red-Headed League" for both "The Stock-Broker's Clerk" and "The Three Garridebs." Few, however, have noted Doyle's hard-boiled innovation in "The Three Garridebs." Though the plots are essentially the same, the tone of each story couldn't be more different.

In both "The Red-Headed League" and "The Three Garridebs," a victim is presented with a too-good-to-be-true opportunity that requires him to be out of his normal home or workplace. This opportunity is a diversion, allowing the criminals access to the victim's property in order to commit a crime.

The early passages in "The Red-Headed League" read like comedy. The pompous, slow-witted Jabez Wilson's statement of the case even causes Holmes and Watson to burst out laughing! It only gets serious at the end of the tale. When the criminal appears he's quickly apprehended, with any gunplay efficiently quashed with a strike from Holmes's riding crop.

But now, over 30 years later in "The Three Garridebs," it's a much different scenario. True, a victim is again presented with a too-good-to-be-true opportunity that requires him to be out of his normal home or workplace. But the story has no comic elements and little sympathy for the object of the deception. And unlike "The Red-Headed League," the story's climax doesn't end so quickly and cleanly. There is, indeed, gunplay, and it's Watson who is hit:

> In an instant he had whisked out a revolver from his breast and had fired two shots. I felt a sudden hot sear as if a red-hot iron had been pressed to my thigh. There was a crash as Holmes's pistol came down on the man's head. I had a vision of him sprawling upon the floor with blood running down his face. . . .

"The Three Garridebs" was written and published right in the middle of the 1920s, and shortly after its author had made two extensive tours of America promoting spiritualism. These tours took Doyle and his family across the length and breadth of the U.S. This lengthy exposure to 1920s America is clearly reflected in the *Case-Book* tales and especially "The Three Garridebs."

"The Three Garridebs" was actually first published in *Collier's Weekly* on October 25, 1924, fittingly enough in America. Its appearance in *The Strand Magazine* came on January 19, 1925, where it was illustrated by Howard K. Elcock.

"The Three Garridebs" isn't merely the reflection of Doyle's experiences of America in the 1920s. It wasn't the tours through Chicago and Los Angeles alone that imparted the harder, more violent spirit to the *Case-Book* tales in general, and "The Three Garridebs" in particular. Instead, this story betrays the conscious influence of the hard-boiled detective story.

A change in tone

That traces of *Black Mask* found their way, consciously or unconsciously, into the stories from *Case-Book,* and especially "The Three Garridebs," seems obvious upon examination. You can almost hear the tough-guy hard-boiled detective delivering Watson's opening lines:

It may have been a comedy, or it may have been a tragedy. It cost one man his reason, it cost me a blood-letting, and it cost yet another man the penalties of the law. Yet there was certainly an element of comedy. Well, you shall judge for yourselves.

Then there is the name . . . no, not "Garrideb." The villain's name . . . the blunt, crude, frightening name of "Killer Evans," a hardened criminal, "aged forty-four. Native of Chicago. Known to have shot three men in the States. Escaped from penitentiary through political influence." No retired colonels, professors, or politicians here. Instead, it's a "very dangerous man, [who] usually carries arms and is prepared to use them."

Elcock's illustrations for "The Three Garridebs" also reflect this new tone (see Figure 10-2 and Figure 10-3). The drawings illustrating the moments just before the arrest of Killer Evans show drawn guns, flying chairs, a gunshot victim, and the detective pistol-whipping the perpetrator. It's a moment that Holmes punctuates by saying, "If you had killed Watson, you would not have got out of this room alive."

Figure 10-2:
The climactic gunplay from "The Three Garridebs," originally in *The Strand Magazine*.

Illustration by Sidney Paget, The Strand Magazine.

Illustration by Sidney Paget, The Strand Magazine.

"The Illustrious Client" — A canonical villain gets really creepy

"The Illustrious Client" is a very late adventure of Sherlock Holmes, published in 1924. As far as Holmes stories go, it stands out for featuring a villain who is utterly unique in the canon: Baron Adelbert Gruner, a sexual predator.

Holmes is approached by an anonymous "illustrious client" (it doesn't take a Sherlock Holmes to figure out that this is Edward the VII, King of England) to prevent the upcoming wedding of Violet de Merville to Baron Gruner. Miss de Merville's father is a friend of the "illustrious client," and so as a favor to all concerned, Gruner must be warned off.

Holmes, who already is aware of the baron's reputation, refers to him as "the Austrian murderer" and believes he killed his previous wife on a journey through the Alps. Holmes takes the case.

Gone are the charming street urchins from the early canon who help out the Great Detective when needed. Now Holmes turns to Shinwell Johnson, who "made his name first as a very dangerous villain and served two terms at Parkhurst," as Watson says, but then who "repented and allied himself to Holmes, acting as his agent in the huge criminal underworld of London." Yes, indeed — things are a bit rougher in the 1920s.

Johnson connects Holmes with Kitty Winter, a woman down and out. "What I am Adelbert Gruner made me," she tells Holmes. Gruner, it seems, "collects women, and takes a pride in his collection, as some men collect moths or butterflies." Kitty Winter knows all about it, saying, "He had it all in [a] book. Snapshot photographs, names, details, everything about them. It was a beastly book — a book no man, even if he had come from the gutter, could have put together. But it was Adelbert Gruner's book all the same. 'Souls I have ruined.'"

A villain who "collects women," who takes photographs and keeps them in a book, who "ruins" them and moves on to the next. This is amazing, almost unbelievable material for the adventures of Sherlock Holmes.

But then, the same can be said about many of the stories found in the later part of the canon. In addition to great stories about Holmes and Watson, the later stories have increased violence and more mature themes, and some are even hard-boiled detective tales, all showing that Sherlock Holmes changed with the times. His adventures were written not as Victorian period pieces, but as vital, modern crime stories.

Chapter 11

Common Themes and Threads

In This Chapter

▶ Looking at elements of the stories that remain constant

▶ Combining rationalism and religion in the tales

▶ Paying attention to the little things: Holmes's reliance on trifles

*V*illains come and go. Clients come and go. Times change, and so does the tone of the canon itself. And yet, within the Sherlock Holmes stories, it wasn't all change all the time. Despite this ever-changing, ever-evolving kaleidoscope of characters and events, some things were constant.

In this chapter, I look at those elements — persons, places, and things — that were constants throughout the course of the Holmes stories. I also examine themes and motifs that characterize not only individual characters but also the stories as a whole.

Some Things Never Change

Part of the appeal of the Sherlock Holmes stories has to do with a cozy familiarity with certain elements found in the tales. This is particularly true for repeat readers. Why would a person come back, over and over again, to a set of stories, particularly *mystery* stories, after the solution has been revealed, the stolen jewel recovered, and the murderer apprehended?

Elements, ideas, and themes are repeated throughout the canon that draw the reader back. For some, it's like visiting old, familiar friends. For others, perhaps the ideals embodied and promoted by the tales (whether overtly or subtly) offer reassurance and pleasure. Whatever the reason is, it's often rooted in the enduring elements of the Sherlockian canon, elements that appear throughout the stories, offering a sense of continuity to an otherwise constantly changing panorama.

Persons

Readers meet a lot of people in the Holmes stories — Arthur Conan Doyle introduces at least 300 characters over the course of the canon's 60 stories. Most are story-specific, meaning they show up in an individual story, only to vanish from the scene when the adventure is concluded.

Some go on to be remembered, even if they never make an actual personal appearance. Holmes remembers and references Professor Moriarty and his right-hand man, Col. Sebastian Moran, well past their appearances.

But among the parade of characters that the reader encounters in Watson's accounts of the Great Detective, a handful are, more or less, around from beginning to end. For the faithful reader, this core of canonical characters forms the nucleus around which the rest of the names orbit.

Sherlock Holmes

Of course, these *are* the adventures of Sherlock Holmes, so naturally, Holmes features in every tale. Holmes springs to life in *A Study in Scarlet,* and from the beginning, he's a masterful, fully realized character. The power of Sherlock Holmes as a character draws readers back time and again to his adventures.

As a character, Holmes is moody (maybe even manic at times) and unapologetically indulges in several bad habits, including tobacco and drugs. He's eccentric, vain, and susceptible to flattery. He can be petulant and rude. And yet, his natural empathy for the victimized and his unfailing sense of fair play and justice make him the man to turn to. "I have heard of you, Mr. Holmes," says Violet Hunter from "The Speckled Band." "I have heard of you from Mrs. Farintosh, whom you helped in the hour of her sore need. Oh, sir, do you not think that you could help me, too," she pleads, "and at least throw a little light through the dense darkness which surrounds me?"

Sherlock Holmes is so real to his readers that he holds a number of distinctions unique in all of literature:

✔ **He not only lived, but he's still alive.** Despite being a fictional character of the late 19th and early 20th centuries, he remains a living person in the minds of many. In 2008, a survey in England revealed that 58 percent of British citizens believed Sherlock Holmes was a real, historical figure. To this day, letters to Holmes arrive at 221b Baker Street (originally the home office of the Abbey National Building Society, and now home to the Sherlock Holmes Museum). These letters ask for interviews, autographs, and, most amazing of all, advice or help in solving a mystery. They contain invitations, birthday and Christmas cards, and occasionally presents. They arrive from every corner of the world and have been doing so for over 50 years.

✔ **The books have never gone out of print.** Since their original publication, the Sherlock Holmes stories have never been out of print. In addition to English-language editions, the canon has been translated into over 65 languages. Nearly every language on earth — from Afrikaans to Yiddish — has produced an edition of the Holmes stories. The canon has even been translated into Braille, shorthand, and Latin!

✔ **Sherlock Holmes is a movie star.** More than 260 movies, hundreds of television episodes, two musicals, and even a ballet have featured the exploits of Sherlock Holmes. (For more on dramatic adaptations of Holmes, see Chapter 14.)

John H. Watson, MD

John H. Watson is the loyal companion and stalwart friend of detective Sherlock Holmes. Indeed, though Holmes has a wide circle of acquaintances because of his profession, when it comes to friends, Watson is it. As Holmes characterized his friendship to Watson, "Except yourself I have none."

Despite the popular misconception of Holmes's sidekick as a dimwitted old man, Watson is an intelligent man who plays a vital role in the crime-solving partnership. And a partnership it is. Time and again, Watson accompanies Holmes on cases, stands in for the detective when needed, acts as a sounding board when Sherlock is working out a problem, runs errands, leaves his own medical practice at the drop of a hat to assist Holmes in an investigation, and even breaks the law with him (all in the name of a good cause). And, most important, Watson is Holmes's biographer — he tells the tales.

The good doctor's admiration for his friend is frank and unapologetic. In *A Study in Scarlet,* toward the end of the book, after Holmes has successfully apprehended the criminal, Watson says, "Your merits should be publicly recognized. You should publish an account of the case. If you won't, I will for you." And when he believes Holmes has died ridding the world of Professor Moriarty, he movingly writes he "shall ever regard [Sherlock Holmes] as the best and the wisest man whom I have ever known."

Watson remains remarkably steady throughout the canon. He marries, he moves out, he finds himself single again, he moves back in, and all the while, like the reader, he finds the lure of Baker Street and Sherlock Holmes irresistible. Even when Holmes heaps abuse on Watson's writing or points out all the doctor's mistakes in trying to use observation and deduction as Holmes does, Watson remains loyal. Holmes knows it, too. In their final recorded adventure together, "His Last Bow," Holmes says to his friend, "Good old Watson! You are the one fixed point in a changing age."

Inspector Lestrade

Inspector G. Lestrade is the best-known Scotland Yard detective in the canon. In fact, he may be the best-known Scotland Yard detective in either fiction or real life.

Lestrade is in the very first story, *A Study in Scarlet,* where he appears with his professional rival, Inspector Gregson. In this early tale, neither of the two official officers gets much praise from Sherlock Holmes. Holmes refers to them as "the best of a bad lot," adding that they're "both quick and energetic, but conventional — shockingly so." But in those early days the relationship between the gifted consulting detective and the veteran Scotland Yarder was still new.

However, over time, Lestrade grows on Holmes — so much so that Sherlock regularly allows Lestrade to take credit for solving cases that Holmes has cracked, and he's often hailed in the papers as one of the best detectives at Scotland Yard. By the time of *The Hound of the Baskervilles,* Holmes openly states that Lestrade "is the best of the professionals," and at another time, while decrying his lack of imagination, Holmes acknowledges that the little ferret-faced detective is "as tenacious as a bulldog when he once understands what he has to do."

Inspector Lestrade has a long, continuing presence in the canon. Indeed, he's one of the fixtures of the Baker Street scene, a continuing character whose entry into the story is always welcome, by both readers and Holmes himself. And over time, their mutual enmity softens, and the sneering, scoffing, professional rival morphs into an admiring, professional colleague.

Mrs. Hudson

The landlady of 221b Baker Street is, as Watson puts it, "a long-suffering woman." The list of grievances is long: "Not only was her first floor flat invaded at all hours by throngs of singular and often undesirable characters," elaborates Watson, "but her remarkable lodger showed an eccentricity and irregularity in his life which must have sorely tried her patience. His incredible untidyness, his addiction to music at all hours, his occasional rifle practice within doors, his weird and often malodorous scientific experiments, and the atmosphere of violence and danger which hung around him, made him the very worst tenant in London."

With this laundry list of reasons for eviction, why does Mrs. Hudson allow Sherlock Holmes to remain at Baker Street? For readers of the canon, the answer is simple — Holmes has the same hold on her imagination and affection as he does on readers. "The landlady stood in the deepest awe of him," says Watson, who also adds a final, and crucial, element. "She was fond of him, too, for he had a remarkable gentleness and courtesy in his dealings with women."

The popular image of Mrs. Hudson is one of a plump, sixtyish woman with a Scotch accent who acts as a sort of den mother to the boys of Baker Street. But this image is in some respects inaccurate. For instance, about her age — she probably isn't much more than ten years older than Sherlock. And as for ruling Baker Street like a den mother, we know from Watson's ironclad authority that Mrs. Hudson "never dared to interfere with him, however outrageous his proceedings might seem."

Who is Martha?

The first name of Mrs. Hudson is never stated in the canon. However, since the 1930s, Sherlockians have presumed that it's Martha. How did the landlady of 221b get this name? Blame it on a Sherlockian named Vincent Starrett. In 1933, Starrett wrote an essay titled "The Singular Adventures of Martha Hudson." This essay first appeared in *Baker Street Studies,* a book of Sherlockiana by H.W. Bell, and it was reprinted in a later edition of Starrett's own landmark volume, *The Private Life of Sherlock Holmes.*

In the short story "His Last Bow," the German spy's English housekeeper is actually an agent of Sherlock Holmes, and her name is Martha. "Old Martha," as Holmes refers to her, "has played her part to admiration. I got her the situation here when first I took the matter up." Starrett, in his essay, assumes that Martha is none other than Mrs. Hudson, who Holmes takes with him in retirement and then places as his own spy in the house of the German agent. Thus, Martha Hudson.

Unfortunately, there's no evidence whatsoever that the woman in "His Last Bow" really is Mrs. Hudson. It's true that Mrs. Hudson would have been up to the task, but the fact that Holmes calls her "Martha" when he never, ever addressed his landlady by anything but the respectful "Mrs. Hudson" weighs heavily against them being the same person. Whoever Martha was, she wasn't Mrs. Hudson.

However, there's no denying that Mrs. Hudson provides a much needed touch of domesticity to the very masculine residence of Holmes and Watson. She certainly does the cooking and eventually protests when the general untidiness of their apartments reaches a critical mass. She's a true member of the Baker Street family: Whether it's cooking the Christmas goose or moving a wax dummy while crawling on the floor to avoid air guns, Mrs. Hudson could always be counted on.

Places

The 60 Sherlock Holmes adventures take the reader to many places — Dartmoor, the Reichenbach Falls, even the United States. But despite the ever-changing locations and scenery, some places are consistent throughout the adventures.

221b Baker Street

The residence of Holmes and Watson is perhaps the most unchanging element in all the stories. Watson describes the apartment as "consisting of a couple of comfortable bed-rooms and a single large airy sitting-room, cheerfully furnished, and illuminated by two broad windows."

Throughout the tales, nearly every adventure either begins or ends in 221b. And despite the fact that Holmes and Watson live there for nearly 20 years (well, Watson keeps moving in and out, depending on his marital status!), the apartment remains virtually unchanged from when they move in to the last glimpse the reader sees of it decades later. Oh sure, there are some modernizations along the way — like Holmes getting a telephone — but in nearly every way, 221b Baker Street remains timeless.

London

In "The Red-Headed League," Holmes remarks to Watson, "It is a hobby of mine to have an exact knowledge of London." For Holmes, London is the great city. In it he sees romance, adventure, mystery, and crime continually playing out all around him. In "A Case of Identity," he articulates his feelings about London and what it offers:

> "If we could fly out of that window hand in hand," he explains, "hover over this great city, gently remove the roofs, and peep in at the queer things which are going on, the strange coincidences, the plannings, the cross-purposes, the wonderful chains of events, working through generation, and leading to the most outré results, it would make all fiction with its conventionalities and foreseen conclusions most stale and unprofitable."

And he's right. In "The Blue Carbuncle," when Watson finds Holmes examining a battered hat one December morning, he asks if it's connected to a crime. No, explains Holmes. It's "only one of those whimsical little incidents which will happen when you have four million human beings all jostling each other within the space of a few square miles. Amid the action and reaction of so dense a swarm of humanity, every possible combination of events may be expected to take place, and many a little problem will be presented which may be striking and bizarre without being criminal."

Sherlock Holmes has always been associated with London. It's where he lived and worked, and it's the city he loved. In "The Final Problem," when he's well aware that his battle with Professor Moriarty could end in his death, he remarks, "If my record were closed to-night I could still survey it with equanimity. The air of London is the sweeter for my presence."

Things

Certain things — certain objects — are universally associated with Sherlock Holmes and appear throughout the stories, offering continuity and familiarity. All these items help build up a mental picture of the Great Detective and give insight into his habits and surroundings.

Violin

One of the most iconic items associated with Holmes is the violin. Holmes was an accomplished musician, and right at the very first meeting of Holmes and Watson, an anxious Sherlock asks Watson if he minds violin playing.

> "It depends on the player," answers Watson. "A well-played violin is a treat for the gods — a badly played one —"

> "Oh, that's all right," replies Holmes with a laugh, "I think we may consider the thing as settled. . . ."

Sherlock wrote articles on music for publication and was an unconventional violinist. Watson remarks that Holmes's powers on the instrument were "very remarkable, but as eccentric as all his other accomplishments. That he could play pieces, and difficult pieces, I knew well, because at my request he has played me some of Mendelssohn's *Lieder,* and other favorites." But when left to his own devices, "he would seldom produce any music or attempt any recognized air. Leaning back in his armchair of an evening, he would close his eyes and scrape carelessly at the fiddle which was thrown across his knee. Sometimes the chords were sonorous and melancholy. Occasionally they were fantastic and cheerful. Clearly they reflected the thoughts which possessed him, but whether the music aided those thoughts, or whether the playing was simply the result of a whim or fancy, was more than I could determine."

Just when Watson began to find these strange concerts almost unbearable, Holmes "terminated them by playing in quick succession a whole series of my favourite airs as a slight compensation for the trial upon my patience."

Dressing gown

Another iconic item associated with Holmes is the dressing gown. Holmes was in the habit of wearing his dressing gown at home, even when being visited by a client or performing some chemical experiment.

A *dressing gown* was a robe that people wore, especially while dressing or resting at home. It was often made of silk, sometimes quilted, and usually elegant and expensive. Today, the closest thing to the dressing gown is the bathrobe, but they aren't quite the same thing.

It was a common occurrence for Watson to return to Baker Street to find the room full of tobacco smoke, and "Holmes in his dressing-gown coiled up in an armchair with his black clay pipe between his lips."

Sherlockians have debated whether Holmes owned three dressing gowns or just one. Over the course of the stories, Holmes's gown is described as being blue, then purple, and then "mouse-colored." Some believe this points to three separate gowns. Others, however, theorize that Holmes had just one gown and it was originally blue, then faded to purple, and finally turned to mouse-color with age.

Smoking (pipes, cigars, cigarettes)

Next to the deerstalker cap, which I talk about later in the chapter, no object is more associated with Sherlock Holmes than a pipe. Throughout the canon, smoking in all its forms is a constant cultural presence. Of the 60 cases, only 4 are without some reference to smoking. Tobacco smoke is the very atmosphere of Baker Street.

Holmes was a world-class smoker, enjoying pipes, cigars, and cigarettes. Smoking was, for him, not only a pleasant pastime but also actually part of the intellectual process. In "The Red-Headed League," when contemplating his client's peculiar case, Holmes says to Watson, "It is quite a three pipe problem, and I beg that you won't speak to me for fifty minutes." The sedative nature of nicotine must have helped relax and focus his mind. In addition to the physical effects, there almost certainly was a psychological one as well.

Pipes

Holmes is remembered primarily as a pipe smoker, and pipe smoking shows up in over 22 cases. Sherlock smoked a variety of pipes, depending on his mood. His favorites include an old black, oily clay pipe, a briar (a pipe made from the root of a briar plant), and less frequently, a long-stemmed cherry-wood. When it came to tobacco, he preferred the strong, smelly version called "shag."

But you may be wondering, "Where is the big curly yellow pipe with the white top? Isn't that what Sherlock Holmes smokes?" That big, distinctive pipe is called a *calabash*. The main body of the calabash pipe is the curving, yellow or golden stem of the African calabash gourd. The white bowl, which is on the top of the pipe, is where the tobacco goes. It's usually made of meerschaum, which is a soft white mineral. The bowl is inserted into the hollowed-out gourd stem.

In popular mythology, it's the Sherlock Holmes pipe. The only problem is, Holmes never smoked a calabash pipe. That bit of apocryphal lore comes from the actor William Gillette, who became famous playing the Great Detective on stage in the late 19th and early 20th centuries. The calabash's low center of gravity made it an easy one for the actor to hold in his mouth while on stage. To his generation, William Gillette *was* Sherlock Holmes, and his hundreds of performances forever fixed the large, curly calabash as the image of Holmes's pipe.

Cigars

Holmes does smoke cigars, but they don't seem to be his first choice. Unlike his choice in pipe tobacco, Holmes's taste in cigars seems to be a little better. For instance, in one scene, Watson joins Holmes at an Italian restaurant before heading out on a night of burglary.

As Watson enters, he sees Holmes "at a little round table near the door of the garish Italian restaurant."

"Have you had something to eat? Then join me in a coffee and curacao. Try one of the proprietor's cigars. They are less poisonous than one would expect."

That Holmes commented on the "less-poisonous" quality of the cigars indicates that, at least when it comes to cigars, Holmes has standards!

Cigarettes

Sherlock Holmes also smokes cigarettes. Indeed, cigarettes may have been his favorite smoke. Holmes's consumption of cigarettes seems to have been as great as his consumption of pipe tobacco. In "The Boscombe Valley Mystery," he tells Lestrade that he has "a caseful of cigarettes here which need smoking," truly the words of a champion smoker.

In "The Golden Pince-Nez," Holmes uses his love of cigarette smoking to lay down a field of ash on the floor in order to detect footprints. This took a lot of cigarettes in a very small amount of time, something that a light smoker would have done with difficulty. However, Holmes rather enjoys the experience, and the pricey imported cigarettes of Professor Coram.

Chemical experiments

According to Watson's friend, Stamford, Holmes is a "first class chemist," a pursuit he enjoys throughout the canon. According to all the evidence of the stories, Stamford is right. Holmes's use of logic and scientific method demonstrates a discipline and skill that he obviously makes good use of in the chemical corner of 221b Baker Street. Watson's own rating of Holmes's chemical abilities is "profound," and later "eccentric." But the evidence is good that Holmes was a very good chemist.

For instance, in *The Sign of the Four*, Holmes tells Watson, "I gave my mind a thorough rest by plunging into a chemical analysis." Later, in "The Gloria Scott," Holmes tells how, while in college, he took "the long vacation between semesters" and "spent seven weeks working out a few experiments in Organic Chemistry."

About that blood test

Back in Victorian times, it was almost impossible to test a stain to determine if it was blood, let alone what type of blood it was. This was way before DNA analysis and blood typing. So being able to tell if a stain on a suspect's clothes was indeed blood and not some other stain like ink or rust would be a huge advance in the detection of crime. It was in the very first book, *A Study in Scarlet,* that Holmes is at the moment of his big breakthrough, when, just as Watson enters the room, Holmes shouts out:

"I've found it. I've found it . . . I have found a reagent which is precipitated by haemoglobin and by nothing else . . . No doubt you see the significance of this discovery of mine?"

Watson, a trained doctor, didn't get it, saying, "It is interesting chemically no doubt, but practically —"

Holmes quickly replies, "Why, man, it is the most practical medico-legal discovery for years. Don't you see that it gives us an infallible test for blood stains?"

Capable of detecting one part in a million, the Sherlock Holmes blood test was a revolutionary step forward over the guaiacum test, which was, at that time, the gold standard of blood testing. The guaiacum test was only good for one part in one hundred thousand.

Holmes worked on a variety of chemical experiments and challenges. Throughout the 60 stories, he plunges into experiments involving acetones, coal tar derivatives, the analysis of barium compounds, and, not least of all, a radical new blood test.

Finally, the canon has many references to Holmes's chemical bench in the corner of their Baker Street sitting room, and it was not uncommon for Watson to come home and find their chambers stinking to high heaven with some smelly, noxious chemical experiment that Holmes was running. Poor Watson!

The deerstalker cap

Nothing invokes the image of Sherlock Holmes like the famous deerstalker hat. The deerstalker's best-known features are the fore and aft brims, and its two side flaps that tie up on the top with a ribbon (see Figure 11-1).

Originally created for hunters and outdoorsmen, the cap has dual brims that provide protection from the sun on the face and neck. When it's cold, the wearer can tie the side flaps below the chin, helping to keep the ears warmer in cold weather and high winds. Otherwise, the side flaps are kept out of the way by keeping them tied up over the crown of the hat. Most deerstalkers come in a checkered or plaid pattern, and it's believed that, for hunters, this provides camouflage.

Figure 11-1:
The iconic
deerstalker
cap.

This style of hat existed before Sherlock Holmes, but ever since the Great Detective was depicted wearing it, the deerstalker has been identified with Holmes. But here's the surprise: Arthur Conan Doyle never actually wrote that Sherlock Holmes wore a deerstalker! So, how did this distinctive headgear become associated so firmly with Holmes? It all has to do with the original illustrator of the stories.

Sidney Paget was the original illustrator of the Holmes stories in *The Strand Magazine.* His brother Walter was also an illustrator and was the artist the *Strand* editors originally intended to hire. However, they accidentally wrote to Sidney instead, and the die was cast. It turned out to be a fateful mistake, as Sidney (who used his brother Walter as his model) created the popular image of the detective — a model that illustrators, actors, and filmmakers have been imitating to this day (see Figure 11-2).

It was Paget who put first put Holmes in the deerstalker. In several stories, Doyle described Holmes as wearing an "ear-flapped travelling cap." Paget, who himself wore a deerstalker at his home in the country, interpreted this as his own favorite hat and stuck it on Sherlock's head. And there it has been ever since.

Figure 11-2:
Sidney
Paget
wearing his
deerstalker
cap.

Rationalism and Religion in the Canon of Sherlock Holmes

When discussing Sherlock Holmes, many cite the fact that he's a "scientific" detective. Logic, deduction, evidence — these are the hallmarks defining the nature of the Great Detective. But this is an incomplete picture. In reality, the canon has twin threads running through it. At certain times those threads are in harmony, and at other times they seem to conflict. These are the themes of rationalism and religion, and both inform the nature of the Holmes stories.

The rational detective

Certainly, the best-known and most obvious theme running through the canon is rationalism. *Rationalism* is a means of knowing the universe that appeals to reason as a source of knowledge and understanding. Truth is derived by a method (there's Holmes's own word: "You know my methods, Watson") of intellectual and deductive reasoning.

Holmes's own method was based on drawing inferences from the careful study of evidence. When faced with more than one possible theory, he would choose the one that covered the most. "It is an old maxim of mine," he tells Watson, "that when you have excluded the impossible, whatever remains, however improbable, must be the truth."

One tenet of rationalism argues that it's possible to deduce full knowledge on a subject by learning a few fundamental principles about it. And sure enough, right there in the very first Holmes story, Holmes has written an article in a magazine titled "The Book of Life," in which he writes:

> From a drop of water a logician could infer the possibility of an Atlantic or a Niagara without having seen or heard of one or the other. So all life is a great chain, the nature of which is known whenever we are shown a single link of it.

Watson, upon reading this, is skeptical. But after he's seen Sherlock in action and experienced firsthand the results of Holmes's "method," he exclaims, "you have brought detection as near an exact science as it ever will be brought in this world." In a later story, Holmes tells Watson that "true cold reason" is that "which I place above all things." There's no doubt Holmes was a rationalist when it came to his craft.

Holmes's rationalism and the supernatural

On three occasions in the canon, cases come to Baker Street that have supernatural overtones. These bizarre cases present situations that, at first glance, seem to defy Sherlock Holmes's belief in "cold true logic." When these seemingly supernatural events invade the familiar, known world of 19th-century England, the implications are terrifying. Fortunately, we have Sherlock Holmes on our side.

Doyle's personal belief in spiritualism and psychic phenomenon seems to fly in the face of Holmes's scientific rationalism. In certain stories, which I discuss in the following sections, and especially in *The Hound of the Baskervilles,* Doyle's most famous tale, the reader sees what is surely a reflection of the author's own struggles with the subject — belief in the supernatural colliding with the philosophy of rationalism. Doyle found a way to reconcile the two, and he had Sherlock Holmes do the same.

The Hound of the Baskervilles

The most famous of all the Holmes stories begins with the presentation of the Baskerville curse, preserved on an ancient parchment. Right out of the gate, readers are absorbed in not only a tale of Gothic mystery but also a creepy, supernatural horror story. After reading the document, Dr. Mortimer, a trained man of science, confesses his belief that the hound is supernatural.

Sherlock Holmes is skeptical. When Mortimer wonders whether Sir Henry Baskerville, the new heir, will be safe out on the moors of Baskerville Hall, Holmes replies by saying, "But surely, if your supernatural theory be correct, it could work the young man evil in London as easily as in Devonshire. A devil with merely local powers like a parish vestry would be too inconceivable a thing."

The Devil's Foot

In this tale, Holmes and Watson investigate the mysterious and disturbing case of an entire family being driven out of their minds (one of them to death). The surviving family member, Mr. Mortimer Tregennis, and the local vicar, a Mr. Roundhay, come to solicit Holmes's help. It seems the Tregennis family had been playing cards in the evening. When it got late, Mortimer Tregennis left, leaving his two brothers and sister around the table. In the morning, he found them still at the table, the brothers completely insane, and the sister dead.

"I take it that you have no theory yourself which can in any way account for them?" asks Holmes.

"It's devilish, Mr. Holmes, devilish!" replies Mortimer Tregennis. "It is not of this world."

Not quite ready to buy into a supernatural cause, Holmes replies by saying, "I fear that if the matter is beyond humanity it is certainly beyond me. Yet we must exhaust all natural explanations before we fall back upon such a theory as this."

The Sussex Vampire

When a new client, Robert Ferguson, becomes convinced that his wife is a vampire preying on their infant son, he comes to Sherlock Holmes for help. He tells Holmes that the baby's mother has been sucking blood from the child's neck, and he even once caught her in the act, crouching over the baby with blood on her lips.

The vampire theory doesn't get much traction with Holmes. "Rubbish, Watson, rubbish! What have we to do with walking corpses who can only be held in their grave by stakes driven through their hearts? It's pure lunacy." He goes on to say quite definitively, "Are we to give serious attention to such things? This agency stands flat-footed upon the ground, and there it must remain. The world is big enough for us. No ghosts need apply."

Sherlock Holmes and religion

Much speculation has gone into the religious views and beliefs of Sherlock Holmes since he first appeared. Many have pondered what, if any, religious faith Holmes held. Did he adopt some form of eastern religion following his three-year hiatus? Was he an atheist? Just what *were* his views? It's possible to understand the true religious philosophy of Holmes — you just need to look at what the man himself said on the subject.

On the subject of religion, Holmes, like many of his contemporaries, reflects the views of William Paley, an English philosopher and theologian from the preceding century. Regarding the existence of God, Paley, in his landmark work *Natural Theology* (1802), uses the analogy of a watch. To paraphrase, if a man walking across a field finds a watch, based on the intricacy of its design and interrelated moving parts, the man would naturally conclude that "the watch must have had a maker: that there must have existed, at some time, and at some place or other, an artificer or artificers, who formed it for the purpose which we find it actually to answer; who comprehended its construction, and designed its use." He adds that, as further evidence, the "design of the contrivance is beneficial" and the designer "has superadded *pleasure* to animal sensations beyond what was necessary for any other purpose."

William Paley

Born in Peterborough, England, and educated at Christ's College, University of Cambridge, where he later lectured, William Paley was ordained in the Church of England in 1767. Paley published numerous popular and respected books on science and religion over the course of his lifetime, but it was in 1802 that he published his most important work, *Natural Theology; or, Evidences of the Existence and Attributes of the Deity.*

Natural Theology is Paley's attempt to show that theistic belief rests on a logical basis of observation and reason, and need not be a matter of pure faith alone. He argues that an examination of nature itself reveals evidence of design. Appearing nearly six decades before Darwin's *The Origin of Species,* Paley's book cast a long shadow on the philosophical, religious, and scientific thought of his age. Charles Darwin, the giant of late-19th-century thought whose theory of natural selection and evolution went so far to challenge Paley's argument, admits to having memorized long passages of *Natural Theology.*

For many familiar with Holmes's comments on religious matters, Paley's argument sounds familiar. Two excerpts follow illustrating this point. The first is Holmes's remarks at the conclusion of "The Cardboard Box":

> "What is the meaning of it, Watson?" said Holmes solemnly as he laid down the paper. "What object is served by this circle of misery and violence and fear? It must tend to some end, or else our universe is ruled by chance, which is unthinkable. But what end? There is the great standing perennial problem to which human reason is as far from an answer as ever."

The second is his monologue on the moss rose from "The Naval Treaty":

> "What a lovely thing a rose is!"
>
> He walked past the couch to the open window and held up the drooping stalk of a moss-rose, looking down at the dainty blend of crimson and green. It was a new phase of his character to me, for I had never before seen him show any keen interest in natural objects.
>
> "There is nothing in which deduction is so necessary as in religion," said he, leaning with his back against the shutters. "It can be built up as an exact science by the reasoner. Our highest assurance of the goodness of Providence seems to me to rest in the flowers. All other things, our powers, our desires, our food, are all really necessary for our existence in the first instance. But this rose is an extra. Its smell and its colour are an embellishment of life, not a condition of it. It is only goodness which gives extras, and so I say again that we have much to hope from the flowers."

Holmes's deduction from the flowers was not unique to him — in fact, it was a commonplace notion widely held by people in the Victorian age. Though these are perhaps the most concise expressions of Holmes's own religious feelings, they certainly aren't the only ones, and they give us a pretty good idea of Holmes's religious philosophy.

 That Holmes was a theist — that he believed in the divine creation of the universe, that he was in some sense religious, that he was in agreement with the concept that nature revealed evidence of both the existence and attributes of God — is apparent from his own words. And despite the growing influence of Darwin and the growing trend of Victorian scientific thought, Holmes's views are also consistent with the majority of his fellow Englishmen at that time.

Sherlock Holmes expresses religious sentiment in many instances throughout the canon. Some examples include:

✔ **"The Boscombe Valley Mystery":** Following the pathetic confession of John Turner comes the following passage:

"God help us!" said Holmes after a long silence. "Why does fate play such tricks with poor, helpless worms? I never hear of such a case as this that I do not think of Baxter's words, and say, 'There, but for the grace of God, goes Sherlock Holmes.'"

✔ **"The Empty House":** As Holmes recounts his fateful escape from the Reichenbach Falls, he clearly credits his survival:

"[Climbing down] was a hundred times more difficult than getting up. But I had no time to think of the danger, for another stone sang past me as I hung by my hands from the edge of the ledge. Halfway down I slipped, but, by the blessing of God, I landed, torn and bleeding, upon the path."

Other theories on Sherlock's religious views

Though the religious views of Sherlock Holmes point to 19th-century Church of England, other theories have been put forward over the years. Some of them include:

✔ **Sherlock Holmes was a spiritualist:** Some commentators attempt to persuade readers that Holmes was in fact a spiritualist, even in the face of Holmes's blunt declaration from "The Sussex Vampire" that "No ghosts need apply!" Because Sir Arthur Conan Doyle was a spiritualist, the argument is that many of Doyle's own beliefs are embedded in his detective. Though this is undoubtedly true as a generalization, it is false in specifics. Doyle himself acknowledged as much, once pointing out that the "creation and creator are not identical."

✔ **Sherlock Holmes was an atheist:** Many point to Holmes's recommendation to Watson of Winwood Reade's book, *The Martyrdom of Man*. In *The Sign of the Four*, Holmes refers to *The Martyrdom of Man* as "one of the most remarkable [books] ever penned." Reade believed that the destruction of both Christianity and a belief in God were essential to the progress of man. However, calling a book "remarkable" is a far cry from agreeing with it.

✔ **Sherlock Holmes was a Buddhist:** Many Sherlockians propose that Holmes, after having traveled for two years in Tibet, amusing himself by visiting Lhasa and spending some days with the head lama, went on to convert to Buddhism. At the center of Buddhism is the belief that the core of human existence is suffering caused by ignorance of and attachment to material reality. Suffering can be ended by overcoming ignorance and attachment through morality, wisdom, and concentration. At its core, Buddhism is a nontheistic religion, and gods aren't creators of the universe or in control of human destiny. But some of Holmes's explicit statements are incompatible with Buddhism's basic tenets. As cited earlier in the chapter in his comments from "The Cardboard Box," Holmes rules out our fates being determined by impersonal chance, and his monologue on the moss rose from "The Naval Treaty" is a direct argument for a theistic understanding of the universe.

Holmes's stated beliefs are consistent with Christianity, and our best bet is that Holmes was raised in the Church of England (Anglican). Whether he remained within that denomination is unknown, but he clearly retained a Christian worldview in adulthood, right through to the conclusion of his very last recorded case.

"There's an east wind coming, Watson," said Sherlock Holmes in the last quiet talk he ever had with his old friend. "Such a wind as never blew on England yet. It will be cold and bitter, Watson and a good many of us may wither before its blast. But it's God's own wind none the less. . . ."

The Importance of Trifles

Throughout the canon, Holmes demonstrates over and over that the little things, what he calls the "trifles," provide the most valuable information in an investigation. Whether it's making deductions about a new client, examining evidence, or researching a particular topic of forensic science, Holmes always makes note of the little things. For example:

- ✔ In "The Blue Carbuncle," Holmes uses trifling details to draw a conclusion about the goose-seller. "When you see a man with whiskers of that cut and the 'Pink 'un' protruding out of his pocket, you can always draw him by a bet."

- ✔ In "The Copper Beeches," he tells Violet Hunter, "I am glad of all details, whether they seem to you to be relevant or not."

- ✔ In "A Case of Identity," it's clear Holmes has noticed the minute differences between typewriters. "I think of writing another little monograph some of these days on the typewriter and its relation to crime. It is a subject to which I have devoted some little attention."

- ✔ In "The Priory School," he does the same with bike tires! "I am familiar with forty-two different impressions left by tires."

- ✔ In "The Red-Headed League," Holmes confesses to Watson, "I hardly looked at his face. His knees were what I wished to see."

- ✔ In *A Study in Scarlet,* Holmes explains to Watson that "they say that genius is an infinite capacity for taking pains. It's a very bad definition, but it does apply to detective work. "

- ✔ In "The Yellow Face," he gives another lesson in trifles: "Pipes are occasionally of extraordinary interest. Nothing has more individuality save, perhaps, watches and bootlaces."

- ✔ And again in "The Red-Headed League," nothing gets past the eagle-eyed Sherlock Holmes: "If you wish to preserve your incognito, I suggest that you cease to write your name upon the lining of your hat, or else that you turn the crown towards the person whom you are addressing."

Chapter 12

The Rivals of Sherlock Holmes

● ●

In This Chapter

▶ Checking out some of the detectives inspired by Sherlock Holmes

▶ Regarding Raffles, an early antihero in the Holmes mold

▶ Noting a few detectives who transcend Sherlock's influence

● ●

*W*hen coming clean about his profession as "the world's only consulting detective" in *A Study in Scarlet,* Sherlock Holmes says to Watson that "here in London we have lots of government detectives and lots of private ones." And as usual, Holmes was right. When Holmes exploded onto the scene in 1891, Victorian and Edwardian England had *dozens* of incredibly talented, idiosyncratic investigators at work.

In this chapter I look at the many detectives whose creation was inspired by Sherlock Holmes, as well as a memorable villain who turned the Sherlock Holmes model on its head.

Brand New Detectives, Yet Strangely Familiar: Investigating the Rivals

You've seen it over and over. Just think of the glut of space opera films and TV shows (like the original *Battlestar Galactica*) that followed the premiere of the first *Star Wars* movie in 1977. Or better yet, the British Invasion that followed the meteoric rise of the Beatles in 1964. The same phenomenon was in play at the turn of the 20th century, following the incredible popularity of Sherlock Holmes. When Holmes hit it big in *The Strand Magazine,* new writers introduced dozens of new detectives to the public. And just as in the cases of *Star Wars* and the Beatles, a public hungry for the original gratefully embraced the tag-alongs, but rarely did these followers equal the original.

In the case of most of these Holmes wannabes, you can easily spot the influence of the Great Detective. The common, familiar elements include:

- The detective not being an official Scotland Yard detective
- A character similar to Watson
- The detective having at least one of Sherlock's abilities (deductive reasoning, "scientific" investigation, and so on)
- An equally brilliant but unique method of investigation
- Idiosyncratic personal habits or hobbies
- Lodgings similar to 221b Baker Street

Many of the new detectives from this era are clearly created in the image of Sherlock Holmes. They either blatantly imitate the style and spirit of Arthur Conan Doyle's creation and storytelling, or they self-consciously react against it. They may invert some element of the Holmes canon, or flip the form to make the detective the criminal. But even the most successful of these efforts (and some were *very* successful) come from the Sherlock Holmes mold. It wasn't until the hard-boiled detective stories appeared in the 1920s that the genre of crime fiction invented a form not rooted in the classic model of the Holmes adventures. (For more on the hard-boiled detective style and its relationship to Holmes, see Chapter 10.)

So who are these newcomers, these *other* detectives, these rivals of Sherlock Holmes?

Martin Hewitt

None of Sherlock Holmes's rivals is more clearly an imitation of Holmes than the detective Martin Hewitt (shown in Figure 12-1). Created by writer Arthur Morrison, Hewitt is, like Holmes, not a Scotland Yard detective; he's a lawyer who, like Sherlock, has an amazing faculty for deduction. Ergo, he decides to put his extraordinary ability to use as a private detective.

Just as in the Holmes stories, Hewitt has his own version of 221b. His office is on the Strand, near Charing Cross station. The Strand is perhaps the second street most identified with Holmes after Baker Street. (The Holmes stories were published in *The Strand Magazine,* after all.)

And just in case the reader were to think that Hewitt was too much of a Holmes imitation, author Morrison made his detective a physical and emotional opposite. Holmes was tall; Hewitt was of average height. Holmes was lean; Hewitt was stout. Whereas Holmes had a prickly, uneasy relationship with the police, Hewitt and Scotland Yard got along just fine. And finally, whereas Holmes was moody and prone to episodes of depression, Morrison made sure that Hewitt was happy and cheerful.

Original? Hardly. But to be fair, despite being utterly derivative, the Martin Hewitt stories were very popular, and several of them aren't just good but very good.

Before he turned to detective stories, Morrison earned a living first as a journalist at the *Evening Globe* and then as an author of novels set in the gritty East End of London, where he was born and raised. He began writing his Martin Hewitt mysteries shortly after readers learned that Sherlock Holmes had died at the Reichenbach Falls. With grief-stricken readers longing for more Holmes, the editors of *The Strand Magazine* jumped on the opportunity to publish Morrison's new detective stories, and the adventures of Martin Hewitt soon appeared in the same pages as Holmes's adventures.

Figure 12-1:
Martin Hewitt, illustrated by Sidney Paget, the same illustrator who drew Holmes.

Illustration by Sidney Paget, The Strand Magazine.

Dr. Thorndyke

If Arthur Morrison glommed onto Holmes's celebrated deductive ability in creating his own detective, Martin Hewitt, R. Austin Freeman did something similar with his detective, Dr. John Evelyn Thorndyke. Beginning with the novel *The Red Thumb Mark* in 1907, Freeman's detective appeared in 21 novels and 38 short stories — almost as many tales as Sherlock Holmes.

One of the pioneering aspects of Holmes's approach was the use of science and forensic crime scene analysis when investigating a mystery. This was the angle Freeman seized upon, and ultimately amplified, with Thorndyke. Some commentators on the mystery genre refer to Thorndyke as the "first real scientific detective." This is, of course, nonsense, as Thorndyke wouldn't have existed without Holmes. But what they're getting at is how Freeman elevated this single aspect of the Holmes character to a new level. Indeed, Dr. Thorndyke often reads like a textbook of forensic science.

Freeman describes Thorndyke, shown in Figure 12-2, as "a medical jurispractitioner," meaning a doctor who is trained in both medicine and law and who uses this training to solve crimes. Freeman himself was a doctor who served in West Africa with the Colonial Office, and his training shows. It's true that, compared to Holmes, Thorndyke's forensic methods are explained in much greater technical detail. For instance, Freeman gives his detective a portable crime scene laboratory that he always carries with him and that holds everything he could need.

Despite the technical improvements in this single aspect, Thorndyke is clearly a derivative of Sherlock Holmes. Like Holmes, Thorndyke has his Watson — in this case his devoted assistant, Dr. Jervis (who also usually acts as narrator). He also has his own version of Lestrade, in this case named Superintendent Miller. And like Holmes, Thorndyke has an oft-emphasized residence — his being at 5A King's Bench Walk, Inner Temple. Thorndyke's relationship with the police is on better terms than Holmes's, but, as with Holmes, Thorndyke usually proves the official police wrong.

The "medical jurispractitioner" is, like Holmes, tall, naturally athletic, and a committed bachelor. And like Holmes, Thorndyke has an encyclopedic knowledge in an astonishing array of topics. Finally, the Thorndyke stories follow a loose pattern, just as the Holmes stories do. A crime is brought to the attention of Thorndyke at 5A King's Bench Walk, and he hears the details over cigars. He then seizes on some thread to follow in the tale, concocts a scientific investigation, and lays out his results.

One innovation that's clearly original is Freeman's creation of the "inverted" detective story. In this form, the first half of the story outlines the actual commission of the crime, including who the criminal is. The second half of the tale is the detailed investigation by Thorndyke.

All in all, though enjoyable and in one or two instances innovative, the Thorndyke stories are a bit bloodless and clinical. This isn't to say that they aren't entertaining, but they sure aren't Sherlock Holmes.

Figure 12-2:
Dr.
Thorndyke
(center)
photograph-
ing a crime
scene.

Dixon Druce

After *The Strand Magazine* lost Sherlock Holmes at the Reichenbach Falls,
the editors churned through a number of imitative replacements. One of the
more popular Holmes stand-ins was detective Dixon Druce, distinguished not
so much by his originality (the character didn't have much of that) but by the
fact that he was created by one of the few successful women mystery writers
working at the time, L. T. Meade.

Of course, just a few decades later, women mystery writers became
commonplace and eventually began to dominate the field. (For example,
there's Agatha Christie's Hercule Poirot and Dorothy Sayers's Lord Peter
Wimsey, both admittedly inspired by Sherlock Holmes.) But to her credit, L.
T. Meade was a prolific author of crime fiction all the way back in the 1890s.
After appearing serially in *The Strand Magazine,* the adventures of Dixon
Druce were published in a volume entitled *The Sorceress of the Strand.*

Dixon Druce was the manager of Werner's Agency, "the Solveney Inquiry Agency for all British Trade." Like Holmes, he was unmarried and had his own personal Watson in the form of Eric Vandeleur, old friend and police surgeon for the Westminster district. However, unlike Watson, Vandeleur isn't the author of the stories, as Dixon Druce narrates in the first person.

Professor Augustus S. F. X. Van Dusen

Perhaps no character in all of detective fiction has a longer name than Professor Augustus S. F. X. Van Dusen, PhD, LLD, FRS, MD, otherwise known as the "thinking machine." Created by the writer Jacques Futrelle, Van Dusen has the distinction of being the only American in this roster of Sherlockian rivals. Futrelle was born in Georgia and began as a sportswriter for the *Atlanta Journal.* He worked his way through a number of newspapers in the ensuing years, and in 1905, while he was at the *Boston American,* he created Van Dusen. The first story was "The Problem of Cell 13."

Don't let Futrelle's American citizenship fool you into believing his detective doesn't belong in this discussion. Professor Van Dusen's main claim to fame is his relentless use of logic to solve a mystery. And of course, he has his own Watson, in the person of his good friend Hutchinson Hatch.

Jacques Futrelle also holds a special place in history beyond his literary creation. While in Europe, Futrelle booked passage home on the maiden voyage of the RMS *Titanic.* Despite being a first-class passenger, Futrelle, after getting his wife into a lifeboat, stayed behind, perishing when the ill-fated ship sank.

Max Carrados

It was 1914 and author Ernest Bramah had decided to write his own detective stories. Holmes was still appearing in *The Strand Magazine* (in fact, *The Valley of Fear* was enjoying its run that year), and the big question for Bramah was how to distinguish his detective from *the* detective, Sherlock Holmes. As I mention previously, other authors chose to emphasize certain aspects of Holmes's character, such as deduction or forensic science. Bramah chose to go the route of the peculiar quirk — in his case, he chose to make his detective blind!

Despite this seemingly debilitating condition (for a detective, at least), Max Carrados, Bramah's creation, still betrays the influence of Holmes on his creator. As usual, Carrados has a sidekick/collaborator in the Watson role. In these stories, it's Carlyle, an ex-lawyer who now runs their detective agency.

And Bramah's detective has his own set of amazing abilities. His remaining senses are so developed that many times, others don't even realize he's blind. For instance, Carrados's sense of touch is so refined that he can read print by touch and has mastered the typewriter. And like Holmes, he's a smoker (for him, it's fine cigars).

While Holmes uses his powers of observation and deduction, Carrados employs his powers of *perception*. Just as Holmes repeatedly admonishes Watson that anyone could, with practice, develop similar abilities, Carrados uses information gathered through his heightened senses.

The adventures of Max Carrados were collected into four volumes, spanning 1914 to 1934. They show how far authors were beginning to push the Sherlock Holmes model in creating their own detectives.

Carnacki the ghost finder

You can find another example of stretching the form in English fantasy writer William Hope Hodgson's detective, Thomas Carnacki. Carnacki, a detective of supernatural phenomenon, starred in six short stories that appeared in *The Idler* magazine and *The New Magazine* beginning in 1910. They were later collected as a book under the title *Carnacki the Ghost-Finder,* published in 1913.

Like the Holmes stories, the Carnacki stories include a Watson figure, and author Hodgson gave him the sound-alike name of Dodgson. Dodgson, like Watson, narrates the stories of his remarkable friend. And in keeping with the form, Carnacki has his own version of 221b, his being a flat in Cheyne Walk, Chelsea.

Though it may seem weird to equate a ghost-hunting detective with the ultra-rational Sherlock Holmes (who flatly stated, "No ghosts need apply!"), Carnacki is simply going a few steps beyond where the canon occasionally went. In several stories, it appears that Holmes and Watson have stumbled into a supernatural situation. "The Devil's Foot," "The Sussex Vampire," and *The Hound of the Baskervilles* are fraught with what seems to be paranormal evil. For some readers, that the solutions to these stories always end up being explained by earthly causes may have been a disappointment. Hodgson's ghost-detecting Carnacki takes the whole concept one step further.

The old man in the corner

In "The Greek Interpreter," Holmes reveals to Watson that he has a brother named Mycroft Holmes. In broaching the subject of his brother, Sherlock explains that Mycroft's gifts of observation and deduction are even greater than his own. When Watson asks why he isn't an even greater detective than Sherlock, Holmes explains that Mycroft has no ambition and no energy — that for Mycroft it's just a mental exercise. His brother is just too lazy to run around looking for clues or to track down suspects. He sums up Mycroft's ambition by saying, "If the art of the detective began and ended in reasoning from an armchair, my brother would be the greatest criminal agent that ever lived." And thus was born the concept of the "armchair detective."

Baroness Emmuska Orczy, the British author and playwright better known for her immortal character, the Scarlet Pimpernel, created her own version of the armchair detective known as "the old man in the corner" (see Figure 12-3).

Sitting endlessly in the corner of a London tea shop, the old man in the corner pushes the Mycroft Holmes model to its limit. By relying on the gruesome and sensationalized crime accounts in the newspapers, the old man uses Holmes-like deduction to deduce the solutions to a variety of crimes, ranging from blackmail to murder.

Though the old man is more Mycroft than Sherlock, the stories have a (sort of) Watson character in the person of Miss Polly Burton. The first six stories (published in 1901 in the *Royal Magazine*) were narrated in the third person. Polly is a female journalist who just happens to frequent the old man's tea shop. She and the old man usually discuss a crime, and in the course of their conversation, the old man solves the mystery. But in the next seven stories, published a year later, Polly is the narrator of the stories, stepping into a more Watson-like role. Additionally, the tea shop serves as a pseudo-221b, offering a familiar and regular venue in which the characters live and act.

Though all this is pretty derivative, Orczy's one true innovation is that no villain is ever found guilty or brought to justice, an occurrence that only happens occasionally in the Holmes adventures.

The experiences of Loveday Brooke, lady detective

A host of imitators and rivals swept into the void that Holmes's supposed death in 1893 left behind. The Great Detective, even in death, cast a long shadow, and his successors were, for decades, merely offering up variations on Sherlock's theme. One of the earliest rivals to appear was also, at least on the surface, one of the most different. But first impressions can be deceiving.

Figure 12-3:
The old man
in the
corner.

Loveday Brooke, lady detective, was the creation of British author Catherine Louisa Pirkis. Pirkis had authored both short stories and novels prior to 1894, but it's Loveday Brooke that she's remembered for to this day.

The seven stories featuring this early female detective began in February 1893, ten months *before* the death of Sherlock Holmes. They were published in *The Ludgate Monthly* magazine. The following year, they were collected into book form as *The Experiences of Loveday Brooke, Lady Detective.*

Other female detectives were around at this time, but most of them relied on good looks and "feminine intuition," and most are entirely forgotten. Loveday Brooke was different. When investigating a crime, Loveday relies on logic and observation, just like her famous male colleague, Sherlock Holmes.

While maintaining a youthful appearance, Loveday Brooke is past 30, unmarried, and considered by Victorian standards to be a spinster. But this maturity and life experience give her tools to be a good detective: "For five or six years she had drudged away patiently in the lower walks of her profession; then chance, or to speak more precisely, an intricate criminal case, had introduced her to the notice of the experienced head of the flourishing detective agency in Lynch court. He quickly found out the stuff she was made of, and threw her in the way of better class work."

Loveday is described as rather plain in appearance. "She was not tall, she was not short; she was not dark, she was not fair; she was neither handsome nor ugly. Her features were altogether non-descript," giving her a sort of invisibility in society that she uses as a detective. Like Holmes, she often used disguises, passing herself off as a nurse, a governess, or some other anonymous role, allowing her to gain the confidence of household servants and to gather vital clues. She's described by her employer, Mr. Ebenezer Dyer, as "the most sensible and practical woman I ever met." He goes on to say that "she has a clear, shrewd brain, unhampered by any hard-and-fast theories." Finally, and in his opinion most importantly, "she has so much common sense that it amounts to genius — positively to genius."

And like Holmes, she makes deductions based on careful observation of clues and crime scenes. Her Sherlockian influence is seen in her examination of furniture, impressions in the grass, and ashes in the fireplace, as well as her frequent disagreements with the official police's evidence interpretation.

Loveday Brooke was indeed a female variation of the Sherlockian detective model, but she was more than that. Brooke paved the way for other women detectives over the years, including the next one on our list, Lady Molly of Scotland Yard.

Lady Molly of Scotland Yard

The old man in the corner, which I describe earlier, wasn't the only detective created by the Baroness Orczy. In addition to her armchair detective, the baroness also created Molly Robertson-Kirk, better known as Lady Molly of Scotland Yard.

Orczy's heroine first appeared in 1910 in the book *Lady Molly of Scotland Yard* and was contemporaneous with the ongoing adventures of Sherlock Holmes. And like her predecessor, Loveday Brooke, Lady Molly relied on her intelligence and deductive ability. However, she is perhaps the least successful of the Holmes rivals. Like most of her fictional feminine contemporaries, she usually solved the case because she was able recognize evidence of a domestic nature that was alien to the men of that era. Despite acting independently and successfully as a detective, at the end of the book, when her case is complete, she leaves Scotland Yard for marriage.

One of the First Antiheroes: A. J. Raffles

J. Raffles, the "amateur cracksman," was the creation of Ernest William ("Willie") Hornung (1866–1921). Hornung is perhaps best known to the followers of Sherlock Holmes as Sir Arthur Conan Doyle's brother-in-law, having married Doyle's sister. Before becoming a professional author, Hornung was a journalist with a worldly personality and dapper manner. Hornung's relationship with his brother-in-law was a turbulent one. Nevertheless, Hornung acknowledges Doyle's detective as the inspiration for his own literary creation in the dedication in the first Raffles book, *The Amateur Cracksman.* The dedication reads, "To A.C.D. This Form of Flattery."

The three collections of Raffles short stories are *The Amateur Cracksman, The Black Mask* (sometimes known simply as *Raffles*), and *A Thief in the Night.* Later, Hornung added a final Raffles novel, *Mr. Justice Raffles.* As a testament to the character's enduring popularity, just like the Holmes tales, the Raffles stories have remained in print since their original publication.

The adventures of A. J. Raffles, the amateur cracksman, are an important set of crime and mystery stories not only for their fine writing and high adventure but also for their undeniable link to Sherlock Holmes, amateur detective. By taking the Sherlockian model and turning it on its head, Hornung created a dark mirror of the Great Detective, as well as his most memorable rival.

The amateur cracksman: Standing the Holmes stories on their head

Hornung's stories turn the Sherlock Holmes detective stories on their head by taking the form and utterly inverting it. Instead of a gifted detective, the protagonist is a master thief. Just as Doyle took pains to distinguish Holmes from his fellow detectives (both official and private) by referring to him as a "consulting detective," Raffles is called the "amateur cracksman" (see Figure 12-4), setting him apart from lower-class professional criminals.

In Victorian and Edwardian society, it was better to be an amateur. If your pursuit, whatever it was, was an avocation rather than a vocation, it showed you were wealthy enough to do it by choice rather than necessity. Thus, Raffles is the upper crust of burglars.

Just as Holmes marked a major shift in crime fiction, in his own inverted way, so did Raffles. Living an upper-class life, being a well-known cricket player (amateur, of course), and having a public school background gave a completely different perspective to the portrayal of crime in fiction. Crime was rampant in Victorian and Edwardian London, and it was this criminality that helped give rise to the popularity of the crime fiction genre. It felt good to read stories where the thieves and burglars and murderers got caught. But with Hornung's character, suddenly readers found themselves rooting for a crook. Raffles is one of modern literature's first antiheroes.

Raffles has been described by crime fiction historians Chris Steinbrunner and Otto Penzler as "the greatest of all fictional thieves," and *The Armchair Detective* magazine described Raffles as "unquestionably the greatest rogue in detective fiction."

Figure 12-4:
A. J. Raffles, the amateur cracksman.

Just as the Holmes stories first appeared in *The Strand Magazine* prior to publication in book form, the adventures of Raffles were originally serialized in *Cassell's Magazine,* with the first set of stories running between June and November of 1898. The series ran under the title *In the Chains of Crime.* Given the moral climate of late-Victorian England, the magazine felt it needed to present the stories as examples of the evil of crime.

They weren't the only ones conflicted about the tales. Doyle himself felt that Hornung's stories set a bad example for young readers and that the gentleman burglar was an unsatisfactory role model. As Holmes and Watson often reflect the character of Doyle, Raffles, to some degree, reflects his creator as well. This isn't to say that Hornung was a criminal, but just as Raffles is the mirror image of Holmes, Hornung was in many ways the opposite of Doyle in personality.

Some modern-day authors have written new adventures of Raffles in which they've reformed the character, making him commit criminal acts only when a greater good is at stake. However, as originally conceived by Hornung, Raffles is undoubtedly a criminal who's in it purely for the money, or sometimes just for the thrill of it. Even modern writers feel guilty enjoying the adventures of the amateur cracksman, seduced by his charisma and personality. Raffles's partner, Harry "Bunny" Manders, describes him as having "the subtle power of making himself irresistible at will. He was beyond comparison the most masterful man whom I have ever known." It sounds like Watson describing Sherlock Holmes!

Raffles's popularity

Many readers will be astonished to know that, at his height, Raffles was as popular as Sherlock Holmes. But if you read the stories you'll understand why. Though they're clearly imitative of the Sherlockian canon, the stories themselves are exceptionally well written.

The concept of the amateur cracksman or gentleman burglar became a well-known one in Victorian and Edwardian England. During this time, crime was rampant, and the growing middle-class felt that society was under siege by social disorder.

The popular magazines of the day were full of both true-life and fictional accounts of crime and punishment. For example, in 1894, *The Strand Magazine* ran a four-part series titled *Crimes and Criminals.* The second installment, "Burglars and Burgling," gave a fully illustrated survey of burgling tools and techniques (see Figure 12-5), as well as a list of the most famous burglars in London history. Raffles would have been right at home. Later, *The Strand* contained an article titled "Does Raffles Exist? or The Myth of the Gentleman Burglar." It was written by real-life detective M. Alphonse Bertillon, who pioneered the use of fingerprints in crime detection. It goes to show that, at least for the years Hornung was writing his stories, the *idea* of Raffles was as strong as Sherlock Holmes.

Figure 12-5:
Actual bur-
glar tools:
skeleton
keys (on the
left) and a
black silk
mask.

The detective versus the cracksman

A. J. Raffles and Bunny Manders are clearly modeled on Sherlock Holmes and Dr. Watson. Despite being on opposite sides of the law, the similarities between the Sherlockian canon and the Raffles stories (which number only 27 tales), as well as the characters of Holmes and Raffles, are so striking that it's instructive to compare their similarities and differences.

Individual traits

Raffles and Holmes have individual traits that are strikingly similar. One of the most obvious is Raffles's use of tobacco. The aristocratic, cricket-playing amateur cracksman has a preference for Sullivan cigarettes. Like Holmes, Raffles is an enthusiastic user of tobacco. In the story "The Ides of March," to calm a nearly hysterical Bunny, Raffles pushes him into a chair and says, "Sit down, my good fellow, and have a cigarette to sooth your nerves." Raffles, like Holmes, often smoked while deep in thought, working out his latest "case."

Also like Holmes, Raffles is a master of disguise, has a knack for deductive reasoning, frequents Turkish baths, has a fondness for using telegrams, and is alternately patronizing and rude or affectionate and kind to his friend.

Arch enemies and sidekicks

Just like Holmes, Raffles has his own enemy on the opposite side of the law (in his case a police detective) who pursues him relentlessly after he sets his mind to it.

And, as Holmes is assisted by Watson, Raffles is helped in his cases by his faithful biographer Bunny Manders. Both Manders and Watson are the intellectual inferiors to their partners; however, whatever they lack in brains, they make up for in loyalty and companionship. Manders, like Watson, narrates their adventures in the first person.

The residence

As any good Sherlock-inspired creation does, Raffles has a residence clearly identified and described, standing in as his version of 221b Baker Street. Raffles's rooms are in the Albany, a building of fashionable bachelor apartments in London. Manders describes the rooms as having "the right amount of negligence and the right amount of taste," having "a carved bookcase, with every shelf in a litter." He adds that he found reproductions of famous paintings on the walls, leading him to conclude that "the man might have been a minor poet." Although the address is more socially upscale, the rooms at the Albany are used precisely as they are in the Holmes stories — to begin and end the adventure in familiar surroundings, to see glimpses of the protagonists in a comfortable setting, and to give a subconscious base from which the characters operate. The Albany has the same kind of familiar, welcoming atmosphere as Baker Street.

The Albany is a real place, and over the years, it has had such famous residents as the poet Lord Byron and Prime Minister William Gladstone.

The big picture: Similar story arcs

Not only do Raffles and Bunny mirror Holmes and Watson, but the entire *cycle* of the Raffles stories is also an imitation of the Holmes saga. The following points apply to both sets of stories:

- ✓ Desperate financial circumstances bring the two partners together in the first story.

- ✓ It is the biographer's (Watson/Bunny) first experience of this kind, while the subject of the stories (Holmes/Raffles) is obviously experienced at the sort of adventure that follows. As the stories progress, a natural partnership, as well as a friendship, develops.

- ✓ The first round of stories end with the hero's nemesis pursuing them to the continent. The series supposedly ends when the hero plunges into a body of water and is presumed dead.

- ✓ After a period of mourning, the biographer (Watson/Bunny) discovers that the hero (Holmes/Raffles) is really alive and in hiding, after the hero appears in disguise before dramatically revealing himself to his friend.

- ✓ They resume their partnership, and the series continues, with the later stories being told well after the hero has discontinued his adventures.

- ✓ The last recorded adventure has the hero serving his country nobly during a time of war.

Holmes's Enduring Influence

Of course, Arthur Conan Doyle's creation continued to inspire imitations well after the Sherlock Holmes canon was closed. In fact, it's been suggested that every fictional detective owes *something* to Holmes. Although they're entertaining, none of the rivals I mention in this chapter ever really achieved true greatness, undoubtedly because of the fact that they really were, in the end, just imitations.

Others came along later in the 1920s that transcended the inspiration of Holmes to become legends of the genre in their own right. In the following sections I discuss some of these detectives.

Lord Peter Wimsey

His full name is Lord Peter Death Bredon Wimsey. He's the hero of Dorothy L. Sayers's series of novels and short stories in which an upper-class amateur takes up detection as a hobby. Wimsey is, in the first few novels, a sort of high-society clown (at least on the surface), but over the course of the novels, both the character and the plots evolve into something far more mature and compelling.

Of course, Wimsey has his Watson. Early on it's his manservant, Bunter. Later, after he falls in love with detective writer Harriet Vane, Harriet begins to take on the role. Ultimately, Harriet herself begins to operate independently as a crime investigator.

Dorothy Sayers is on record as having been inspired by Sherlock Holmes. In fact, she's famous as a Sherlockian, having deduced that John H. Watson's middle name is "Hamish" (Scottish for James).

Father Brown

G. K. Chesterton, the English novelist, journalist, and Catholic apologist, is also the creator of the fictional detective Father Brown. Chesterton, like Sayers, was a Sherlockian and admirer of the detective story. Among his countless essays and articles, Chesterton wrote several on Sherlock Holmes.

Father Brown is a short, rather featureless Catholic priest whose dumpy clothes and umbrella mask an amazing ability to look into the human heart. And though Holmes couldn't, on the surface, be further from a priest, the two detectives have similarities (refer to Chapter 11 for a discussion of Holmes's religious views). Like Holmes, Father Brown has his own master criminal to deal with and has his own unique methods of solving crime. But while Holmes's method is based on observation and deduction, Father Brown's is clearly intuitive.

Hercule Poirot

Poirot is the first of the great mystery writer Agatha Christie's legendary detectives (the second is Miss Marple). Poirot starred in an astounding 33 novels and 51 short stories that Christie wrote between 1920 and 1975. Poirot remains enormously popular to this day — so much so that, like the Holmes adventures, the Poirot stories have been adapted into plays, feature films, and TV shows many, many times.

Christie is on record admitting that Sherlock Holmes was an inspiration for Hercule Poirot, saying in her autobiography that, in the early days, when she invented the little Belgian detective, "I was still writing in the Sherlock Holmes tradition — eccentric detective, stooge assistant, with a Lestrade-type Scotland Yard detective, Inspector Japp." However, Poirot, like Wimsey and Father Brown, outgrew the Holmes tradition and went on to become his own detective.

Part IV
Beyond Baker Street

The 5th Wave   By Rich Tennant

"Ahhh, Mr. Dorfman. Already I can tell you're just the sort of person we're looking for to own a McFee Detective Agency franchise."

In this part . . .

From the beginning, Sherlock Holmes has cast a large shadow, and his influence has been felt far beyond the original stories, and even beyond the printed page. In this part, you see how Holmes has inspired thousands of imitators, both in parody and pastiche. I look at the influence of Holmes on other mystery writers, who created entirely new detectives that resemble Sherlock. I also examine Sherlock Holmes on the stage and screen and look at the character's unprecedented fan following.

Chapter 13

The Sincerest Form of Flattery

The charisma and popularity of Sherlock Holmes spawned a host of detectives stamped out of the Holmes model. These "rival" detectives began showing up even before Holmes "died" at the Reichenbach Falls, but after Holmes was believed dead, his imitators really took off. Most of these new detectives were enjoyable but forgettable, but others went on to become classics of the genre in their own right. (For more on the rivals of Sherlock Holmes, see Chapter 12.)

But running parallel to the creation of new, look-alike detectives was an even stranger, more surprising occurrence — writers began penning their own Sherlock Holmes adventures. This urge for authors to write their own Holmes stories was, like so many other aspects of Sherlock Holmes, an amazing and nearly unprecedented phenomenon, and it's more prominent now than ever before.

In this chapter, I look at the two types of these new Holmes stories — pastiche and parody — and discuss the characteristics unique to each form. Get ready — it's a strange subject!

Two Types of New Tales: Pastiche and Parody

When an author takes pen in hand to write a Sherlock Holmes adventure of his own, this new, unofficial, extra-canonical Sherlockian adventure falls into one of two broad categories: parody and pastiche.

> ✔ In literature, a *parody* is a work in which the characteristics of another author's writing are imitated, mocked, or made to seem ridiculous, especially by applying them to absurd or inappropriate subjects.
>
> ✔ A *pastiche,* on the other hand, is a work — whether literary, artistic, musical, or architectural — that imitates the styles of previous work.

Within five years of Holmes appearing in *The Strand Magazine,* both Sherlockian parody and pastiche began showing up in newspapers, magazines, and even books. With the death of Arthur Conan Doyle in 1930 and the subsequent realization that there would be no further official adventures of Sherlock Holmes, authors began churning out their own versions of Holmes in earnest. Ever since then, new adventures of Holmes have been appearing — beginning as a trickle in the 1890s and growing to a tidal wave by the 21st century.

The Sherlock Holmes pastiche and parody works pioneered the modern phenomenon known as "fan fiction," which, in the 21st century, is a thriving genre most commonly associated with (but certainly not limited to) science fiction and fantasy. Even within this broader genre, Holmes is one of the most popular characters.

Holmes's identifying characteristics proved to be irresistible to both pastiche writers and parodists. In literature, the sheer quantity of this body of writing is utterly unique. Philip K. Jones, a researcher and scholar of the phenomenon of Sherlockian pastiche, has identified approximately 8,000 examples of Holmes parody and pastiche, with more appearing, quite literally, every month.

Whether parody or pastiche, this urge to extend the canon beyond the original 60 stories stems from a simple desire for more Sherlock Holmes stories. Thousands of people — from rank amateurs to established, bestselling authors — have written their own versions of the Great Detective. Sometimes these new tales are wonderful. More often than not, they're terrible! But good or bad, the genre itself remains popular.

Sherlockian Pastiche: The Continuing Adventures of Sherlock Holmes

When a pastiche author decides to write his own Holmes tale, he can follow two possible paths: relate one of the many untold tales that Watson refers to within the canon but chose not to write himself, or construct a wholly new tale.

✔ **The untold tales:** Doyle built into the canon itself a motivation and opportunity for Sherlockian pastiche. Watson says that "somewhere in the vaults of the bank of Cox and Co., at Charing Cross, there is a travel-worn and battered tin dispatch-box with my name, John H. Watson, M. D., Late Indian Army, painted upon the lid. It is crammed with papers, nearly all of which are records of cases to illustrate the curious problems which Mr. Sherlock Holmes had at various times to examine."

This treasure trove of a dispatch box has become legendary. Over the course of the stories, Watson refers to over 100 cases of Holmes that, for one reason or another, Watson chose not to write about. Though Watson may have passed on these adventures, the bottomless dispatch box has offered opportunities for writers wanting to take a crack at these untold tales.

✔ **The brand new stories:** The second option is to simply write a completely original Sherlock Holmes adventure. Since 1893, hundreds, if not thousands, of writers have done exactly that. Over time, the style of these new tales has evolved beyond strict pastiche to explore plots, locations, eras, and even other genres of fiction that Doyle never dreamed of.

The many forms of pastiche

Five basic categories, more or less, fall under the umbrella of Sherlockian pastiche. The following sections have them covered.

The classic Watsonian style

Within this first category are works that adhere to a strict interpretation, meaning a Holmes story written in the style of the originals. The stories are set in the proper Victorian (or Edwardian) time period, and Watson is the narrator. Although some pastiche efforts are novels, generally, the most successful examples of the classic pastiche are short stories, which happens to be the case with the original canon as well.

You can find countless examples of new Holmes stories written in this fashion, but perhaps the best examples are by Denis O. Smith. His short story "The Purple Hand" is nearly perfect. Look for it in *The Further Adventures of Sherlock Holmes,* edited by Richard Lancelyn Green (Penguin).

Ten rules for writing Sherlockian pastiche

In 1976, historian and scholar Jacques Barzun offered ten rules for writing serious Sherlock Holmes pastiches. For all you budding authors out there, ignore them at your peril!

1. No shilly-shallying between pastiche and parody.

2. Whether in pastiche or parody, no fancy writing; plain language is safest.

3. No recourse merely to the well-known tricks of speech and action in the original.

4. No incessant effort to squeeze comedy out of every remark or incident.

5. No gross or grotesque proper names.

6. No expressions of recent coinage, high or low (that is, no anachronisms).

7. No technical terms thrown about needlessly.

8. No pastiche without the Holmes touch (for example, remarks such as, "My charges are upon a fixed scale; I do not alter them save when I remit them altogether.").

9. No pastiche that degrades Holmes through any piece of feeble or patently false reasoning.

10. No pastiche without at least one Sherlockismus, the equivalent of one truffle in each pâté de foie gras. (*Sherlockismus:* Any of several kinds of memorable quotes or phrases attributed to, or characteristic of, Sherlock Holmes.)

Holmes meets history

Beginning in the mid-1970s, following the tremendous success of the bestselling pastiche novel *The Seven-Per-Cent Solution,* a new trend in Sherlockian pastiche appeared. *The Seven-Per-Cent Solution,* by Nicholas Meyer, told an alternative version of "The Final Problem" which has the fictional Sherlock Holmes joining forces with the very real, historical Sigmund Freud (you find out more about this landmark work in the later section "The Sherlockian pastiche hall of fame"). Meyer's plot device was a unique innovation, and in a short time other authors were pairing Holmes with other contemporary historical characters. It wasn't long before what was an innovation had turned into a gimmick, as a parade of historical characters encountered the Great Detective.

In this now large body of stories, Holmes has encountered Teddy Roosevelt, Harry Houdini, Jacques Futrelle, Rasputin, Lillie Langtry, Benjamin Disraeli, Albert Einstein, Jack the Ripper, Bram Stoker, Gilbert and Sullivan, and virtually every member of royalty and every major British politician. And that's merely the tip of the iceberg.

Sherlock Holmes versus the Ripper

In the alternative universe of Sherlockian pastiche, Sherlock Holmes, the world's greatest detective, and Jack the Ripper, the most famous serial killer of them all, have squared off against each other many times. Perhaps it's only natural — if Holmes really had been working in Victorian London during that autumn of terror, surely he would have brought the Whitechapel killer to justice. That's certainly the belief of pastiche authors over the last 50 years, for Holmes and the Ripper have been paired many, many times. Some of the more notable examples include

✔ *Sherlock Holmes of Baker Street,* by William S. Baring-Gould (1962). This biography of Holmes offers one of the earliest accounts of Sherlock's involvement with the Ripper.

✔ *A Study in Terror,* by Ellery Queen (1966). This is actually the novelization of the film by the same name.

✔ *The Return of Moriarty,* by John Gardner (1974). Jack the Ripper features into the plot of this novel centered on Professor Moriarty.

✔ *The Last Sherlock Holmes Story,* by Michael Dibdin (1978). This disturbing book chronicles the investigation by Holmes and Watson into the Ripper crimes. You won't believe the ending of this one!

✔ *An East Wind Coming: Sherlock Holmes and Jack the Ripper,* by Arthur Byron (1979). The advertising blurb says it all in this science-fiction adventure: "An immortal Sherlock Holmes. A deathless Jack the Ripper! In a fantasy duel through the corridors of time." Hmm. . . .

✔ *The Mycroft Memoranda,* by Ray Walsh (1984). This novel sets out to solve two of the most perplexing riddles of the Victorian era. First, who was Jack the Ripper? And second, why didn't Sherlock Holmes hunt down the killer?

✔ *The Whitechapel Horrors,* by Edward B. Hanna (1993). This book blends Holmes and Watson into a very detailed, factually accurate account of the Ripper murders.

✔ *Bloodguilty,* by Raymond Thor (1997). A modern-day writer is transported back to the London of Jack the Ripper in 1888. This book gives details of the Ripper crimes and posits that Holmes actually existed.

✔ *Chapel Noir: A Novel of Suspense Featuring Sherlock Holmes, Irene Adler, and Jack the Ripper,* by Carole Nelson Douglas (2002). When Irene Adler (the woman from "A Scandal in Bohemia") investigates a brutal murder in Paris, she comes to believe it's the work of London's Ripper. She also finds that she's in competition with Holmes. Carole Nelson Douglas followed this with a sequel in 2003, *Castle Rouge: A Novel of Suspense Featuring Sherlock Holmes, Irene Adler, and Jack the Ripper.* Altogether, Douglas's Irene Adler series numbers eight volumes.

✔ *Sherlock Holmes: The Unauthorized Biography,* by Nick Rennison (2005). Another Holmes biography revealing Sherlock's contact with Jack the Ripper.

✔ *The Shadow of Reichenbach Falls,* by John R. King (2008). In this story, Professor Moriarty's wife is a victim of Jack the Ripper.

(continued)

(continued)

> ✔ *Dust and Shadow: An Account of the Ripper Killings,* by Lyndsay Faye (2009). One of the best Holmes/Ripper pairings is an account of Sherlock's attempt to hunt down the Ripper. Faye's Sherlock Holmes uses a Whitechapel streetwalker as an assistant and relies on Watson after surviving a terrible attack by none other than Jack the Ripper himself!
>
> Beyond this list, over 30 additional novels and short stories connect the canon to Jack the Ripper, as well as 6 Sherlockian parodies. Additionally, Sherlock Holmes has investigated the Whitechapel murders twice on the big screen, in *A Study in Terror* (1965) and *Murder by Decree* (1979). (For more about these films, see Chapter 14.)
>
> The pairing of the legendary detective and the legendary serial killer seems irresistible to would-be Watsons, guaranteeing repeated rematches in the years ahead.

In addition to having Holmes encounter historic characters, writers also began concocting plots placing Holmes at major historical events. Holmes became sort of a literary version of Woody Allen's film character, Zelig, showing up in an amazing number of historical situations. A fan of the Sherlockian pastiche discovers Holmes's involvement in the notorious Lizzie Borden murder case in Fall River, Massachusetts; the investigation of the John F. Kennedy assassination (yeah, I know — the timeline is all wrong!); the sinking of the Titanic (where he and Watson supposedly went down with the ship); and the overthrow of the czar by the Communists, to name just a few of the dozens of examples.

Zelig is a character from the 1983 Woody Allen film of the same name. Leonard Zelig is known as "the human chameleon" because of his ability to blend into whatever social situation he finds himself in. In the film, Zelig shows up in a variety of situations, from a party at the home of F. Scott Fitzgerald to sitting behind Adolf Hitler at a rally in Nazi Germany. Wherever you looked, there was Leonard Zelig in the background.

Variations on this category also brought a number of books featuring Arthur Conan Doyle himself as a character, as well as adventures placing the Great Detective in improbable places such as Minnesota and Mexico!

Sherlock Holmes saves London/the British Empire/the world . . . take your pick!

A number of Sherlockian novels don't concern themselves with cases as mundane as stolen jewels or murder. No, in these adventures, Holmes's investigations have much larger consequences.

Perhaps no better example falls into this category than *The Earthquake Machine* by Austin Mitchelson and Nicholas Utechin, published in 1976. Holmes and Watson are directed by Mycroft to infiltrate a group of revolutionaries. The trail lands them in the court of the tsar of Russia, where they discover the existence of an atomic bomb! When the inventor (guess who) threatens to use it on London, Holmes races to evacuate the city and disarm the bomb. This story has so many features found in Sherlockian pastiche that it's almost a category-buster! It has historical figures (Karl Marx, Winston Churchill), a science-fiction slant with the atom bomb, and, most important for this category, Holmes saving London, the British Empire, heck . . . maybe even the world!

The supernatural/sci-fi Sherlock

Though Holmes himself declared, "This agency stands flat-footed upon the ground, and there it must remain . . . no ghosts need apply," this hasn't stopped the many pastiche writers from giving Holmes cases supernatural or science-fiction overtones.

One of the most popular and compelling scenarios pits Sherlock Holmes against Count Dracula. The count and the detective have been brought together at least a dozen times in short stories and novels, and that doesn't even include comic books. The most noteworthy examples include

- *The Holmes-Dracula File,* by Fred Saberhagen (1978). Who knew that the untold tale of the giant rat of Sumatra had anything to do with Dracula?

- *Sherlock Holmes vs. Dracula: The Adventure of the Sanguinary Count,* by Loren D. Estleman (1978). Despite the lurid title, this is one of the best examples in this category, seamlessly blending the canon with Bram Stoker's novel.

- *The Dracula Caper,* by Simon Hawke (1988). Here you get both science fiction *and* the supernatural! Arthur Conan Doyle joins forces with Bram Stoker and H. G. Wells, battling not only Dracula but also vampires from the future.

- *Anno Dracula,* by Kim Newman (1992). In this mesmerizing, supernatural, alternative history novel, Queen Victoria is married to Count Dracula. Vampires have become high society, and vampirism is fashionable. And Sherlock Holmes has been sent to a concentration camp.

- *Séance for a Vampire,* by Fred Saberhagen (1994). When Holmes vanishes after attending a séance, a desperate Dr. Watson appeals to Count Dracula for help in finding his friend.

- *The Tangled Skein,* by David Stuart Davies (1995). After a series of mysterious murders, the trail leads to a battle between Holmes and Dracula.

Another popular supernatural and science-fiction encounter occurs when Holmes is paired with the work of American horror, fantasy, and science fiction author H. P. Lovecraft. Lovecraft wrote in the early part of the 20th century, and his weird tales have inspired many writers of the macabre. Lovecraft has a longstanding cult following.

In *Pulptime,* published in 1984, novelist P. H. Cannon tells a story that brings Holmes into contact with Lovecraft as he investigates the case of a missing gangster. The novel is set in 1925 New York, and Harry Houdini makes an appearance as well.

But it's *Shadows Over Baker Street: New Tales of Terror* (published in 2003) that showcases the full marriage of Holmes and Lovecraft. This anthology, edited by Michael Reaves and John Pelan, includes 14 short stories by modern horror writers who all blend the Lovecraft mythos with the Sherlockian canon.

Finally, no discussion of science fiction-tinged pastiche can leave out *Sherlock Holmes's War of the Worlds* by Manly Wade Wellman and Wade Wellman, published in 1975. Written as a sequel to H. G. Wells's *The War of the Worlds,* this story teams Holmes and Watson with another of Doyle's great characters, Professor George Challenger, hero of *The Lost World.* Here, the two great intellects work together to defeat the Martian invasion.

Sherlockian by association

As the term *pastiche* has, at least in the Sherlockian universe, become more elastic, more and more variations have appeared. One of the most interesting includes works of fiction that don't feature Sherlock Holmes himself but are, in plot or character, loaded with the spirit of Baker Street. Holmes looms large in the following stories, which feature everyone from Harry Houdini to Orson Welles to an autistic boy to turn-of-the-century cowboys:

- *The War of the Worlds Mystery,* by Philip Shreffler (Wessex Press, 1998). In this fine novel (as well as in its sequel, *The Twentieth Century Limited Mystery*), the *fans* of Sherlock Holmes solve a crime and get the same treatment as Holmes does — real-life, historic characters and events used as a launching pad for a mystery story. Members of the legendary Sherlock Holmes literary society, the Baker Street Irregulars, get caught up in a perplexing case of murder amid the famous cast of Orson Welles's famous 1938 radio broadcast. (For more on the Baker Street Irregulars and other Holmes societies, see Chapter 15.)

- *The Curious Incident of the Dog in the Night-time,* by Mark Haddon (Doubleday, 2003). With its title taken from a quote by Holmes in the story "Silver Blaze," this award-winning novel tells the story of a 15-year-old boy with autism who is fascinated with Sherlock Holmes and

The Hound of the Baskervilles. When someone kills a neighborhood dog, the boy sets out to solve the mystery of who did it, and along the way he discovers the secret to his dysfunctional family. It's a fine book, and it shows just how the Sherlockian motif can be adapted beyond traditional boundaries.

✔ *The Man from Beyond,* by Gabriel Brownstein (W. W. Norton, 2005). Inspired by the true-life yet contentious friendship between Sir Arthur Conan Doyle and Harry Houdini, this award-winning novel reimagines the consequences of an actual séance held by Doyle and his wife for the celebrated magician. In 1922, Doyle, the world's most famous spiritualist, and his wife Jean, delivered a message from beyond to Houdini. The message was from his late mother. Houdini didn't believe it was true, and the subsequent falling out between the author and the magician caused a fascinating series of events, both in real life and in this novel.

✔ *Holmes on the Range,* by Steve Hockensmith (Thorndike Press, 2006). Set in 1892, this novel introduces detective cowboys Gustav "Old Red" Amlingmeyer and his younger brother, Otto "Big Red" Amlingmeyer. Old Red is obsessed with Sherlock Holmes, having discovered his hero through copies of *The Strand Magazine.* The two brothers act as cowboy versions of Holmes and Watson when they take up "deducifyin." *Holmes on the Range* was nominated for an Edgar Award and is the first in a series of novels featuring the Sherlock-loving Amlingmeyer brothers.

The Sherlockian pastiche hall of fame

Literally thousands upon thousands of new adventures of Sherlock Holmes have been written. And though many, if not most, are forgettable except as examples of the phenomenon in general, a number have stood the test of time by being both historically significant and well written. Though no list could be comprehensive (the sheer volume of Sherlockian pastiche makes it impossible to be comprehensive — entire books have been devoted to the subject), I discuss a number of the most important in the following sections.

The Unique Hamlet: A Hitherto Unchronicled Adventure of Mr. Sherlock Holmes

Vincent Starrett was a distinguished newspaperman, literary critic, poet, mystery writer, and book collector. Starrett is also one of the most important Sherlockians of all time, best-known for his 1933 book *The Private Life of Sherlock Holmes.* This volume helped jump-start the amazing, unprecedented phenomenon of Holmes societies and inspired the unending body of Sherlockian scholarship enjoyed by fans around the world. Starrett was a charter member of the famous Holmes society, the Baker Street Irregulars.

But *The Private Life of Sherlock Holmes* wasn't Starrett's first published Sherlockian effort. In 1920, Starrett wrote *The Unique Hamlet: A Hitherto Unchronicled Adventure of Mr. Sherlock Holmes* and had it privately printed. The plot deals with Holmes and Watson investigating a missing 1604 edition of Shakespeare's play, which includes an inscription by Shakespeare himself. Many Sherlockians regard *The Unique Hamlet* as the finest pastiche ever written.

The Solar Pons books

When Wisconsin teenager August Derleth learned in 1928 that there would be no further Sherlock Holmes stories, he decided to do something about it. Derleth sat down and created Solar Pons, the "Sherlock Holmes of Praed Street." Pons's resemblance to Holmes is no accident — like Holmes, he smokes a pipe, wears an Inverness cape and deerstalker hat, and is a master of observation and deduction. He's aided by his friend, Dr. Parker, who shares rooms with him at 7B Praed Street. They even have a long-suffering landlady named Mrs. Johnson. The Solar Pons adventures are set in the late 1920s and number 70 stories published over a number of volumes, including one novel.

The spirit of Baker Street lives in Derleth's affectionate stories, and indeed, so successful is he that Pons has gone on to gather his own body of devoted followers, the Praed Street Irregulars.

The Misadventures of Sherlock

By 1944, enough Sherlockian parodies and pastiches had been written that it was time to publish a best-of collection. This brainwave came to Ellery Queen, who put together what is still one of the best collections of this type of Sherlockian writing. Queen titled the book *The Misadventures of Sherlock Holmes* (Little, Brown and Company), and the contributors are a who's who of famous names, including John Kendrick Bangs, Robert Barr, James M. Barrie, Anthony Berkeley, Anthony Boucher, Agatha Christie, August Derleth, Bret Harte, O. Henry, Maurice Leblanc, R. C. Lehmann, Stuart Palmer, Ellery Queen, Vincent Starrett, Mark Twain, Manly Wade Wellman, Carolyn Wells, and many others.

Unfortunately, Doyle's estate didn't see the book as the tribute to their late father that it was intended to be. Viewing it instead as a copyright infringement, the estate had the book suppressed, but not before some copies made it out. It isn't impossible to find a copy, and reading *The Misadventures of Sherlock Holmes* shows how good Sherlockian parody and pastiche can be.

Ellery Queen is the pseudonym of Frederic Dannay and Manfred Bennington Lee, two American cousins who are giants in the genre of detective and crime fiction. Dannay and Lee also used the name for their own fictional detective.

The Exploits of Sherlock Holmes

For well over a decade after Doyle's death, the Doyle estate (which was managed by Doyle's sons Dennis and Adrian Conan Doyle) resisted the idea of any writer presuming to author Sherlock Holmes stories. In 1944 the sons successfully quashed the release of Ellery Queen's *The Misadventures of Sherlock Holmes,* but ten years later the financial lure of Holmes and a market for officially sanctioned Holmes stories had them rethink their position. Thus came *The Exploits of Sherlock Holmes* (Random House), written by Adrian Conan Doyle and John Dickson Carr (a famous author of detective fiction).

Doyle and Carr had already worked together when Adrian commissioned the mystery author to write the official biography of Sir Arthur. The result was a serviceable biography that, thanks to the heavy hand of Adrian, bordered on hagiography. Nonetheless, the book sold well, and so now it was time for them to officially cowrite a new set of Sherlockian pastiche.

The 12 short stories that comprise *The Exploits of Sherlock Holmes* were first serialized in *Collier's* magazine and then collected and issued in book form in 1954. Among Sherlockians, the reputation of the stories is only so-so, primarily because of animosity between the Doyle estate and the Baker Street Irregulars. But as pastiches go, *The Exploits of Sherlock Holmes* isn't bad.

The Seven-Per-Cent Solution: Being a Reprint from the Reminiscences of John H. Watson, MD

No Sherlockian pastiche is more important, and more influential, than Nicholas Meyer's 1974 novel, *The Seven-Per-Cent Solution* (E. P. Dutton). You could also argue that no Sherlockian pastiche is better. This landmark title landed at the top of the *New York Times* Best Seller list and stayed there for nearly a year. Virtually every Sherlock Holmes pastiche published since 1974 owes something to *The Seven-Per-Cent Solution.*

The Seven-Per-Cent Solution established many conventions of modern Holmes pastiche that are taken for granted today. However, they were fresh and new in 1974. For instance, the novel begins by explaining that what follows is a lost manuscript of Dr. John H. Watson. Watson is even credited as author. Virtually every pastiche since has come with an explanation of the story's origin, usually mimicking the lost-manuscript-recently-found convention of *The Seven-Per-Cent Solution.*

It was the first major pastiche to wholeheartedly indulge in revisionism, stating that *The Seven-Per-Cent Solution* is the true story of what happened in Holmes's deadly encounter with Professor Moriarty. Moriarty himself is cast in an entirely different light as well. According to Meyer, "The Final Problem" and "The Empty House" were fabrications by Watson to cover what really happened.

It was also the first Sherlockian pastiche to face head-on Holmes's addiction to cocaine (a cold dash of reality that didn't sit well with old-line Sherlockians, who were always in a bit of denial over Holmes's bad habit). Nowadays, Sherlock's drug abuse is a favorite idiosyncrasy that probably gets too much attention, thanks to the path blazed by *The Seven-Per-Cent Solution.*

For all the aforementioned elements, and for the mystery that's woven into the story, *The Seven-Per-Cent Solution* really takes off with its final innovation. Prior to Meyer's book, the idea of pairing Holmes with real-life characters hardly went further than Jack the Ripper. But here, Holmes is brought together with Dr. Sigmund Freud, the revolutionary psychoanalyst who, in the 1890s, was curing cocaine addiction with hypnosis. Meyer's novel has Freud helping Holmes beat his addiction to the deadly drug, and along the way the book provides insight into what makes the eccentric, brilliant detective tick. Ever since *The Seven-Per-Cent Solution,* authors have sent an unending (and increasingly improbable) parade of eminent Victorians through Baker Street.

The Seven-Per-Cent Solution was made into a successful Hollywood film in 1976 (for more on this film, see Chapter 14) and was followed by two sequels, *The West End Horror* and *The Canary Trainer.* But it was *The Seven-Per-Cent Solution* that not only set a new standard for Sherlockian pastiche but also in many ways resuscitated the popularity of Sherlock Holmes.

The Mary Russell novels

Mary Russell is the heroine in a mystery series by award-winning author Laurie R. King. Set in the first two decades of the 20th century, King's series recounts the adventures of Mary Russell and Sherlock Holmes.

The first novel in the series, *The Beekeeper's Apprentice,* appeared in 1994. It tells of a teenage Mary Russell meeting Holmes on the Sussex Downs, where he now lives in retirement. As the middle-aged Sherlock and the teenage Mary get to know each other, he comes to believe that she has what it takes to make a good detective and starts to teach her his methods. Naturally, they eventually find themselves investigating a mystery together.

In the first few books, Holmes is a mentor to the girl, but later in the series, the elderly Holmes actually takes the young Mary Russell as his bride.

Despite the improbability of the romance, or perhaps because of it, King's books have attracted a legion of fans who now write their own pastiches of the series.

Spoofing the Great Detective: The Parodies

Only a very small number of fictional detectives have invited parodying like Sherlock Holmes has. Hard-boiled detectives Philip Marlowe and Sam Spade come to mind, but this probably has more to do with their portrayals in film by Humphrey Bogart than the actual literary works themselves. Agatha Christie's Hercule Poirot ("Haircurler Poirot," "Hercules Popeau") has also been spoofed, but Christie's little Belgian detective is almost a parody in his own right. And of course, Ian Fleming's James Bond 007 has been copied and satirized, again mostly due to his long film career (the Matt Helm series of books and movies, and, more recently, the Austin Powers films.) But you can count these examples on one hand. Not so with Sherlock Holmes.

So what is it about Holmes that inspires writers to keep authoring his continuing adventures, whether serious or comical? The answer is found in the specific traits of both the canon and Holmes's character. Holmes's methods of observation and deduction, his personal habits (smoking, drug use, violin playing, and so on), his cold, aloof manner — all these are powerful lures for aspiring authors and the perfect opportunity for lampooning.

And surely the name "Sherlock Holmes" itself is an inspiration. The peculiar construction of that name has conjured up an astonishing — and seemingly endless — number of variations! Picklock Holes, Hemlock Jones, Ham Hock Bones . . . these names both invoke the spirit of the Great Detective and simultaneously poke fun at him.

While taking the conventions of the Holmes canon and the character of Holmes himself and making it all look ridiculous, the vast majority of these works are done out of admiration and love of the character. Only an aficionado with an intimate and thorough knowledge of the stories is able to pull it off successfully.

Classic Sherlock short story parodies

Sherlock Holmes has been a favorite target of spoofers, and understandably so. In the very early days of Sherlock's popularity, many of these authors were anonymous. And of course, some were better at it than others. Following is a small sample of some of the most memorable to appear over the years. You may be surprised at a few of the names who've taken on the Great Detective.

The crazy pseudonyms of Sherlock Holmes

The name "Sherlock Holmes" offers a seemingly endless array of ways to spoof it. Twisting the name is high sport for Sherlockian parody, and you could undoubtedly come up with a few variants yourself. Following is a (not even close to being complete) list of the various takes on the Sherlockian name that authors have come up with over the past century, along with the story in which the name appeared.

- **Sherlock Bones:** "The Case of Vamberry, the Wine Merchant," by Ian Charnock

- **Thinlock Bones:** "The Adventure of the Table Foot," by Allan Ramsay

- **Warlock Bones:** "The Adventure of the Diamond Necklace," by G. F. Forrest

- **Hemlock Booms:** "Holmes and the Startled Banker," by Anonymous

- **Padlock Booms:** "Holmes and the Startled Banker," by Anonymous

- **Sheerluck Coames:** "The Modern Radio Sleuth," by Jay Coote

- **Sherlog Combes:** "Baffled," by Anonymous

- **Oilock Combs:** "The Succored Beauty," by William B. Kahn

- **Hemlock Coombs:** "Holmes and the Startled Banker," by Anonymous

- **Forelock Domes:** "The Case of the Poisoned Finger," by Exile

- **Hemlock Foames:** "The Murder of Conan Doyle," by Ray Russell

- **Townclock Fumes:** "Holmes and the Startled Banker," by Anonymous

- **Sureluck Gommes:** "Wilde About Holmes," by Milo Yelesiyevich

- **Shylock Haynes:** "W. G. Grace's Last Case," by William Rushton

- **Picklock Holes:** "The Hungarian Diamond," by R. C. Lehmann

- **Shamrock Holes:** "The Marischal Manor Mystery," by Anonymous

- **Hemlock Holmes:** *The Adventure of the Eleven Cuff-Buttons,* by James Francis Thierry

- **Shedlock Holmes:** "Shedlock Holmes and Louisiana Raffles: The Great Sausage Mystery," by Ed Carey

- **Doorlock Homes:** "The Adventures of the Five Puce Map Tacks," by Paul Nizza

- **Shylock Homes:** "Mr. Homes Makes an Important Confession," by John Kendrick Bangs

- **Unlock Homes:** "The Great Flea Mystery," by Snowshoe Al

- **Shylock Hommes:** "The Adventure of the Ripper's Scrawl," by Michael Mallory

- **Purlock Hone:** In the introduction to *The Revelations of Inspector Morgan,* by Oswald Crawfurd

- **Shylock Hound:** "Hound in the Highlands," by Brenda Sivers

- **Boothcut Hoyle:** "The Cat of the Baskervilles," by Boothcut Hoyle

- **Shamrock Jolnes:** "The Adventures of Shamrock Jolnes," by O. Henry

- **Dudley Jones:** "Dudley Jones, Bore-Hunter," by P. G. Wodehouse

- **Fetlock Jones:** *A Double Barrelled Detective Story,* by Mark Twain

- **Hemlock Jones:** "The Stolen Cigar Case," by Bret Harte

- **Padlock Jones:** "An Easy Case for Padlock Jones," by Anonymous

- **Sheerluck Jones:** *Holmes on the Range,* by Steve Hockensmith

- **Surelock Keys:** *The Adventures of Surelock Keys,* by Herbert Beeman

- **Sherlaw Kombs:** "The Great Pegram Mystery," by Robert Barr

- **Sure Luck:** "The Master Sleuth on the Trail of Edwin Drood," by Robert F. Fleissner

- **Sherk Oms:** "The Greatest Tertian," by Anthony Boucher

- **Spitlock Phones:** "The Scarlet Drop," by Fibulous

- **Shylock Plumes:** "Holmes and the Startled Banker," by Anonymous

- **Solar Pons:** "The Adventure of the Frightened Baronet," by August Derleth

- **Hamlock Shears:** "The Marischal Manor Mystery," by Anonymous

- **Hamrock Shoals:** "The Marischal Manor Mystery," by Anonymous

- **Hurlock Shoams:** "Hurlock Shoams — One of His Adventures," by "Sir Arthur Cannon Ball"

- **Herlock Sholmes:** *Arsene Lupin versus Herlock Sholmes,* by Maurice Leblanc

- **Herlock Soames:** *The Arsene Lepine–Herlock Soames Affair,* by S. Chester Beach

- **Picklock Soles:** "The Marischal Manor Mystery," by Anonymous

- **Smallpox Soles:** "The Marischal Manor Mystery," by Anonymous

- **Badlock Tombs:** "Holmes and the Startled Banker," by Anonymous

- **Mereluck Tombs:** "The Missing Group," by A. S. Reeve

- **Shamrock Wolmbs:** "The Singularge Experience of Miss Anne Duffield," by John Lennon

And even Watson gets his share of name variations. Here are but a few:

- **Goswell:** Sidekick of Warlock Bones

- **Dr. Jobson:** Sidekick of Purlock Hone

- **Dr. Potson:** Sidekick of Sherlog Combes

- **Dr. Spotson:** Sidekick of Oilock Combs

- **Dr. Squatson:** Sidekick of Hurlock Shoams

- **Swatson:** Sidekick of Fetlock Jones

- **Waddus:** Sidekick of Dudley Jones

- **Dr. Watts:** Sidekick of Herlock Soams

- **Dr. Whatsoname:** Sidekick of Thinlock Bones

- **Dr. Whatsup:** Sidekick of Shamrock Jolnes

- **Dr. Whenson:** Sidekick of Surelock Keys

The Adventure of the Eleven Cuff-Buttons

James Francis Thierry's *The Adventure of the Eleven Cuff-Buttons* claims to hold the distinction of being the very first full-length Holmes parody ever published. The short novel highlights the exploits of Hemlock Holmes. What's unusual about *The Adventure of the Eleven Cuff-Buttons* is the name of Hemlock's sidekick. He's named Dr. Watson. That's right . . . no ridiculous variation, but just good old Dr. Watson. *The Adventure of the Eleven Cuff-Buttons* was published in 1918.

Sherlock Holmes meets the Beatles

You're likely to encounter Sherlock Holmes in the most unlikely places. In the massive *Beatles Anthology* volume, there is mentioned, almost in passing, a reference to a Holmes parody written by John Lennon. In 1964, Lennon published his first book, *In His Own Write,* a collection of James Joyce-like verse, Thurberesque cartoons, and silly short stories. The book was a bestseller, and so he followed it up with a similar volume called *A Spaniard in the Works.* It was for *Spaniard* that Lennon penned "The Singularge Experience of Miss Anne Duffield." Lennon wrote it while on a boating holiday in Tahiti. "I read one or two Conan Doyle books when I was younger," he writes, "but on the boat that we'd hired there was a set of them." He tells how, despite the allure of "Tahiti and all those islands," he still preferred to read the book on the boat. "There just happened to be a big volume of Sherlock Holmes, a sort of madman's Sherlock Holmes where you get all the stories in one; and I realized that every story was the same. They're all pretty similar; and that's what I was doing, writing them all into one. So I wrote Shamrock Wolmbs after three weeks of Sherlock Holmes in Tahiti."

Peter Pan parodies Sherlock Holmes

One of the best Holmes parodies of all time was written by James Barrie, friend and collaborator of Arthur Conan Doyle. It was 1893, still 16 years before Barrie conceived his classic *Peter Pan.* Nonetheless, Barrie was already a well-known author, but he aspired to be a playwright. He had written a few early plays, but they had met with only moderate success. Finally, Barrie pitched his play *Jane Annie or The Good Conduct Prize* to the famous Richard D'oyly Carte, of the D'oyly Carte Opera Company. This was the opera company that made its name by producing the operettas of Gilbert and Sullivan. D'oyly Carte agreed to produce the play, but shortly after Barrie began work, Carte suffered a nervous breakdown. Desperately needing to get the play written, Barrie turned to Doyle.

Doyle, who had just killed his famous detective, agreed to collaborate on *Jane Annie.* Unfortunately, the experiment was not a success. Barrie's notes on the story were confusing, and the storyline was a point of contention between the two friends. When it finally reached the stage it was a disaster and a box-office bomb.

Arthur Conan Doyle's own Sherlockian spoof

Even Arthur Conan Doyle himself indulged in Sherlockian parody! Well aware of the fun authors (and readers) were having at the expense of his detective, Doyle finally got in on the act. When in 1923, as a tribute to Queen Mary, wife of King George V, a dollhouse demonstrating British skill and craftsmanship was created, books were needed for its library. Well-known authors of the day were commissioned to write original works to be put into miniature books on the room's shelves. Doyle's contribution was a parody of his own creation titled "How Watson Learned the Trick," which was later published in a full-size book, *The Book of the Queen's Dolls' House.* In "How Watson Learned the Trick," Watson tries to show Sherlock how he's "learned the trick" of making incredible deductions from seemingly trifling evidence. Alas for poor old Watson — he fails miserably!

Fortunately, Barrie and Doyle remained friends throughout the ordeal, and as a token of his gratitude, Barrie presented Doyle with a copy of his book *A Window in Thrums.* Inside, on the flyleaf, Barrie had written a Sherlockian parody, "The Adventure of the Two Collaborators." It wasn't until 1924 that the story was finally published, appearing in Doyle's autobiography *Memories and Adventures.* "The Adventure of the Two Collaborators" is a reflection of the ill-fated partnership of the creator of Sherlock Holmes and the future creator of Peter Pan. It's considered to be one of the best examples of Sherlockian parody ever written. (You can read "The Adventure of the Two Collaborators" in the sidebar at the end of this chapter.)

Schlock Homes

Robert L. Fish was a 47-year-old civil engineer when he sat down to create his own take on the Great Detective, "Schlock Homes." How good is his homage to Holmes? Good enough for his parodies to win three Edgar Allan Poe Awards from the Mystery Writers of America. Fish's detective lives on Bagel Street and is joined by his friend and partner, Dr. Watney; Inspector Balustrade of Scotland Yard; and bad guys Professor Marty and Colonel Moron. Fish wrote his Bagel Street saga from 1959 to 1981, with the whole Schlock Homes canon numbering 32 stories.

The Adventures of Turlock Loams

John Ruyle's *The Adventures of Turlock Loams* is a series of 24 pastiches featuring his Holmes-parodying detective. Turlock Loams books were published by Pequod Press, Ruyle's own private press. All the books are hand-set, printed letter press, and hand-bound in limited editions, with the maximum press run being 252 copies. These books are highly collectible by Sherlockians and book collectors. Turlock Loams stories all employ puns of actual canonical titles for their own titles. Examples include "The Adventure of the Five Buffalo Chips," "The Adventure of the Frying Detective," and "The Adventure of the Cardboard Lox."

Other parodies

Sherlockian parody isn't confined to short stories. Some of the very best examples are found in comic strips (see Figures 13-1 and 13-2), cartoons, TV comedy skits, and even feature films like *The Adventure of Sherlock Holmes' Smarter Brother* and *Without a Clue*. (For more about Sherlockian film and TV, see Chapter 14.) Even advertising offers opportunity to spoof the iconic elements of the Sherlockian mythos. Sherlock Holmes has been used to sell everything from chewing gum to washing machines, all the while parodying the iconography, methods, and spirit of Holmes and the Sherlockian canon.

Figure 13-1:
Gus Mager's "Sherlocko Monk" appeared in this single panel cartoon in the *New York Evening Journal* on January 20, 1912.

Figure 13-2:
H. A. MacGill's comic strip "Padlock Bones, the Dead-Sure Detective" ran only three weeks in 1904.

"The Adventure of the Two Collaborators," by James M. Barrie

In bringing to a close the adventures of my friend Sherlock Holmes I am perforce reminded that he never, save on the occasion which, as you will now hear, brought his singular career to an end, consented to act in any mystery which was concerned with persons who made a livelihood by their pen.

"I am not particular about the people I mix among for business purposes," he would say, "but at literary characters I draw the line."

We were in our rooms in Baker Street one evening. I was (I remember) by the centre table writing out "The Adventure of the Man without a Cork Leg" (which had so puzzled the Royal Society and all the other scientific bodies of Europe), and Holmes was amusing himself with a little revolver practice. It was his custom of a summer evening to fire round my head, just shaving my face, until he had made a photograph of me on the opposite wall, and it is a slight proof of his skill that many of these portraits in pistol shots are considered admirable likenesses.

I happened to look out of the window, and, perceiving two gentlemen advancing rapidly along Baker Street, asked him who they were. He immediately lit his pipe, and, twisting himself on a chair into the figure 8, replied:

(continued)

(continued)

"They are two collaborators in comic opera, and their play has not been a triumph."

I sprang from my chair to the ceiling in amazement, and he then explained:

"My dear Watson, they are obviously men who follow some low calling. That much even you should be able to read in their faces. Those little pieces of blue paper which they fling angrily from them are Durrant's Press Notices. Of these they have obviously hundreds about their person (see how their pockets bulge). They would not dance on them if they were pleasant reading."

I again sprang to the ceiling (which is much dented), and shouted: "Amazing! but they may be mere authors."

"No," said Holmes, "for mere authors only get one press notice a week. Only criminals, dramatists and actors get them by the hundred."

"Then they may be actors."

"No, actors would come in a carriage."

"Can you tell me anything else about them?"

"A great deal. From the mud on the boots of the tall one I perceive that he comes from South Norwood. The other is as obviously a Scotch author."

"How can you tell that?"

"He is carrying in his pocket a book called (I clearly see) *Auld Licht Something*. Would any one but the author be likely to carry about a book with such a title?"

I had to confess that this was improbable.

It was now evident that the two men (if such they can be called) were seeking our lodgings. I have said (often) that my friend Holmes seldom gave way to emotion of any kind, but he now turned livid with passion. Presently this gave place to a strange look of triumph.

"Watson," he said, "that big fellow has for years taken the credit for my most remarkable doings, but at last I have him — at last!"

Up I went to the ceiling, and when I returned the strangers were in the room.

"I perceive, gentlemen," said Mr. Sherlock Holmes, "that you are at present afflicted by an extraordinary novelty."

The handsomer of our visitors asked in amazement how he knew this, but the big one only scowled.

"You forget that you wear a ring on your fourth finger," replied Mr. Holmes calmly.

I was about to jump to the ceiling when the big brute interposed.

"That Tommy-rot is all very well for the public, Holmes," said he, "but you can drop it before me. And, Watson, if you go up to the ceiling again I shall make you stay there."

Here I observed a curious phenomenon. My friend Sherlock Holmes shrank. He became small before my eyes. I looked longingly at the ceiling, but dared not.

"Let us cut the first four pages," said the big man, "and proceed to business. I want to know why — "

"Allow me," said Mr. Holmes, with some of his old courage. "You want to know why the public does not go to your opera."

"Exactly," said the other ironically, "as you perceive by my shirt stud." He added more gravely, "And as you can only find out in one way I must insist on your witnessing an entire performance of the piece."

It was an anxious moment for me. I shuddered, for I knew that if Holmes went I should have to go with him. But my friend had a heart of gold.

"Never," he cried fiercely, "I will do anything for you save that."

"Your continued existence depends on it," said the big man menacingly.

"I would rather melt into air," replied Holmes, proudly taking another chair. "But I can tell you why the public don't go to your piece without sitting the thing out myself."

"Why?"

"Because," replied Holmes calmly, "they prefer to stay away."

A dead silence followed that extraordinary remark. For a moment the two intruders gazed with awe upon the man who had unravelled their mystery so wonderfully. Then drawing their knives —

Holmes grew less and less, until nothing was left save a ring of smoke which slowly circled to the ceiling.

The last words of great men are often noteworthy. These were the last words of Sherlock Holmes: "Fool, fool! I have kept you in luxury for years. By my help you have ridden extensively in cabs, where no author was ever seen before. *Henceforth you will ride in buses!*"

The brute sunk into a chair aghast.

The other author did not turn a hair.

Chapter 14

Adapting Holmes for Stage and Screen

In This Chapter

▶ The dramatic Sherlock Holmes adaptations

▶ The Great Detective on the big screen

▶ The televised history of Sherlock Holmes

*S*hortly after he first rose to prominence in the pages of *The Strand Magazine,* Sherlock Holmes became a favorite of dramatists. His public career in front of an audience closely tracks every form of drama and performance over the 20th century.

- ✔ **The stage:** Sherlock Holmes trod the boards with the best of them.

- ✔ **Motion pictures:** Within a decade after the invention of the motion picture camera, the first Holmes film was made.

- ✔ **Radio:** Sherlock was a staple of the wireless well into the 1950s, appearing hundreds of times.

- ✔ **TV:** Holmes was there at the beginning. A Sherlock Holmes story was the first drama broadcast in the U.S.

Indeed, since the closing of the canon, Sherlockian drama — be it stage or screen — has proved almost as popular as the written adventures.

Though it's common for fictional characters to be adapted for the stage or screen, Arthur Conan Doyle's detective, Sherlock Holmes, holds the unique position of being the world's most adapted literary character in history.

Sherlock Holmes on the Stage

When Holmes was presumed dead at the Reichenbach Falls, the doors opened to adapting him for the stage. Stage adaptations were part of the same phenomenon as Sherlockian parody and new, look-alike rival detectives — they all were created to fill the void left by Holmes and to meet the public's desire for more Holmes adventures.

In retrospect, it's obvious — Sherlock Holmes is the perfect vehicle for adapting to the stage. With an endless supply of colorful characters (including Sherlock himself), the tight plots of the short stories, and the canon's great dialogue, bringing Holmes to life on the stage is a natural. Just a few of the more notable examples of early Sherlockian plays include *Under the Clock* (1893), *Sherlock Holmes* (1893), and *Sherlock Holmes: A Drama in Four Acts* (1899).

Curiously, it was that last play, *Sherlock Holmes: A Drama in Four Acts,* that may have contributed to a few decades of Holmes being absent from the stage. The play, written by and starring William Gillette, was so popular that producers and the public were more interested in repeated revivals of it than new adaptations. That fact, combined with Sherlock's success on the big screen, led to a few decades of little Sherlockian activity in the theater.

But eventually, Holmes did return, and since then, he has appeared in dozens of adaptations, the most important of which include *Baker Street: The Musical* (1965), *The Crucifer of Blood* (1978), *Sherlock's Last Case* (1987), and *Sherlock Holmes: The Final Adventure* (2007).

Today, the Great Detective remains a popular source of inspiration and adaptation for playwrights.

Under the Clock (1893)

Written by Seymour Hicks, *Under the Clock* was billed as an "extravaganza" in one act. It starred Charles H. E. Brookfield, who gets credit as the first actor to portray Sherlock Holmes on the stage, and Hicks himself played Watson. *Under the Clock* premiered on November 25, 1893, at the Royal Court Theatre in London. Little else is known about the production.

Sherlock Holmes (1893)

The first known drama featuring Holmes was written by Charles Rogers, a rather pedestrian author of standard Victorian melodrama. His play, *Sherlock Holmes,* was exactly that. Rogers filled the plot with a series of exciting, if improbable, incidents, and, as many have done since then, he took liberties with characters. In his story, Watson is married to a woman named Amy. But more shocking is Rogers's innovation that Holmes was in love with Watson's wife! The story features a Jack the Ripper-like killer who kidnaps Watson, an arrest of Holmes for Watson's murder, Holmes's escape from prison, and a whole slew of other outlandish plot twists. One reviewer wrote, "Nervous people should not go to see *Sherlock Holmes.*"

Sherlock Holmes: A Drama in Four Acts (1899)

Hands down, the most famous stage production of Sherlock Holmes was this play written and performed by William Gillette (see Figure 14-1). *Sherlock Holmes* debuted on Broadway at the Garrick Theater on November 6, 1899. It was a smashing success, lasting over seven months in its first run.

The creation of the play

When Doyle "killed" Holmes in "The Final Problem," he knew dramatic productions starring his detective would be lucrative, so he decided to take his character to the stage. After completing the play, his literary agent, A. P. Watt, sent the script to producer Charles Frohman. Frohman, who found Doyle's original draft to be a bit dry, felt that it would benefit from a professional playwright's input. Thus, Frohman suggested giving the project to William Gillette. Doyle agreed, and Gillette, who was in San Francisco touring with his play, *Secret Service,* began adapting Doyle's script. Ultimately, Gillette sent Doyle a telegram asking, "May I marry Holmes?" Doyle's famous answer was, "You can marry him, or murder him, or anything you want."

Not much is known about Doyle's original version before Gillette worked on it. No known copy of the play survives. Gillette's adaption is believed, however, to be extensive, combining "A Scandal in Bohemia" and "The Final Problem," as well as several other tales. He also added entirely new elements and characters. Rather than making the heroine Irene Adler, for example, Gillette invented Alice Faulkner who, by play's end, falls in love with Holmes.

While Gillette was staying in San Francisco's Baldwin Hotel, the hotel caught fire and burned down, incinerating Gillette's script, as well as Doyle's original version. Undaunted, Gillette went back to work, rewriting the entire play in a few weeks.

Following its run on Broadway, the play toured across America, and then Gillette took it for a brief stay in Australia. When the play debuted in London, it was a triumph. The original 12-week scheduled was extended, and touring companies were sent out across England with the play.

It has been estimated that Gillette performed as Holmes approximately 1,300 times over the next 30 years. The (for that time) unprecedented notoriety from the play, along with the promotional material that went with it, cemented Gillette as *the* image of Sherlock Holmes, and in many ways, his influence is felt to this day.

Figure 14-1:
A vintage poster promoting William Gillette in *Sherlock Holmes.*

What Sherlock Holmes did for Gillette

Well before *Sherlock Holmes,* Gillette was famous both as an actor and a playwright in the U.S. In addition, he helped bring live drama into the modern era by using realistic sets, sound effects, and revolutionary lighting, particularly for scene changes. He also introduced a more realistic acting technique. In his productions, he abandoned the traditional, but hokey, bombastic style for a more natural, realistic one, having his characters walk, talk, and act like real-life people.

Despite his large body of work prior to *Sherlock Holmes,* because of the play's popularity, Gillette became identified with the role in the mind of the public. He was the first actor to be known as the "Sherlock Holmes of his generation." In addition to his theater work, Gillette starred as the Great Detective in a silent movie and twice on the radio.

What Gillette gave Sherlock Holmes

The impact that Gillette's play had on the popular perception of Sherlock Holmes — indeed, the *popularity* of Holmes — can't be overstated. Many of the iconic elements that conjure the image of the Great Detective in the public's consciousness were either popularized or invented by Gillette. These include

- ✔ **The deerstalker cap:** Despite Sidney Paget's illustrations showing Holmes wearing the deerstalker, it was Gillette's adoption of the distinctive headgear that forever identified it with Holmes.

- ✔ **The calabash pipe:** Doyle never described Holmes using this odd, curved pipe. Neither the briarwood or cherry pipe was described as curved, and clay pipes are straight-stemmed. It was Gillette who introduced the curved calabash, the style of which made it easier to say his lines and kept the pipe from being out in front of his face.

- ✔ **Romance:** The overwhelming popularity of *Sherlock Holmes: A Drama in Four Acts* opened the door to the public's acceptance of Holmes falling in love. For strict Sherlockians, this is anathema to Doyle's image of Holmes. However, Doyle gave the go-ahead, and dramatists and pastiche writers have been pairing Holmes up with women (usually Irene Adler) ever since.

- ✔ **The American image of Sherlock Holmes:** When the stories were originally published in the U.S., they were illustrated by an artist named Frederic Dorr Steele. Steele used Gillette as his model, thus amplifying the image of Gillette as Sherlock Holmes.

Arsène Lupin versus Sherlock Holmes (1910)

French playwrights Victor Darlay and Henri de Gorsse produced this early pairing of Arsène Lupin, France's popular "gentleman burglar," created by Maurice Leblanc, and Doyle's Sherlock Holmes. In this freely adapted work, Holmes's partner isn't Watson but instead the Great Detective's son, "Frederick." *Arsène Lupin versus Sherlock Holmes* is half mystery, half comedy, with Holmes out to recover the sultan diamond, which has been stolen by Lupin. The outcome is, of course, a draw. Holmes does manage to arrest Lupin and recover the diamond. But once in custody, he escapes!

The Adventure of the Speckled Band (1910)

Based on his short story of the same name, *The Adventure of the Speckled Band* was written by Sir Arthur himself. Originally titled *The Stonor Case,* Doyle's adaptation elaborates on and takes liberty with some elements in the original tale. (For instance, the spelling of both Helen Stoner's last name and Dr. Roylott's last name are slightly different.) One of the more interesting features of the play was the use of a live snake at the production's climax! Unfortunately, the real snake looked fake, and so to make it look real, they ended up using a fake!

It took Doyle two weeks to write the play, and on June 4, 1910, *The Speckled Band* came to life at the Adelphi Theater in London. An anxious and excited audience held its breath as the house lights fell and Sherlock Holmes walked onto the stage. Holmes and Watson were recognizably themselves, but as the story unfolded, the Great Detective was nearly overshadowed, in both stage presence and popularity, by the memorable villain, Dr. Grimesby Rylott. Not only did the character scene-steal from Holmes, but at the opening night curtain call, Doyle himself was upstaged when the villain, sporting the speckled band itself around his neck, made his appearance!

The actors

So . . . who played Holmes? The detective was played by H. A. Saintsbury, a very popular Sherlock Holmes of the day, starring in productions of William Gillette's *Sherlock Holmes* play before taking on *The Speckled Band.* Scholars believe he portrayed the Great Detective over 1,400 times. Based on Saintsbury's popularity in the role, Doyle gave him the lead in *The Speckled Band.*

And who played Rylott? The evil stepfather was played by Lyn Harding. It was a stroke of genius to cast the popular Shakespearian actor as the evil doctor. At first, Doyle and Harding disagreed on the character's interpretation. Sir Arthur envisioned Rylott as he had written him in the story. Harding, on the other hand, clearly was taking the role over the top, and there was real tension between the author and the actor. Finally, mutual theatrical friend J. M. Barrie, the author of *Peter Pan,* arbitrated the dispute. Before rendering a verdict, Barrie attended a pre-opening performance of the play. Upon its conclusion he turned to Doyle and said, "Let Harding have it his own way." Doyle took his advice. On opening night, as Harding received over a dozen curtain calls, Doyle sent him a congratulatory note.

The villain of the play version of *The Speckled Band* spells his name differently from his counterpart in the original story. In the written story, his last name is Roylott. However, in the play, Arthur Conan Doyle changed the spelling to Rylott. Why? Nobody knows, but the name change has been causing confusion ever since!

Rodney Stone

The Speckled Band wasn't Arthur Conan Doyle's first foray into the theatrical world. In 1909, Doyle adapted his prizefighting novel, *Rodney Stone,* for the stage. Renaming it *The House of Temperly: A Melodrama of the Ring,* the author took out a six-month lease on the Adelphi Theater to house his boxing drama. At that time boxing was illegal in England. The play opened on February 11, 1910, and from the start, attendance was poor. Despite the fact that the play featured real boxing on stage — or perhaps because of it — the play did very poorly at the box office. Given that few women enjoy boxing, perhaps a stage play centered on prizefighting wasn't such a good idea. To add to the play's difficulties, King Edward the VII died during the run, and all theaters closed in mourning. Facing utter ruin, Sir Arthur did what many people in dire circumstances did — he turned to Sherlock Holmes for help, and the result was the stage adaptation of one of the greatest Holmes tales of them all.

The reviews

The play was a huge hit, and the fortunes of Doyle and his lease on the Adelphi Theater were saved. It's arguable that, had Doyle gotten his way and reigned in Lyn Harding, the fortunes of *The Speckled Band* may well have been different. Deferring to the veteran actor's instincts most certainly saved the day.

Harding's portrayal of Dr. Rylott made such an impression on the public that he was tapped to reprise the role in the 1931 film version of the play, starring opposite Raymond Massey as Holmes. But his canonical villainy didn't end there — he graduated from Grimesby Rylott to Professor Moriarty in two later films starring Arthur Wontner as Holmes. He deserves special recognition in the pantheon of Sherlockian dramatics for giving a performance that upstaged not only Sherlock Holmes but also Doyle himself.

Baker Street: The Musical (1965)

Baker Street: The Musical is based on the story "A Scandal in Bohemia." It was written by Jerome Coopersmith, with music by Marian Grudeff and Raymond Jessel. The early previews had mixed reviews, compelling the producers to have new songs written by Sheldon Harnick and Jerry Bock, who composed the music for *Fiddler on the Roof.*

The plot diverges from the original story when Irene Adler becomes an assistant of Sherlock Holmes. Naturally, as often happens in Sherlockian drama, a romance blossoms between them. Holmes was played by Fritz Weaver, and Inga Swenson was Irene Adler.

The Crucifer of Blood (1978)

The Crucifer of Blood, by Paul Giovanni, is an adaptation of *The Sign of the Four.* Tinkering with the plot, Giovanni's play includes a woman named Irene St. Claire, who hires Holmes to investigate the events that resulted from a cursed treasure chest her father and his three cohorts stole during the Indian Rebellion of 1857. The play opened on Broadway and starred Paxton Whitehead as Holmes and Glenn Close as Irene St. Claire. *The Crucifer of Blood* won four Tony Awards.

Sherlock's Last Case (1987)

Debuting on Broadway to scathing reviews, *Sherlock's Last Case* nonetheless remains a popular Sherlockian play. The original production starred Frank Langella, fresh off his turn in *Dracula,* as Holmes. Written by Charles Marowitz, *Sherlock's Last Case* is described as a black comedy and centers on a death threat against Holmes by the son of Professor Moriarty. After many plot twists, Holmes finds himself imprisoned not by Moriarty's son but instead by Dr. Watson! It seems that Watson has had it with being Holmes's flunky. Mixing humor and mystery, the play concludes with a stunning ending.

Sherlock Holmes: The Final Adventure (2007)

Adapted by Steven Dietz and based on the play by William Gillette, *Sherlock Holmes: The Final Adventure* is a conflation of the stories "A Scandal in Bohemia" and "The Final Problem." The king of Bohemia hires Holmes to recover a scandalous photograph from Irene Adler and keep it out of the hands of Professor Moriarty. Along the way, Holmes falls in love with Miss Adler before the play climaxes at the Reichenbach Falls. *Sherlock Holmes: The Final Adventure* won the 2007 Edgar Award for best mystery play.

Sherlock Holmes at the Movies

The history of Sherlock Holmes films is almost as long as the history of Sherlock Holmes. Within a decade of the invention of motion pictures, the very first Holmes film had been shot. *Sherlock Holmes Baffled* was produced in 1900 by the American Mutoscope & Biograph Company. It ran all of 30 seconds and was made to show in arcades on Mutoscope machines.

The cinematographer for *Sherlock Holmes Baffled* was a man named Arthur Marvin, but no record exists that reveals who played the first cinematic Sherlock. The plot, such as it is, has Holmes trying to catch a criminal, who keeps disappearing and reappearing, using the camera trick of stopping and starting the camera.

The Mutoscope was an early device made for viewing motion pictures. The individual frames were black-and-white photographs on cards. These cards were attached to a circular drum, which was turned by a crank. The viewer saw the movie through a lens enclosed by a hood. Only one viewer could watch at a time.

As crude as *Sherlock Holmes Baffled* was, it wasn't long before motion picture technology matured, bringing us silent movies, then sound and color. And Sherlock Holmes was there every step of the way.

The silent era

Sherlock Holmes had a thriving motion picture career in the era of silent films. In fact, some of the most important installments of Sherlockian cinema came before the movies learned to talk.

Sherlock Holmes (1922)

A lot of great actors have donned the deerstalker over the last century. The first great film actor to do so was the legendary John Barrymore, who starred in the 1922 film *Sherlock Holmes.* Barrymore, who made his fame on the stage in Shakespeare's *Hamlet,* was at the height of his fame when he was cast as the Great Detective. Roland Young was his Dr. Watson. Barrymore's film was, by the standards of the day, ambitious, with some scenes being filmed on location in London.

The movie starts with Holmes and Watson as college students, where they first meet Moriarty, setting up the deadly clash with the professor years later. Even as silent films go, this one is slow and the plot is clumsy. Barrymore is a pretty good Sherlock, but he can't overcome the deficiencies of the script. The film was thought to be lost for decades, but with the discovery of a print, it has been restored and is available to a new generation of Sherlockian cinema buffs.

The films of Eille Norwood (1921–1923)

The 1920s are considered the golden age of silent movies. In that decade, this new medium was maturing — filmmakers had discovered the potential of the motion picture, and technology was making it possible to tell ever more sophisticated stories. It was also during this decade that the first great

Sherlock Holmes of film appeared. English actor Eille Norwood was 60 when he first stepped before the cameras as the Great Detective. Norwood starred in a staggering 47 Holmes films from 1921 to 1923 — a feat that was not to be equaled until Jeremy Brett played Holmes on TV over 60 years later.

His real name was Anthony Edward Brett, but he took his stage name by combining his girlfriend's first name, Eileen, with the town of Norwood, in southern England. Of his understated (for silent movies) performance, he said, "My idea of Holmes is that he is absolutely quiet. Nothing ruffles him." Norwood studied the canon, learned to play the violin, and shaved the temples of his hairline to more closely approximate the illustrations of Sidney Paget. His approach paid off. Even Arthur Conan Doyle was bowled over. "He has that rare quality which can be described as glamour," said Sir Arthur, "which compels you to watch the actor eagerly when he is doing nothing. He has a brooding eye which excites expectation and he has a quite unrivalled power of disguise. His impersonation of Holmes amazes me."

Norwood starred in three film series for the British company Stoll Picture Productions. Founded in 1918, Stoll was a major player of the silent era. It was a prolific company, too — between 1918 and 1921, when it began its Holmes films, Stoll had cranked out over 175 motion pictures!

Each Norwood series had 15 films. The first series appeared in 1921, *The Adventures of Sherlock Holmes.* It was followed the next year by *The Further Adventures of Sherlock Holmes,* and then finally, in 1923, *The Last Adventures of Sherlock Holmes.* In addition, Norwood starred in Stoll's version of *The Hound of the Baskervilles* and *The Sign of the Four.* Unfortunately, very few of Norwood's films survive. But if you can find a copy, you won't be disappointed. Eille Norwood as Sherlock Holmes is a revelation.

The 1930s: The talkies

The first feature-length movie with sound was 1927's *The Jazz Singer.* It was a sensation, and by the 1930s, sound films had come of age. For fans of the Great Detective, that meant that Sherlock Holmes had found his voice.

The Speckled Band (1931)

With Doyle's 1910 stage play of "The Speckled Band" being such a success (see the earlier section "The Adventure of the Speckled Band"), it was a no-brainer to eventually produce a film version. As in the original story and the play, the movie has all the familiar elements — the dying sister who, with her last breath, cries, "It was the Speckled Band!"; the weird animals on the estate; Helen Stoner being forced to sleep in the dead sister's room; and especially, the evil stepfather, Dr. Grimesby Rylott. As in the play, the film features Lyn Harding as the sinister Dr. Rylott. Instead of H. A. Saintsbury, who played Holmes on the stage, the film version has Raymond Massey as

Holmes. This was the third film role for Massey (and his first talkie), who went on to a very successful career, first in Hollwood and later on TV. His Holmes is serviceable but undermined by the filmmaker's decision to turn 221b into an honest-to-goodness detective agency, with secretaries and other modern innovations.

A Study in Scarlet (1933)

Despite the title, this film has nothing in common with the first Sherlock Holmes novel. Holmes is played by Reginald Owen, a popular Hollywood character actor. Owen had played Dr. Watson in a previous production and wanted to begin his own series with himself as the Great Detective. Unfortunately for Owen, he was horribly miscast — rather tubby, let's face it, and a bit boring. Owens's Sherlockian feature film debut was also his swan song.

The films of Arthur Wontner (1931–1937)

The second great Sherlock Holmes of the screen, Arthur Wontner, stepped before the cameras in 1931, just after the dawn of the sound era in movies. Wontner was already in his mid-50s when he took on the role. Both he and Norwood contributed to the still popular impression of Sherlock being much older than he is in the canon.

Wontner's Holmes films are

- ✔ *The Sleeping Cardinal* (1931): Retitled *Sherlock Holmes' Fatal Hour* in the U.S., this is an original story, although it borrows elements from the stories "The Empty House" and "The Final Problem." Holmes is hired by the sister of Ronald Adair to investigate why her brother is gambling so much. Along the way is a plot involving counterfeit money, foreign intrigue, and a suicide. And let's not forget Professor Moriarty.

- ✔ *The Missing Rembrandt* (1932): When the evil Baron von Guntermann, known as "the worst man in London," decorates his home with a recently stolen Rembrandt, Holmes takes up the case. He does so after an American detective hits a dead end. The baron is a blackmailer who has become wealthy and powerful through his evil trade. Based on the original story "The Adventure of Charles Augustus Milverton," *The Missing Rembrandt* has plenty of plot twists. Unfortunately, the film is lost, with no known print in existence.

- ✔ *The Sign of the Four* (1932): Though this movie isn't a completely faithful adaptation, the source material is still recognizable, despite being updated to the 1930s. Holmes and Watson set out to protect Mary Morstan, who is being menaced by an escaped murderer looking for a stolen treasure. The plot goes through familiar scenes, as well as some surprising new ones, including a strange carnival. When Miss Morstan is kidnapped, Holmes and Watson must work quickly to save her.

✔ *The Triumph of Sherlock Holmes* (1935): This adaptation of the novel *The Valley of Fear* opens with Holmes in retirement. His peace is interrupted when a country squire named John Douglas is murdered. Holmes's investigation reveals the involvement of a murderous American secret society, and worse, the intervention of Professor Moriarty.

✔ *Silver Blaze* (1937): Though this film, retitled *Murder at the Baskervilles* in the U.S., is primarily an adaptation of the original story "Silver Blaze," the screenwriters threw in the character of Henry Baskerville (and his daughter!) and mixed in, yet again, Professor Moriarty. While on vacation visiting Sir Henry, Holmes ends up investigating a double-murder, a stolen racehorse, and Moriarty's illegal betting scheme.

Wontner was a favorite of early Sherlockians. Vincent Starrett, author of *The Private Life of Sherlock Holmes,* wrote, "No better Sherlock Holmes than Wontner is likely to be seen and heard in pictures, in our time. Sentimentalized, as is imperative, his detective is the veritable fathomer of Baker Street in person. The keen, worn, kindly face and quiet, prescient smile are out of the very pages of the book."

Arthur Wontner had two Watsons over the years. Ian Fleming (no relation to the creator of James Bond) played Watson in all the films except *The Sign of the Four.* In that film, Watson was played by Ian Hunter.

Just who was Basil Rathbone?

Philip St. John Basil Rathbone was born in Johannesburg, South Africa. His parents were English, and when Basil was 3, the family returned to England. Rathbone enlisted in the army in 1916 during World War I, eventually retiring with the rank of captain.

His acting career started before the war. In 1911, Rathbone made his first stage appearance in a production of *The Taming of the Shrew.* Throughout the ensuing years, before and after the war, Rathbone had steady, and steadily better, acting roles on the stage. In 1923, he was able to tour America with his theater company, and from then on he was frequently working in the U.S.

Leading up to Sherlock Holmes, Rathbone built a memorable film career. Among the titles he appeared in are *The Bishop Murder Case, David Copperfield* (in a harrowing role as the abusive stepfather Mr. Murdstone), *Anna Karenina, Captain Blood, A Tale of Two Cities, The Adventures of Robin Hood* (playing the villainous Sheriff of Nottingham), *The Mark of Zorro, Tower of London,* and the underappreciated *Son of Frankenstein.* Rathbone excelled as a villain and was known for his skill as a swordsman.

The 1940s: Basil Rathbone and the first golden age of Sherlockian cinema

By the late 1930s and into the 1940s, moviemaking had grown up. The technical difficulties of first shooting moving pictures and then adding sound had been mastered. The end of the decade gave viewers arguably the greatest single year of film releases in history. Among the many landmark films released in 1939 were *Gone with the Wind, The Wizard of Oz, Mr. Smith Goes to Washington, The Hunchback of Notre Dame, Goodbye, Mr. Chips,* and *The Hound of the Baskervilles.* And as seen in that last title listed, it was the dawn of the first golden age of Sherlockian cinema. This was the era of Basil Rathbone, shown in Figure 14-2, as Sherlock Holmes.

Figure 14-2:
Nigel Bruce
as Watson
and Basil
Rathbone
as Sherlock
Holmes.

Despite an outstanding credit list that includes such films as *Anna Karenina* and *The Adventures of Robin Hood,* Rathbone is best remembered for his portrayal of the Great Detective. Between 1939 and 1946, he starred in 14 Holmes films with his friend Nigel Bruce, who played Dr. Watson. With his angled face and crisp vocal delivery, Rathbone looked as if he had been torn from the pages of *The Strand Magazine.* To the moviegoing public, with his 14 Holmes films (and hundreds of Holmes radio shows), Basil Rathbone and Sherlock Holmes were one.

Here's a list of Rathbone's Holmes films, the first two of which were produced by 20th Century Fox and the rest by Universal Studios:

- *The Hound of the Baskervilles* (1939): This is still arguably the best adaptation of this famous Sherlock Holmes story. *The Hound* was never intended to kick off a new film series, but when it became a surprise hit, the studio decided to make a sequel. It's set in the proper Victorian time period.

- *The Adventures of Sherlock Holmes* (1939): Also set in the proper Victorian time period, *Adventures* combines plot elements from several Holmes stories. It claims to be based on William Gillette's play, but it bears absolutely no resemblance. It is, however, a great Sherlock Holmes film.

- *Sherlock Holmes and the Voice of Terror* (1942): This film marks the point where the series left 20th Century Fox for Universal Studios. The change was drastic. No more big-budget productions were planned. Instead, the series was moved to the modern-day 1940s, and starting with *Voice of Terror,* Holmes and Watson became propagandists for the war effort. Here Holmes is brought in to foil a Nazi radio broadcast used to spread war propaganda and demoralize Britain.

- *Sherlock Holmes and the Secret Weapon* (1943): Holmes leads the race to secure the plans for a revolutionary new bomb sight. Who will get it first, the British or the Nazis?

- *Sherlock Holmes in Washington* (1943): Holmes's investigation into the kidnapping of a British government courier brings him to Washington, DC.

- *Sherlock Holmes Faces Death* (1943): Watson volunteers to help out at a convalescent home during the war, but when people start to get murdered, he calls for help from his friend, Sherlock Holmes.

- *The Spider Woman* (1944): Britain is still at war when the nation's attention focuses on a series of suicides. Dubbed the "pyjama suicides" by the press, these baffling deaths draw the attention of Holmes.

- *The Scarlet Claw* (1944): When Holmes and Watson travel to Canada to attend the meeting of the Royal Canadian Occult Society, they find themselves investigating the murder of their host's wife. Was her killer the glowing, throat-slashing phantom the nearby villagers fear? With similarities to *The Hound of the Baskervilles,* this is the best of the Universal Studios films.

- *The Pearl of Death* (1944): When a valuable pearl is stolen from a museum, right out from under Holmes's nose, he sets out to recover it. Toss in a string of brutal murders and a menacing killer known as the Creeper, and you have a nice, scary Sherlock Holmes movie.

✔ *The House of Fear* (1945): When the "good comrades" gather together in a gloomy castle, one by one they start to drop dead. Just before they die, an envelope of orange pips is delivered to the next victim. Holmes investigates this case, which is clearly inspired by Agatha Christie's classic, *Ten Little Indians*.

✔ *The Woman in Green* (1945): When it appears that a serial killer is loose in London, Holmes is called in by Scotland Yard for help. The investigation leads to a mysterious woman, an evil hypnotist, and ultimately, Professor Moriarty.

✔ *Pursuit to Algiers* (1945): In what is, hands down, the weakest film in the series, Holmes and Watson get mixed up in the plot to assassinate Nikolas, an heir to a foreign throne, who they are escorting on an ocean liner.

✔ *Terror by Night* (1946): The series bounces back with this low-budget but highly effective entry. While taking the overnight train to Edinburgh, Scotland, Holmes and Watson escort Roland Carstairs and his mother, owners of the famed diamond known as the Star of Rhodesia. When the diamond is stolen and Carstairs is murdered, Holmes sets out to catch the killer.

✔ *Dressed to Kill* (1946): The series draws to a close with *Dressed to Kill*. When the purchasers of a certain type of music box end up murdered, Holmes and Watson set out to discover the link between the victims and the motive for their deaths.

Rathbone's Watson problem

Basil Rathbone didn't get typecast and permanently identified with his character all alone. No — his Watson did, too, much to the consternation of Sherlockians. Nigel Bruce's portrayal of Dr. Watson was about as far from the literary original as you could get. Doyle's Watson is a practical, practicing doctor, about the same age as Holmes, attractive to women, and of average intelligence. Bruce, however, depicts Watson as an old, doddering, absent-minded buffoon. One insightful critic characterized his portrayal as "Boobus Britannicus." Many more have asked the obvious question, "Why would someone like Holmes hang around with this idiot?"

But Bruce's performance has to be evaluated in another way. To understand it only in comparison to the written Watson is to see it as an obvious failure. But these were popular movies, and Bruce's screen Watson was pure entertainment, offering comic relief in times of tension and fear. And besides, he and Rathbone had terrific chemistry — their real-life friendship comes through on the screen. It's no wonder that the public loved *both* of them. For the Sherlockian purists, however, Bruce's inauthentic portrayal stamped Watson as an old fool for decades.

Despite the great popularity of Rathbone's Holmes series, by *Dressed to Kill,* he had grown sick of Sherlock. He had become so permanently identified with the character (much as Nigel Bruce had with Watson) that in the minds of the public, he *was* Sherlock Holmes. Rathbone found himself typecast as the Great Detective, and his film career, which had burned so bright before playing Holmes, was a mere shadow of itself to the end of his life. Eventually, he reconciled himself to Holmes and even embraced the character again in later years. He should have been proud. He created a role that to this day is, for many, the greatest screen Sherlock of all time.

The 1950s and 1960s: Holmes gets color

In the two decades following the end of the Basil Rathbone film series, only two major Sherlock Holmes films were made. This undoubtedly had to do with Rathbone's image of Holmes being so overwhelming in the public's consciousness. But it also had to do with the onset of the TV age. Starting in the 1950s, Sherlock Holmes became a fixture on TV. Nonetheless, the two films that were produced are important in the history of Sherlockian cinema.

The Hound of the Baskervilles (1958)

Leave it to Britain's Hammer Film Productions to produce the first color Sherlock Holmes movie. The studio is best-known for a series of lurid, Gothic horror films made from the mid-1950s into the 1970s. When Hammer decided to add Holmes to its roster, it turned to *The Hound of the Baskervilles,* producing the first big-screen Holmes film since Basil Rathbone had retired from the role 13 years earlier. Peter Cushing, a Hammer regular, was tapped to play Sherlock. Opposite him, as an intelligent, competent Dr. Watson, was Andre Morell. Hammer sensationalized the horror elements in *The Hound* and added a few of their own, including human sacrifices and a tarantula — but the spirit of the novel remains. One of its strongest moments comes in telling the story of Sir Hugo Baskerville and the origins of the hound. Hammer's take on Sherlock Holmes comes highly recommended.

A Study in Terror (1965)

Despite an advertising campaign influenced by the campy hit TV show *Batman* ("He's the original Caped Crusader! He's Batman with brains!"), *A Study in Terror* is the first time that Sherlock Holmes was injected into a real-life, historical story. Starring John Neville as a rather refined Sherlock and Donald Houston as a Nigel Bruce-like Watson, the film centers on the Jack the Ripper crimes. What seems like a cliché now was utterly original in 1965, as the film follows Holmes on his investigation into the seedy underworld of Whitechapel. Though the victims of the Ripper seem a bit too pretty, and their hair and makeup is of a mid-1960s vintage, *A Study in Terror* has its creepy moments. And of course, Holmes gets his man, all in glorious Technicolor.

The 1970s: The second golden age of Sherlockian cinema

Though Sherlock Holmes appeared regularly on TV during the 1950s and 1960s, his popularity seemed to have dimmed. This is reflected in his lack of big-screen appearances. Hollywood is a perfect barometer for measuring popular culture — when something, somewhere gets popular, Hollywood makes movies about it. So when Holmes became a hot property again in the 1970s (triggered by the success of Nicholas Meyer's novel *The Seven-Per-Cent-Solution;* refer to Chapter 13), Hollywood jumped on the bandwagon, ushering in the second golden age of Sherlockian cinema.

The Private Life of Sherlock Holmes (1970)

Over the years, Sherlock Holmes films have drawn many famous actors to the role. *The Private Life of Sherlock Holmes* showed that Holmes can land famous directors as well. *Private Life* is Billy Wilder's melancholy, controversial, landmark study of the Great Detective. Holmes is played by Robert Stephens, a star of the British stage. Colin Blakely provides an entertaining, intelligent Dr. Watson, and the two have the best screen chemistry since Rathbone and Bruce.

The plot is entirely original. *Private Life* begins with a set piece involving a Russian ballerina who wants Holmes to father her child, and then it moves on to investigating the disappearance of a woman's husband. The woman is played by Genevieve Page, and the romantic sparks between Holmes and his client fly as the investigation takes them to Scotland, where Mycroft, the Loch Ness Monster, and a German spy plot all figure into the story. Let's just say it isn't a happy ending for either Holmes or his leading lady.

The film wasn't well received on release by either critics or moviegoers. The movie's failure distressed Wilder so greatly that for decades he refused to talk about it. However, its reputation has only grown with time, and for Sherlockians and film aficionados alike, *The Private Life of Sherlock Holmes* is now seen as a near-masterpiece.

They Might Be Giants (1971)

Starring George C. Scott as a mentally ill man who believes he's Sherlock Holmes and Joanne Woodward as a modern-day psychiatrist named Dr. Watson, *They Might Be Giants* explores the boundary between myth and reality. When Woodward's Watson finds herself drawn into Scott's delusion and into a real-life mystery as well, she and the viewer wonder just what *is* reality. Released just six months after *The Private Life of Sherlock Holmes, They Might Be Giants* continues and extends the exploration of the Holmes character. Where *Private Life* looked at Holmes in ways never before done on screen, *Giants* looked at Holmes as an icon, presenting an odd yet entertaining film.

The Adventure of Sherlock Holmes' Smarter Brother (1975)

Hot on the heels of *Young Frankenstein* came *The Adventure of Sherlock Holmes' Smarter Brother,* which attempted to do for Sherlock Holmes what *Young Frankenstein* did for, well, Frankenstein. Gene Wilder, a confessed Sherlockian, plays Sigerson Holmes, the jealous, not-quite-as-talented younger brother of Sherlock. Resentful at living in his famous brother's shadow, Sigerson sets up his own detective agency. When Sherlock sends a case to his brother, Sigerson teams up with Scotland Yard detective Sgt. Orville Stanley Sacker, played by the scene-stealing Marty Feldman. Together (and with the secret help of Sherlock), they set out to solve the case of their beautiful client, played by Madeline Kahn. Chock-full of Sherlockian references, *The Adventure of Sherlock Holmes' Smarter Brother* is clearly made by, and for, fans of the Great Detective.

The Seven-Per-Cent-Solution (1976)

Based on the bestselling novel, *The Seven-Per-Cent Solution* pairs Sherlock Holmes with Dr. Sigmund Freud in a mystery that rewrites Sherlockian history and answers questions about Holmes's personality. The film's script was written by Nicholas Meyer, author of the novel. The film adaptation tweaks some of the story's plot points and offers up a lavish, full-blown Hollywood extravaganza. Nicol Williamson stars as a wonderfully eccentric Sherlock Holmes, Alan Arkin is Freud, a terrific Robert Duvall plays Watson, Vanessa Redgrave is the beautiful damsel in distress, and none other than Sir Laurence Olivier plays Professor Moriarty. Shot on location in Vienna, this big-budget film is a romp and one of the favorites in all of Sherlockian cinema.

The Strange Case of the End of Civilization as We Know It (1977)

By 1977, the cycle of Sherlockian cinema had come full circle. Cinematic spoofs and parodies were common in the earliest, crude silent films, and now they were popular again. *The Strange Case of the End of Civilization as We Know It* was the second big-screen farce in three years. John Cleese plays Arthur Sherlock Holmes, the grandson of the great Sherlock. When the grandson of Professor Moriarty announces that the world will come to an end in five days, the president summons Arthur Sherlock Holmes to help. Nothing deep here — just plain Sherlockian fun.

The Hound of the Baskervilles (1978)

This comic adaption of *The Hound of the Baskervilles,* the third Holmes spoof of the decade, is best remembered as one of the biggest misfires in Sherlockian filmmaking history. Peter Cook, the great English satirist, writer, and comedian, plays Sherlock Holmes. Dudley Moore is Dr. Watson. Cook was legendary in Britain as a comedian in the 1960s, but this joint effort with Moore resulted in a sophomoric, self-indulgent mess. Some say the blame belongs to director Paul Morrissey, who denied Cook and Moore the creative control they wanted. But given the fact that Cook's and Moore's names are all over it, from the script to the score to the acting, they own it.

Murder by Decree (1979)

Think of this as the post-Watergate Sherlock Holmes film. *Murder by Decree* stars the great Christopher Plummer as Holmes and James Mason as a steady, believable Watson. Once again, Holmes finds himself on the trail of Jack the Ripper. However, unlike in *A Study in Terror,* the trail is darker, and the mystery of the Whitechapel killer even deeper, as Holmes uncovers a government conspiracy to cover up the crimes and shield the killer. Rife with political intrigue, *Murder by Decree* offers a 1970s, blow-dried, sensitive Sherlock. But don't be put off by that — it's also a creepy, effective mystery.

The 1980s: The golden age continues

Although the 1980s didn't produce the quantity (or the quality) of Sherlock Holmes films as the preceding decade, Hollywood still cranked out films about the Great Detective. This is remarkable, given that Holmes had been migrating from the big screen to TV. Here are three major examples of Sherlockian cinema from the 1980s:

- ✔ *Young Sherlock Holmes* (1985): When producer Steven Spielberg asked, "What if Sherlock Holmes and Dr. Watson met in boarding school?" the answer was *Young Sherlock Holmes.* In the Chris Columbus-written script, Holmes, famous among his peers for his deductive methods, battles an evil Egyptian cult. Along the way there's a primitive flying machine, hallucinatory drugs, and stained-glass knights. Critics claimed that the film, directed by Barry Levinson, was a bit too Indiana Jones-like. It clearly was intended to be the start of a franchise, but given its disappointing reception, *Young Sherlock Holmes* was a one-off effort.

- ✔ *The Great Mouse Detective* (1986): Based on the books by Eve Titus, *The Great Mouse Detective* is the Disney version of *Basil of Baker Street.* Basil is the detective mouse that lives within the walls of 221b Baker Street. Basil is enlisted to help find a girl mouse friend's missing father, uncovering a larger plot along the way. At one point, the voice of Basil Rathbone makes a cameo as the off-screen Sherlock Holmes, making this his last turn as Holmes.

- ✔ *Without a Clue* (1988): The last big-screen Holmes film for over 20 years stars Michael Caine as Sherlock and Ben Kingsley as Watson. *Without a Clue,* however, turns the entire canon on its head by portraying Watson as the brilliant crime solver and Holmes as a drunken lout who only *portrays* the Great Detective in public.

And so ended the last golden age of Sherlockian cinema, with Holmes and Watson as boys, a cartoon mouse, and Holmes as a drunken idiot. Perhaps it was time for a retreat after all.

But maybe another golden age of Sherlockian cinema in just around the corner. After 21 years, Holmes finally returned to the big screen in *Sherlock Holmes,* the action-packed blockbuster from 2009. Emphasizing the more physical aspects of Holmes's character (sword fighting, martial arts, boxing, and so on), this film stars Robert Downey, Jr. as Holmes and Jude Law as Dr. Watson. Director Guy Ritchie brings a fresh interpretation of Holmes and Watson to a new generation of fans.

Sherlock Holmes on TV

The Great Detective holds an honored place in TV history. Though you may know that the character has been the star of a number of well-known TV series produced over the decades, you may be surprised to discover that Holmes was instrumental in the early development of TV broadcasting in America, which is where Sherlock Holmes launched his TV career.

TV technology began to be seriously developed in the 1920s, close on the heels of wireless radio communication. The first truly successful TV technologies were invented by the Russian-born American physicist Vladimir Kosma Zworykin in 1923 and by the American radio engineer Philo Taylor Farnsworth shortly thereafter. TV broadcasting on a regular basis began in England in 1936 and in the U.S. in 1939, but these regularly scheduled broadcasts were interrupted by World War II.

The National Broadcasting Company began trial TV broadcasts in New York City in 1937. On November 27 of that year, NBC aired the very first "teleplay," a production of the Sherlock Holmes short story "The Three Garridebs." Prior to this, TV broadcasts were news, or merely technical tests. This was the very first production of a TV drama. Holmes was chosen as a subject because of his popularity, and "The Three Garridebs" was selected because it had an American angle. There are no records of how many people actually saw it.

NBC's production starred Louis Hector as Holmes and William Podmore as Watson. One of the members of the small audience was a reporter for *The New York Times,* who the next day described it as "an ambitious experiment in teleshowmanship." He went on to add, "The presentation revealed how a skillful TV producer may make use of the best of two mediums, how viewers may witness the realism of flesh and blood acting allied with the more spectacular scenic effects achieved by the screen." Though the picture was a little fuzzy and crude, *The Three Garridebs* was a success.

Holmes next appeared on TV on March 12, 1948, in a production titled *Tea Time for Baker Street,* which aired on WWJ-TV in Detroit. It was created and produced by a well-known Sherlockian named Russell McLaughlin, founder of the Detroit Holmes club called the Amateur Mendicant Society. *Tea Time for Baker Street* is an adventure in which Holmes and Watson are out on a case. The main character is Mrs. Hudson, who, with the aid of her friend

Mrs. Wiggins, solves a crime in their absence. The entire cast was made up of members of the Amateur Mendicant Society. The second-ever Sherlockian-themed telecast was written, produced, and acted by Sherlockians.

Since these early productions, Sherlock Holmes has been featured in numerous TV series. I discuss the four most important in the following sections.

The New Adventures of Sherlock Holmes (1954–1955)

Although Sherlock Holmes had popped up a few times in the early days of TV, it was producer Sheldon Reynolds who first set out to create an entire TV series for Sherlock. Ronald Howard, the son of actor Leslie Howard, was cast as Holmes. His Watson was played by H. Marion Crawford, a familiar character actor in British TV, film, and radio drama. The series lasted for an impressive 39 episodes. Reynolds chose to shoot the show in France, where it was cheaper to produce. Often you'll see French actors in bit parts struggling to hold onto their English accents. But it wasn't the production values that hurt the show — it was the writing. Many of the episodes were adaptations of the canonical tales, but many more were original stories that played Holmes and Watson for camp or comedy. When you see a title like "The Case of the Baker Street Bachelors," you know you're in trouble!

Howard's portrayal of Holmes emphasized his youth and sincerity and downplayed the mood swings, drug abuse, and rudeness found in the character. Crawford's Watson swings wildly from the traditional blustering sidekick in some episodes to a steady, reliable partner in others. But overall, *The New Adventures of Sherlock Holmes* is an entertaining, if often eyebrow-raising, early Sherlock Holmes TV series.

Sherlock Holmes (1964–65)

In 1964, the BBC decided to bring Sherlock Holmes back to the small screen in a regular series. One of its promises was that it would be as true to the spirit of the canon as possible, including the sexual undertones and violence that do, indeed, happen in the tales. In their promotion of the show, the BBC announced that late-Victorian and early-Edwardian London would be accurately reproduced, making this the most accurate adaptation ever. The producers cast Douglas Wilmer as Holmes and Nigel Stock as Dr. Watson.

Wilmer, who was a fan of Holmes, is an excellent Sherlock, often portraying the many sides of the detective's complicated personality — even his unflattering ones. Stock gives a fine performance as Watson, helping with the long rehabilitation of the character after Nigel Bruce's bumbling duffer opposite Basil Rathbone.

Wilmer starred in 13 episodes of the series but declined to reprise the role when the series was renewed. It was then that the BBC turned to another actor familiar with the role of Holmes, Peter Cushing, when the series was revived in 1968.

Sherlock Holmes (1968)

When Douglas Wilmer bowed out of the BBC's Holmes series after one season, the BBC turned to an actor who had already played Sherlock on the big screen — Peter Cushing. It was a good choice. Cushing had risen to fame in a long string of horror movies produced by Hammer Studios. Best-known for playing Baron Frankenstein and Dr. Van Helsing, Cushing donned the deerstalker in the 1958 Hammer version of *The Hound of the Baskervilles.* (Of course, to later generations, Cushing would be remembered as Grand Moff Tarkin, commander of the Death Star in *Star Wars.*)

If anything, Cushing was an even greater fan of Holmes than Wilmer was, often changing the script to conform to the text of the canon. In later interviews, Cushing claims the short shooting schedule, coupled with personal concerns (his wife was extremely ill at the time), resulted in only mediocre performances on his part. But he's wrong. Cushing is terrific in the role, and his 16-episode series is one of the best adaptations of the adventures of Sherlock Holmes.

The Granada Television "Sherlock Holmes" series (1984–1995)

At the beginning of the 1980s, Michael Cox of Britain's Granada Television set out to do what no one had done before — produce the most faithful, accurate adaptation of Sherlock Holmes ever brought to screen. To do this, Cox assembled the cream of British TV talent — writers, directors, and cinematographers with credits and experience on some of Britain's most famous productions.

Cox took a significant first step when his team compiled *The Baker Street File: A Guide to the Appearance and Habits of Sherlock Holmes and Dr. Watson.* Using the original 60 stories, they compiled a list of character traits, descriptions of persons and places, and other details. This became the "bible" that scriptwriters, actors, and the production team used to maintain authenticity. Whenever a question arose about a set or a character's clothing or personality, the team could find the answer in *The Baker Street File.* It also allowed them to build believable interior sets for 221b Baker Street, and further research resulted in an amazing block-long exterior reconstruction of Baker Street itself.

Despite this unprecedented effort, it would have all been in vain without the final piece of the puzzle — actors who would play Sherlock Holmes, Dr. Watson, and the other regular characters.

The cast and the chemistry

In the role of Sherlock Holmes, Cox and company cast Jeremy Brett (see Figure 14-3), a classically trained actor perhaps best-known for playing Freddy Eynsford-Hill, Audrey Hepburn's lovesick suitor from *My Fair Lady*. Brett's performance came like a thunderclap to viewers used to the traditional interpretation of Holmes. Whereas previous Sherlocks tended to fix on individual characteristics of Holmes's complex personality, Brett presented the full character, warts and all. Not only did Brett's performance finally replace Rathbone's as Sherlock Holmes in the public's mind, but it also changed the public's *understanding* of Holmes. No longer was Sherlock a stuffy, old-fashioned straight arrow, saying, "Elementary, my dear Watson," while being followed around by a doddering old duffer. No, Brett's Holmes was mesmerizing, brilliant, moody, drug-abusing, and, to be honest, a bit scary.

No other actor struggled with the role of Sherlock Holmes as much as Brett did. In a 1987 interview for *The Sherlock Holmes Review*, Brett spoke about his thoughts on playing the Great Detective. "I was never really turned on to Sherlock," said Brett. "I find him a cold fish. It's only later, when I was offered the part and started to read the stories again, that I began to find lots of chinks in the armor which made it more human to play." Brett immersed himself in the role, and by the end of the series, the line between the actor and the role had, for actor and viewer alike, become a bit blurred. His interpretation has colored the performance of every actor who has portrayed the Great Detective in his wake.

As important to Cox as getting Holmes right was the rehabilitation of Dr. Watson. Gone was Nigel Bruce's entertaining but moronic portrayal. Instead, Cox cast David Burke, who gave an utterly believable portrayal of the good Doctor. Burke made viewers believe that the Watson on screen could have actually written the stories and was the kind of man who could forge a friendship with the Great Detective. After the first 13 installments, Burke left the show, and Cox hit another home run by casting Edward Hardwicke as Granada's second Dr. John Watson. Hardwicke was up to the task and continued to redefine the character. Watson was elevated from the bumbling comic-relief character familiar to generations and was rightfully reinstated as Doyle's original vision from the canon.

With Holmes and Watson cast, the final piece of the puzzle fell into place. Brett and Burke, and then Brett and Hardwicke, got the relationship — the *friendship* — right. It's this friendship that drives the entire canon and keeps readers (and viewers) coming back to the stories again and again. Granada got it right.

Figure 14-3:
Jeremy
Brett as
Sherlock
Holmes.

The results

The first episode of this landmark series debuted in Britain on April 24, 1984, and in the U.S. on May 14, 1985. Over the next ten years, Granada adapted 41 of the 60 canonical adventures for the small screen, with many memorable episodes. Perhaps your favorite is "A Scandal in Bohemia" (the first adventure to air), with the beautiful Gayle Hunnicutt as Irene Adler. Or is it "The Final Problem," the first to actually shoot the climactic meeting between Sherlock Holmes and Professor Moriarty where it happened at the Reichenbach Falls? Who can forget the horror and grief of Watson as he calls to his friend down in that fearful chasm? Or maybe, as many fans of the show will tell you, it's impossible to pick a favorite, so great is the quality of this series.

Granada's series is not only the best Sherlock Holmes TV series produced to date but also one of the most successful historical TV series ever produced. Seen in over 50 countries around the world, it stands as a shining example of how a faithful adaptation of a literary classic can work wonders on the screen.

The complete Granada series (12 DVDs!) is available from Amazon at www. amazon.com/Sherlock-Holmes-Complete-Granada-Television/dp/ B000RPCJB6. Also, some of the episodes are available from Netflix — go to www.netflix.com.

The made-for-TV movies

The 1970s were a golden age of Sherlockian cinema, with seven major Holmes films appearing on the big screen during the decade. But that wasn't the only screen that Holmes appeared on at that time. The decade that gave us Jimmy Carter, the pet rock, and disco also gave us a long run of made-for-TV Sherlock Holmes movies. Film and TV producers like nothing better than a trend, and in the 1970s, Holmes was hot. In fact, the made-for-TV Sherlock Holmes movie phenomenon continued right through the next three decades, into the new millennium. Following are some of the highlights.

Sherlock Holmes in New York (1976)

With the big-budget theatrical release of *The Seven-Per-Cent-Solution* set for October 24, 1976, 20th Century Fox Television had to work fast to cash in. Their efforts paid off — *Sherlock Holmes in New York* aired on October 18, 1976, exactly six days before *The Seven-Per-Cent-Solution* hit theater screens. For a TV movie, *Sherlock Holmes in New York* looks great.

By having a first-rate cast of real, Hollywood actors, as well as reusing the sets from the film *Hello Dolly!,* this quickie TV movie looks like a theatrical film. Roger Moore, the James Bond of the 1970s and early 1980s, is a bit stiff in the role of Sherlock (and he might sport the worst hair in any Holmes film, ever). Opposite is Patrick Macnee, who is a serviceable, if forgettable, Watson. John Huston, the great film director, steals every scene he's in as Professor Moriarty, shamelessly (and entertainingly) chewing the scenery. But the plot is the weak link. With a Machiavellian plan by Moriarty to steal gold in New York City and a romance between Irene Adler and Holmes, *Sherlock Holmes in New York* is a combination of camp, melodrama, and clever mystery plotting.

The Return of the World's Greatest Detective (1976)

This made-for-TV movie borrows the premise of the theatrical *They Might Be Giants* and gives it a more lighthearted spin. In *The Return of the World's Greatest Detective,* the pre-*Dallas* Larry Hagman stars as the bumbling LAPD motorcycle officer Sherman Holmes. Sherman, who loves Sherlock Holmes, has his motorcycle fall on his head while he's reading the canon. After getting knocked on the head, he believes he is Sherlock Holmes. The injury has somehow given him Holmes's abilities of observation and deduction, as well as a British accent!

As in *They Might Be Giants,* Sherman/Sherlock is assigned a police psychiatrist named Dr. Watson (played by Jenny O'Hara), and before too long, Holmes and Watson are on a real murder case. *The Return of the World's Greatest Detective* was a pilot for an intended series. Unfortunately for Sherlockians, Hagman got another job — the character of J. R. Ewing on *Dallas* — and the show never materialized.

The Hound of the Baskervilles/The Sign of the Four (1983)

In the early 1980s, Sy Weintraub, an American producer, began working on a series of six Sherlock Holmes TV movies. These programs were to be faithful adaptations of original canonical stories. Casting was complete, with the outstanding Ian Richardson set to play Holmes, and production had begun. Unfortunately, Weintraub wasn't the only one with the idea — it turned out that Granada Television was beginning work on their own Holmes series, starring Jeremy Brett. After a long, contentious legal battle, a settlement was reached, with Granada going on to produce its series and Weintraub settling for just his version of *The Sign of the Four* and *The Hound of the Baskervilles.*

Looking remarkably like Basil Rathbone, Richardson strikes a good balance between Holmes the moody eccentric and Holmes the brilliant, single-minded detective. Even though Richardson never played Holmes again, he went on to play the inspiration for Holmes, Dr. Joseph Bell in the 1999 series *The Dark Beginnings of Sherlock Holmes.* It's a shame that more installments in this series weren't made, as Richardson is an outstanding Sherlock, and both these made-for-TV films are solid, entertaining productions.

The Masks of Death (1984)

Nearly 20 years after Peter Cushing last played Sherlock Holmes on TV, he donned the deerstalker one last time in *The Masks of Death.* The movie starts with Holmes in retirement, until, that is, he is visited by Inspector MacDonald. It seems there's a case that's crying out for assistance from Sherlock Holmes. Holmes agrees to MacDonald's request to come out of retirement, and the game is afoot! A string of mysterious murders, with no detectable way for the victims to have died, has Scotland Yard stumped. As Holmes and Watson get to work, things get complicated as the detective searches for a missing prince, and Germany and England find themselves on the brink of war.

The Crucifer of Blood (1999)

This made-for-TV version of the stage play starred Charlton Heston — yes, that's right, Charlton Heston — as Sherlock Holmes. Heston, better known for *The Ten Commandments* and *Planet of the Apes,* wasn't a stranger to the Great Detective, having played the part on stage 11 years earlier in Los Angeles's acclaimed Ahmanson Theatre production of *The Crucifer of Blood.* Coincidentally, it was in that play that Jeremy Brett, who went on to play Holmes in the Granada Television series, played Dr. Watson to Heston's Holmes. The TV movie of *The Crucifer of Blood* was adapted, directed, and produced by Heston's son Fraser.

Chapter 15

Communities of Sherlockians

From the moment his popularity exploded with his first appearance in *The Strand Magazine,* Sherlock Holmes has commanded an enthusiastic following. As early as 1902, the term *Sherlockian* was used in print to describe those Holmes fans afflicted with a devotion to the world's greatest detective. This devotion has engendered an unprecedented phenomenon of literary societies, fan clubs, and publications about Sherlock that span the globe. It all began in the 1930s with a single, and singular, organization — the Baker Street Irregulars — and the game was afoot!

In this chapter, I look at Sherlock Holmes's devoted following, from its start back in the 1930s up into the 21st century.

The Baker Street Irregulars

Any look at the phenomenal following of Sherlock Holmes must start with the Baker Street Irregulars, the premier Holmes society in the world. Membership numbers just a few hundred worldwide and is by invitation only.

Christopher Morley, the group's founder

Any look at the Baker Street Irregulars must begin with the point man of the entire Sherlockian movement: Christopher Morley.

Christopher Morley's many clubs

Christopher Morley had many friends and acquaintances, and one of his favorite pastimes was starting clubs. Most were short-lived, meeting only once or twice, but two of his groups ended up being direct precursors to the Baker Street Irregulars. The first was the *Grillparzer Morals-Police Association* (named after a secondhand book he had just purchased), and the second was the *Three Hours for Lunch Club*. The latter society's rationale was "to be truant from one's workplace with agreeable friends doing agreeable things: lunching, drinking, sightseeing, book shopping." The membership of these two clubs was largely intertwined, and none of his clubs had regular schedules, instead meeting only when the spirit moved Morley to call up his friends. Recounting the adventures of the Three Hours for Lunch Club in Morley's "Bowling Green" column became a regular feature and was a favorite of his readership. Both the Grillparzer Morals-Police Association and the Three Hours for Lunch Club had members who were also in the first ranks of Baker Street Irregulars membership.

Christopher Morley was born May 5, 1890, in Haverford, Pennsylvania. He was among that fortunate generation of children who were raised on the Sherlock Holmes stories as they were being published. In adulthood, Morley was one of the most popular writers of the early 20th century — a best-selling author, book reviewer, poet, playwright, literary columnist, and, later in life, a television game-show panelist.

Morley wrote a long list of popular novels and was a columnist for newspapers and magazines. He had a regular column in several publications, including *The Saturday Review of Literature* and *The Evening Post,* both of which featured a great deal of Sherlockian commentary, before and after the Baker Street Irregulars had been established. In his *Saturday Review of Literature* column of January 7, 1933, Morley wrote a piece speculating when the birthday of Sherlock Holmes was. (Morley proposed January 6, a date that Sherlockians have largely accepted.) Readers immediately began responding, and many of these correspondents later became members of the Baker Street Irregulars.

So it was Christopher Morley's regular injection of Sherlockiana into his magazine columns that helped light the fuse for the creation of the first, and most famous, Sherlock Holmes society.

The members

According to the history of the Baker Street Irregulars (or BSI), the group's first official meeting was held on January 6, 1934, at the Hotel Duane in Manhattan. Though it was a memorable affair for those who attended, it really wasn't much more than a cocktail party celebrating the birthday of Sherlock Holmes. It wasn't until December 7, 1934, that the Irregulars held their first annual dinner at Christ Cella restaurant. Eighteen members were present.

By the end of the 1940s, the Sherlockian movement had spawned local chapters all across the country, and eventually, all around the world, and the Sherlockian universe had been established. Since 1946, the Irregulars have published a quarterly journal, *The Baker Street Journal,* that contains articles analyzing and commenting on the Holmes stories as if they were real, historic events. Sherlockians call this "playing the game."

You can subscribe to *The Baker Street Journal* at www.bakerstreet journal.com.

For decades, membership in the BSI was male-only, but in 1991, the Irregulars went coeducational (see the sidebar "The Adventuresses of Sherlock Holmes" for details). Over the years, the BSI membership has included many famous authors — Poul Anderson, Isaac Asimov, August Derleth, Neil Gaiman, John Gardner, Howard Haycraft, Ellery Queen, Rex Stout — as well as publishers, journalists, book dealers, politicians, businessmen, and actors. The BSI have even included two U.S. presidents (Franklin Delano Roosevelt and Harry S. Truman).

The Adventuresses of Sherlock Holmes

The decade of the 1960s was an era of social revolution, and these winds of change were felt even in the world of Sherlock Holmes. When the (at that time) all-male Baker Street Irregulars refused to admit women, a small group of female college students picketed the annual dinner of the BSI, urging a change in policy. When the demands of these young women, all from Albertus Magnus College (a small, private, liberal arts college in New Haven, Connecticut), fell on deaf ears, they responded by founding the Adventuresses of Sherlock Holmes (ASH), a women-only alternative, with membership granted by invitation. For 25 years, ASH held a dinner meeting on the same night as the BSI, somewhere across Manhattan. The Adventuresses' dinner, however, was open to both men and women. Finally, when the BSI opened its doors to women in 1991, four men were in turn made special members of ASH. It wasn't until 2008, however, that ASH became fully coeducational. The Adventuresses continue on today, with annual spring and autumn dinners and lunches throughout the year. In addition, they publish their own quarterly journal, *The Serpentine Muse,* and have issued a two-volume anthology of Sherlockian essays. You can find out more about ASH at www. ash-nyc.com.

The meetings

The BSI meet every January in New York City for their annual dinner celebrating the birthday of Sherlock Holmes. The one-night affair has grown over the years, as other events have been added and other Sherlockian organizations have scheduled meetings and dinners around the BSI's. From Christopher Morley's modest beginnings has grown a prestigious society devoted to keeping green the memory of Sherlock Holmes.

The Scion Societies

Shortly after the Baker Street Irregulars began, local chapters started springing up across the country. These small groups quickly became known as *scion societies.* The dictionary defines the word *scion* as "a descendant of a wealthy, aristocratic, or influential family," and that was, especially in the early days, a good way to understand the relationship between the BSI and the local organizations. When local Sherlockians founded their own Holmes club, they petitioned the parent organization for official recognition as a scion society of the Baker Street Irregulars.

Being affiliated with the BSI imposed no requirements, rules, or criteria upon the scion society. (Every Sherlock Holmes club is free to engage in Sherlockian pursuits according to its own lights.) What it did, and still does, is unite the local club in spirit with the legendary group that started it all.

Many Sherlock Holmes clubs remain independent of the BSI. Indeed, sometimes fans of Holmes come together and form a club with no knowledge of this network of Holmes societies, living in a sort of Sherlockian Galapagos Islands, without any contact with the larger world of Sherlock Holmes. Other clubs remain independent by choice. There's even a new phenomenon of Sherlockian organizations being formed in ways, and for motivations, not seen in the past. Consider these examples:

✔ Some Sherlock Holmes clubs have been formed specifically around the Granada Television *Sherlock Holmes* series starring Jeremy Brett.

✔ A considerable group of fans have little interest in the original canon but are instead organized around the Sherlock Holmes/Mary Russell novels of Laurie King. (Local chapters are called *hives.*)

✔ Some science fiction fans cross over, forming clubs blending the worlds of Holmes and *Star Trek,* again with little interest in the original canon or the traditional Holmes clubs.

The great thing is that the Sherlockian universe is big enough for everyone.

How scion societies start

There are as many ways to start a Sherlock Holmes club as there are Sherlock Holmes clubs. One often starts when a couple of Sherlockians meet and discover their mutual love of the canon. A poster in the public library or local mystery bookstore can be the key to discovering a number of like-minded people with an interest in the Great Detective. Sending notices of the new group's first meeting to your town's community event calendars in the newspaper and on the radio can bring you members as well. Any method of getting the word out to the public about a new Sherlock Holmes club often does the trick — Sherlockians are everywhere!

When it comes to Sherlockian groups, new members are often pleasantly surprised that most scion societies have a huge social component to them. Spending time with fellow Sherlockians is almost as much fun as reading the stories themselves.

John Bennett Shaw was a popular and revered member of the Baker Street Irregulars. Shaw's minimum criteria for starting your own scion society was "two Sherlockians, a copy of the canon, and a bottle. In a pinch you can dispense with one of the Sherlockians."

What's in a name?

To the outsider, the cryptic names that Sherlock Holmes societies adopt for themselves seem strange. But in reality, most of the names are drawn from the canon. Some of the best examples of the whimsical phenomenon of Sherlockian scion society names include

- **The Goose Club of the Alpha Inn:** This California club takes its name from the organization that Henry Baker purchased his goose from in "The Blue Carbuncle."

- **The Double-Barrelled Tiger Cubs:** Based in Urbana, Illinois, this club's name is inspired by Watson's tongue-tied storytelling (in an effort to impress Mary Morstan) in *The Sign of the Four.*

- **The Amateur Mendicant Society:** This scion society, based in the Detroit area, has adopted the name of a mysterious organization mentioned in one of Watson's untold tales.

- **The Giant Rats of Sumatra:** One of the best-known untold tales also provides this Memphis, Tennessee, club with its picturesque name.

- **The Cornish Horrors:** This Scotch Plains, New Jersey, group was inspired by Holmes's name for the case recorded in "The Devil's Foot."

Most Sherlock Holmes organizations take their name from something in the canon — either the name of a story (for instance, the Illustrious Clients of Indianapolis, the group your author belongs to), a character, or an event. Some have names that seem to indicate a numerically limited membership, but this usually isn't the case. For instance:

- Three Garridebs of Westchester, New York, have way more than three members.
- The Scion of the Four, in Morgantown, West Virginia. Only four members? Nope . . . way more than four!
- The Six Napoleons of Baltimore, Maryland . . . likewise.
- The 140 Varieties of Tobacco Ash have a long way to go before they reach 140 members. Current membership is a canonical 17 (as in the 17 steps up to Holmes's rooms at 221b Baker Street).

Where and when and what?

Okay, so you want to start a Sherlock Holmes club, and you know how to promote it. But newcomers to the Sherlockian universe often wonder about some nuts-and-bolts questions, which I cover in the following sections.

Where do these groups meet?

The rule of thumb is whatever works for your group is where you should meet. Many clubs meet in members' homes, particularly if the group is small enough. Others regularly gather in a restaurant, holding a dinner meeting in the tradition of the Baker Street Irregulars' annual dinner. Others convene in private clubs, meeting rooms of the public library, or their local bookstore.

What do Sherlockians do at meetings?

Most Sherlockians will agree that one of the favorite activities of a Sherlockian scion society is simply socializing with your friends and fellow Holmes fans. However, most clubs do indeed do more than that. Some of the most common activities include

- **Presenting scholarly papers:** Researching and writing essays and articles about Sherlock Holmes, whether it's mock-scholarship or serious research, is one of the longstanding traditions of Sherlockiana. Many Sherlockians will, at one time or another, find some aspect of the canon that intrigues them, look into it, and write it up. These works often find their way into journals, books, and other publications, but many also debut as presentations at a local meeting.

✔ **Taking the Sherlockian quiz:** Another favorite activity is a brief quiz challenging the knowledge and ingenuity of the group's members. This quiz is often on a story that's up for discussion or some other topic, like Sherlockian cinema, characters from the canon, or story titles. The subjects for composing a Sherlockian quiz are endless.

✔ **Discussing a story:** Often, scion societies will select a story from the canon in advance for discussion at the meeting. This allows the members to debate the finer points of the story, as well as the numerous inconsistencies and ongoing mysteries the tales present.

✔ **Presenting skits, plays, or reader's theater:** Many Sherlockians are moved to present dramatic enactments of the adventures of Sherlock Holmes. Brief comic skits, full-length plays, and group readings of a story are all activities that have occurred in Sherlockian scion societies.

✔ **Showing and telling:** One common activity is sharing newly discovered Sherlockiana with your fellow enthusiasts. Sherlock Holmes is perennially popular, and new books of pastiche adventures of scholarship and commentary regularly appear. Keeping up can be difficult, so sharing the news is a great idea! In addition, many Sherlockians are collectors, and showing off a recent acquisition of rare, collectible Sherlockiana is always appreciated.

✔ **Viewing Sherlockian movies or TV:** Of course, gathering to watch a Sherlock Holmes movie as a group is great fun, and many Holmes societies hold annual Sherlockian film meetings.

✔ **Engaging in other unusual pursuits:** Sherlockians rarely have an interest in only Sherlock Holmes. Those with other hobbies and interests often find ways of combining their love of Sherlock with other pursuits. For instance, some scions are organized around professions, including librarians, undertakers, and geologists! Other clubs combine a passion for Holmes with such interests as magic and magicians, the music of Gilbert and Sullivan, the stories of P. G. Wodehouse, or the appreciation of fine cigars. There's even a Sherlock Holmes society for members of the high IQ organization Mensa!

The Sherlock Holmes Society of London

In England, the preeminent Sherlock Holmes society is, well . . . the Sherlock Holmes Society of London, which was founded in 1951. (There had once been a Sherlock Holmes Society back in the 1930s, but the onset of World War II ended the small group's short existence.) Unlike the Baker Street Irregulars, the SHSL's membership is open to any interested Sherlockian (or, as they say in England, "Holmesian").

In May 1951, to celebrate the Great Exhibition, London hosted an event called the Festival of Britain. It was only a few years after the end of World War II, and London was still recovering from the bombing and devastation of the war. It was felt that this exhibition could instill a feeling of progress, spur recovery, and lift the morale of the nation. Events and exhibitions happened at various sites around London and nearby.

The St. Marylebone Borough Council decided that an exhibition devoted to Sherlock Holmes should be installed. Marylebone was the neighborhood of Baker Street and Sherlock Holmes, so what could be more appropriate? After the decision was made, a group of local Holmesians in charge of planning the exhibition decided to re-create the sitting room at 221b Baker Street. Combing the canon for information, they gathered all the material mentioned in the stories — everything from the jackknife on the fireplace mantel to the wax dummy with a bullet hole in its head. The exhibit was installed in the Abbey National headquarters, which stood on the site of 221b Baker Street. (Abbey National was a British bank and building company at the time.) The exhibition was a smash hit, drawing more than 50,000 people.

The excitement generated by the Festival of Britain inspired those Holmesians who worked on it to start a new group, and shortly thereafter, the Sherlock Holmes Society of London was born. Within a very short time, the SHSL began publishing its own journal (*The Sherlock Holmes Journal*, which appears twice a year), and the group established an annual dinner in January, often on the same weekend as the Baker Street Irregulars. It was common for congratulatory telegrams to be exchanged between the groups on the evening of their festivities. The organization started with 100 members. Today, the membership list tops 1,000!

Over the course of the society's history, pilgrimages have been made to Sherlockian locations on the continent, especially to Switzerland to see the Reichenbach Falls, site of the deadly encounter between Sherlock Holmes and Professor Moriarty.

In addition to an annual meeting, the SHSL holds dinner meetings featuring papers or other presentations and plenty of socializing. And once a year, the SHSL holds a Sherlock Holmes film evening devoted to the cinematic adventures of the Great Detective.

You can find out more about the Sherlock Holmes Society of London at its Web site: www.sherlock-holmes.org.uk.

A Web of Intrigue: Virtual Sherlock Holmes Societies

Though Sherlock Holmes appeared way back in the 1880s, his popularity is as strong as ever, lasting well into the 21st century. As technology and society both evolve, Holmes — and his fans — evolve as well. With the explosion of Internet usage, Sherlockians have found ways to share their enthusiasm for Holmes over the Web.

The Hounds of the Internet

The earliest manifestation of Web-based Sherlockian organizations belongs to the Hounds of the Internet. The Hounds is an online discussion group devoted to the study and enjoyment of Sherlock Holmes. Founded in 1992, right at the dawn of the Internet age, the group formed with a mere six members. Today, membership is in the hundreds, and the Hounds of the Internet is recognized as an official scion society of the Baker Street Irregulars. (For more information, see www.sherlockian.net/hounds/.)

Yahoo! Sherlock Holmes group listings

Other Sherlockian Internet discussion groups, fan clubs, and Web-based societies have appeared since the founding of the Hounds of the Internet. On the Web portal Yahoo!, you can find over 40 Sherlock Holmes groups, including

- **sherlockholmesclub:** This group has over 260 members and is open to all fans of Sherlock Holmes. Its aim is to invite comments and opinions on the canon, reflect on various Sherlockian issues, and bring noteworthy pastiches to the attention of club members.

- **WelcomeHolmes:** This popular online group boasts over 600 active members and makes a point to say that, while following the adventures of Sherlock Holmes, the members also "honor Sir Arthur Conan Doyle, author and 'teller of tales.'"

- **Brett Rathbone Sherlock Holmes Baker Street Club:** It's pretty clear from this group's title what its focus is. In addition to the canon itself, the group, which has over 180 members, places a heavy emphasis on the actors who've portrayed Holmes and Watson throughout the history of the motion picture.

- **Sherlock Everywhere:** This group stands at over 40 members, and the site is a "news exchange for collectors of all things Sherlockian." It offers a place to report on new Sherlockiana and discuss "discoveries of both new Holmes items and old, publications currently arriving in Sherlockian mailboxes, and other news for the collector."

- **Baker Street:** With over 75 members, this site offers a place to share your Sherlockian Web links, discuss theories about the stories, post essays, and, for collectors, advertise want lists and items for sale or trade.

- **sherlockholmessittingroom:** At 130 members, this site attempts to create a Sherlockian club room where members "can come in, sit a while, talk with some friends, leave messages, read others."

The Sherlock Holmes Social Network

The Sherlock Holmes Social Network is a Facebook-like service hosted on ning, an online site that allows users to create their own social networks. The Sherlock Holmes Social Network (`http://sherlockholmes.ning.com/`) describes itself as "part discussion group, part social network," adding that it exists "for one reason: Sherlock Holmes." The site urges users to "bring up topics of interest to you, start discussions, share media files, start your own groups, make blog posts, etc."

On the network, you can find even more Holmes groups, including the Jeremy Brett Fan Club (devoted to Brett and his interpretation of Sherlock Holmes), and Art in the Blood, an online Sherlockian gallery that allows artists to post drawings, paintings, sculpture, costumes, and other items of Sherlockian artwork.

As seems pretty clear, Sherlock Holmes is here to stay, and his admirers continue to get together and celebrate the Great Detective in ways both traditional and modern. Perhaps it's time for you to start your own Sherlock Holmes society!

Part V
The Part of Tens

The 5th Wave   By Rich Tennant

"The body's been contaminated, Detective. Apparently all the King's men tried putting it back together, and— get this— some of the horses got in on the action."

In this part . . .

This part offers immediate answers to questions that many readers will have in mind. These include: What are the ten unsolved mysteries found in the canon? Where would you go if you wanted to visit the actual places where the stories happened? What are the ten most important books about Sherlock Holmes that you should have on your shelf? And what are some of the most memorable quotes of Sherlock Holmes?

I also include an appendix in this part that lists the active Sherlockian societies in the United States.

Chapter 16

Ten Unsolved Mysteries

When it came to Sherlock Holmes, Arthur Conan Doyle worked almost solely within the limits of the short story (remember, only 4 of the 60 tales were novels). The demanding schedule of cranking out short stories for monthly publication required Sir Arthur to write quickly and often away from his writing desk at home. He once complained that cooking up plots for short stories was just as difficult as it was for the novels. He also considered the Holmes stories to be lesser works — merely adventure tales he knocked off between his more serious writing.

All of this adds up to Doyle boldly writing away without double-checking his earlier writings, thereby creating quite a few situations that you might call "gaps in continuity" today. Hashing out the details Doyle did provide and trying to reconcile the contradictions are favorite hobbies of fans and scholars alike.

The Missing Pup

Doyle seemed to forget that in *A Study in Scarlet,* Watson told Holmes that he had a dog. When they first meet, the two tell each other a bit about themselves to see if they'll be good potential roommates. In addition to specifying various annoying habits, Watson says, "I keep a bull pup." However, on moving-in day, the dog is gone, never to be seen. Ever. He's not mentioned again in any story, not even by the most tenuously stretched reference.

Some Sherlockians have suggested that by "bull pup," Watson wasn't referring to a dog but to a firearm of that name. However, Watson likely wouldn't have been referring to a gun under the circumstances. Not only would it be more appropriate for him to "own" or "carry" a weapon than to "keep" one, but also, Holmes had no problem with weapons.

In "The Musgrave Ritual," Watson speaks of the one time when his roommate Holmes fired a gun indoors:

> I have always held, too, that pistol practice should be distinctly an open-air pastime; and when Holmes, in one of his queer humours, would sit in an armchair with his hair-trigger and a hundred Boxer cartridges and proceed to adorn the opposite wall with a patriotic V. R. [Victoria Regina, or Queen Victoria] done in bullet-pocks, I felt strongly that neither the atmosphere nor the appearance of our room was improved by it.

This is hardly the attitude of a man who would warn his roommate that he liked to fire his gun in the apartment, yet anyone who has raised a puppy knows how it can disrupt the routines of daily life. I believe Watson decided to find a new home for his dog when he remembered his friend Stamford saying of Holmes, "I could imagine [Holmes] giving a friend a little pinch of the latest vegetable alkaloid, not out of malevolence, you understand, but simply out of a spirit of inquiry in order to have an accurate idea of the effects."

Watson's Wound

In the opening lines of *A Study in Scarlet*, the reader finds out that Watson had been wounded in battle in Afghanistan, where he was "struck on the shoulder by a Jezail bullet, which shattered the bone and grazed the subclavian artery." In the later novel *The Sign of the Four*, however, he describes himself as "nursing my wounded leg. I had had a Jezail bullet through it some time before, and though it did not prevent me from walking it ached wearily at every change of the weather." Later, in "The Noble Bachelor," Doyle, perhaps realizing the inconsistency he had introduced, vaguely alludes to the Jezail bullet as being "in one of his limbs."

So, what was it? This question has been hotly debated for decades! My personal favorite explanation is that *both* places are right. It happened like this — Watson must have been shot while he was bending over a wounded soldier during the battle. That way, the bullet passed clean through his upper leg and lodged in his shoulder. Voilà! One bullet, two distinct wounds.

The Great Hiatus

Following the fateful showdown between Sherlock Holmes and Professor Moriarty at the Reichenbach Falls in 1891, Holmes disappeared for three years. The period of time between "The Final Problem," in which Holmes presumably died, and "The Empty House," which relates the details of his disappearance, is known by Sherlockians as "The Great Hiatus."

What Holmes did to occupy those missing three years has led to unending debate and continued research in Sherlockian circles. Holmes's own version is as follows:

> I traveled for two years in Tibet, therefore, and amused myself by visiting Lhasa, and spending some days with the head lama. You may have read of the remarkable explorations of a Norwegian named Sigerson, but I am sure that it never occurred to you that you were receiving news of your friend. I then passed through Persia, looked in at Mecca, and paid a short but interesting visit to the Khalifa at Khartoum, the results of which I have communicated to the Foreign Office. Returning to France, I spent some months in a research into the coal-tar derivatives, which I conducted in a laboratory at Montpellier, in the south of France.

Uh . . . right. Somehow this account just hasn't rung true with Sherlockians, and some writers have come up with alternative explanations for this hiatus. In Nicholas Meyer's novel *The Seven-Per-Cent Solution,* the hiatus is depicted as a private sabbatical following Holmes's treatment for cocaine addiction at the hands of Sigmund Freud. Other fantastical, alternative explanations have been offered, and these missing years have a hold on the imagination of countless Sherlockians. Come on, Holmes . . . what were you *really* doing?

The Good Doctor's Wives

It's never been clear exactly how many wives Dr. Watson had during the course of his life. At the end of *The Sign of the Four,* he's engaged to be married to Mary Marston, but readers never actually read about him marrying her. It's a reasonable assumption that he did, because he's married at the beginning of the next story, "A Scandal in Bohemia," the first story in the collection *The Adventures of Sherlock Holmes.*

One of the only things that appears definite is that Mary Marston seems to have died in 1894 during the three-year period when Holmes was presumed dead. Even this is little more than supposition, as Holmes simply expresses condolences to Watson for his "bereavement" in the story "The Empty House." Nowhere is it actually said that it was Watson's wife who had died, and some writers have interpreted "bereavement" to mean something other than death — perhaps merely marital separation.

However, in "The Blanched Soldier," set in 1903, Holmes is chagrined when Watson marries, so it seems clear that something had happened to Mary Marston by at least the early 1900s, and thus Dr. Watson had at least two wives during the course of his life.

Beyond that, Doyle's careless continuity within the stories has led scholars to deduce that there were more than two Mrs. Watsons. Some of these theories are based on what story happened when. Others are dependent on even more tenuous clues. Part of the confusion regarding Watson's wives is that he never once mentioned any of them by name, and all this has led some to claim that there were up to half a dozen Watsonian marriages!

Sherlock and Irene: Did Holmes Fall in Love?

Despite Watson's firm denial, many readers just can't help it. There's something about the mysterious Irene Adler that they just can't let go of. Something tells them that Holmes fell for her.

Right at the beginning of "A Scandal in Bohemia," Watson says, "It was not that he felt any emotion akin to love for Irene Adler. All emotions, and that one particularly, were abhorrent to his cold, precise but admirably balanced mind." But most readers don't buy it. Watson works hard to convince them, saying, "Grit in a sensitive instrument, or a crack in one of his own high-power lenses, would not be more disturbing than a strong emotion in a nature such as his." But even the Good Doctor has doubts. He quickly adds, "And yet there was but one woman to him, and that woman was the late Irene Adler, of dubious and questionable memory."

Sherlockian scholars, pastiche writers, and moviemakers have romantically paired the Great Detective with the beautiful, iron-willed, resourceful "adventuress" over and over again. But don't blame them; blame Watson. Despite his claims to the contrary, it's clear that he knew something was up between the two. He mentions a secret about Sherlock — that he keeps Irene's picture locked in his desk drawer. "And when he speaks of Irene Adler," he adds, "or when he refers to her photograph, it is always under the honourable title of *the* woman."

Oh, yeah . . . he fell for her.

The Moriarty Brothers

How many Moriarty brothers were there? And what were their names? As trivial as this may sound, the question has vexed Sherlockians for decades. It all stems, once again, from sloppy continuity on the part of Arthur Conan Doyle.

In "The Final Problem," Watson tells of how he's moved to write the story because of "the recent letters in which Colonel James Moriarty defends the memory of his brother." Then, in "The Empty House," the professor's first name is finally revealed — it's James, just like his aforementioned brother!

And finally, in *The Valley of Fear,* Holmes says that the professor "is unmarried. His younger brother is a stationmaster in the west of England." So, there were three Moriarty brothers, and at least two of them had the first name of James. But is this so? The question of how many Moriarty brothers there were, and how many of them were called James (the favorite theory is that they were *all* named James!), has provided much amusement for Sherlock Holmes fans in the years since the stories were first published.

Canonical Chronology

Almost from when the Holmes stories were first being written, readers and commentators began trying to determine when the stories took place, and in what order they actually happened. Of course, such inquiry depends on treating the stories as accounts of real events and real people. This intellectual game has been a hallmark of Sherlockian fandom from the beginning, and one of its earliest manifestations was working out the canonical chronology.

Since the publication of the final Sherlock Holmes story, at least 17 full canonical chronologies have been completed. Each one tries to date all 60 stories by day, month, and year. You would think this would be pretty easy, right? Just read the stories, make a note of when Watson says they took place, and by the final story, you'll have a chronology.

If only it were that easy. Doyle's internal inconsistencies and Watson's admission to fudging dates, facts, and names to protect the identities of those involved have led to a wide disagreement among the chronologists, who concur on only about 40 percent of the stories.

Two Sherlockians who've actually studied the various canonical chronologies, Andrew J. Peck and Leslie S. Klinger, list the elements that most chronologists use to make their list. These include

✔ References to newspapers, letters, and real-life publications like *Whitaker's Almanack*

✔ Statements by Holmes or Watson that are backed up by evidence from other places in the canon

✔ Claims by any character that can be confirmed by independent sources

✔ Unverifiable, uncorroborated statements

In the end, does it matter? Not really, but once the notion of treating the Sherlock Holmes stories as reality takes root, the puzzle of what happened when becomes almost addictive.

What Color Was Holmes's Dressing Gown?

Most people know the iconography that immediately calls to mind Sherlock Holmes — deerstalker hat; big, curvy calabash pipe; magnifying glass. Right behind these items is Sherlock's favorite around-the-house wardrobe article, the dressing gown. Throughout the canon, Holmes is portrayed wearing it over his clothes. He wears it while doing chemical experiments, smoking during a "three-pipe problem," working on updating his scrapbooks, and even interviewing new clients. Holmes wore it not only for comfort but also, undoubtedly, to keep away the chill of his 19th-century flat.

But what color was it? At various times his dressing gown has been described as being blue, purple, and "mouse," which most people agree is a grey/brown color. As trivial as it may seem, even this question has taxed the minds of Sherlockian scholars. Were there three separate gowns, or is the theory of Christopher Morley, the founder of the Baker Street Irregulars, correct? His theory is that there was only one gown, which began life as blue, faded over time to purple, and then finally ended up being "mouse."

The official colors of the Baker Street Irregulars' club tie are blue, purple, and grey, reflecting the different shades of Holmes's dressing gown.

The Knighthood Question: Why French and Not English?

At the beginning of "The Three Garridebs," Doyle writes that Holmes had been offered knighthood for his services to the country over the years. To the reader's shock, however, Holmes refused the honor, and Doyle offers no explanation for why Holmes turned it down.

Some Sherlockians have speculated that Holmes's rejection of the honor shows his contempt for authority. Others have proposed that public honors such as knighthood went against his more private nature. The question becomes more difficult when you consider that earlier, in "The Golden Pince-Nez," Watson says that Holmes accepted the highest honor the French government can bestow, the legendary *Legion d'honneur.* Which begs the question: Why accept such an honor from France and not from your own country?

Perhaps something happened during those eight years that altered his perspective on such things. And after all, Holmes's grandmother was French, which may have been a factor in his acceptance of the Legion of Honor. In real life, when Doyle himself was offered knighthood, his first inclination was to turn it down. However, his mother was shocked that her son would insult the king of England in such a way, and she insisted that he accept. And so he did. But evidently, his mother's influence couldn't keep Doyle from having Sherlock turn it down! Surely, Holmes's refusal of knighthood is a projection of Doyle's own feelings about the award.

Where Was 221b Baker Street?

Originally, 221b Baker Street existed only in the world of Sir Arthur's imagination. When Doyle first worked up the location of Holmes's rooms, he mentioned in his notes the area of "Upper Baker Street." At that time, however, no such number as 221 (with or without a letter) really existed on that street; it was just something he made up.

Through an odd series of coincidences over the decades, Baker Street underwent some alterations that resulted in the appearance of a real 221b — in the area that was called "Upper Baker Street." Thus, Holmes finally came home to where he had been all along.

Chapter 17

Ten Sherlockian Places to Visit

*I*n this chapter, you find a potpourri of Sherlockian sites — actual physical locations to visit that are mentioned in various Holmes stories. Not surprisingly, most are located in London, where Sherlock Holmes lived and worked. However, there are canonical sites all over England and Europe and, as you'll see in this list, even in the United States!

You may find it astonishing how much of Sherlockian London still exists. For the Holmesian, visiting these places makes the stories come alive.

The Baker Street Tube Station

The number one location on most Sherlockians' list of places to visit is Baker Street. The mere mention of this commercial thoroughfare conjures a magical image of gas lamps and hansom cabs, deadly villains and desperate clients, and, of course, Sherlock Holmes and Dr. Watson. When traveling to Baker Street, most pilgrims take the Underground (the London subway), arriving at the Baker Street Tube station.

The station is located at the intersection of Baker Street and Marylebone Road and is one of the original stations of the Underground system. It was built in 1863, back when the Underground was known as the Metropolitan Railway.

Upon arrival, you'll see that the station embraces its association with Sherlock Holmes. The walls of the platforms are decorated with ceramic tile images of the Great Detective's profile (see Figure 17-1).

Figure 17-1:
Sherlock
Holmes
greets
travelers on
the platform
of the Baker
Street Tube
Station.

When you exit the station, you'll notice the large statue of Holmes, commemorating the station's famous neighbor. A few doors east of the station, on Marylebone Road, is Madame Tussauds Wax Museum, which has an exhibit featuring Robert Downey Jr. as Sherlock Holmes.

The Sherlock Holmes Museum, 221b Baker Street

If you visit only one place in your Sherlock Holmes quest, it has to be the most famous Sherlockian address — 221b Baker Street, London, England.

Despite the amount of time that has passed since the Great Detective lived there (fictional or not, he seems real to his fans), the rooms where he and Watson spent so much time together have been meticulously kept by the careful — one might even say worshipful — curators of the Sherlock Holmes Museum (see Figure 17-2). The location was actually a boardinghouse back when Holmes and Watson were busy solving crimes, and it was acquired by the Sherlock Holmes International Society, which took a lot of care to make it seem real.

And it does seem real. Here, you can step back in time to that wonderful era when anxious supplicants were escorted by Mrs. Hudson up the 17 steps (yes, there really are 17, just like in the stories) to appeal for help from the world's first consulting detective. You can see the acid-stained table where Holmes pursued his chemical experiments, marvel at the odd souvenirs of his life that line the walls and shelves, and get a real sense of what Holmes's Victorian living quarters were like — from the size of the rooms to the floor plan and layout. It's as if Holmes and Watson had just stepped out on a case before you arrived.

And after you've toured the rooms, the ground floor gift shop will satisfy your need for Sherlockian souvenirs!

The museum is open from 9:30 a.m. to 6 p.m. daily except Christmas. Admission is £6 for adults and £4 for children under 16 (roughly $8.58 and $5.72 at the time of publication). If you can't make it in person, you can see a video tour by going to www.sherlock-holmes.co.uk/video.html.

Technically, the museum's address, by modern numbering standards, should be 239 Baker Street, but the government allows it to use the real number out of respect for its most famous resident.

Figure 17-2:
The Sherlock Holmes Museum at 221b Baker Street, London.

Photo courtesy of Steven Doyle.

The Strand

Next to Baker Street, the street most associated with Sherlock Holmes is the Strand, running from Trafalgar Square east for three-quarters of a mile, where it intersects with Fleet Street. This famous street is mentioned in 8 of the 60 stories. For instance, in *A Study in Scarlet,* Watson says that, when he returned to London after being discharged from the army, he lived for a while in a hotel in the Strand. Henry Baskerville purchased new boots in a shoe shop in the Strand. Simpson's, Sherlock Holmes's favorite restaurant, is still in business, located in the Strand. And in "The Resident Patient," Holmes and Watson take a stroll through London, watching the ebb and flow of life as it moves through the Strand. Obviously, this area was a favorite of Holmes's.

And of course, the Holmes stories were published in *The Strand Magazine,* whose offices were just one block off the Strand on Burleigh Street. An illustration of the famous street, showing St. Mary le Strand Church in the distance, was on the magazine's cover. To walk down the Strand today is, for the Sherlockian, like walking into the cover of *The Strand Magazine* itself, so similar is the streetscape (see Figure 17-3).

Figure 17-3: The iconic street scene on the cover of *The Strand Magazine,* and the same, virtually unchanged view today.

Photo courtesy of Steven Doyle.

The Lyceum Theatre

On Wellington Street, near the Strand, is the Lyceum Theatre, a location with strong Sherlockian associations. It's here that Holmes, Watson, and Mary Morstan had their fateful rendezvous with Thaddeus Sholto in *The Sign of the Four*. Sholto instructed Miss Morstan to "be at the third pillar from the left outside the Lyceum Theatre to-night at seven o'clock. If you are distrustful bring two friends." She was distrustful, and therefore, she brought Holmes and Watson. The third pillar from the left is still there, as is the theater itself.

The Lyceum (see Figure 17-4) is also famous for having been the venue of William Gillette's play, *Sherlock Holmes,* during its run in London. The theater is still a working venue, so if you're visiting London you can take in a show at this famous location.

Figure 17-4:
The Lyceum Theatre, where Holmes, Watson, and Mary Morstan began the case known as *The Sign of the Four*.

Photo courtesy of Steven Doyle.

The Sherlock Holmes Pub

Located at 10-11 Northumberland Street, the Sherlock Holmes Pub is a mandatory pilgrimage site for all Sherlockians. Back in Holmes's day, it was known as the Northumberland Arms and was the hotel that Sir Henry Baskerville stayed in while in London. It was here that his boot was stolen, and Holmes himself visited Sir Henry here while investigating the case. This hotel is also where Holmes tracked down the mysterious stranger from the short story "The Noble Bachelors." It's a true Sherlockian landmark, but its history doesn't end there.

In 1957, the Sherlock Holmes exhibit from the Festival of Britain was installed on the second floor of the building, and the name was changed to the Sherlock Holmes Pub. (See Chapter 15 for more on the Festival of Britain and this exhibit.) The entire pub became Sherlockian-themed, with memorabilia throughout the ground floor and the world's first replica of the 221b sitting room visible to diners through a large glass window (see Figure 17-5). Stop in for lunch and a pint!

Figure 17-5:
The
Sherlock
Holmes Pub.

Photo courtesy of Steven Doyle.

While you're there, step outside and look to the building next door. This is the location of Neville's Turkish Bath (see Figure 17-6), which Holmes and Watson patronized at the beginning of "The Illustrious Client."

A Turkish bath is a style of bathing imported from the East. The bather is exposed to heat and steam to induce perspiration. This is followed by washing, massaging, and drying in a drying room. It was known to leave patrons extremely relaxed and seems to have been a favorite experience of both Holmes and Watson.

Figure 17-6:
The sight
of Neville's
Turkish
Bath.

Photo courtesy of Steven Doyle.

St. Bartholomew's Hospital

This famous hospital — popularly known as "St. Bart's" — is another prime Sherlockian location (in the Smithfield area of London). When Holmes and Watson first met, the Great Detective was studying chemistry there, and the doctor naturally assumed that the eager young man performing an experiment on human blood was a medical student.

St. Bart's (see Figure 17-7) dates all the way back to the 12th century, and the fact that Holmes studied there implies that he was the recipient of the totality of British biochemical research over long centuries of time.

Although the hospital itself is off-limits to tourists, as it's still an actual working medical facility, researchers have identified a small room that was the site of Holmes and Watson's fateful first meeting. Years ago, a plaque commemorating the occasion was installed in the room, but it has now been moved to the hospital's museum.

You can visit the museum and see the plaque (see Figure 17-8) Tuesday through Friday from 10 a.m. to 4 p.m., except on holidays (admission is free). In the museum, you can see the kinds of medical equipment that Dr. Watson would have used in his medical practice and the chemical apparatus that Holmes trained on.

Figure 17-7:
The entrance to St. Bartholomew's Hospital.

Photo courtesy of Steven Doyle.

AT THIS PLACE NEW YEARS DAY, 1881
WERE SPOKEN THESE DEATHLESS WORDS

"YOU HAVE BEEN
IN AFGHANISTAN, I PERCEIVE."
BY
Mr. SHERLOCK HOLMES
IN GREETING TO
JOHN H. WATSON, M.D.
AT THEIR FIRST MEETING

THE BAKER STREET IRREGULARS — 1953
BY THE AMATEUR MENDICANTS AT THE CAUCUS CLUB.

Figure 17-8:
The plaque commemorating Holmes and Watson's first meeting.

Photo courtesy of Steven Doyle.

The Langham Hotel

One of the grandest hotels of Victorian London is still one of London's finest. Built at a cost of £300,000 (that's over $31 million in today's money), the Langham (see Figure 17-9) was the most luxurious, modern hotel in the city. Its opening ceremony was conducted by the Prince of Wales. It was, indeed, fit for a king. That's why Arthur Conan Doyle had the king of Bohemia reside at the Langham during "A Scandal in Bohemia," and the famous hotel is also featured in *The Sign of the Four*.

Doyle knew the hotel firsthand. It was at the Langham that the author attended a famous dinner party hosted by the publisher of *Lippincott's Monthly Magazine* and was commissioned (along with Oscar Wilde) to write for the magazine. Doyle wrote *The Sign of the Four,* and Wilde wrote *The Picture of Dorian Gray.*

Figure 17-9:
The
Langham
Hotel.

Photo courtesy of Steven Doyle.

The Criterion Bar

Located in Piccadilly Circus, the Criterion Bar is the fateful place where the entire canon got started. Watson says in *A Study in Scarlet* that "I was standing at the Criterion Bar, when someone tapped me on the shoulder, and turning round I recognized young Stamford, who had been a dresser under me at Bart's." Watson tells his old friend that he's looking for a roommate to save money, and Stamford replies that he knows someone else who is looking for a roommate, and he'll introduce him to Watson. That someone is Sherlock Holmes.

The Criterion Bar (see Figures 17-10 and 17-11) is still there, and you can go inside and have a drink at the bar, just as Watson did so many years ago.

Photo courtesy of Steven Doyle.

Figure 17-10:
The entrance to the Criterion Bar.

Figure 17-11:
The inside of the Criterion Bar, where Watson met his friend Stamford.

Photo courtesy of Steven Doyle.

The British Museum

When the young Sherlock Holmes first came to London, determined to become a detective, he rented an apartment near one of that city's great centers of knowledge. In "The Musgrave Ritual," he tells Watson, "I had rooms in Montague Street, just round the corner from the British Museum, and there I waited, filling in my too abundant leisure time by studying all those branches of science which might make me more efficient."

The British Museum (see Figure 17-12) had been open to the public for around a century before England's most famous sleuth took up his studies in its storied halls. Happily, the museum has no general admission charge (although some special exhibits do have a fee). Located on Great Russell Street, its hours are 10 a.m. to 8:30 p.m. on Thursday and Friday and 10 a.m. to 5:30 p.m. every other day of the week. For more information, see www. britishmuseum.org/.

Figure 17-12: The British Museum.

Photo courtesy of Steven Doyle.

After you finish your visit to the museum, head across the street to the Museum Tavern (see Figure 17-13). Sherlockian scholars have identified this location as the best candidate for the Alpha Inn, the favorite bar of Henry Baker of "The Blue Carbuncle." This spot was where the famous goose with the jewel in its crop came from and where Holmes and Watson questioned the landlord about his goose club.

Figure 17-13:
The
Museum
Tavern.

Photo courtesy of Steven Doyle.

Salt Lake City, Utah

When Doyle wrote *A Study in Scarlet,* the novel that introduced Sherlock Holmes, he was relying on secondhand information about the history behind the founding of Salt Lake City, the famous Mormon city in the American desert. Nonetheless, and despite the 19th-century prejudices that permeate that novel, any Sherlockian worth his or her salt should pay a visit to the area that inspired Doyle to give Sherlock Holmes to the world.

While you're there, you may want to drop in on the Joseph Smith Memorial Building on Main Street and South Temple. Back in Sir Arthur's day, this was the Hotel Utah, where Doyle stayed when he visited on a speaking tour in 1923. Doyle was invited to speak at the Salt Lake Tabernacle then, and it's another must-see site. The invitation and its acceptance were undertaken in the spirit of putting to rest the enmity that *A Study in Scarlet* had generated in Utah.

For a real idea of what the Mormon part of the story was like, don't miss This Is The Place Heritage Park at 2601 E. Sunnyside Avenue (see Figure 17-14), which re-creates early Mormon settlements dating from the time of *A Study in Scarlet*.

Figure 17-14: A re-created Mormon settlement from the days of *A Study in Scarlet*.

Photo courtesy of Steven Doyle.

Chapter 18

Ten Books Every Sherlockian Should Have

*I*f you're a die-hard Sherlock Holmes fan, or even if you're just curious to dig a little bit deeper into the world he lived in, this chapter lists some books you've just got to have in your library. Some of these books are rare, older classics of Sherlockiana, and others are more modern.

The older books may cost you a fortune at a rare bookshop, but many of the old classic titles have been reissued in new editions over the years. I provide links to online copies wherever possible to save you both money and trouble.

The Baker Street Journal

Okay, so this first one isn't a book. Nonetheless, *The Baker Street Journal* is a *publication* every Sherlockian should have. *The Baker Street Journal* (or BSJ) is the official publication of the Baker Street Irregulars and the premier publication of scholarship about Sherlock Holmes. The Baker Street Irregulars have been publishing *The Baker Street Journal*, billed as an "irregular quarterly of Sherlockiana," since 1946. With both serious scholarship and articles that play the game that Holmes was real, the *Journal* is essential reading for anyone interested in Sherlock Holmes, Sir Arthur Conan Doyle, and a world where it's always 1895.

The Baker Street Journal is published quarterly, with a bonus *Baker Street Journal Christmas Annual* published in December. A subscription to the BSJ is $37.50 in the United States and $47.50 everywhere else in the world. You can subscribe by going to this Web site: www.bakerstreetjournal.com/.

The Complete Sherlock Holmes

Although you can pick up copies of the individual Holmes books, such as *The Adventures of Sherlock Holmes* or *The Memoirs of Sherlock Holmes,* there's nothing like having the whole shebang all rolled together into one neat package. Like the title says, you get every single story that Arthur Conan Doyle wrote about the Great Detective in one volume. Originally published by Doubleday in 1930 after Doyle's death, *The Complete Sherlock Holmes* has now been issued in various volumes by a number of publishers. You should have no problem getting a copy. The one-volume edition is really handy!

The Sherlock Holmes Reference Library/ The New Annotated Sherlock Holmes

William S. Baring-Gould, who wrote *The Annotated Sherlock Holmes* in 1967, may have been the quintessential Holmes scholar of his time, but new times generate new ways of looking at things and new values to explore. Leslie Klinger has annotated not one, but *two* editions of the Sherlock Holmes canon.

The first is *The Sherlock Holmes Reference Library,* a staggering, ten-volume, 3,000-page set that features over 9,000 annotations, as well as charts, illustrations, and appendixes. Aimed at the hard-core Sherlockian, it's the most complete collection of canonical scholarship and commentary ever assembled. You can purchase it on the publisher's Web site: www. wessexpress.com.

Klinger's second annotated edition is *The New Annotated Sherlock Holmes,* published in 2004. This 3-book set (with 2 volumes covering the 56 short stories and another covering the 4 novels) takes much of the material from *The Sherlock Holmes Reference Library* and refocuses it for a more general audience. In doing so, Klinger adds new material on Victorian customs and history, providing context and background. Upon publication, *The New Annotated Sherlock Holmes* was an instant classic to a new generation of readers and writers, and it has gone on to win several awards.

You can find this more modern look at Holmes and Watson in most retail bookstores or online at Amazon.com.

The Private Life of Sherlock Holmes

Julian Wolff, the legendary leader of the Baker Street Irregulars, called Vincent Starrett's landmark book, *The Private Life of Sherlock Holmes,* "the greatest book about Sherlock Holmes that has ever been written!" Its publication in 1933 inspired and motivated those kindred spirits to come together as the Baker Street Irregulars. As one of the first books of Sherlockiana, *Private Life* encouraged fans of Holmes to indulge in the intellectual game of Sherlockian studies. It has remained a beloved favorite and cornerstone work in any Holmes collection, and nearly everything written about the Great Detective since its publication owes something to it. Over the years, several editions have been issued, but most are expensive and difficult to find.

A magnificent 75th anniversary facsimile edition is now available at www.wessexpress.com.

The Baker Street Reader: Cornerstone Writings about Sherlock Holmes

This anthology of Sherlockian writing, compiled and edited by Philip A. Shreffler, is one of the best collections on the subject ever assembled. It covers all the burning topics in the Sherlockian universe — When was Holmes born? Where did he go to school? Where is 221b Baker Street? What's up with Watson's wounds? And what about Sherlock's cocaine use? — and on and on. You'll be surprised at some of the authors, too, which include Edmund Wilson, T. S. Eliot, and other recognizable names.

The Misadventures of Sherlock Holmes

This collection of parodies and pastiche published by Ellery Queen is the first anthology of its kind.

The Misadventures of Sherlock Holmes immediately had its own misadventure when it was published in 1944: Doyle's estate (at that time run by his two sons, Denis and Adrian Conan Doyle) felt that this book somehow infringed upon the rights of the estate, and through a threat of litigation, the estate had the publisher pull and suppress the volume. But not before a good number of them got out.

Thank goodness they did, because *The Misadventures of Sherlock Holmes* is a classic! You'll pay a premium for a good copy from a used book dealer, but if you're building a cornerstone collection, it's a must-have.

The Seven-Per-Cent Solution

When Nicholas Meyer's *The Seven-Per-Cent Solution* hit the bookstores in 1974, it exploded as a bestseller and kicked off a Sherlockian golden age that lasted for a decade. The book itself spent the better part of the year on *The New York Times* Best Seller List.

The Seven-Per-Cent Solution is a pastiche presented as a recently recovered lost manuscript of Dr. John H. Watson. (This gimmick has been imitated by pastiche authors so often that it's now a cliché, but Meyer was the first to use it, and in his novel, the idea is still fresh.) *The Seven-Per-Cent Solution* tells of Holmes's heroic fight to kick his addiction to cocaine by seeking the help of Sigmund Freud. Along the way he solves a kidnapping and prevents a European war. The book was so popular that it was adapted into a successful Hollywood film (see Chapter 14). If you include only one Sherlockian pastiche on your bookshelf, make it *The Seven-Per-Cent Solution*.

The Life of Sir Arthur Conan Doyle

This official biography by the great mystery author John Dickson Carr is still one of the best of the many Doyle biographies. Despite being over 60 years old, it's still an exciting read. Doyle is given a sympathetic treatment by a fellow mystery author who provides a fair overview of Sir Arthur's life, taking into account both his foibles and his strengths and making it easy for the modern reader to understand Doyle's drives, obsessions, triumphs, and tragedies. Carr's work traces Doyle's life from his sometimes turbulent childhood through his medical training and into his literary success, and it portrays its subject as a many-sided individual shaped by complex forces.

The Encyclopaedia Sherlockiana

Its full title is *The Encyclopaedia Sherlockiana; or, A Universal Dictionary of the State of Knowledge of Sherlock Holmes and His Biographer, John H. Watson, M.D.* Although there have been numerous Sherlockian handbooks and encyclopedias, Jack Tracy's volume takes a unique approach by using the idea that the book was written during the Victorian era. Thus, from A to Z, all the information between the covers is state-of-the-art circa 1895. For those who value the smallest of details in the Holmes stories, this book has remained a cornerstone for over 30 years.

Starring Sherlock Holmes

No Sherlockian library is complete without at least one book on the films of Sherlock Holmes. In *Starring Sherlock Holmes,* British cinephile David Stuart Davies serves up a big, lavishly illustrated survey of the film and TV portrayals of Holmes. Full of interesting nuggets of Sherlockian cinematic trivia, the book presents the full sweep of this large subject — from *Sherlock Holmes Baffled* up through the TV series starring Jeremy Brett, and beyond. As much fun to look at as it is to read, *Starring Sherlock Holmes* comes highly recommended.

Chapter 19

Ten Notable Quotes and Passages

In This Chapter

▶ A few famous quotes

▶ Several revealing passages

▶ One undying myth

You could easily fill a book with memorable quotations and passages from the Sherlock Holmes stories. I don't have that much space, though, so you'll have to settle for a handful of the best ones. Some are just so Holmesian that they simply can't be left out, while others give you a revealing glimpse inside our good friends Holmes and Watson.

Holmes's Literary Game

One of the most famous moments in the canon appears in "The Abbey Grange," when Holmes rouses Watson from a sound sleep, crying, "Come, Watson, come! The game is afoot. Not a word! Into your clothes and come!"

"The game is afoot" — "game" in this case meaning the hunting of an animal — isn't an original saying by the detective, however. It's actually one of Holmes's many allusions to Shakespeare. This quote comes from *Henry V,* Act 3, Scene I, when King Henry rouses his troops to battle:

> I see you stand like greyhounds in the slips,
>
> Straining upon the start. The game's afoot:
>
> Follow your spirit, and upon this charge
>
> Cry 'God for Harry, England, and Saint George!'

The Dog That Didn't Bark

In one adventure, everyone else is trying to figure out what happened, but Holmes solves the mystery by noticing what didn't happen. In "Silver Blaze," a police inspector asks Holmes, "Is there any other point to which you would wish to draw my attention?" Then the following exchange occurs:

"To the curious incident of the dog in the night-time."

"The dog did nothing in the night-time."

"That was the curious incident," remarked Sherlock Holmes.

This is one of the greatest passages in mystery literature, its very brevity making it so eminently quotable. As Holmes explains in greater detail later on,

" . . . I had grasped the significance of the silence of the dog, for one true inference invariably suggests others. The Simpson incident had shown me that a dog was kept in the stables, and yet, though someone had been in and had fetched out a horse, he had not barked enough to arouse the two lads in the loft. Obviously the midnight visitor was someone whom the dog knew well."

The Impossible and the Improbable

One of Holmes's basic investigative principles is that you absolutely have to face the facts whether you like them or not. He expresses this idea over and over again, but his favorite way of putting it is: "When you have eliminated all which is impossible, then whatever remains, however improbable, must be the truth."

That particular phrasing comes from "The Blanched Soldier," but he said the same thing nearly verbatim in "The Beryl Coronet" and in *The Sign of the Four* as well.

In the movie *Star Trek VI: The Undiscovered Country,* the half-human Mr. Spock, no slouch himself when it comes to logic, attributes this saying to one of his ancestors. This claim of Spock's is a bit outside the canon because Holmes never married nor had children, so it would be impossible for him to be anyone's ancestor, Vulcan or not.

Keeping an Uncluttered Brain

While most scholars try to cram their heads with as many facts as possible, Holmes expresses a different view of the workings of the human mind — namely, that unnecessary knowledge (sorry, trivia fans) not only clutters the brain but also crowds out more important information. When they first meet in *A Study in Scarlet,* Watson expresses his horror at how ignorant Holmes is of the science of astronomy, and the Great Detective replies:

> "I consider that a man's brain originally is like a little empty attic, and you have to stock it with such furniture as you choose. A fool takes in all the lumber of every sort that he comes across, so that the knowledge which might be useful to him gets crowded out, or at best is jumbled up with a lot of other things, so that he has a difficulty in laying his hands upon it. Now the skilful workman is very careful indeed as to what he takes into his brain attic. He will have nothing but the tools which may help him in doing his work, but of these he has a large assortment, and all in the most perfect order. It is a mistake to think that that little room has elastic walls and can distend to any extent. Depend upon it there comes a time when for every addition of knowledge you forget something that you knew before. It is of the highest importance, therefore, not to have useless facts elbowing out the useful ones."

Holmes was just at the beginning of his career at the time he said this and seems to have decided to expand his horizons along the way, eventually acquiring expertise on such topics as warships of the future and "the causes of the obliquity in the ecliptic" (the latter much to Watson's relief, no doubt).

Proves or Disproves?

You just gotta love Holmes for getting this one right. In *The Sign of the Four,* the Great Detective observes, "I never make exceptions. An exception disproves the rule."

Almost anyone else would have spoken of "the exception that proves the rule," a reversal of meaning whose enduring popularity — despite its obvious self-contradiction — is amazing. The Great Detective knew that a rule is only a rule if it's always true.

Dr. Gregory House, TV's modern version of Sherlock Holmes from the show *House,* addresses this issue when one of his subordinates says that "there's an exception to every rule." He replies, "Actually, there isn't. That's what makes it a rule."

A Look in the Mirror

Holmes's self-confident ego is apparent in many cases, a fact that he freely acknowledges to his friend Watson. From "The Greek Interpreter":

> "My dear Watson," said he, "I cannot agree with those who rank modesty among the virtues. To the logician all things should be seen exactly as they are, and to underestimate one's self is as much a departure from truth as to exaggerate one's own powers."

Although Holmes is not given to false modesty, he's rarely the one through whom readers discover his remarkable powers of perception. Instead, readers normally see Holmes's greatness through Watson's eyes. As the narrator of most of the tales, one of Watson's roles is to reveal Holmes's extraordinary abilities in a way that Holmes himself can't — at least not without sounding arrogant and unlikable.

The First Handshake

Holmes sets the pattern for his relationship with Watson the very instant they first meet. In *A Study in Scarlet,* when Stamford, an old acquaintance of Watson's, somewhat hesitantly introduces the two, Holmes asks Watson, "How are you?" as they shake hands. He then casually adds, "You have been in Afghanistan, I perceive."

> "How on earth did you know that?" I [Watson] asked in astonishment.
>
> "Never mind," said he, chuckling to himself. . . .

Throughout the stories, Watson asks Holmes essentially the same question — how does Holmes know what he knows? — and it's a question that many readers want to know the answer to as well. This setup enables Holmes to share his reasoning and reveal the clues that matter to him when solving mysteries.

In this case, it's obvious to Holmes that Watson has been involved in the British Army's recent troubles at the battle of Maiwand, because he perceives that Watson is:

> ". . . a gentleman of the medical type, but with the air of a military man. Clearly an army doctor, then. He has just come from the tropics, for his face is dark, and that is not the natural tint of his skin, for his wrists are fair. He has undergone hardship and sickness, as his haggard face says clearly. His left arm has been injured: He holds it in a stiff and unnatural manner. Where in the tropics could an English army doctor have seen much hardship and got his arm wounded? Clearly in Afghanistan."

The Obvious Facts

Watson often tries to imitate his friend's amazing knack for seeing what's in front of his eyes. Holmes encourages the good doctor in this pastime. In "The Red-Headed League," Watson's careful observation of a client doesn't give him much information. In the end, all he can really say is that the man is pretty average except that he has bright red hair and looks unhappy.

Holmes takes his turn next, seeming to toy a bit with his friend as he reels off a long list of things that are obvious to him, followed by a questionably modest disclaimer: "Beyond the obvious facts that he has at some time done manual labour, that he takes snuff, that he is a Freemason, that he has been in China, and that he has done a considerable amount of writing lately, I can deduce nothing else."

Knowledge Is My Business

When Holmes meets a distraught man in "The Blue Carbuncle," he says to him, "I think that I could be of assistance to you," leading to the classic exchange:

> "You? Who are you? How could you know anything of the matter?"

> "My name is Sherlock Holmes. It is my business to know what other people don't know."

Elementary, My Dear Watson

This is the most enduring Holmes quotation, the one that everybody knows. The only problem is, Holmes never said it. Well, not in Doyle's novels, anyway, and not in any of his short stories, either.

The Great Detective was rather fond of the word "elementary," however, and this faux signature phrase isn't really so out of place. Even in the canonical stories, you find an occasional scene like this one from "The Crooked Man," in which Holmes has once again amazed Watson with some keen observation:

> "I have the advantage of knowing your habits, my dear Watson," said he. "When your round is a short one you walk, and when it is a long one you use a hansom. As I perceive that your boots, although used, are by no means dirty, I cannot doubt that you are at present busy enough to justify the hansom."

> "Excellent!" I cried.

"Elementary," said he. "It is one of those instances where the reasoner can produce an effect which seems remarkable to his neighbour, because the latter has missed the one little point which is the basis of the deduction."

Appendix

Active Sherlock Holmes Societies in North America

*W*hat follows is a listing of all active Sherlock Holmes societies in North America. If you want to pursue your interest in the Great Detective further, participating in a local Sherlock Holmes club is a great way to do just that!

**The Singular Society
of the Lion's Mane**
Erin Bentley
7500 Trenton Lane
Anchorage, AK 99502-3142

The Genius Loci
Lee Eric Shackleford
P.O. Box 55704
Birmingham, AL 35255-5704

**The Eastern Shore
Irregulars**
Philip Ellis
P.O. Box 2661
Daphne, AL 36526-2661

**The Arkansas Valley
Investors, Ltd.**
Jason Rouby
11 McKinley Circle
Little Rock, AR 72207-6333

**Harding Brothers
of High Street**
Paul D. Haynie
P.O. Box 12247
Harding University
Searcy, AR 72149-0001

**The Baker Street Arabs
of the Western Desert**
Paul C. Smedegaard
40339 Hickok Ct.
Anthem, AZ 85086-3606

The Desert Beekeepers
Doris and Richard Dale
P.O. Box 18635
Fountain Hills, AZ 85269-8635

**The Trained Cormorants of
Long Beach, California**
Jim Coffin
US CA Long Beach
6570 E. Paseo Alcazaa
Anaheim Hills, CA 92807-4910

**The Loungers and Idlers
of the Empire**
Edna Jukofsky
5316 Huddart Ave.
Arcadia, CA 91006-5953

The Blind German Mechanics
Wally Conger
2650 Brentwood Circle
Arroyo Grande, CA 93420-5543

The Persian Slipper Club of San Francisco
Raymond A. de Groat
19147 Crest Ave.
Castro Valley, CA 94546-2816

Bow Street Runners
Fred H. Holt
350 Minnewawa Ave. #133
Clovis, CA 93612-0958

The Noble West Enders
Jim Ferreira
573 Oriole Ave.
Livermore, CA 94550-2684

The Scowrers and Molly Maguires of San Francisco
Jim Ferreira
753 Oriole Ave.
Livermore, CA 94550-2684

The Tigers of San Pedro
John Farrell
1826 E. Third Street #1
Long Beach, CA 90802-3968

The Curious Collectors of Baker Street
Jerry and Chrys Kegley
US CA Los Angeles
9338 Sophia Ave.
North Hills, CA 91343-2821

The Diogenes Club of the Monterey Peninsula
Michael H. Kean
3040 Sloat Rd.
Pebble Beach, CA 93953-2837

The Knights of the Gnomon
Richard R. Rutter
2 Rock Creek Ct.
Redwood City, CA 94602-4051

The Napa Valley Napoleons of S.H.
Donald A. Yates
555 Canon Park Dr.
Saint Helena, CA 94574-9726

The Christopher Morley Whiskey & Sodality Club
Steven E. Whiting
9528 Miramar Rd. #180
San Diego, CA 92126-4599

The Grimpen Admirers of Sherlock Holmes
Steven E. Whiting
9528 Miramar Rd. #180
San Diego, CA 92126-4599

The Blustering Gales from the South-West
Paula Salo
435 W. Eighth St. #401
San Pedro, CA 90731-3209

The Pips of Orange County
Robert A. Dunning
2025 Martha Lane
Santa Ana, CA 92706-3219

The Scion of the Green Dragon
Mary Ellen and Walt Daugherty
1305 Mira Flores Dr.
Santa Maria, CA 93455-5609

The Legends of the West Country
Howard Lachtman
926 W. Mendocino Ave.
Stockton, CA 95204-3024

**The Cardboard Boxers
of Susanville**
William Ballew
P.O. Box 1954
Susanville, CA 96130-1954

The Family of Col. Moran
Gordon H. Palmer
111 Apache Circle
Thousand Oaks, CA
91362-3210

**The Wax Vestas of the
Dartmoor Professor**
Michael J. Brady
8551 California Ave.
Whittier, CA 90605-1518

**The Goose Club of
the Alpha Inn**
John P. Sohl
20446 Orey Place
Winnetka, CA 91306-4246

The Wisteria-Hysteria
Marilyn Genaro
19944-A Sherman Way
Winnetka, CA 91306-3606

**Dr. Watson's Neglected
Patients**
William S. Dorn
2045 S. Monroe St.
Denver, CO 80210-3734

**The Winter Assizes
at Norwich**
Charles A. Adams
60 River Rd.
East Haddam, CT 06423-1403

**The Yale Sherlock Holmes
Society**
David F. Musto
P.O. Box 207900
New Haven, CT 06520-7900

The Men on the Tor
Harold E. Niver
29 Woodhaven Rd.
Rocky Hill, CT 06067-1045

**The Friends of Sherlock
Holmes**
Les Moskowitz
10346 Utopia Circle North
Boynton Beach, FL 33437-5548

**The Sherlock Holmes
Mystery Club**
Howard S. Schoen
7833 Whispering Palms Dr.
#202
Boynton Beach, FL
33437-3842

**Sherlock Holmes' Dumber
Brothers**
Richard Bryer
2026 Gray Ct.
Fort Myers, FL 33903-6436

**The Pleasant Places of
Florida**
Carl L. Heifetz
1220 Winding Willow Dr.
New Port Richey, FL
34655-7120

**The House of Stuart: The
Sherlockian Society of the
Treasure Coast**
Mr. S. Holmes
P.O. Box 221
Palm City, FL 34990-0221

The Plant Plotters
Ann Evelyn Morris
12524 Lovers Lane
Riverview, FL 33569-6813

The Beach Hounds Society
Chick Huettel
71 E. Mitchell Ave.
Santa Rosa Beach, FL
32459-5691

The Tropical Deerstalkers
Robert S. Ennis
3455 Stallion Lane
Weston, FL 33331-3035

**The Confederates of
Wisteria Lodge**
Mary Leonard
Mycroft Manor
1265 Willow Park Way
Cumming, GA 30041-7911

The Keepers of the Bullpup
Ira Block
406 Pine St.
Madison, GA 30650-1614

The Priory School Dropouts
B. Dean Wortman
223 Lynn Ave.
Ames, IA 50014-7166

The Younger Stamfords
Richard M. Caplan
701 Oaknoll Dr.
Iowa City, IA 52246-5168

The Iowa Valley of Fear
Carolyn McCracken
3700 S. Center St.
Marshalltown, IA 50158-4760

**The Criterion Bar
Association**
Allan T. Devitt
16W603 Third Ave.
Bensenville, IL 60106-2327

**The Occupants of
the Empty House**
William R. Cochran
614 S. Terrace Dr.
Carbondale, IL 62901-2117

**The Chester Baskerville
Society**
Michael W. McClure
1415 Swanwick St.
Chester, IL 62233-1317

The Camford Scholars
Elizabeth A. Burns
Bloomington-Normal
R.R. 3, P.O. Box 221
Clinton, IL 61727-9300

**The Solar Pons
Breakfast Club**
Bernadette Donze
7224 S. Kidwell Rd.
Downers Grove, IL
60516-3766

The Sons of Baker Street
Wayne B. Siatt
2310 W. Burlington Ave.
Downers Grove, IL
60515-2444

**Watson's Bull Pups of
Elmhurst**
James Cunningham
26 Windsor Dr.
Elmhurst, IL 60126-3971

Hugo's Companions
William Sawisch
149 Rockford Ave.
Forest Park, IL 60130-1263

**The STUD Sherlockian
Society**
Sawisch, William E.
149 Rockford Ave.
Forest Park, IL 60130-1263

**The Pinkertons of the Fox
River Valley**
Barton A. Eberman
405 S. First St.
Geneva, IL 60134-2707

The Baker Street Pages
Tim O'Connor
6015 W. Route 115
Herscher, IL 60941-6139

The Scotland Yarders
Susan Richman
472 Burton Ave.
Highland Park, IL 60035-4939

**The Dedicated Associates
of Lomax**
Richard A. Myhre
1319 Poplar Ct.
Homewood, IL 60430-4221

**The Fellowship of
the Fallen Elm**
Tom Tully
12981 Woodland Trail
Huntley, IL 60142-7818

The South Downers
John Ambrose
20135 Wolf Rd.
Mokena, IL 60448-9402

**Colonel Sebastian Moran's
Secret Gun Club**
Elliott M. Black
2511 Windsor Lane
Northbrook, IL 60062-7040

**Altamont's Agents of
Chicago**
John N. Wilson
11837 W. 118th Street
Palos Park, IL 60464-1401

**The Sherlockians by
Invitation Only Society
(SBIOS)**
Donald B. Izban
1012 Rene Ct.
Park Ridge, IL 60068-2068

The Torists International, S.S.
Donald B. Izban
1012 Rene Ct.
Park Ridge, IL 60068-2068

**The Hansoms of
John Clayton**
Robert C. Burr
4010 Devon Lane
Peoria, IL 61614-7109

**The Alpha Public
House Goose Club**
John Bowen
109 E. Prairie St.
Roodhouse, IL 62082-1135

Pondicherry Lodge
Mary Denham
40 Westwood Terrace
Springfield, IL 62702-4611

**The Double-Barrelled
Tiger Cubs**
John F. Wyman
508 W. Elm St.
Urbana, IL 61801-3134

**The Hounds of
the Baskerville**
Robert J. Mangler
103 Broadway Ave.
Wilmette, IL 60091-3462

**The Friends of Baron
Gruner**
Brian R. MacDonald
7801 N. 700-W
Fairland, IN 46126-9544

The Retired Colourmen
Michael F. Whelan
7938 Mill Stream Circle
Indianapolis, IN 46278-2105

The Illustrious Clients of Indianapolis
Steven Doyle
9 Calumet Ct.
Zionsville, IN 46077

The Agra Treasurers
Tom McElfresh
P.O. Box 2604
Covington, KY 41012-2604

The Silver Blazers
Ralph Hall
2906 Wallingford Ct.
Louisville, KY 40218-2363

Le Cercle de Sherlock Holmes
R. W. Culver
4324 Loveland St.
Metairie, LA 70006-4122

The Speckled Band of Boston
Richard M. Olken
1313 Washington St. #306
Boston, MA 02118-2153

Dr. Watson's Stethoscope
Frank Medlar
Bapst Library
Boston College
Chestnut Hill, MA 02167

The Red Circle of Washington, D.C.
Peter E. Blau
7103 Endicott Ct.
Bethesda, MD 20817-4401

The Denizens of the Bar of Gold
Art Renkwitz
1908 Pig Neck Rd.
Cambridge, MD 21613-3644

The Six Napoleons of Baltimore
William Hyder
5488 Cedar Lane #C-3
Columbia, MD 21044-1374

Society of the Naval Treaty
Lynn Whitall
562 Maynadier Lane
Crownsville, MD 21032-2136

Watson's Tin Box
Paul Churchill
2118 Carroll Dale Rd.
Eldersburg, MD 21784-7033

The Carlton Club
Karen Lane
837 Bear Cabin Dr.
Forest Hill, MD 21050-2732

The Friends of Irene Adler
Daniel Posnansky
11 Goosefair Lane
Kennebunkport, ME 04046-5730

The Arcadia Mixture
Stephen Landes
1260 Barrister Rd.
Ann Arbor, MI 48105-2820

McMurdo's Camp
Bill Briggs
13595 Phelps Rd.
Charlevoix, MI 49720-9201

The Ribston-Pippins
Regina Stinson
715 Amelia Ave.
Royal Oak, MI 48073-2756

The Amateur Mendicant Society
Raymond Mandziuk
43133 Napa Dr.
Sterling Heights, MI 48314-1942

The Violet Entrapment
Diane E. Edward
16917 Pierce St.
West Olive, MI 49460-9510

**The Greek Interpreters
of East Lansing**
Shari Conroy
4440 Beeman Rd.
Williamston, MI 48895-9607

The Wandering Gypsies
Julie A. McKuras
13512 Granada Ave.
Apple Valley, MN 55124-7664

**The Lady Frances
Carfax Society**
Linda J. Reed
2809 Fremont Ave. S. #211
Minneapolis, MN 55408-2036

Martha Hudson's Cronies
Julia Carraher
4242 Stevens Ave. S. #2
Minneapolis, MN 55409-2004

**The Norwegian Explorers
of Minnesota**
Gary K. Thaden
111 Elmer L. Andersen
Library
222 Twenty-first Ave. S.,
Univ. Minn.
Minneapolis, MN 55455

**The Parallel Case
of St. Louis**
Joseph J. Eckrich
914 Oakmoor Dr.
Fenton, MO 63026-7008

**The Great Alkali Plainsmen
of Greater Kansas City**
Stan Carmack
2393 N.W. Summerfield Dr.
Lee's Summit, MO
64081-1923

**The Harpooners of
the Sea Unicorn**
Michael E. Bragg
P.O. Box 256
Saint Charles, MO
63302-0256

**The Jefferson Hopes
of St. Louis**
Michael Waxenberg
7353 Princeton Ave.
Saint Louis, MO 63130-2923

**The Noble Bachelors
of St. Louis**
Randall Getz
7456 Cornell Ave.
University City, MO
63130-2914

**Diogenes Club
Excommunicants**
Tommy Cheshire
921 Nottingham Dr.
Charlotte, NC 28211-4124

The Maiwand Jezails
Lee Polikov
Office of the County
Attorney
1210 Golden Gate Dr.
Papillon, NE

**Sherlock Holmes Club of
the Upper Valley**
Tom Brydges
12 Ferson Rd.
Hanover, NH 03755-3901

Cox & Co. of New England
Robert F. Fritsch
P.O. Box 3003
Nashua, NH 03061-3003

The Retired Colourpeople
Irving Kamil
250 Gorge Rd. #27-D
Cliffside Park, NJ 07010-1312

**The Red-Headed League
of Jersey**
Steve and Linda Morris
723 Drake Ave.
Middlesex, NJ 08846-2143

**The Epilogues of Sherlock
Holmes**
Robert S. Katz
11 Van Beuren Rd.
Morristown, NJ 07960-7008

The Cornish Horrors
Burt Wolder
8 Essex Rd.
Scotch Plains, NJ 07076-2547

Mycroft's League
Frank Ferry
885 Marion Rd.
Woodbury, NJ 08096-3136

The Sloane Rangers
Trisha Stanton
4133 Seneca Dr.
Las Cruces, NM 88005-0818

The Dog(s) in the Night
Graham Sudbury
P.O. Box 506
Taos, NM 87571-0506

The Mexborough Lodgers
John D. Whitehouse
6334 Cranberry Lane
Las Vegas, NV 89156-5923

Altamont's Agents
Thomas A. Dandrew II
375 Langley Rd.
Amsterdam, NY 12010-7915

The Three Garridebs
Dante M. Torrese
US NY Eastchester
11 Chestnut St.
Ardsley, NY 10502-1001

**The Montague Street
Lodgers of Brooklyn**
Thom Utecht
1676 E. 55th St.
Brooklyn, NY 11234-3906

Round the Fire
Dolores Rossi Script
887 W. Ferry St.
Buffalo, NY 14209-1409

**Mrs. Hudson's Cliffdwellers
of New Jersey**
Ron Fish
P.O. Box 4
Circleville, NY 10919-0004

The Consulting Detectives
Herbert M. Levy
P.O. Box 197
East Meadow, NY 11554-0197

The Delaware Deerstalkers
Leonard E. Sienko, Jr.
12 E. Main St.
Hancock, NY 13783-1128

**The Young Sherlockians
of New York**
Mohamad Bazzi
8008 35th Ave. #5-F
Jackson Heights, NY
11372-4934

The Priory Scholars
Joseph W. Moran
67 Hickory Grove Dr. West
Larchmont, NY 10538-1706

**The Keepers of the
Segregated Queen**
Fred J. Serafin
127 Grant St.
Lockport, NY 14094-5032

**The Baker Street
Underground**
Andrew Jay Peck
185 W. End Ave. #11-F
New York, NY 10023-5544

**The Isle of Uffa Chowder
and Marching Society**
Susan Rice
125 Washington Place #2-E
New York, NY 10014-3838

**An Irish Secret Society
at Buffalo**
Bruce D. Aikin
P.O. Box 26
Newfane, NY 14108-0026

Rochester Row
Lewis Neisner
501 Rivers Run
Rochester, NY 14523-4935

**The Long Island Cave
Dwellers**
Warren Randall
15 Fawn Lane West
South Setauket, NY
11720-1346

**The Hudson Valley
Sciontists**
Nancy C. Alden
P.O. Box 365, 7 High St.
Staatsburg-on-Hudson, NY
12580-0365

**The Mycroft Holmes
Society of Syracuse**
Carol Cavalluzzi
300 Heroy Lab
Syracuse University
Syracuse, NY

Dr. Watson's Holmestead
Alfred N. Weiner
4105 Marietta Dr.
Vestal, NY 13850-4032

The Students of Deduction
Stephen Imburgia
1055 Klem Rd.
Webster, NY 14580-8628

The Inverness Capers
Michael Senuta
881 Columbine Dr.
Barberton, OH 44203-4320

**Mycroft's Isolated
Companions**
Dwight J. McDonald
1711 Cypress Ave.
Cleveland, OH 44109-4409

**The Clients of Sherlock
Holmes**
Sherry Rose-Bond
5471 Riverport Dr.
Columbus, OH 43221-5625

The Darlington Substitutes
Martin Arbagi
History Department
Wright State University
Dayton, OH 45435-0001

Mrs. Hudson's Lodgers
The Stetaks
15529 Diagonal Rd.
La Grange, OH 44050-9531

The Tankerville Club
Paul D. Herbert
734 Alpine Dr.
Milford, OH 45150-1401

**The Stormy Petrels
of Maumee Bay**
Mark J. McGovern
3033 Sherbrooke Rd.
Toledo, OH 43606-3772

**The Afghanistan Perceivers
of Oklahoma**
Vic Lahti
8515 E. 64th St.
Tulsa, OK 74133-7634

**The Vamberry Wine
Merchants**
Drucilla Weiland
21760 SW Elwert Rd.
Sherwood, OR 97140-3618

**The Fifth Northumberland
Fusiliers**
William H. Conway
5383 Library Rd.
Bethel Park, PA 15102-3607

**The Goose Club of the
Alpha Inn of Princeton
University**
Thomas Drucker
304 S. Hanover St.
Carlisle, PA 17013-3938

**The E. Hopkins Trust
Company**
Jeff Decker
14 Racehorse Dr.
Jonestown, PA 17038-9227

The White Rose Irregulars
F. B. Spector
45-5 Holly Dr.
Reading, PA 19606-3249

**The Diogenes Club
of Scranton**
Alan Sweeney
105 Washington Rd.
Scranton, PA 18509

The Bitches of the Beeches
Barbara S. Koelle
801 Yale Ave. #1008
Swarthmore, PA 19081-1822

The Abbey Grangers
Thomas R. Smith
7520 Rogers Ave.
Upper Darby, PA 19082-1907

**Boss McGinty's Bird
Watchers**
Frederick C. Sauls
Department of Chemistry
King's College
Wilkes-Barre, PA 18711-0802

**The Residents of
York College**
David M. Hershey
1708 W. Market St.
York, PA 17404-5419

The Hansom Wheels
Myrtle Robinson
6117 Lakeshore Dr.
Columbia, SC 29206-4331

The Knights of Shag
C. A. Lewis, Sr.
P.O. Box 9041
Greenville, SC 29604-9041

The Strand's Sherlockians
Randy Howell
304 Saint Andrews Lane
Myrtle Beach, SC 29757-6306

**The Survivors of the
Gloria Scott**
David J. Milner
P.O. Box 515
Taylors, SC 29687-0515

The Sign of the Four Faces
Cary J. Wencil
5009 S. Caraway Dr.
Sioux Falls, SD 57108-2822

**The Fresh Rashers of
Nashville**
Bill Mason
2367 Lights Chapel Rd.
Greenbrier, TN 37073-4926

The Baker Street Volunteers
Stefanie Kate Hawks
P.O. Box 9486
Knoxville, TN 37940-9486

The Giant Rats of Sumatra
Robert A. Lanier
635 West Dr.
Memphis, TN 38112-1728

The Nashville Scholars of the Three Pipe Problem
Gael B. Stahl
1763 Needmore Rd.
Old Hickory, TN 37138-1126

The Waterloo Station
Carolyn Hoehn
11208 Amethyst Trail
Austin, TX 78750-1425

The Diogenes Club of Dallas
Jim Webb
3811 Wooded Creek Dr.
Dallas, TX 75244-4751

The Crew of the Barque "Lone Star"
Donald J. Hobbs
2100 Elm Creek Lane
Flower Mound, TX
75028-4680

The Maniac Collectors
Don Hobbs
2100 Elm Creek Lane
Flower Mound, TX
75028-4680

The John Openshaw Society
Thomas L. Harman
University of Houston/
Clear Lake
2700 Bay Area Blvd. (P.O.
Box 161)
Houston, TX 77058-1098

The Strange Old Book Collectors
Ben Fairbank
P.O. Box 15075
San Antonio, TX 78212-8275

The Country of the Saints
Kevin John
637 N. 200 West
Brigham City, UT 84302-1415

The Avenging Angels
Heidi-Marie Mason
5556 Marshwood Lane #4-E
Murray, UT 84107-6461

The Game Is Afoot
Richard R. Morrison, Jr.
144 Woodlake Dr.
Charlottesville, VA
22901-1342

The Cremona Fiddlers of Williamsburg
David F. Morrill
17 James Square
Williamsburg, VA
23185-3346

The Goose Club of the Alpha Inn
William E. Wicker
140 Birchwood Dr.
Colchester, VT 05446-6255

The Baker Street Breakfast Club
Sally Sugarman
P.O. Box 407
Shaftsbury, VT 05262-0407

The Loungers and Idlers
Janet Bailey
4320 Old Mill Rd. NE
Bainbridge Island, WA
98110-3128

The Sherlock Holmes League
Michael Meaney
4094 W. Lake Sammish
Parkway SE
Bellevue, WA 98008-5938

**The Sound of the
Baskervilles**
David N. Haugen
3606 Harborcrest Court NW
Gig Harbor, WA 98332-8981

**The Conductors of
Aldersgate Street Station**
Fred Zensen
15103 N.E. 27th Ave.
Vancouver, WA 98686-1524

**The Noble and Most
Singular Order of the
Blue Carbuncle**
Terri Zensen
15103 N.E. 27th Ave.
Vancouver, WA 98686-1524

The Thor Bridge Fishers
Alan J. Block
1419 Chapin St.
Beloit, WI 53511-5601

**The Notorious Canary-
Trainers**
Thomas M. Boykoff
221 South High Point Rd. #305
Madison, WI 53717-2087

The Merripit House Guests
Ed Christenson
2230 Meadowbrook Ct. #A
Oshkosh, WI 54904-7839

**The People of the Drama:
The Valley Dwellers**
James A. Pabian
S 12595 Davies Rd.
Spring Green, WI, 53588-9761

The Bagatelle Card Club
Daniel P. King
5125 N. Cumberland Blvd.
Whitefish Bay, WI 53217-5747

The Scion of the Four
Andrew G. Fusco
2400 Cranberry Square
Morgantown, WV 26505-9209

**The Norwood Building
Inspectors**
Richard Hartman
305 Highland Ave.
South Charleston, WV 25303-
1911

Index

• *C* •

• Y •

• Z •

Business/Accounting & Bookkeeping

Bookkeeping For Dummies
978-0-7645-9848-7

eBay Business
All-in-One For Dummies,
2nd Edition
978-0-470-38536-4

Job Interviews
For Dummies,
3rd Edition
978-0-470-17748-8

Resumes For Dummies,
5th Edition
978-0-470-08037-5

Stock Investing
For Dummies,
3rd Edition
978-0-470-40114-9

Successful Time
Management
For Dummies
978-0-470-29034-7

Computer Hardware

BlackBerry For Dummies,
3rd Edition
978-0-470-45762-7

Computers For Seniors
For Dummies
978-0-470-24055-7

iPhone For Dummies,
2nd Edition
978-0-470-42342-4

Laptops For Dummies,
3rd Edition
978-0-470-27759-1

Macs For Dummies,
10th Edition
978-0-470-27817-8

Cooking & Entertaining

Cooking Basics
For Dummies,
3rd Edition
978-0-7645-7206-7

Wine For Dummies,
4th Edition
978-0-470-04579-4

Diet & Nutrition

Dieting For Dummies,
2nd Edition
978-0-7645-4149-0

Nutrition For Dummies,
4th Edition
978-0-471-79868-2

Weight Training
For Dummies,
3rd Edition
978-0-471-76845-6

Digital Photography

Digital Photography
For Dummies,
6th Edition
978-0-470-25074-7

Photoshop Elements 7
For Dummies
978-0-470-39700-8

Gardening

Gardening Basics
For Dummies
978-0-470-03749-2

Organic Gardening
For Dummies,
2nd Edition
978-0-470-43067-5

Green/Sustainable

Green Building
& Remodeling
For Dummies
978-0-470-17559-0

Green Cleaning
For Dummies
978-0-470-39106-8

Green IT For Dummies
978-0-470-38688-0

Health

Diabetes For Dummies,
3rd Edition
978-0-470-27086-8

Food Allergies
For Dummies
978-0-470-09584-3

Living Gluten-Free
For Dummies
978-0-471-77383-2

Hobbies/General

Chess For Dummies,
2nd Edition
978-0-7645-8404-6

Drawing For Dummies
978-0-7645-5476-6

Knitting For Dummies,
2nd Edition
978-0-470-28747-7

Organizing For Dummies
978-0-7645-5300-4

SuDoku For Dummies
978-0-470-01892-7

Home Improvement

Energy Efficient Homes
For Dummies
978-0-470-37602-7

Home Theater
For Dummies,
3rd Edition
978-0-470-41189-6

Living the Country Lifestyle
All-in-One For Dummies
978-0-470-43061-3

Solar Power Your Home
For Dummies
978-0-470-17569-9

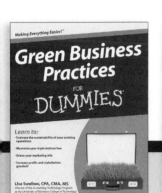

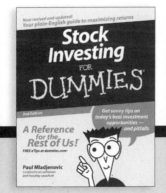

Internet

Blogging For Dummies,
2nd Edition
978-0-470-23017-6

eBay For Dummies,
6th Edition
978-0-470-49741-8

Facebook For Dummies
978-0-470-26273-3

Google Blogger
For Dummies
978-0-470-40742-4

Web Marketing
For Dummies,
2nd Edition
978-0-470-37181-7

WordPress For Dummies,
2nd Edition
978-0-470-40296-2

Language & Foreign Language

French For Dummies
978-0-7645-5193-2

Italian Phrases
For Dummies
978-0-7645-7203-6

Spanish For Dummies
978-0-7645-5194-9

Spanish For Dummies,
Audio Set
978-0-470-09585-0

Macintosh

Mac OS X Snow Leopard
For Dummies
978-0-470-43543-4

Math & Science

Algebra I For Dummies,
2nd Edition
978-0-470-55964-2

Biology For Dummies
978-0-7645-5326-4

Calculus For Dummies
978-0-7645-2498-1

Chemistry For Dummies
978-0-7645-5430-8

Microsoft Office

Excel 2007 For Dummies
978-0-470-03737-9

Office 2007 All-in-One
Desk Reference
For Dummies
978-0-471-78279-7

Music

Guitar For Dummies,
2nd Edition
978-0-7645-9904-0

iPod & iTunes
For Dummies,
6th Edition
978-0-470-39062-7

Piano Exercises
For Dummies
978-0-470-38765-8

Parenting & Education

Parenting For Dummies,
2nd Edition
978-0-7645-5418-6

Type 1 Diabetes
For Dummies
978-0-470-17811-9

Pets

Cats For Dummies,
2nd Edition
978-0-7645-5275-5

Dog Training For Dummies,
2nd Edition
978-0-7645-8418-3

Puppies For Dummies,
2nd Edition
978-0-470-03717-1

Religion & Inspiration

The Bible For Dummies
978-0-7645-5296-0

Catholicism For Dummies
978-0-7645-5391-2

Women in the Bible
For Dummies
978-0-7645-8475-6

Self-Help & Relationship

Anger Management
For Dummies
978-0-470-03715-7

Overcoming Anxiety
For Dummies
978-0-7645-5447-6

Sports

Baseball For Dummies,
3rd Edition
978-0-7645-7537-2

Basketball For Dummies,
2nd Edition
978-0-7645-5248-9

Golf For Dummies,
3rd Edition
978-0-471-76871-5

Web Development

Web Design All-in-One
For Dummies
978-0-470-41796-6

Windows Vista

Windows Vista
For Dummies
978-0-471-75421-3

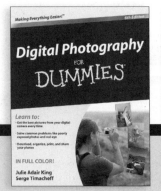

DUMMIES.COM

How-to?
How Easy.

From hooking up a modem to cooking up a casserole, knitting a scarf to navigating an iPod, you can trust Dummies.com to show you how to get things done the easy way.

Visit us at Dummies.com

Go to www.Dummies.com

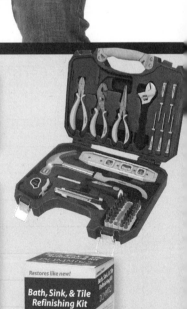

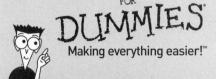

Notes

Notes